D1553779

THE BOMB IN BENGAL

The Rise of Revolutionary Terrorism in India
1900–1910

THE BOMB IN BENGAL

The Rise of Revolutionary Terrorism in India
1900–1910

PETER HEEHS

DELHI
OXFORD UNIVERSITY PRESS
OXFORD NEW YORK
1993

Oxford University Press, Walton Street, Oxford OX2 6DP
New York Toronto
Delhi Bombay Calcutta Madras Karachi
Kuala Lumpur Singapore Hong Kong Tokyo
Nairobi Dar es Salaam
Melbourne Auckland
and associates in
Berlin Ibadan

ISBN 019 563350 4

Typeset by the author and
Printed at Sri Aurobindo Ashram Press, Pondicherry 605002
Published by Neil O'Brien, Oxford University Press
YMCA Library Building, Jai Singh Road, New Delhi 110001

CONTENTS

PART FOUR: THE AFTERMATH

List of Illustrations

For sources, see list of abbreviations, pages 275-6

Preface

This book is a narrative history of the revolutionary movement in Bengal from its origins around 1900 to the close of its first phase in 1910. This decade was among the most interesting and important in the course of India's struggle for freedom. Many books and articles have been written about the men and events of the period, some so uncritically laudatory that legend has taken the place of history. I believe this book will provide a more accurate account than any found in previous narratives and also correct certain mistakes made by academic historians. But I have tried to make it as vivid and fast-moving as the events themselves. When factual history is as absorbing as this, the embellishments of the myth-maker are unnecessary.

Most histories of the freedom movement published during the two decades following 1947 were nationalist in approach and commemorative in nature. The purpose of the writers was to eulogize the struggles and sufferings of the men and women who helped free India from British rule. Much attention was given to the participants' personalities and to the loftiness of the ideals that impelled them. This motive is not unworthy, but it does not always produce reliable results.

Over the last quarter-century a new generation of scholars has published an impressive body of work which has placed the study of the period on a more solid basis. Three main schools of interpretation have emerged: the neo-imperialist, the nationalist and the Marxist. Recently a fourth school has mounted a vigorous attack on its predecessors, charging them all with élitism and championing the role of the nameless 'subaltern' classes. The ongoing hermeneutic debate has greatly enriched our understanding of the economic and social background of the period. But it has been confined for the most part to scholarly journals and conferences and so far has had little influence on the general public.

My approach in this book is nationalist in focus, narrative in form and chronological in presentation. I offer no apologies for any of these choices. Although somewhat out of fashion in academic circles, the nationalist approach has revealed much, and has more to reveal, about how men and women responded to the challenges of colonial rule. Narrative history, never abandoned by popular writers, has recently found defenders among historiographers and philosophers. And the very school that condemned chronological history as incurably 'eventish' (*événementielle*) not long ago announced 'the return of the event'. Perhaps it never went away.

In choosing to concentrate on men and events I in no way deny the importance of social, economic or political structures. I have placed my data in this larger framework in a series of papers that are listed in the bibliography. But in this book my primary aim has been to arrange the factual data in the form of a narrative accessible, interesting and perhaps even inspiring to the non-academic reader. I have avoided the weakness of commemorative histories by basing myself entirely on primary sources. I have made use not only of the familiar government records but also hitherto untapped collections of judicial and police documents. I have also sought out and read the papers and published accounts of participants and eyewitnesses. The two main types of material —official documents and the writings of participants—are complementary. Government sources provide a reliable skeleton of fact (events, dates, etc.); the participants' accounts flesh this out with inside details. Yet even both types of material together do not provide clear answers to every question. In particular I have not been able to establish the dates or even the sequence of some significant events. In the text I take them up in what seems to be the correct sequence without encumbering the flow of the narrative with scholarly argumentation. Where discussions of chronology or other controversial matters were unavoidable, I have relegated them to the notes or appendixes.

The same desire to keep the text free from unnecessary argumentation has led me to avoid direct involvement in current academic debate. I have however given some attention to two major problems in the study of the freedom movement: the relationship between revolution and religion and the relative importance of violent and non-violent methods. I deal with the first of these questions in chapter 7. The second forms the subject of chapter 24; but the entire book may be said to be a non-analytical case study of one group of violent revolutionaries.

I have not hesitated to use the word 'terrorism' to refer to the activities of these men. It was avoided by the commemorative historians, who preferred the cumbersome and inaccurate 'militant nationalism'. Many readers will feel that their squeamishness was justified. Terrorists have given their trade such a bad name that it would seem best to avoid the word when referring to a legitimate freedom struggle. Sidestepping the impossible task of assigning absolute legitimacy or illegitimacy to a historical movement, I simply point out that I employ the word 'terrorism' in the sociological and not the journalistic sense. In the social sciences 'terrorism' means the use of small-scale violence, generally in the form of assassination and robbery, by small, urban groups to achieve political ends. This definition exactly fits the activities of the group under study and in the interests of exactitude I use the word 'terrorism' to describe their work.

In transliterating Indian words and names, I have used a common-sense system that ought to satisfy those who speak the languages and not baffle those who do not. Basically I have followed the international system of Sanskrit transliteration, but avoided diacritical marks. I have used 'b' and 'j' to represent those sounds in Bengali regardless of their etymological origin. (Thus *Bande Mataram*, not *Vande Mataram*; *Jugantar*, not *Yugantar*—except sometimes in quotations.) I have generally spelled personal names the way the person did if he wrote in English. If he did not, I have used the spelling most frequently encountered in secondary sources. For place names I have used spellings current during the period under study and not the more correct forms introduced in recent years. In quotations I have of course followed the documents verbatim. Thus in quoted material 'Aurobindo' is spelled 'Arabinda', 'Arabindo' and several other ways as well.

It is not possible for me to list the names of all those who have helped me in the writing of this book. But I must acknowledge my indebtedness to those who assisted me in research in non-English sources. Aloka Ghosh, Ela Ghosh, Arup Mitra and Maurice Shukla provided me with summaries of Bengali books and articles. Without their help I could never have gone through the extensive

Bengali literature on the subject. I used these summaries as well as printed translations while rendering passages from Bengali into English but am responsible for the final form of the translated passages. I received help with Marathi and Gujarati sources from B. D. Limaye, Ganapati Pattegar, Sreehari Marathe, Jayantilal Parekh and Sanjay Bhatt. Needless to say none of the researchers named is in any way responsible for the use I have made of her or his material. Among the many people who have helped me to obtain documents, Joya Mitter and Lalita Roy deserve special mention. I am grateful to Bob Zwicker, Barbie Daily, Arup Mitra and Ashok Acharya for reading all or parts of the manuscript, proofs or both; to Ulrich Mohrhoff for help with the typesetting; and to Jacques Pouchepadass for sharing with me his knowledge of historiography.

PART ONE
Origins

1

A Golden Sunset

Disraeli wanted a symbol for his new concept of imperialism. Victoria wanted a style befitting her more-than-queenly dignity. The Royal Titles Act of 1876 gratified them both. That year the royal Christmas cards were signed 'V. R. & I': *Victoria Regina et Imperatrix*. The Queen of Great Britain and Ireland was now Empress of India as well.[1]

The Crown's representative was not long in acquainting her Indian subjects with the news. Four months after the passage of the Act, Lord Lytton convoked a durbar or royal levée in Delhi. On 23 December Lytton made his ceremonial entrance into the city. First came columns of cavalry, then the viceroy and vicereine in a silver howdah on the back of a magnificent elephant. They were followed by their bodyguard, 'then the governors and swells on other elephants to the number of fifty; then more cavalry and artillery, &c.' This was enough to impress an artist who observed the spectacle from the city's principal mosque. But, he continued, 'nothing I ever saw or have dreamed of could equal the rush of native chiefs' elephants that closed the procession.' On the animals' backs were 'magnificent and sometimes magnificently grotesque *howdahs*, and in the *howdahs* a motley crew, men in armour, men with shields and large swords, men with trumpets 8 feet long, all sorts of wild men shouting and scuffling and behind all the golden sunset.'[2]

The climax of all this pomp, and the pomp of the days that followed, came on the first of January 1877. In a pavilion that was 'like a gigantic circus', the viceroy announced to the assembled 'governors, heads of administration, notables, princes and chiefs' that henceforth their sovereign would be known as Empress of

India or *Kaiser-i-Hind*. The most prominent of her Indian 'allies' were granted titles such as *Farzand-i-Khas-i-Daulat-i-Inglishia* or 'Own favoured son of the British Empire'. Some were given further recognition as 'Concilliors of the Empress'.[3] It was all a fine example of the verbal legerdemain at which the British in India excelled. Far from being an affirmation of the 'rights, dignity and honour of Native Princes', to which the Crown had been committed on paper since 1858, the assumption of the imperial title was an announcement that India was and would remain a British possession.

It was a possession more than ten times the size of the mother country, with a population of 250 million—one-fifth of the inhabitants of the globe. These people, the heritors of rich and ancient cultures, enjoyed a life-expectancy that at the end of the century was calculated at 23.7 years. This alarming statistic was due in part to the famines that since the middle of the century had made the population of the country actually decline. The worst was the famine of 1876–7. While the Durbar celebrations were being planned and carried out, some five million men, women and children perished. Entire villages were wiped out. 'I do not know what we should have done without the dogs and vultures', declared a British witness. Lord Lytton eventually appointed a famine commission, but his overworked officials could not do much. There was simply not enough money to feed all the starving people.[4]

2

Militancy in a Vanquished Land

In 1883, six years after the Durbar, John Seeley published his memorable observation: 'We [English] seem, as it were, to have conquered and peopled half the world in a fit of absence of mind.'[1] Of no part of the Empire was this statement more appropriate than India. The British were latecomers to the region when they founded the East India Company on the first day of 1600. For most of the next two centuries Company merchants remained interested mostly in 'a quiet trade'. It was not until Clive showed how easy it was to conquer a rich province that the British began thinking seriously of empire. Success came more swiftly than anyone could have imagined. In 1754, eight years after the victory at Plassey, the Company gained possession of most of eastern India. By 1818 it had replaced Mysore and the Marathas as the dominant power in the South and West, and by 1856 it was master of all the North. Ill-equipped and without patriotic sentiment, Indian soldiers were no match for Company regulars armed with modern weapons and loyal to their British officers. Early on the invaders learned that they did not even have to do much of the fighting themselves. It was more efficient to let soldiers of one province kill soldiers of another, and then step in and confiscate the prize.

But it did take some presence of mind to parlay a few commercial outposts into an empire. Faced with resolute armies in Punjab, Maharashtra and Nepal, the Company always managed to end up on top. Appreciative of a valiant foe, the British rewarded the Sikhs, Gurkhas and others with the designation 'martial race' and made them the mainstays of their army. It was the loyalty of such regiments that allowed them to weather the storm of 1857 and to keep the country's restive populace under control before and after.

The Revolt of 1857 or 'Indian Mutiny' was by no means the first revolt against British rule in India. In the hundred years between Plassey and Meerut, Company soldiers were almost always on call in one part of the country or another. In Bengal they had to face starving peasants led by saffron-robed holy men in the so-called 'Sannyasi rebellion'. In the hills of Bihar and central India they turned their muskets against the bows and arrows of the Santals and other 'primitive' tribes. Around the same time they had to deal with peasant rebellions in Tripura, Bengal and Mysore; troop mutinies in Vellore and Barrackpore; and crusades of the Farazi and Wahabi cults. But these upheavals and dozens of others were isolated, badly organized, easily suppressed. The same was true of the various encounters that made up the Revolt of 1857. This widespread insurrection might have succeeded if leaders in different parts of the country had worked together. In fact even allies like Tatya Tope and the Rani of Jhansi were unable to cooperate.

Sporadic uprisings continued to occur in the years that followed the suppression of the Revolt. There was the Indigo Rebellion of 1859–62; a recrudescence of Wahabi unrest in the early sixties; peasant upheavals in Bengal, Maharashtra and Andhra; and tribal revolts in the North-West, North-East, and Chota Nagpur. Most of these uprisings were caused by local grievances and could be quelled more or less easily by local forces. There was as yet no organized opposition to the British. The closest thing to a true rebellion in the late nineteenth century was the quixotic crusade of Wasudeo Balwant Phadke.

Phadke was a Chitpavan Brahmin living in Poona, the former capital of the Maratha empire. Originally confined to a narrow strip in the West, the Marathas extended their territory under Shivaji and his successors northward to Rajasthan, eastward to Bengal and as far south as Tanjore. Successful chieftains took control of the lands they subjugated but remained united in a confederacy under the Peshwa, a hereditary prime minister belonging to the Chitpavan Brahmin caste. During the heyday of the Peshwas it seemed as though the Marathas would replace the Mughals as the predominant power in the land. But the British were able to play one Maratha chief off against the other and finally to defeat them all.

Even after the Marathas' defeat the Chitpavans remained one of the most powerful groups in western India. Late-nineteenth-century Britons knew them to be 'inspired with national sentiment and with an ambition bounded only with the bounds of India itself'.[2] But the rulers found the talents of this well-educated community indispensible to the efficient running of their bureaucracy. Some Chitpavans, for example Mahadeo Govind Ranade, rose to high positions in the British government. Others, like the rustic Wasudeo Balwant Phadke, earned paltry salaries in the lower echelons of the administration.

In 1870 the twenty-four-year-old Phadke was working as a clerk in the Poona office of the Commissariat Department. His British superiors treated him and other 'natives' with undisguised contempt. His dislike of them turned to hatred when his ailing mother died while his leave application was under review. During the famine of 1876–7, which struck Maharashtra with particular severity, Phadke became obsessed with thoughts of revenge. 'My mind turned against the English, and I wished to ruin them,' he wrote. 'From morning to night, bathing, eating, sleeping, I was brooding over this, and could get no proper rest.'[3] Unable to arouse the interest of the educated, Phadke put together a band of Ramoshis and other backward peoples and supplied them with guns, swords, spears and staves. Knowing he was not yet ready to meet the British, he began leading his men in dacoities against moneylenders and other rich Indians. He hoped in this way to obtain the funds he needed to carry out a full-scale rebellion. His plan was to send parties of raiders in every direction, 'from which great fear would come to the English'. He would disrupt communications and free prisoners, thousands of whom would flock to his banner. Then he could realize his ill-defined intention of ridding the country of the foreign enemies of Hinduism.[4] His Ramoshis however were more interested in gathering booty than in taking part in a disciplined campaign. Abandoned by his men, pursued by the British police, Phadke fled to Hyderabad where he made a last effort to raise an army. Captured in July 1879, he was sentenced to life imprisonment and transported to Aden where he died in 1883.

The last quarter of the nineteenth century was a time of growing political consciousness in the country. The Indian National Congress (founded in 1885) gave a forum to English-educated professionals but made little effort to reach the common people. In 1893 Bal Gangadhar Tilak (another Chitpavan Brahmin) sought to involve the masses in quasi-political activities by turning the domestic worship of Ganapati into a public festival. Three years later he started another festival in honour of Shivaji. At the Congress session held in Poona in 1895 Tilak emerged as the leader of the breakaway party that opposed the linkage of Congress to a conference promoting Western-style social reform.

During these years of political development there were no major episodes of violent rebellion. One reason was the passage of the Arms Act of 1878, which made it illegal for 'natives of India' (some dignitaries excepted) to possess firearms, swords and other weapons. This effectively disarmed the country. The British looked with disfavour even on traditional Indian exercises and sports, promoting games like cricket instead. In some parts of the country youths of the upper classes stopped going to the neighbourhood *akhara* (open-air gymnasium) to learn wrestling and other manly skills.[5] But the traditions of physical culture did not die out completely in Maharashtra. Youth clubs were founded in places like Kolhapur that developed into centres of pro-Hindu and anti-British feeling.[6]

The most notorious of these clubs was started in Poona by Damodar and Balkrishna Chapekar around 1895. From their childhoods the brothers, members of a poor Chitpavan family, had looked upon the English as their 'implacable enemies'. Their hatred had no specific cause, but it was certainly connected with their orthodox Hindu beliefs. They had a 'most secret' feeling that they were divinely appointed to defend their faith, which was under attack by non-Hindus as well as 'perfidious' Hindus favouring reform. In order to drive these noxious elements from the country the Chapekars resolved to build up their bodies and to gather young men to assist them. They did exercises, as many as twelve hundred *suryanamaskars* a day, and tried unsuccessfully to obtain military training. Recruiting in playgrounds they managed to gather twenty-five or thirty 'fairly proficient lads' whom they formed into a club whose tutelary deity was the god Maruti. They taught the boys traditional Indian games and encouraged them to break up cricket matches. Later they led them in stone-slinging free-for-alls. When they had grown sufficiently bold, members started intimidating or attacking passers-by. Most of the victims were Indian Christians or reformers, along with the occasional British missionary or woman.

When the Chapekars found that their 'lads' did not show them proper respect they severed their connection with the club and continued on their own. In the autumn of 1895 they tarred a statue of Queen Victoria and garlanded it with shoes. Later that year, at the Poona Congress, they attacked two reformist editors, smashing one from behind with an iron pipe. Soon afterwards they meted out similar punishment to an Indian convert to Christianity.[7]

On the surface there was little to distinguish the Chapekars from a simple gang of hooligans. But the brothers were capable of acute if rudely expressed political thinking. In his Marathi autobiography Damodar wrote that the speechifying and resolution-passing of the 'self-styled educated men' of the Congress could best be compared to the make-believe ceremonies of girls playing with dolls. He wanted to ask the university graduates of Congress whether there was 'any instance in history wherein empty talk and indulgence in eating and drinking has accomplished the good of one's country'. Even the strength of the 'Extremist' party 'was of no avail because efforts not backed by physical force are doomed to failure. The demands of the Indian National Congress have proved futile for this reason.'[8]

The Chapekars did not have access to the English-language press where members of Congress published their speeches and petitions. Their preferred medium of instruction was the *katha*, a traditional storytelling performance. At the Ganapati and Shivaji festivals they recited verses that openly expressed their aim. As the image of the elephant-headed god was carried to the river they sang: 'Alas. Like butchers the wicked in their monstrous atrocity kill calves and kine. Free her (the cow) from her trouble, die (but) kill the English. . . . This is called Hindustan (land of the Hindus). How is it that the English rule here? It is a great shame.' At the birth festival of Maharashtra's hero they reproached their countrymen: 'Merely reciting Shivaji's story like a bard does not secure independence; it is necessary to be prompt in engaging in desperate enterprises.' To those who asked them what they were doing themselves, the brothers promised: 'Listen. We shall risk our lives on the battle-field in a national war.'[9]

The Chapekars were hardly prepared to wage war, but by 1897 they were ready for desperate enterprises. That year bubonic plague broke out virulently in Bombay and Poona. The government took swift and drastic steps to stop the progress of the disease, which not only endangered 'native' lives but hurt trade and threatened to spread abroad. At first local leaders, including the orthodox Tilak, supported the government's actions. But later Tilak's *Kesari* and other Indian newspapers began featuring reports of atrocities committed by soldiers conducting house-to-house searches. The Chapekars became incensed by what they read, heard, and observed, and they resolved to kill the chairman of Poona's plague commission, W. C. Rand. After invoking the blessings of Bhawani, the terrible form of the Mother goddess, they lay in wait for Rand on the evening of 22 June 1897. As his carriage drove past, Damodar ran up and shot him in the back, wounding him fatally. Noticing that the couple in the next carriage had witnessed the deed, Balkrishna shot and killed the man, Lieutenant C. E. Ayerst.[10] In the confusion that followed the assassins made good their escape.

The police were without clues until Damodar sought publicity by writing to a newspaper editor. An investigation was set on foot and soon the brothers were betrayed by one of their former comrades. Damodar was arrested and 'with a view to earn renown' confessed to the murders. Later he admitted he had been aided by Balkrishna. Damodar was tried, sentenced to death, and hanged on 18 April 1898. The next year Balkrishna along with another brother and one of their friends followed Damodar to the gallows.

In many respects the campaigns of Phadke and the Chapekars set the pattern for future terrorist outbreaks in India. Both conspiracies were hatched by men who had a gut hatred of the British people and who attributed all the country's ills to them. Both leaders laid stress on physical development and the cultivation of manly qualities. Both established secret organizations sworn to the use of force against their foreign enemies. But unlike later terrorists neither Phadke nor the Chapekars had a clear political aim. It took the personal tragedy of the death of his mother and the larger tragedy of a widespread famine to bring home to Phadke the oppressiveness of the British Raj. His anger might equally have been directed against an Indian regime. The British were seen as odious more on account of their religion than their administration. According to one of his Ramoshi conscripts, Phadke's goal was 'to have a Hindu raj, and establish the Hindu religion'.[11]

Damodar Chapekar had a clearer grasp of politics than Phadke, but it is impossible to read his autobiography without feeling that his chief concern was the protection of orthodox Hinduism. His hatred of Hindu reformers and converts was as strong as or stronger than his hatred of the British. He justified his attack on the reformist editors of Poona in the following words:

> Like your association for removing the obstacles in the way of widow-remarriage (we also) have formed a society for removing the obstacles in the way of the Aryan religion,* that is to say, a league, prepared to lay down their lives as well as take the lives of others for the sake of that religion.... We like all the Hindu customs including even the evil practices... condemned by the reformers. There is no necessity for any innovation whatever either in our religious observances or our customs of the present day.[12]

This intense if not fanatical fundamentalism was behind all the Chapekars' activities, most of which were directed against their own countrymen. They killed Rand because he 'made himself an enemy of our religion', not because he represented the government that ruled India.

Hatred and other gut feelings play a part in most if not all revolutions; but a successful political revolution requires a deeper foundation. The most that can be said of the crusades of Phadke and the Chapekars is that they were semi-political revolts actuated largely by personal resentment and religious enthusiasm.

The inextricable tangle of religion and politics in India was brought to light in Tilak's 1897 sedition trial. On 15 June 1897, a week before the Rand-Ayerst murders, he published some speeches and a patriotic poem that had been delivered at that year's Shivaji festival. Two of the speeches dealt with the most controversial episode in Shivaji's career—his killing of the Mughal general Afzal Khan. Tilak said that the act had to be viewed not with an eye to the penal code but in the light of the *Bhagavad Gita*. He endorsed Sri Krishna's teaching that killing was legitimate if done without selfish motive and for the good of society. A month

* This passage from Damodar's 'Autobiography' should correct the misconception, created by the authors of the Rowlatt Report and repeated by many historians, that the *name* of the Chapekar club was 'Society for the removal of obstacles to the Hindu Religion'.

after the murders he was arrested. It was widely believed that he was being singled out for punishment because of the anti-government stance of his newspaper and because the police had made no progress in the case. The government in fact believed that Tilak and his associates, the Natu brothers, were at 'the bottom of the whole matter'.[13] The Natus were deported without trial; Tilak was tried, convicted of sedition and sentenced to eighteen months imprisonment. By the time of his release in September 1898 he was looked on by many as a hero.

It has never been determined whether Tilak conspired with the Chapekars in the murder of Rand. He certainly had known Damodar for several years before 1897 and is said to have been informed of the success of his 'mission' shortly after it occurred. He met the convicted assassin in jail and drafted his application to the High Court. Later he helped Balkrishna Chapekar find temporary refuge in Hyderabad State.[14] None of this proves Tilak's complicity but suggests that he did not disapprove of the Chapekars' methods.

3

A Bengali in the Maratha Country

In the beginning of the eighteenth century, as the Mughal empire began to disintegrate, armed bands of Marathas rode out from their mountain kingdom. East to Vidarbha, north to Malwa and Gujarat they rode and conquered. The chieftains who occupied these regions soon freed themselves from the overlordship of the Peshwa. Before long they were fighting among themselves. In these struggles the East India Company was glad to lend its army in exchange for certain favours. Those who accepted British help soon discovered that the foreigners were more dangerous than their neighbours. By 1820 the Maratha kingdoms had either been annexed or reduced to puppet principalities allied to the Company by treaties of 'perpetual friendship'.

One of the largest of these client states was the kingdom of Baroda. Founded in 1723 by an adventurer named Pilajirao Gaekwar, it passed through a century of intrigues and betrayals before being carved up by its British protector.[1] What remained of the kingdom became the 'native state' of Baroda. Its ruler, the Maharaja (often called 'the Gaekwar' by the British), was entitled to the highest honours at imperial functions, but his orders and actions were subject to the approval of the agent of the Company or Crown. The Gaekwars tended more than most 'princes' to bridle at British interference. In 1874 the strong-headed Malharrao was accused of maladministration and deposed. His successor, selected from a collateral branch of the family, was a boy of 'malleable age' with no experience of court-life. In 1875 he ascended the throne as Sayajirao III.[2] During his minority the ruler was tutored by an Englishman while his state was run by a British-approved Diwan. Taking up the reins of government in

1881 Sayajirao soon won praise for his progressive policies. But like his predecessors he chafed at any attempt by the British to limit his royal prerogatives.

One of these was foreign travel. In 1892 the Gaekwar embarked on the first of many tours of the West. While passing through London in December he was approached by a young Bengali in need of employment. Aurobindo Acroyd Ghose had lived in England for most of his twenty-one years. Taken to Manchester at the age of seven by his anglophile father, he was educated at St Paul's School, London, and King's College, Cambridge. Groomed for the exclusive Indian Civil Service, he passed the written examinations but was rejected for his failure to take the horse-riding test. The Gaekwar engaged this talented young man for a trifling two hundred rupees a month. Returning to India in 1893, Aurobindo began his service in the state's land-revenue department.

He found the work unspeakably boring. In England Aurobindo had developed two passions: literature and nationalist politics. Fluent in English, French, Greek and Latin, conversant with German, Spanish and Italian, he had read most of the masterpieces of European literature in the original languages. In addition he had learned Bengali—the 'mother tongue' his father had never allowed him to speak—as well as Hindustani and Sanskrit. His early poetical efforts bear the imprint of these various literary traditions. But some of his best student verse was topical. Home Rule was the dominant political issue of the 1880s and Aurobindo made his Irish sympathies clear by writing two elegies on Parnell, whose rise and fall he had followed in the newspapers.[3] At school and university Aurobindo read widely in the history of Europe from the Persian Wars to the Revolutions of 1848. His heroes were Jeanne d'Arc, Mazzini and others who fought for the liberation of their countries.[4] Convinced that India's civilization was superior to Britain's, he cultivated a contempt for the philistine traders who had made themselves the rulers of his homeland. At Cambridge he delivered patriotic speeches to a group of Indian students and in London helped organize a short-lived 'secret society', romantically dubbed the 'Lotus and Dagger', whose members 'vowed to work for the liberation of India'.[5]

In August 1893, six months after his return from England, Aurobindo put his literary and political passions to work by writing a series of articles on the Indian National Congress. *New Lamps for Old*, as the series was called, was not the first criticism of Congress in the Indian press; but it may have been the first systematic critique written in English from a nationalist viewpoint. It was also significant as an open challenge to the authority of Congress leaders, whose vapid utterances Aurobindo pilloried in scornful language. Apropos of remarks by Pherozshah Mehta and Mano Mohun Ghose about what 'history teaches us', Aurobindo quipped: 'When we find the intellectual princes of the nation light-heartedly propagating such gross inaccuracies, we are really tempted to inquire if high education is after all of any use. History teaches us! Why, these gentlemen can never have studied any history at all except that of England.'[6] It was broadly true that the lawyers and journalists who made up the Congress élite knew little of the history of continental Europe and about England only what they could read in books. Those who had gone to London had remained just long enough to be called to the Bar. They went through Mill's *On Liberty* and returned home with the sanguine notion that in India, just as in England, freedom would slowly broaden down from precedent to precedent.

Aurobindo's knowledge of the British personality and his study of Britain's political system made him doubt whether meaningful political change could be achieved by constitutional means. 'From Runnymede to the Hull Riots is a far cry,' he wrote; 'yet these seven centuries have done less to change partially the social and political exterior of England, than five short years to change entirely the political and social exterior of her immediate neighbour.' France gained freedom 'not through any decent and orderly expansion, but through a purification by blood and fire' in a revolution led by 'the vast and ignorant proletariate'. So in Rome the oppressed plebeians broke out in 'a wild storm of rebellion' when they realized that orations in the Senate were not going to help them. In Ireland too political change was initiated by 'men who preferred action to long speeches and appealed . . . not to the British sense of justice but to their own sense of manhood'.[7] In each instance it was revolutionary action that brought results.

It is hardly surprising that Aurobindo was not permitted to continue in this vein for long. After the appearance of two or three instalments of *New Lamps for Old*, M. G. Ranade, a former editor of the paper, warned its owner that he might be charged with sedition. Aurobindo agreed to tone down his language, but soon lost interest and abandoned the series. If he could not speak his mind about politics he could still write with enthusiasm about literature. His articles on Bankim Chandra Chatterjee (1894) show he was already familiar with the leading figures of the 'Bengal Renaissance'. This nineteenth-century religious, social, and literary awakening had inaugurated an era of tradition-breaking inquiry in all parts of India. Aurobindo found much to like in some of the writers of the period but he turned in disgust from 'the generation formed in the schools of Keshab Chandra Sen and Kristo Das Pal, with its religious shallowness, its literary sterility and its madness in social reform'.[8] The inspiration of Keshab and his Brahmo compeers was Western, even Christian. What Aurobindo was looking for was an impulse based on the greatness of the Bengali and Indian past. He found this to some extent in the writings of his grandfather Rajnarain Bose, a Brahmo leader who championed Hindu culture. But while he respected Rajnarain, Aurobindo 'learned nothing new' from him, having 'gone in England far beyond his stock of ideas which belonged to an earlier period'.[9]

He did learn a great deal from Bankim. Like other Bengali intellectuals of his generation, Bankim was profoundly influenced by Western thought and literature. But eventually he rejected the teachings of Comte and Mill for those of Sri Krishna, just as he rejected English as a medium of expression by writing his mature works in Bengali. Together with the poet Michael Madhusudan Dutt, Bankim created the modern Bengali language and thereby set in motion 'the revolution of sentiment which promises to make the Bengalis a nation'.[10]

No work of Bankim's did more to promote this pre-nationalistic revival than the novel *Ananda Math* (1882). Basing himself on accounts of the Sannyasi Rebellion of the 1770s, Bankim transformed the bands of brigands that roamed Bengal in those years, officially described as 'a set of lawless banditti' 'swollen by a crowd of starving peasants',[11] into an Indian version of Robin Hood and his Merry Men. Deep in the jungle, in a ruined monastery called Ananda Math (the Abbey of Bliss), lives an army of ascetics known as the *santans* (children). Although worshippers of Vishnu, they offer their special devotion to the Mother-Goddess, who to them is the same as the Motherland. Their purpose is to restore

Her to Her former glory and prosperity, which have been replaced in these days of Muslim misrule by degradation and poverty. Famine has laid waste to the country but the nawabs of Murshidabad have not reduced their exactions. To bring relief to the helpless and to finance their operations the santans raid government treasuries and convoys. This brings them in conflict with the East India Company, which is now the real power in the land. In the end the santans succeed in wiping out the Muslim presence in the area, but this does not lead immediately to the establishment of a Hindu kingdom. In the last chapter Satyananda, the leader of the santans, realizes it is God's will that the British should rule the country. Their benevolent administration will create the necessary conditions for the re-emergence of the Eternal Religion in its ancient form.

Within this framework Bankim weaves a melodrama of battles and valorous deeds, separations and tearful reunions, tragic deaths and miraculous restorations to life. The book is filled with songs—enough to remind the modern reader of a musical cinema, but of such quality that the comparison is invalidated. The most famous of them is the santans' hymn to the Mother/Motherland: *Bande Mataram* (literally, 'I bow to the Mother'). In this anthem Bankim lauds Mother Bengal as a 'richly-watered, richly fruited' land of beauty and strength and abundance, 'showering wealth from well-stored hands'.[12]

Neither in *New Lamps* nor in the articles on Bankim did Aurobindo give evidence of religious feeling. His father, a rationalist who had repudiated first Hinduism and then Brahmoism, had not allowed his sons to be brought up either as Hindus or Christians. When he took them to England he asked their guardian, a protestant clergyman, to let them choose their own religion when they came of age. When Aurobindo returned to India he considered himself an agnostic. He was introduced to the faith of his forefathers by his study of Indian literature. The songs of Bengali *bhaktas*, the *Ramayana* and *Mahabharata*, the *Upanishads* and the *Bhagavad Gita* convinced the young scholar that the Hindu view of life had more to offer than the dry secularism affected by English-educated Indians. He apparently included himself in the 'new generation' he wrote of in *Bankim Chandra Chatterjee*: 'a generation national to a fault, loving Bengal and her new glories, and if not Hindus themselves, yet zealous for the honour of the ancient religion and hating all that makes war on it'. This acceptance of the cultural value of Hinduism had political overtones. In the same essay he wrote that he saw the Hindu revival movement together with the emerging Indigenous Trade Party as omens 'of good hope for the future'.[13]

Aurobindo's acknowledgment of the centrality of Hinduism to the Indian tradition led to his passive participation in Hindu life and an acceptance of Hindu social forms. When he married he insisted that the ceremony be performed according to Hindu rites—a decision that could not have gratified his Brahmo relatives. A few years later he wrote to his wife that he would prefer not to hire a Muslim servant since 'after so recently being readmitted to Hindu society I cannot risk it'.[14] But for all this social punctiliousness Aurobindo never became an orthodox believer. According to his brother he rarely took part in 'conventional religious ceremonies'. If he happened to enter a temple he never bowed his head to the idol.[15]

Aurobindo was not however immune to the forms of popular religion. He found in Hindu mythology a set of beautiful and meaningful symbols and he made extensive use of them in his writings. But in the years that followed the publication of *Bankim Chandra Chatterjee* he wrote comparatively little. One might speculate that his early experience with political journalism had convinced him that the 'revolution of sentiment' initiated by Bankim and Madhusudan had to precede the political revolution he had hinted at in *New Lamps for Old*. But his inability to write in Bengali made it impossible for him to participate in this movement. So while Tagore and others continued Bankim's work in Bengal and Tilak and others prepared the mind of Maharashtra, Aurobindo remained silent in Baroda, teaching, reading and writing poetry and criticism. Among his manuscripts of the period there is only one fragment—the draft of an unpublished pamphlet—that touches at all upon politics. In it he says that the immediate need of the country is the development of 'strength mental, strength material and strength moral'. The first object was 'to improve the mental force of the race' primarily by means of deep thinking.[16]

Years later Aurobindo wrote that he passed this fallow period studying 'conditions in the country'.[17] He expressed his political ideas only in conversations with friends, in particular three

Marathis: Keshav Ganesh Deshpande, Madhavrao Jadhav, and Khaserao Jadhav. A brilliant mathematician, Deshpande went on a scholarship to Cambridge, where he met Aurobindo. After qualifying for the Bar he returned to Bombay, where besides practising law he helped edit the paper that published *New Lamps for Old*. At this time he became acquainted with the leaders of both Congress factions in Maharashtra, the constitutionalist G. K. Gokhale and the advanced nationalist Tilak. He avoided taking sides in the conflict preceding the 1895 Congress; but he made it clear in a letter to Gokhale that he shared Aurobindo's distaste for Congress's do-nothing ways.[18] In 1897 he was associated with Tilak's defence in the *Kesari* sedition trial.[19] The next year he left Bombay and joined the Gaekwar's service in Baroda. Sharing lodgings with Aurobindo, Deshpande became acquainted with the Jadhav brothers, his host's closest friends. Madhavrao, like Aurobindo three years younger than Deshpande, was a junior officer in the Maharaja's army. Khaserao, oldest of the four, was a ranking civil servant who enjoyed the confidence of the Gaekwar.

The three Maharashtrians and their quiet Bengali friend found such means to amuse themselves as the provinciality of Baroda offered.[20] But they also spent much time discussing the future of the country. They agreed that if India was to prosper the British would have to go. At times they spoke of 'armed rebellion'.[21] Aurobindo, their historian, took it as an axiom that a subject nation has the right to use force to achieve freedom.[22] But conditions in India did not favour the creation of a revolutionary movement. There were not enough men ready to take the necessary risks. In Maharashtra the British had been able to crush the Chapekars and put Tilak in jail after an apparently impartial trial. And Maharashtra was the most disaffected region of the country. During his visits to Bengal Aurobindo saw nothing of the revolutionary temper. The typical educated Bengali was poorly built, unathletic, unassertive and notoriously fainthearted. Throughout India he was scorned as *bhiru Bangla*, 'coward Bengali'. Much of this scorn may be attributed to envy. Bengalis were clever, did well in examinations and picked up a disproportionate number of the government posts open to Indians. But these 'babus' were not loved by their British rulers, who believed them to be cowardly, corrupt, crafty, and loquacious. The *locus classicus* of this prejudice is a passage in Macaulay's essay on Warren Hastings:

> The physical organisation of the Bengalee is feeble even to effeminacy. He lives in a constant vapour bath. His pursuits are sedentary, his limbs delicate, his movements languid. During many ages he has been trampled upon by men of bolder and more hardy breeds. Courage, independence, veracity, are qualities to which his constitution and his situation are equally unfavourable. . . . What the horns are to the buffalo, what the paw is to the tiger, what the sting is to the bee, what beauty, according to the old Greek song, is to woman, deceit is to the Bengalee.[23]

Aurobindo conceded that the 'natural possessions of the cultured Bengali' included 'a frail constitution and a temper mild to the point of passivity'. But the Bengali 'race' (as he called it) also was endowed with 'a boundless intellect'—a gift it shared with the more stalwart Maharashtrian. These two races were therefore those 'which have the destinies of the country in their keeping'.[24] It was true that the Bengali was still caught up in the rounds of qualification and preferment; but it seemed to Aurobindo that 'the desire for a nobler and more inspiring patriotism was growing more intense' in his home province.[25] This trend proved insignificant if not imaginary. Bengalis benefited more from the Raj than any other group in India. This made them more anxious than the rest to preserve the status quo. Bengal was the last place in India where one would expect the revolutionary impulse to arise. It is thus ironic that it was the meeting of two Bengalis in Baroda that provided the spark for India's first true revolutionary movement.

In 1899 there appeared in Baroda a young man from the Burdwan district of Bengal named Jatindra Nath Banerji.* Tall, well-built, and with 'bright penetrating eyes', the twenty-two-year-old Jatin was in appearance and temperament the antithesis of the typical babu.[26] After receiving his early education in Burdwan, he went to Allahabad where he enrolled in the Kayasth Pathashala. Here he became acquainted with Ramananda Chatterjee, later

* In a statement of 1908 (IOR L/PJ/6/883) Jatin said that he arrived in Baroda in 1899. Dinendra Kumar Roy, Aurobindo's Bengali tutor, wrote that Jatin arrived some time after the Rand-Ayerst affair (1897–8) and shortly before Dinendra left Baroda in late 1899 or early 1900. (*Aurobindo Prasanga* 63–4.)

famous as the editor of *The Modern Review*. Finding the youth intelligent but bored by his studies, Ramananda encouraged him to pursue his interest in history. Jatin devoured books on the Dutch Revolts, the Risorgimento, and the French and American revolutions. These fuelled his desire to become a revolutionary.

Jatin's development was similar in several respects to Phadke's and the Chapekars'. At an early age he became fascinated by the life of the soldier. Patriotic pride, based partly on strong religious beliefs, convinced him that India ought to be independent. Stung by the assertion that Bengalis were a 'non-martial' race, he vowed he would obtain military training. The rules prevented him from entering the Indian army; but in a friendly native state he might have a chance. Arriving in Baroda he got himself admitted to the Gaekwar's army through the connivance of the Jadhav brothers and Aurobindo.* Fluent in Hindi Jatindra Nath Bandyopadhyay (the proper form of Banerji) succeeded in passing himself off as the North Indian Yatinder Nath Upadhyay. He entered the 4th Baroda Infantry as a sepoy to learn discipline from the ground up. After a year he was transferred to the Gaekwar's Bodyguard, a cavalry corps whose adjutant was Madhavrao Jadhav. Here Jatin perfected his riding skills while wearing the Bodyguard's splendid gold uniform.[27]

During his two years in Baroda, Jatin spoke often with Aurobindo and his friends. Later he claimed that it was he who convinced Aurobindo 'that it was only by force' that a 'more suitable Government than the present one . . . could be obtained'.[28] Aurobindo's writings in *New Lamps for Old*, published years before Jatin's arrival, show he did not lack conviction on this

* There is some disagreement as to how Jatin came to Baroda. According to one account, he was 'brought' there by Aurobindo and his friends (Sri Aurobindo, talk of 18 December 1938, pubf Nirodbaran, ed., *Talks* 1, 45); according to another he was advised to go to Baroda by Ramananda Chatterjee (GOI HPA March 1910, 33–40: 1; cf. J. Mukhopadhyay, *Srimat Niralamb Swami* 5, where the author, who knew Jatin personally, says that 'a well-wisher' advised him to go to the state); according to a third he came to Baroda on his own after wandering about northern India (B. Ghose, *Agnijug* 33–6; cf. D. Roy, *Aurobindo Prasanga* 64–5). In a statement taken down by a police officer after his arrest (IOR L/PJ/6/883), Jatin says that after leaving Allahabad he 'travelled about as a Brahmin [? sannyasin], visiting many of the sacred places of India. In 1899 I arrived in Baroda.' He gives no explanation for choosing to visit this place, which is not considered especially sacred.

point. It seems likely that each man arrived at his beliefs independently and found them confirmed in the other. But it does appear that Jatin's arrival had a catalytic effect on Aurobindo. Temperamentally unsuited to play a visible role, Aurobindo needed an extrovert like Jatin to do the active work of organization. Young, macho, energetic, Jatin found his complement in Aurobindo, the studious intellectual with his deep knowledge of history and his understanding of the British character.

Little is known of Aurobindo and Jatin's activities before 1902. In April 1901 Aurobindo was married in Calcutta. There were a number of reasons why he took this step at this time. Among them, according to his friends, were a comparative lack of interest in politics, and personal depression.[29] The lack of interest, if present, was short lived. During his honeymoon Aurobindo wrote a postcard to a friend in which he said a certain Banerji was in Calcutta.[30] If this was Jatin, as seems likely, it would appear that the newlywed was mixing revolutionary business with nuptial pleasure.

Jatin appears to have left the Baroda army around this time, possibly because his irregular admission had been discovered.[31] Nothing is known about his activities during the latter half of 1901 except that in October he was in Gwalior, a Maratha native state in Central India. From here he wrote a letter to Bal Gangadhar Tilak asking the Poona leader to send him a book they had spoken of earlier 'in which a Russian Count has most vividly described the effects of the most modern weapons'.[32] It is not known how he and Tilak had become acquainted or how long the two had known one another. But their association comes as no surprise: both believed that India should be free and both were interested in military training. Tilak had long advocated the repeal of the Arms Act and was in favour of opening a Military School for Indian cadets.[33] Privately he went much further. In the early part of 1902 he sent his friends Joshi and Khadilkar to Nepal to open a clandestine munitions factory. Nothing came of this rash attempt.[34]

Jatin did not remain long in Gwalior. It had always been his and Aurobindo's intention to make Bengal their primary field of action. The first step of Aurobindo's 'programme of preparation and action' was 'to establish secretly or . . . under various pretexts and covers, revolutionary propaganda and recruiting throughout Bengal'.[35] He also envisaged open political agitation, but considered this of secondary importance. The first thing to be done was to start 'a secret revolutionary propaganda and organization of which the central object was the preparation of an armed insurrection'.[36] At the beginning of the century this idea was not as quixotic as it would have been twenty years later. Looking back in the 1940s on conditions in India before the First World War, Aurobindo wrote: 'At that time the military organization of the great empires and their means of military action were not so overwhelming and apparently irresistible as they now are: the rifle was still the decisive weapon, air power had not yet been developed and the force of artillery was not so devastating as it afterwards became.' With 'help from outside', presumably from Japan, even the difficulty created by the Arms Act 'might be overcome and in so vast a country as India and with the smallness of the regular British armies, even a guerrilla warfare accompanied by general resistance and revolt might be effective. There was also the possibility of a general revolt in the Indian army.'[37] Aurobindo saw this programme as one that 'might occupy a period of 30 years before fruition could become possible'.[38] It was set in motion when Jatin arrived in Bengal probably towards the end of 1901.* Re-establishing himself in his home province he found stirrings of life that had not been apparent when he left it several years earlier.

* In his statement to the police, Jatin says that he left Baroda 'after two years' (IOR L/PJ/6/883). Ker (p. 7), accepting 1899 as the date of Jatin's arrival in the city, concludes that he arrived in Calcutta in 1901. I assume that Jatin's stay in Gwalior in October 1901 came between his departure from Baroda and his arrival in Calcutta. He certainly was in Calcutta by the beginning of 1902.

4

Seed-Time in Bengal

In May 1893, three months after Aurobindo returned from London to Bombay, a Bengali monastic left that port on his way to North America. Vivekananda, as the traveller was called, was bound for a 'Parliament of Religions' to be held in connection with the Columbian Exposition in Chicago. Visitors at the parliament gaped at the young Indian in his orange silk robes and ochre turban, but it was his commanding voice and presence that made him the most popular speaker in Chicago. His lectures revolutionized Americans' notions about India. No, the people did not feed their children to crocodiles; yes, their ancient civilization was superior in many respects to the Western. Indeed the Vedanta philosophy that lay at the root of the religion non-Indians called Hinduism was the highest expression of spiritual truth ever formulated.

After the parliament Vivekananda went on a three-year tour of America and Europe. The turban and robes remained drawing cards, but the philosophy attracted sincere followers. Returning to India in 1897 he was received by jubilant crowds of thousands. Many believed he had made the Western world acknowledge India's spiritual primacy. This of course he had not done. The next year journalists in London and Detroit had other novelties to write about. But Vivekananda did start a significant trend. For the first time a number of ordinary Westerners (and not just a handful of scholars) began looking to India for spiritual light.

After his return, in speeches delivered 'from Colombo to Almora', Vivekananda gave his Indian listeners a message as new and inspiring as the one he had taken to the West. India's greatness, he said, was its religion. 'In India, religious life forms the centre, the keynote of the whole music of national life.' But now this music had turned to discord. The land of the *rishis* had fallen into poverty and debasement. Who was responsible for this decline? 'The answer comes every time: Not the English; no, they are not responsible; it is we who are responsible for all our misery and all our degradation, and we alone are responsible.'[1] What, the Swami asked elsewhere, was the difference between the Englishman and the Indian? It was 'that the Englishman believes in himself and you do not'. The British in their rash overconfidence presumed to force even their upstart religion on a country that had no need of it. Rather, cried Vivekananda, 'What we want is strength, so believe in yourselves. . . . Make your nerves strong. What we want is muscles of iron and nerves of steel. We have wept long enough. No more weeping, but stand on your feet and be men. It is a man-making religion that we want. It is man-making theories that we want. It is man-making education all round that we want.'[2]

Like many original thinkers, Vivekananda cared little for consistency. On one occasion he made his celebrated statement, 'Heaven is nearer through football than through Gita. We want men of strong biceps.'[3] On another, to those who said of Hinduism: 'What is there in this religion? It does not bring any grist to the grinding mill, any strength to the muscles; what is there in such a religion?', he answered: 'They little dream that that is the very argument with which we prove our religion, because it does not make for this world.'[4] For all his interest in secular matters, this disciple of the mystic Ramakrishna Paramahansa never ceased to regard his mission as spiritual.* Nevertheless the Swami's teachings inspired thousands of young men who had no intention of taking up the spiritual life. What touched them was the man's masculine qualities: fearlessness, rectitude, pride in the greatness of India. Years later, when police began raiding the hideouts of Bengali revolutionaries, they found worn copies of Vivekananda's

* It is possible, by taking passages from Vivekananda's writings out of context, to make him look like a consciously nationalistic figure. But if one goes through the *Complete Works* dispassionately one is forced to conclude that Vivekananda never ceased to regard his mission as a spiritual one. He once said: 'Nationalism of purely agitational pattern cannot carry us far; with patriotism must be associated a real feeling for others. We must not forget that we have also to teach a great lesson to the world. But the gift of India is the gift of religion and philosophy' (q. Isherwood 325).

speeches with disconcerting regularity next to *Ananda Math* and biographies of Mazzini.

One admirer of Vivekananda who did join his order was the Irishwoman Margaret Elizabeth Noble. After meeting the Swami in a West End drawing room in 1895, this earnest Victorian lady became devoted to the man and his teachings. Accepting him as her guru she followed him to India where he initiated her and gave her the name Sister Nivedita. For more than a year she worked and studied in Calcutta. Then, in 1898, she accompanied her master on his second trip to the West. In America and England she delivered many lectures and published a book on Hindu saints and symbolism, *Kali the Mother*.

When Nivedita first came to India she thought herself a loyal subject of the Queen. But a remarkable cultural sympathy induced her to accept not only the forms but also the inner spirit of Indian life. Before long she became convinced of the moral indefensibility of the Raj. In another, such a feeling might have lain dormant or found expression only in literary and social work. But Nivedita's 'volatile' temperament did not permit this.[5] Increasingly she viewed India's troubles in political terms. The British missionary in India was, she wrote, 'a snake to be crushed', the British official 'a fool, playing amidst smoking ruins', the Native Christian 'a traitor in his own land'. What India needed was 'the ringing cry, the passion of the multitude, the *longing* for death' in the country's service. Congress, however well intentioned, could do but little. So far as she could see the 'only person' who went 'to the root of the matter' was Vivekananda, with his doctrine of 'national man-making'. And even he did not endorse the radical political action that Nivedita believed necessary.[6]

The Swami's approach to India's problems was always essentially spiritual. Referring to his years as a wandering monk he once said: 'I have done much more in the way of politics than Nivedita. I roamed all over India to create revolution. But I saw that India is in putrefaction. What I want is a group of workers that will awaken India.'[7] He seems to have hoped that the Ramakrishna Mission would serve this purpose. Nivedita was less sanguine about its possibilities. But so long as her master lived she kept her activities within the bounds he set. This did not prevent her from getting in touch with men of more advanced political views. At the time she wrote the letter cited above, she was in correspondence with two thinkers whose ideas owed nothing to Vedanta: the Russian Peter Kropotkin and the Japanese Kakuzo Okakura.

Kropotkin was the foremost of the philosophical anarchists who exerted great influence in Europe and America at the turn of the century. Now nearing sixty, and mellowed by years of exile, he kept something of the heroic reputation he had won by his escape from a St Petersburg prison. Opposed to the doctrine of 'propaganda by the deed' when solely conceived as terrorism, he never renounced his belief in the legitimacy of tyrannicide.[8] But for several years he had given most of his attention to the scientific bases of anarchism. His latest book, *Mutual Aid*, was an examination of the principle of altruism in animal and human society.

It was perhaps this work to which Nivedita was referring when she wrote in a letter of 1900 that she felt a 'feline possessiveness' towards one of Kropotkin's books.* The Russian, she said, knew 'more than any other man of what India needs'. He confirmed her in her '*determination towards Anarchy*', not necessarily the peaceful kind. But while she was 'glad of every sovereign destroyed' she hoped that India, 'the most civilized country in the world', might be able to enter the promised land without violence. One day, she prophesied, 'We shall . . . peacefully wait upon the Viceroy and inform him, smiling, that his services are no longer required.'[9] Before returning to India in 1902 Nivedita seems to have visited Kropotkin in England.[10]

Meanwhile she had begun corresponding with another well-wisher of oppressed peoples. Kakuzo Okakura was not a revolutionary but an art critic and historian, 'one of the outstanding [artistic] leaders who revived traditional Japanese art in the midst of Japan's westernization'.[11] Once curator of the Imperial Art Museum and president of the Tokyo School of Art, he had been forced to resign when he fell afoul of the pro-Western faction. Later that year he and his friends founded the Fine Arts Academy of Japan. He came in contact with Nivedita in 1901 through her friend and fellow-disciple Josephine MacLeod. In December he

* Atmaprana (p. 125) writes that the book referred to in this letter was *Mutual Aid*, which Nivedita had read in America, evidently during her stay there in 1899–1900. *Mutual Aid* was not published as a book until 1902, but the chapters that compose it appeared serially in *The Nineteenth Century* between 1890 and 1896. It is possible that Nivedita was referring to these chapters in her letter, though it seems odd that she would refer to them as a 'book'.

and his friend Shitoku Hori accompanied Miss MacLeod to India, reaching Calcutta early in January.[12] The official purpose of his visit was to investigate Indian antiquities on behalf of the Imperial Arts Commission;[13] but his chief interest in coming may have been to meet Vivekananda, whom he wanted to invite to Japan. The two men met in Calcutta on 6 January, after which they visited Bodh Gaya and Benares. Later Okakura made a tour of northern and western India, stopping at Agra, Ajanta and other artistic sites.[14]

By March Okakura was back in Calcutta. Here he met Nivedita, who had returned the previous month. Finding that she had unusual aesthetic sensitivity, he persuaded her to edit his history of Japanese art, which was published under the rather misleading title *The Ideals of the East*. 'Asia is one' the book begins; 'Victory from within, or a mighty death without' it ends. These sentences are often cited as having inspired Bengal's budding revolutionaries.[15] This is possible, but the 227 pages that separated them contained little to excite the imaginations of students uninterested in academic art history. What was of relevance to India in Okakura's study was a suggestion Nivedita brought out in her preface: 'It is of supreme value to show Asia, as Mr. Okakura does, not as the congeries of geographical fragments that we imagined, but as a united living organism, each part dependent on all the others, the whole breathing a single complex life.'[16] If the countries of Asia stood together they might be able to free themselves more swiftly from their cultural and political subservience to Europe.

During his stay in Calcutta Okakura came in touch with the cream of Bengali society. At one reception Nivedita introduced him to Surendranath Tagore. The young Bengali was struck by Okakura's solemn expression, his black silk kimono and hand-painted fan and his ever-present Egyptian cigarettes. Prompted by Nivedita the Japanese asked him, 'What are you thinking of doing for your country?' He was disheartened when Surendranath could only mutter a confused reply.[17] Elsewhere in Calcutta Okakura spoke about art, about his idea of a pan-Asiatic union and about the British domination of India. At a well-attended meeting at the Indian Association Hall,* he told Calcutta's assembled worthies: 'You are such a highly cultivated race. Why

* The writers who mention this meeting give no indication of when it took place.

do you let a handful of Englishmen tread you down? Do everything you can to achieve freedom, openly as well as secretly. Japan will assist you.' Apparently on another occasion he made the meaning of 'secret' more clear when he remarked: 'political assassinations and secret societies are the chief weapons of a powerless and disarmed people, who seek their emancipation from political ills.' Stung by his rebuke and emboldened by his suggestion, the leaders of Bengali society decided that something had to be done.[18]

Okakura's visit to Calcutta was one of several events of 1902 that resulted in the birth of India's first true revolutionary society. The details of this genesis are far from clear. The dates and even the sequence of many of the events are not known. What can be said with some certainty is that early in 1902 several tentative beginnings came together in the formation of the group that became the prototype of all subsequent revolutionary organizations in India.*

Secret societies were not a new phenomenon in Bengal. According to nationalist leader Bipin Chandra Pal, during the 1870s the 'Calcutta student community was... almost honeycombed with these organisations.' Their inspirations were the Carbonari and Mazzini's Young Italy Society; but unlike their Italian exemplars the Bengali groups were 'without any real revolutionary motive', indeed without 'any serious plan or policy of political action aiming at the liberation of their people from the British yoke'. They were in fact simply undergraduate clubs, long on nebulous ideals but short on action. Pal himself joined a group led by Brahmo leader Shivanath Shastri that combined a fashionable interest in social and religious reform with some rather contradictory political notions. 'While boldly asserting India's right to self-government', Shastri's group deemed it necessary 'to render lawful obedience to the laws and institutions of the present

According to Okakura's Japanese biographer, he came to India in January 1902 and left the country in October of the same year, not to return until 1912 (Horioka [1963] 95, 97; Horioka [1975] 32–33). The meeting therefore must have taken place between March and October 1902. In the narrative I have placed the meeting early in March, since it would appear to have taken place before P. Mitra's assumption of the leadership of Anushilan, which seems to have happened near the end of the month.

* See Appendix 1, note 1.

Government.' Like the more militant clubs established around the same time in Maharashtra, several Calcutta groups including Shastri's recognized the importance of cultivating the 'national physique'. Around the turn of the century a number of akharas were set up in the city and in district towns like Hooghly and Mymensingh. Physical culture was also an important element of the Hindu Mela, one of the focal points of late-nineteenth-century Bengal nationalism.[19]

The Mela was inaugurated by Nabagopal Mitra with financial assistance from the Tagore family in 1867. Mitra had been inspired by the writings of Rajnarain Bose, already mentioned as the grandfather of Aurobindo Ghose. Around this time Rajnarain became the head of a 'secret society' founded by Jyotirindranath Tagore, elder brother of Rabindranath. The poet later left an amusing description of the society's activities. These included secret meetings (complete with passwords) and 'hunting expeditions' that usually ended up as picnics. There is no need to question his assertion that 'there was nothing in our activities for the government or the people to worry about.'[20] Indeed none of the Bengali 'secret societies' founded at this time were revolutionary; rather they were pioneer expressions of organized cultural nationalism.

None of the early societies survived till the end of the century. But shortly before 1900 there was a spurt of interest in physical culture in Calcutta. The protagonist of this effort was Sarala Devi Ghosal. Granddaughter of Brahmo patriarch Debendranath Tagore, daughter of Swarnakumari Tagore, a novelist and editor, and Congress leader Janakinath Ghosal, Sarala was exposed from her childhood to the chief cultural and political movements of nineteenth-century Calcutta. In 1890, at the age of eighteen, she took her B.A. with honours in English. In addition she was an accomplished singer and teacher of music. Despite or perhaps because of these attainments, this strikingly beautiful woman remained unmarried until she was well past thirty. She travelled widely at a time when even men rarely left their home provinces. During a visit to Solapur, in Maharashtra, she was much impressed by a physical-culture demonstration that included 'play' with swords and *lathis*. The lathi or singlestick was the basis of a traditional Indian martial-arts system. Since the passage of the Arms Act it had become the principal weapon of self-defence in the country. In Bengal its use was confined mostly to Muslims and lower-class Hindus. Wishing to popularize lathi-play and other manly sports among high-class (*bhadralok*) Bengalis, Sarala Devi opened an akhara in Calcutta sometime around 1897. She engaged a Muslim circus performer and fencing-master named Murtaza to give instruction in the use of the lathi and sword. Before long boys from all over Calcutta were coming to practise on her lawn. As word spread other clubs were started in various parts of the city.[21] One of them was the Atmonnati Samiti or 'Self-Development Society', with which Sarala Devi seems to have had some connection.[22] The groups that sprang up at this time had various objects and orientations. Some put more emphasis on physical training, others on mental and moral development. None was overtly revolutionary but all provided soil for the revolutionary seed.

The man who did most of the sowing was a Calcutta High Court barrister named Pramathanath Mitra. P. Mitra (as he invariably was called) was born in Naihati, 24 Parganas district, in 1853. At the age of fifteen he went to England, and in 1875 was called to the Bar. While abroad he became fascinated by societies like the Carbonari and resolved to found a similar group in India. A strong hefty man with a bulldog expression, he was an expert in the use of the lathi and club.[23] Present at Okakura's talk at the Indian Association Hall, he was selected by those present to be commander-in-chief of the group that was to be formed.[24]

A commander-in-chief needs troops, however, and these were in short supply in 1902. Mitra seems to have got together with Sarala Devi around this time,[25] but little came of their efforts until Mitra came in touch with the leader of one of the new societies. The name eventually adopted by this group, the Anushilan Samiti, became a byword for revolutionary terrorism in Bengal; but its origins were remarkably unmartial. Around 1901 a group of students at the General Assembly's Institution began meeting under the guidance of a clergyman named Wann. Besides taking classes at the Institution, the Reverend Mr Wann was president of its literary society and gymnastic club. One of the most active participants in these extracurricular activities was a student named Satish Chandra Bose. Like many of his classmates Satish had been influenced by Vivekananda's teachings. Once he went to Vivekananda's brother-disciple Saradananda to talk over some ideas he had. Saradananda urged him to follow Vivekananda's precepts and sent him to Nivedita for further advice. Nivedita said, 'You know Swamiji's teachings. Go to the slums and do sanitary work. Work out with lathis and clubs. Build up your bodies.'[26]

Wann did not permit lathi-play in his club, so Satish decided to start one of his own. Early in 1902, apparently in February or March,* he set up a modest akhara on Madan Mitra Lane in north Calcutta. A few boys began to come by. They were encouraged by some prominent adults, who suggested that they perform meritorious deeds such as closing down a brothel. Satish asked one of these advisors, Narendra Chandra Bhattacharya, to give the club a name. Narendra, thinking of the ideal of all-round development and selfless service presented by Bankim in his *Dharmatattwa Anushilan*, suggested the name *Anushilan Samiti* (Cultural Society). Feeling the need for an experienced leader, Satish went for advice to Shashi Chaudhuri and Shashi's brother Ashutosh, the famous barrister. Ashutosh said that the ideal person would be his colleague P. Mitra and gave Satish a letter of introduction. Mitra was overjoyed when Satish came calling and agreed to become the head of the samiti.[27]

Things had hardly got under way again at Madan Mitra Lane when Mitra learned that a member of a Baroda secret society had arrived in Calcutta.[28] This was Jatin Banerji, who had come to town some time earlier. His plan, as formulated by Aurobindo, called for the establishment of revolutionary societies under

* Secondary sources give earlier dates for the founding of the Anushilan Samiti, e.g. the often-cited G. Haldar (p. 236) who without data declares that P. Mitra 'founded the Anushilan society about 1897'. This is unquestionably too early. Haldar's informants may have been thinking of the start of Sarala Devi's group, which later became somewhat intertwined with Anushilan. If Satish Bose spoke to Nivedita before opening his *akhara*, as he says he did in his 'Bibriti' (the most important document dealing with the founding of Anushilan), he cannot have opened it before February 1902, when Nivedita returned to Calcutta from the West where she had been since the middle of 1899. It is hardly possible on the basis of Satish Bose's account as well as generally reliable secondary accounts such as those of J. Haldar and N. Ray to assume a date of 1899 or before. A date this early also would not dovetail with the traditional date of the founding of the Samiti, 24 March 1902 (see next footnote). If Satish did meet Nivedita before opening his *akhara* and if the traditional date of the founding of Anushilan is that of the amalgamation of Satish's and Jatin Banerji's groups (as suggested by N. Ray, p. 23), it follows that Satish's group was active for little more than a month before being amalgamated with Jatin's.

'various ostensible objects, cultural, intellectual or moral'. In addition the various groups 'already existing were to be won over for revolutionary use'. The young recruits 'were to be trained in activities which might be helpful for ultimate military action, such as riding, physical training, athletics of various kinds, drill and organised movement'. While this work was being done 'among the youth of the country', 'the older men who had advanced views or could be won over to them' were to be approached for 'sympathy and support and financial and other assistance'.[29] Jatin had wasted no time getting started. Acquiring a house at 108 Upper Circular Road, he set up an akhara in the opposite lot and began a recruitment drive. His approach to the older leaders was facilitated by Aurobindo, who had given him a letter of introduction to Sarala Ghosal.[30] It was apparently through her that Jatin came in contact with P. Mitra. The barrister saw that the stalwart young man, with his imposing figure and military bearing, would make an invaluable addition to the samiti. He called Satish and told him that he wanted the club at Madan Mitra Lane to be amalgamated with Jatin's. Satish had no objections and on the auspicious day of Dol Purnima (24 March 1902)* the expanded Anushilan Samiti was officially opened.[31]

From this moment the centre of the samiti's activities shifted from Madan Mitter Lane to Upper Circular Road. The former place was kept as a meeting-place for recruits, who were not immediately let in on the society's purpose.[32] Soon the Anushilan Samiti found itself at the centre of Calcutta's nascent cult of revolution. Under its influence 'already existing small groups and associations of young men who had not yet the clear idea or any settled programme of revolution began to turn in this direction' while groups that 'had already the revolutionary aim' began developing their activities 'on organized lines'.[33] But even at Upper Circular Road things remained low key for a number of months. Among the group's activities were lectures by P. Mitra, Nivedita, and others. Mitra spoke mostly on political and military history—the Sikh Khalsa, the French Revolution and the lives of Mazzini and Garibaldi. Nivedita sought to rouse the young men's

* I accept the date of the founding of Anushilan given in two official histories (N. Ray 23; J. Haldar 4). There is no contemporary evidence in support of this date, but it has to recommend it besides its traditional authority the fact that it accords well with Satish Bose's 'Bibriti' and other reliable accounts.

patriotic feelings and their sense of duty to the country.[34] She presented the samiti with her collection of books on revolutionary history. One of the most popular volumes was the autobiography of Mazzini. The chapter on guerilla warfare was often copied out and circulated.[35]

P. Mitra exercised overall control over the samiti and served as the mediator between the members and the older men on whom they depended for financial support. Jatin, the oldest and most impressive looking of the members, was the chief fund raiser. Often he enhanced his soldierly appearance by making his rounds on horseback.[36] But most of his time was devoted to the less glamorous activity of breaking in recruits. He taught horse-riding to the hardier boys, bicycling to the less daring. There was also instruction in lathi, drill, boxing and other martial activities. All this training was presented in the guise of legitimate physical culture. So effective was the artifice that when the samiti wanted to give swimming lessons it asked for and received the help of the police.[37]

Almost from the start there was friction between Jatin and the rank and file. Both physically and psychologically the drillmaster was cast in a different mould from the recruits. Tough and sturdy, with two years of army experience, he was an almost fanatical believer in the value of discipline. But the 'respectable' class that provided him with his material had no military traditions and little inclination to follow orders. Not surprisingly most of the young men came to regard 'Military Jatin' as a martinet.

An important element of Aurobindo and Jatin's long-term plan was to establish centres 'in every town and eventually in every village' in Bengal.[38] Soon after he had established himself in Calcutta, Jatin departed on a recruitment drive in the western districts. Two of his first destinations were Midnapore and Arbelia (24 Parganas). Aurobindo's grandfather Rajnarain had spent most of his working life in Midnapore, instilling the spirit of nationalism into many of its inhabitants. Rajnarain's eldest son Jogindranath had started a 'secret society' in Midnapore around 1900.* Jogin's recruits included his cousins Satyendra Nath and Jnanendra Nath Bose and Hem Chandra Das. The young men began their revolutionary careers with target practice, trekking in the sun and rides

* See Appendix 1, note 2.

on a broken-down pony. They were much encouraged when Jatin paid them a visit. He said he was connected with an enormous revolutionary network that had branches in every part of India except Bengal. He had been sent from Baroda by Aurobindo Ghose, who soon would come to initiate the first Bengalis.[39] Jatin repeated this story when he went to Arbelia. It was time for Bengal to embrace the gospel of revolution. Jatin had come to prepare the way; Aurobindo would follow.[40]

5

A Year in Gujarat

On 28 April 1902 Aurobindo took leave from his work in Baroda and went to Bengal. While in Calcutta he doubtless learned of recent events there and may have met members of the Anushilan Samiti.* But by 30 May he was back in Baroda.[1] One might ask why he continued to work a thousand miles from Bengal when the revolutionary seed he had laboured to plant was finally taking root. His decision may have been due partly to practical considerations; he had a good position in Baroda, none in Calcutta. A recently married man could not look without misgivings on the prospect of hunting for a job.[2] But he may also have felt he was serving the cause better in Gujarat than he could have done in Bengal. It was a time of expanding revolutionary opportunities in Baroda, one of which was provided by his growing intimacy with the ruler of the state.

Since 1895 Aurobindo had been working on and off as the Gaekwar's unofficial English secretary. In April 1901 the Gaekwar transferred him from the college to the state service in order to use his literary talents on a more regular basis.[3] Summoned to the palace by liveried messenger, Aurobindo spent the day writing letters and drafting memoranda. Most of these documents had to do with routine administrative or household matters. He had for example to write dozens of letters relating to the Gaekwar's

* There are no known documents showing what Aurobindo did in Calcutta; indeed there are none showing that he actually went there. A letter from Aurobindo to Jogindranath Bose of 15 August 1902 (*A&R* 1 [April 1977]: 68–74) shows that he spent at least part of his leave in Deoghar. It is highly unlikely that he visited Bihar and not Bengal. Probably he stopped in Deoghar on his way back to Baroda from Calcutta.

grandiose plans for building mansions in Ooty, Mussoorie and other resorts. But the secretary was also entrusted with drafting important letters to the Government of India. While engaged in this work he could observe the Gaekwar's political thinking at first hand.[4]

During his reign Sayajirao Gaekwar was regarded as the most sympathetic of Indian princes to the national movement. Some even thought him a friend of revolutionaries or a revolutionary himself. There were a number of reasons for this reputation, which remains undimmed to this day.[5] The Gaekwar was less obsequious to the British than most if not all other Indian rulers. The viceroy, Lord Curzon, considered him the 'sole important prince' who was 'not loyal to the British Government'. Curzon's successor Lord Minto wrote that the Gaekwar was 'anything but free from suspicion' of involvement in seditious activities.[6] The ruler's 'coolness' towards the government won him the applause of the nationalist press, even as it earned him the animosity of the British.[7]

The best-remembered expression of the Gaekwar's princely pride was an incident of 1911, in which he turned his back on George V during an Imperial Durbar. This was a serious breach of protocol to say the least and it is possible that it was meant as a deliberate insult.* Whether it was also a deliberate act of patriotism is another matter. An earlier affair, with which Aurobindo was connected, can serve as a touchstone for evaluating this and other 'nationalistic' acts of the maharaja.

In August 1900 Lord Curzon visited Baroda while the Gaekwar was in Europe. Curzon requested the ruler to return to India by November in order to receive him when he was again in Western India. The Gaekwar declined, saying that the maharani's health would not permit it. In response Curzon issued a circular requiring native rulers to obtain permission from the government before leaving the country. In this he observed: 'the ruler shall devote his best energies, not in the pursuit of pleasure nor to the cultivation of absentee interest in amusements, but to the welfare of his own subjects and the administration.'[8] This observation, it should be noted, was not only just in principle—all princes, Sayajirao

* The Maharaja of course strenuously denied this afterwards. He was required to make a rather abject apology in order to keep his throne.

included, spent an inordinate amount of their kingdoms' wealth on personal pleasures—but also had special force in 1900, when Western India was experiencing the most devastating famine in its modern history. Curzon had come to the Bombay Presidency precisely 'to see for himself' the 'famine-stricken districts in Guzerat'.[9] But the fact remained that the circular was intended by Curzon to punish a man he resented. To the Gaekwar the issue was whether an 'independent' prince should be subject to the dictates of a British administrator.

Aurobindo may have helped with the correspondence engendered by the Gaekwar's refusal of 1900 and he certainly had a hand in negotiations undertaken three years later, when the Gaekwar desired to return to Europe.[10] In accordance with regulations long in force, he had to submit his itinerary to the resident or agent of the viceroy, When he did so the resident drew his attention to the Curzon circular. The Gaekwar hardly needed to be reminded of this document, which he considered vindictive and humiliating. 'We [princes] are all supposed to be chiefs, but we are treated worse than paid servants,' he wrote in reference to it.[11] Resolved to safeguard his right to act without constraint, the ruler assembled a team of experts to present his case to the government. To Aurobindo fell the task of drafting an official reply to the resident. His letter, well-reasoned and diplomatic, stressed above all the undesirable effect that the circular 'was calculated to produce' on the Gaekwar's 'status and dignity as a Ruler'.[12]

This easily ruffled dignity seems to have been at the root of the Gaekwar's patriotism. He was a proud man, conscious of the noble Maratha blood flowing in his veins. 'Hedged in by difficulties and restrictions, [a prince] loses some of his self-respect and a large share of personal influence which was the heritage of his predecessors', he wrote.[13] Flattered by the suggestion that India could recover its ancient greatness under the rule of enlightened native princes, he cautiously helped a number of nationalist politicians, giving financial support to some and letting others carry out their activities in the relative safety of his domains.[14]

According to Aurobindo the Gaekwar's long-term plan was to create a centre of power within his dominion 'which would serve when the time for revolution came'. This idea, however, 'was not carried through'.[15] The ruler had a difficult game to play. Publicly and officially his attitude towards the government had to be one of absolute loyalty. Privately and indirectly he could make small but telling gestures of dissent. But experience made him cautious and he did much less than others hoped he would. This is illustrated by two incidents of the pivotal year 1902 that involved Aurobindo and Nivedita.

Shortly after his return to Baroda from Bengal in March 1902, Aurobindo was summoned by the Gaekwar to Lonavla, a hill resort in the Western Ghats.* The ruler, possibly brooding over his inability to be in Paris or his beloved St. Moritz, asked his secretary to write a 'document', presumably a memorandum or letter to the government. Aurobindo complied but the Gaekwar changed his mind 'at the last minute' and never sent or made public what Aurobindo wrote. Soon afterwards, as Aurobindo informed his wife, 'another very big and secret work came up'. Aurobindo did not say what this was; but it probably was political and possibly somewhat rash. 'The day of [the Gaekwar's] downfall is coming,' Aurobindo commented; 'all the signs are bad.'[16]

Like Aurobindo, Nivedita had unrealistically high hopes in regard to the Gaekwar. Her life had undergone a great change after 4 July 1902, when her guru Vivekananda passed away. For some time before this unexpected and crushing event, she had become increasingly dissatisfied with the non-political stance her membership in the Ramakrishna Order demanded. Two weeks after Vivekananda's death she wrote to the head of the Order asking for 'complete personal freedom'. The next day it was announced in the *Amrita Bazar Patrika* that the members of the Order and Nivedita had decided 'that her work shall henceforth be regarded as free and entirely independent of their sanction and authority'.[17] Until her death nine years later her activities were centred on the national movement in its various aspects.

* The only source of information on Aurobindo's trip to Lonavla and his work for the Gaekwar there is a letter that Aurobindo wrote to his wife on 25 June 1902, shortly after his return to Baroda (pub. Sri Aurobindo, *Bangla Rachana* 330). In the letter Aurobindo does not mention the Gaekwar by name, but speaks of someone called *kencho* (the Worm). This *kẽncho* had summoned Aurobindo to Lanabali (Bengali for Lonavla) and asked him to draw up a document (*lekh*). The only man who was in a position to do this was the Gaekwar. It is known from other sources that the Gaekwar way staying in Mahabaleshwar, another resort in the Western Ghats, in June 1902. It is safe to assume that he also passed some time in Lonavla.

Two months later Nivedita undertook a fund-raising tour of western India. This brought her on 20 October to Baroda.[18] She was received at the station by Aurobindo. This was the first time the two had met, though they knew of each other already. Aurobindo had read and admired Nivedita's *Kali the Mother*. Nivedita had heard from people in Calcutta that Aurobindo 'believed in strength and was a worshipper of Kali'. This she understood in the intended sense: that he was a revolutionary. The two 'worshippers of force' found that they also shared an interest in Indian art. As they drove by the main building of Baroda College, a ponderous structure with a grotesquely oversized dome, Nivedita cried out against its ugliness. Later, as they passed an unpretentious *dharmasala*, she praised it for being in the true Hindu style. Khaserao Jadhav, who was also in the carriage, thought the woman must be a little cracked, but Aurobindo appreciated her discernment.[19] During her six-day stay in Baroda, Nivedita brought him up to date with developments in Calcutta.[20] The friendship they formed at this time would be renewed often in the years to come.

Nivedita gave three speeches in Baroda but the main reason for her coming seems to have been to meet the Gaekwar and to win him over to the cause. According to Aurobindo, who was present at her interview, Nivedita invited the ruler 'to support the secret revolution'. It was his duty to do so, she said. The Gaekwar expressed interest but refused to commit himself. We learn from Nivedita's diary that on 23 October she received a letter from the Gaekwar that upset her greatly. She saw him again the next day but this meeting also proved fruitless. She and the maharaja agreed that further communications on the subject of revolution could pass through Aurobindo; but the maharaja never spoke to him about it. He was 'much too cunning to plunge into such a dangerous business,' Aurobindo commented later.[21]

This may be taken as the last word on the Gaekwar's connection with the revolutionaries. As the years went by and he grew weary of harassment, he became more and more moderate in speech and action. But he never stopped thinking that the status of native rulers should be enhanced. In August 1904, when Curzon proposed that princes should contribute money and troops to protect British territories, the Gaekwar had Aurobindo, now his Huzur Kamdar or Crown Secretary, draw up a memorandum which said: 'The creation of the new obligation proposed would seem to demand the concession of a corresponding privilege, a recognised voice in the councils of the Empire. This privilege is the natural corollary of any general military federation, and would alone justify the creation of new burdens.'[22] This proposal was ignored by Curzon, but it foreshadowed the creation of the Chamber of Princes seventeen years later.

One morning late in 1902, apparently a short time after Nivedita left Baroda,* a travel-weary youth knocked at the door of Khaserao Jadhav's house. The servant who answered was not sure whether the caller should be admitted. Dressed in dirty clothes and carrying a torn canvas bag, he insisted he was the brother of Ghose Saheb! Ushering him somewhat dubiously into the parlour, the servant went upstairs to inquire. In a moment a surprised Aurobindo came down. Seeing that it was indeed his younger brother Barin he cried out, 'You here? And in such a state! Go immediately to the bathroom and change.' After a shower Barin put on a clean shirt and dhoti borrowed from his brother. He was now ready to meet the master of the house, the witty tormenter Khaserao. Also present at the breakfast table was Khaserao's brother Madhavrao, with whom Barin struck up an immediate friendship. Before long the Jadhav brothers had drawn out the young man's story, and along the way learned more about their reticent house guest Aurobindo.[23]

The fourth son of Kristo Dhone and Swarnalotta Ghose, Barin was born in Upper Norwood, a suburb of London, in January 1880. A few months before this Dr Ghose had completed arrangements for his elder sons to be educated in England. He returned to India alone, leaving his pregnant wife in the care of an English doctor. Partly in honour of this man, Swarnalotta called her newborn Emmanuel Matthew Ghose. Mercifully the name never caught on. When Swarnalotta returned to India the boy became known as Barindra Kumar.[24]

Since 1873 Swarnalotta had been subject to fits of madness. By 1880 she was almost completely insane.[25] Finding it impossible to live with her at Rangpur, Dr Ghose made arrangements for her to live near Deoghar, where her father Rajnarain was staying. Barin

* See Appendix 1, note 3.

remained in Bihar with his mother for almost ten years. It was not a happy childhood. He lived in the perpetual fear that Swarnalotta would thrash him as she thrashed his sister Sarojini. Sometimes the children passed the whole day on the veranda while their mother sat muttering in her room. At night she kept Barin from causing trouble by tying him to his bed.

This nightmare of child-abuse ended when Dr Ghose took possession of the children. They were brought to Calcutta and placed in the care of a young woman who was a friend of their father's. 'Ranga Ma', as Barin and Sarojini called her, gave them the first real love they had ever known. Once or twice a month the doctor came up from Khulna, where he had been posted, to spend a few days. In Calcutta Barin belatedly learned the alphabet and began studying under a private tutor, but he was far more interested in discovering the wonders of India's greatest city.[26]

In 1893 Dr Ghose unexpectedly died. His relations, who had long been scandalized by his liaison with Ranga Ma, took the children away from her. They were brought to Deoghar, where they stayed with their mother's brother Jogindranath. Barin was soon enrolled in the local school. One of his teachers was Sakharam Ganesh Deuskar, a man of Maharashtrian origin who wrote excellent Bengali. Influenced by Rajnarain and Jogindranath, Deuskar became an outspoken nationalist and a proponent of the cult of the lathi.[27] Barin was inspired by Deuskar's patriotism but spent little time at the gymnasium. The dreamy adolescent seems to have given most of his attention to the girls he fell in love with one after another.

At Deoghar Barin got to know his older brothers, who had all returned recently from England. Aurobindo came regularly from Baroda for the Puja holidays. The Cambridge-educated intellectual got along surprisingly well with the unsophisticated youngster. As Barin grew, Aurobindo spoke to him more about the subject that interested him most: the motherland, which had to be freed from British domination.

After several years of school Barin entered Patna College, where he studied for about six months. Later he went to Dacca, where his second brother Manmohan was working as a professor. After a brief stay there he left for Calcutta with the idea of raising money to do some farming. His plans came to nothing and he was soon back in Deoghar—but not for long. After a visit to Ranga

Ma and another stay in Calcutta he went to Cooch Behar where his eldest brother Benoy Bhusan was working. Finding no opening there he returned to Calcutta, where a friend advised him to open a shop in Patna.

Barin thought he would give it a try. Renting two rooms opposite the college he put out a shingle saying 'B. Ghose's Stall'. Students wandered in, looked at the merchandise, and wandered out. Deciding to diversify, he hung up a new sign that read

B. Ghose's
Tea Stall
Half anna cup, rich in cream.

For a while it looked like business was picking up and Barin enlarged the tea-stall into a refreshment stand. But he soon came to grief because he sold too much on credit.

Around this time plague broke out in Patna. It clearly was time for Barin to leave Bihar. But where to go? He already had tried living with two of his brothers. Perhaps he would have better luck with the third. So it was that sometime in 1902 he boarded the train for Bombay. After the cross-country voyage (his first) and the overnight trip to Gujarat he arrived, unannounced, on Aurobindo's doorstep.[28]

At Baroda Barin could live the unstructured sort of life that suited him best. He read, wrote poetry, played the *esraj*, did some gardening and developed a passion for bird-hunting. He also did a fair amount of reading, history being his subject of choice. Burke's *French Revolution*, Ranade's *Rise of the Maratha Power* and William Digby's recently published *'Prosperous' British India* were among the books he read.[29] In the evenings he joined in discussions between Aurobindo and his Maharashtrian friends. He learned that they were in contact with a secret revolutionary society—one that was said (on doubtful authority) to have existed since the Mutiny and to have some sort of connection with the Chapekars' group. Its purpose was 'to prepare a national insurrection'.[30] The leader of this society was a mysterious figure named Thakur Ramsingh.

Thakur Saheb (as he generally was known) was a Rajput noble (*thakur*) of the princely state of Udaipur. His chief revolutionary interest was the subversion of the Indian army. Aurobindo later wrote that the Thakur had 'won over two or three regiments', one of which Aurobindo visited around this time.[31] As overall head of the secret society, Thakur Saheb stood above the revolutionary circles into which the country had been divided. Perhaps the most active of these was the West India circle, which, according to Aurobindo, 'had a Council of Five in Bombay with several prominent Maharatta politicians as its members'.[32] Aurobindo never mentioned the names of these council members, but it is probable that Tilak and his lieutenant G. S. Khaparde were among them.* The council's purpose was to help Thakur Saheb 'organize Maharashtra and the Mahratta States' such as Gwalior and Baroda.[33]

Aurobindo came in contact with Thakur Ramsingh's secret society sometime in 1902. Soon afterwards he took its oath and was introduced to the Council in Bombay.† He was made president of the society's Gujarat circle—an undemanding post, since the region was then 'very moderate'. Aurobindo did occasionally meet men, mostly Maharashtrians, who were interested in the cause. He did not conceal his activities from Barin and the young romantic soon convinced himself that Thakur Saheb's secret society had hundreds of centres, and that 'thousands of revolutionaries' 'were sharpening their swords' in anticipation of the revolution that in two or three years would drive the British

* Aurobindo nowhere said who the 'Maharatta politicians' were but from a reference in a statement by Barindra Kumar Ghose one may assume that G. K. Khaparde was one of them (HFMP IV & V 41/2). Tilak may well have been another. Aurobindo is recorded as saying once that the secret society was 'started by Tilak' (Sri Aurobindo, talk of 12 December 1940, pub. Nirodbaran, ed., *Talks* 4, 279). (Note that like many non-Maharashtrians, Aurobindo used 'Maratha' —old spelling 'Mahratta' or 'Maharatta'—to mean 'Maharashtrian' or 'Marathi-speaking'. Properly 'Maratha' refers to a particular Kshatriya community of Maharashtra. Brahmins like Tilak and Khaparde are not rightly spoken of as 'Marathas'.)

† Aurobindo says he 'contacted and joined' the secret society 'somewhere in 1902–3' (*On Himself* 4). Barin says that he was present when Aurobindo was initiated, adding that Aurobindo had been in contact with the society for some time before that (*Agnijug* 38). If Barin arrived in Baroda in 1902 and was present at the initiation, the earliest possible time for it would be the middle of that year. If (as Barin says) the meeting with Madgavkar at the Taj Mahal Hotel in December 1902 followed Aurobindo's initiation, the latest date for the initiation would be December 1902. Aurobindo says that the person whom he met and who introduced him to the Council was a certain Mr Mandal[e] (Sri Aurobindo, talk of 21 January 1939, pub. Nirodbaran, ed., *Talks* 1, 221).

from India.[34] Aurobindo's own estimate of success after two or three decades was more realistic.[35]

In December, just before the 1902 session of Congress, Aurobindo and Barin went to Bombay to take part in a conclave of revolutionaries. The meeting was held in the Taj Mahal Hotel, in the room of Govind Dinanath Madgavkar. A contemporary of Aurobindo's in England, Madgavkar now was a member of the Bombay cadre of the Indian Civil Service.* He was also a member of Thakur Saheb's society. The chief topic of discussion at the meeting was the society's plan to send Madhavrao Jadhav to Japan for military training. Madgavkar gave Rs 1000 for the purpose and Madhavrao apparently left India soon afterwards.[36]

The 1902 session of Congress was held in Ahmedabad at the end of December. The three-day sitting was preceded by an Industrial Exhibition, which was opened by the Gaekwar of Baroda. Aurobindo, who had written the Gaekwar's speech, accompanied him as part of his retinue. The speech is an example of how Aurobindo's political thinking had an impact on the Gaekwar's public persona and perhaps his private opinions as well. After an unusually brief opening the Gaekwar announced with admirable directness:

> Famine, increasing poverty, widespread disease, all these bring home to us the fact that there is some radical weakness in our system and that something must be done to remedy it. But there is another and a larger aspect of the matter and that is that this economic problem is our last ordeal as a people. It is our last chance. Fail there and what can the future bring us? We can only grow poorer and weaker, more dependent on foreign help; we must watch our industrial freedom fall into extinction and drag out a miserable existence as the hewers of wood and drawers of water to any foreign power which happens to be our master. Solve that problem and you have a great future before you, the future of a great people, worthy of your ancestors and of your old position among the nations.[37]

Why had Indian industry and trade declined to such an extent? Partly because of outmoded methods and machinery. But there

* Govind Dinanath Madgavkar was born in 1871. Along with Aurobindo he passed the ICS entrance examination of June 1890. After completing the course, he was posted first in Burma and later transferred to Bombay. He eventually became officiating Chief Justice of the Bombay High Court (IOR *Record of Services* 746).

was, asserted the Gaekwar, 'a further reason which does not depend on the natural working of economic laws but which is political in its nature, the result of the acquisition of political power by the East India Company and the absorption of India in the growing Indian Empire.'[38] The ruler of a protected state could not go further than this in criticizing the government.

Aurobindo remained in Ahmedabad to observe the session. It was the first time he had witnessed the speech-giving and resolution-passing that still constituted the function of the body he had criticized in *New Lamps for Old*. The proceedings confirmed him in his view that the Congress policy was simply 'a process of futile petition and protest'.[39] The Chairman of the Reception Committee, Ambalal Sakerlal Desai, opened the session with an address that set the tone for what followed. While making the customary plea for superficial government reforms, Desai affirmed that 'the basal idea that underlies and runs through all our actions . . . is that it is for our benefit that the British power should continue to be supreme in our land.' 'Loyalty to the British Government,' he declared, 'is the dominant sentiment of every Congressman.'[40] The president of the session, the veteran orator Surendranath Banerjea, gave no reason for anyone to doubt he approved of Desai's sentiments. At the end of an enormously long address, Surendranath cried: 'We plead for the permanence of British rule in India.' However much he qualified this with an entreaty 'for equal rights and enlarged privileges' the fact remained that the Demosthenes of the Congress advocated India's 'permanent incorporation into the great confederacy of the British Empire'.[41]

It is greatly to be doubted whether Aurobindo stayed long enough to hear this conclusion. Years later, recalling an occasion where he had to listen to Surendranath for half an hour, he said that he 'found no thought—it was all words'.[42] But Aurobindo did pay close attention to another politician at Ahmedabad. Bal Gangadhar Tilak, whom Aurobindo regarded as the 'one possible leader of a revolutionary party', 'took him out of the *pandal* [Congress pavilion] and talked to him for an hour in the grounds expressing his contempt for the Reformist movement and explaining his own line of action in Maharashtra'.[43] This seems to have been the first meeting between the two men. Aurobindo, still unknown outside Baroda, had contacted the celebrated leader before the Congress, apparently through friends in the secret society.[44] In the years that followed the relationship between the Maharashtrian and the Bengali became increasingly important to both.*

Shortly after the Congress session, Aurobindo set down his impressions of the current state of India's political life. The Congress, he said, was a spent force. The wave of the Congress Movement had 'dashed itself against the hard facts of human nature . . . and now there is throughout the country the languor, the weakness, the tendency to break up and discohere of the retiring wave.' But, he added hopefully, 'behind and under cover of this failure and falling back there has been slowly and silently gathering another wave the first voices of which are now being heard, the crests of whose foam are just mounting here and there into view.' He and others of 'the new age' who were destined 'to mount on the rising slope' of the new wave—'even if we do not live to ride on its crest'—had to study the failures of Congress to avoid its mistakes.[45]

Aurobindo did not publish, indeed he did not even complete the article in which these thoughts were expressed. In the beginning of 1903 there was little in the country to justify its optimistic conclusion. To opponents of the British Raj the most heartening of recent developments had taken place on a different continent. The success of the Boers in 1899 had been a blow to British prestige, but the 'Khaki Election' of 1900 was held on the assumption that peace had been restored. Yet a handful of Boer guerrillas were able to harass the British for another two years. In a poem written 'during the course of the Boer War' Aurobindo

* Tilak, preoccupied with the Tai Maharaj case, did not play a major role at the Ahmedabad Congress, but he was present (see List of Delegates, EINC 4: 427). (Note that the Tai Maharaj case was adjourned between 20 December 1902 and 19 January 1903 [*Mahratta* 21 December 1902: 599]). Jatin Banerji's letter to Tilak of December 1901 would suggest that Tilak was acquainted with Aurobindo at least a year before the Congress. They may have met each other even earlier than this. Tilak spent a good amount of time in Baroda in 1894 in connection with the Bapat Case, which involved the head of Baroda's Survey Settlement Department—the department in which Aurobindo then was working. Tilak may have been one of those who knew that Aurobindo was the writer of *New Lamps for Old*. K. G. Deshpande, who helped defend Tilak in the *Kesari* sedition case of 1897, probably spoke to Tilak about his Bengali friend. But the meeting at the Ahmedabad Congress is the first one for which there is any evidence.

praised the 'band of armèd herdsmen small' who faced fearlessly the victors of Waterloo and Trafalgar.[46] Thousands of others in India followed the progress of the war and expressed satisfaction at its outcome. According to Hem Chandra Das of Midnapore, 'When accurate news [of the war] was received in Bengal . . . an invisible pulsation was felt in the heart through a suppressed sense of satisfaction and feeble hope.'[47] If a few Dutch farmers could embarrass the mighty British what might the united power of three hundred million Indians accomplish? But India was not united. Nor was there anywhere in the country an organized force of resistance.

6

Apathy and Despair

In the beginning of 1903, not long after the Ahmedabad Congress, Aurobindo sent Barin to Calcutta to help Jatin Banerji in the work of revolutionary recruitment and organization. Before dispatching the young man on his mission, Aurobindo initiated him into Thakur Saheb's secret society. Holding a copy of the Gita in one hand and a sword in the other, Barin recited a Sanskrit *sloka*, pledging himself to fight for India's freedom as long as there was life in his body.[1]

After arriving in Calcutta, Barin went to the house on Upper Circular Road where Jatin was living. This was the first time the two men had met. There could hardly have been a greater contrast between them. Thin, bespectacled and dreamy, Barin cut a poor figure beside the stalwart Jatin, whose upright figure and penetrating glance made a favourable impression on everyone. The two had one thing in common, however: a contagious enthusiasm for the revolutionary cause. During his tour of western Bengal Jatin had roused a hesitant interest in Abinash Chandra Bhattacharya of Arbelia. Abinash was sufficiently intrigued to make the journey to Calcutta a few weeks later. When he knocked at the door of 108 Upper Circular Road he was met not by Jatin but the recently arrived Barin. After the usual exchange of civilities and some generalized conversation, Barin suddenly exclaimed, 'Brother, if India's bondage makes your heart ache, don't waste any more time, join us in this work today, this very moment.' This decided it for Abinash. Taking hold of Barin's hand, he cried, 'Right, brother! From now on I'm with you.'[2] It was the first of many successful conversions for Barin.

During January 1903 Aurobindo was much occupied with the

Gaekwar's correspondence in regard to the Curzon circular. But by the end of February he was sufficiently free to take privilege leave and go to Bengal.[3] This was his first visit since May of the previous year. In the meantime he had become a member of the secret society of western India. After his arrival 'he spoke of the Society and its aim to P. Mitter [Mitra] and other leading men of the revolutionary group in Bengal and they took the oath of the society and agreed to carry out its object on the lines' he suggested. Aurobindo's current idea was to get in touch with the 'small groups of revolutionaries' that were acting 'without reference to each other' and 'without any clear direction' and to unite them in 'a single organization' with 'a common programme' under Mitra's guidance. As 'leader of the revolution in Bengal', Mitra would be president of a Council of Five similar to the one Aurobindo had contacted in Bombay.[4] According to tradition the other members of the council were Aurobindo, C. R. Das, Surendranath Tagore and Sister Nivedita.*

Nivedita was probably the busiest woman in Calcutta. During the early part of 1903 she gave much of her time to teaching and administration in her girls' school.[5] But she was also working on a book on Indian culture, editing the scientific papers of Dr J. C. Bose, writing articles for several journals, corresponding with men like Moderate politician G. K. Gokhale and British journalist William Stead, delivering lectures, and through it all finding time for her spiritual practices. Her crowded schedule made it difficult for her to give as much time as she would have liked to national work; but she remained a dedicated revolutionary. Her outward appearance belied the intensity of her convictions. Thoroughly feminine, with a 'charming face' that radiated intelligence, she dressed habitually in unadorned white, a string of *rudraksha* beads across her bosom. But 'her very soul came out' when she spoke of revolution. Describing her later, Aurobindo said simply, 'That was fire.' While she seems to have been somewhat ambivalent about the use of arms, there was, Aurobindo said, 'no non-violence about her'.[6]†

If Nivedita was one of the most radical of the council's members, Chittaranjan Das was perhaps the least. Unlike his High Court colleague P. Mitra, Das was by temperament more a man of

* See Appendix 1, note 4.

† See Appendix 1, note 5.

letters than a man of action. An outstanding student at Calcutta University, he had gone to England in 1890 to take the ICS examination. Two year later he met Aurobindo, then in the process of getting rejected from the service. Unsuccessful in his effort to enter the ICS, Das joined the Inner Temple and in 1893 was called to the Bar. He returned home to find the legal profession overcrowded and his family's finances in ruins. Unable to get cases, he struggled for several years to recoup his fortunes. But by 1902 he was doing well enough to make generous donations to the cause.

A more important financial supporter was Surendranath Tagore, scion of one of the richest and most prominent families of Bengal.[7] Since his graduation from St Xavier's College in Bombay, Surendranath had been involved in various enterprises of the House of Tagore. Contact with Okakura, Nivedita and his cousin Sarala Devi helped stimulate his interest in national work. Sarala Devi was not directly connected with Mitra's samiti, but she gave financial and other forms of support to all the Calcutta groups and allowed them to borrow her martial-arts instructor 'Professor' Murtaza.[8] Her own Birastami Samiti gave physical demonstrations at a festival of the same name, which evidently was modelled on the festival she had witnessed years earlier in Solapur. She also borrowed from Maharashtra the idea of the hero-cult, inaugurating a Pratapaditya Utsab on the lines of the Shivaji festival. A tireless proponent of physical culture, she urged her brother-in-law A. C. Banerjee to learn and teach the use of the lathi, the sword, and the gun. But all this, she told him, was of minor importance compared to 'the high thing we wish to do'.[9] Jatin Banerji would have agreed with her in this, though they differed as to how the 'high thing' was to be accomplished. She seems to have looked upon the martial arts chiefly as means of developing physical strength and manly attitudes. Jatin and Aurobindo accepted these aims but they also thought that military skills could be put to practical use in the coming insurrection. In the beginning Jatin occasionally went to Sarala Devi for advice; but the two parted ways over the question of whether it was proper to gather funds by means of dacoities. Sarala Devi was vehemently opposed to this.* From this point 'nobody went to Sarala Devi any more', though she remained involved in other aspects of the movement.[10]

* See Appendix 1, note 6.

While Aurobindo was in Bengal in March 1903 he met some of the new recruits. One of them was Abinash Bhattacharya. Taken to Jatin's place, Abinash found 'Aurobindo-babu and Jatin-babu sitting on a mat spread out on the floor, talking and laughing'. Aurobindo examined the nervous youngster and spoke a few words to him.[11] Later he had a more significant meeting with Jatindra Nath Mukherjee. A handsome young man whose 'stature was like that of a warrior', Jatin excelled in physical activities and was practically fearless. He earned his nickname, 'Bagha Jatin', by singlehandedly killing a leopard (*chitra-bagha*) with a knife. In Calcutta Jatin learned stenography and typing and got work in a government department. Eventually he became the confidential clerk to Bengal's Financial Secretary. It never occurred to his employers that the efficient young 'steno' harboured a burning desire to drive the British from India. After his meeting with Aurobindo and Jatin Banerji, Jatin Mukherjee became one of the most active revolutionaries in Bengal.[12]

Jatin Mukherjee was connected with a secret society in Kushtia, one of the first to be founded outside Calcutta.[13] Centres also were active in Chandernagore, a French enclave north of the metropolis, and other *mofussil* (district) towns.[14] Apparently during his leave of February-March 1903,* Aurobindo and Barin visited the centre in Midnapore. Their uncle Jogin, the founder of the centre, took them to meet the local recruits, one of whom was Hem Chandra Das. At one point the men retired to a nearby ravine to try some target practice. 'When I saw the way [Aurobindo] and Barin held and aimed the gun, I realized that this was the first time they had handled one,' noted Hem, who nevertheless was thrilled to have the leaders in his home town. Aurobindo spoke of his plans for a revolutionary organization. Bengal would be divided into six regions, each of which would be further subdivided. Midnapore would be one of the regional headquarters.[15]

* Hem Chandra says that K-babu (certainly Aurobindo) and Barin came to Midnapore in 1902, a few months before a second visit which he places 'perhaps at the end of 1902' (*Banglay Biplab* 20). However it is clear from Barin's *Agnijug* (p. 73) that the first visit was after Barin came to Calcutta to join Jatin's society. This happened after the Ahmedabad Congress of December 1902. Aurobindo was on leave for a month from 22 February 1903 (BSR, below English Educational Department Tippan 26 March 1903, letter Aurobindo to Dewan 4 June 1903). This was the first occasion after the Congress when he might have visited Bengal.

When Aurobindo returned to Baroda Barin and others continued to tour the districts to set up centres. They had indifferent luck in unrevolutionary Orissa, better results in Mymensingh, Chandernagore and other places where the samiti idea had already caught on.[16] Their method was to preach the benefits of physical exercise to school and college students and other young bhadralok. Once an akhara had been started and recruits were coming in, they exposed them to political propaganda. In Calcutta Barin combed College Square and other student hangouts, engaging young men in conversation and making a few converts. But he had difficulty convincing them that a radical change of government was more important than passing marks in the First Arts examination.[17]

Barin had been given the work of touring the districts by Jatin Banerji, who remained in active charge of the Calcutta centre. In the light of later events, it seems likely that Jatin gave him this work at least partly because they got on each other's nerves. Misunderstandings caused by differences of temperament were aggravated by Barin's refusal to take orders from anyone but Aurobindo. Barin later complained that the older men talked big and never listened to the opinions of newcomers.[18] Presumably the newcomer he had chiefly in mind was himself. It certainly was true that there was lots of big talk going around. Hem Das noted this when he came up from Midnapore and soon he was adding to the sum. When Calcutta men gave him amazing reports of their progress, he gave them equally amazing reports of his own. Since he knew his own accounts were inflated, he assumed that the others' were as well. Looking around the Calcutta centre he saw little to get excited about. After two years they had succeeded in obtaining 'one horse, one bicycle . . . and a dozen or so leaders great and small'.[19]

This comment, delivered in the sarcastic tone Hem perfected during his years in prison, makes the centre seem more ridiculous than it was. A good number of branches had been opened and some significant additions made to the staff. One was Sakharam Ganesh Deuskar, the journalist from Deoghar who was introduced to the group by his former student Barin.[20] Deuskar became the samiti's expert on economic history. In 1904 he set down his ideas—essentially the 'drain theory' of Naoroji, Dutt and Digby—in a book called *Desher Katha*. This became enormously popular and had the distinction of being the first book to be banned under the Press Act of 1910.[21] Another important recruit of the 1903 period was Bhupendranath Dutt, younger brother of Swami Vivekananda. Dutt spent much of his time touring the districts doing essential but unglamorous grassroots work.[22] It was however true that there were too many generals and too few soldiers at Grey Street, where the Calcutta centre had shifted. Besides Aurobindo and P. Mitra, there were field marshals Jatin and Barin, and a newly recruited brigadier named Debavrata Bose. No wonder communications at headquarters were often confused. No wonder, too, that the officers found it hard to get along with one another.

The conflict that developed between Jatin and Barin has become famous in the annals of the revolution. Much has been written on the subject without the central issues being resolved or even identified. The two major first-hand accounts are confusing and contradictory; later observers are left to judge in accordance with their predilections.* Historians agree in labelling it a 'sordid' matter,[23] but it is possible to look on it instead as slightly ludicrous. Yet it cannot be denied that the clash resulted in the division of the party and the loss of much time and work.

* The main sources for the Jatin-Barin feud are Hem Chandra Das Kanungo's *Banglay Biplab Pracheshta* (p. 36 ff) and Barin Ghose's *Agnijug* (p. 78 ff, 99 ff). Bhupendranath Dutt (*Dwitiya Swadhinatar Sangram* 128–9) supports Hem while Abinash Bhattacharya ('Aurobindo' 832, 'Baiplabik Samiti' 192–3) supports Barin. Jadugopal Mukhopadhyay gives an informed second-hand account that is closer to Barin's version than Hem's (*Biplabi Jibaner Smriti* 168). Barin's account was written in the 1940s to answer charges leveled by Hem twenty years earlier. There was evidently much bad blood between the two. If Barin's account is marred by self-justification, Hem's is marred by rancour. In my account I follow Barin's version of the events but not his interpretation. Hem does not seem to have been in Calcutta at the time and several of the particulars in which his version differs from Barin's are rather dubious. He says for instance that Barin reported Jatin's misconduct first to Aurobindo, who ruled in Barin's favour, causing many including P. Mitra to break with Aurobindo (*Banglay Biplab* 38). It seems unlikely that the matter was referred to Aurobindo before Mitra, since Aurobindo was a thousand miles away in Baroda and had to make a trip to Bengal specifically to adjudicate the matter. Nevertheless many of Hem's criticisms of Barin seem to be well taken. I doubt whether Barin succeeded as well as Hem alleges in making Aurobindo the tool of his machinations, but it is likely that he tried his best to do so. Other points of difference are of only incidental importance.

As in many quarrels the real issue was masked by a squabble over an affair of little importance. Briefly, the faction led by Barin accused Jatin of harbouring a woman of doubtful virtue. Jatin insisted she was his relative and ignored the accusations. Finding him adamant Barin and his friends took their tales to commander-in-chief P. Mitra. Mitra took an especially serious view of sexual misconduct, having in his youth repudiated a guru who showed weakness in this respect. Aggrieved by Barin's report, he ruled that the woman would have to go or Jatin leave the centre. Jatin chose the latter alternative. He shifted to a mess on Sitaram Ghose Street, while Barin and his supporter Abinash moved to Madan Mitter Lane. Here they could remain for only two or three months, after which they wandered off in search of a permanent home. During this period the work of the society was practically at a standstill.

When the confrontation between Barin and Jatin first came to a head, Barin wrote to Aurobindo giving him his side of the story. Aurobindo asked the disputants to settle things among themselves. Six months later, with no settlement in sight, he took leave from his work and came to Calcutta. According to Barin Aurobindo rebuked him for picking a quarrel with Jatin and succeeded in bringing the two together. But the truce proved to be short-lived. 'The breach was healed only to gape wider as soon as his [Aurobindo's] back was turned,' wrote Barin.[24]

During the peace-parlays Jatin was able to convince Barin that the woman who was the 'cause' of it all was indeed his relative, since their feet had the same peculiar shape. But by now it was obvious that the conflict had little to do with the lady. Barin and Hem, whose accounts are poles apart in most respects, agree that Jatin was much resented for his military ways. Hem claims further that Barin used Jatin's unpopularity as a rallying point in his effort to capture the leadership of the society, making use of his relationship with Aurobindo to further this end. But Hem was intelligent enough to recognize that the real cause of the dissension was 'the desire of [Jatin and Barin] to boss other people around'. This desire 'was so great that they refused to listen to anybody else's suggestions'.[25]

It is a common observation that revolutionary parties tend to break apart into factions that often spend more time in internecine feuds than in action against the enemy.* This is especially true when victory seems near and the overriding concern is which faction is going to assume power. According to Hem some of the members of the society thought success so certain in 1904 that they already were exercised over this.[26] Factionalism has always found the soil of Bengal unusually fertile. The historian Niharranjan Ray is probably right in considering the conflict between Barin and Jatin the precursor of 'those personalistic feuds characterized by individual likes and dislikes . . . which have been plaguing politics in Bengal ever since'.[27]

The negotiations in Calcutta between Aurobindo, Jatin and Barin seem to have taken place in October 1904.† Around the middle of that month Aurobindo and Barin went from Calcutta to Deoghar to pass the *puja* holidays with their family. Soon letters arrived from Calcutta containing fresh complaints against Jatin. At this point, according to Barin, Aurobindo said: 'I can see that nothing will ever come of Bengal. Let's go back to Baroda.'[28] It may be doubted whether these were Aurobindo's exact words, but they seem to represent his current state of mind. Some time previously, possibly during the same trip, Aurobindo had made a tour of eastern Bengal with Debavrata Bose.‡ His purpose was 'to

* Examples could be provided from virtually every revolutionary movement in history. The classic cases are of course the French and Russian revolutions. In relation to the revolution under study, see B. Ghose, 'Sri Aurobindo as I Understand Him' 37; B. Ghose, *Wounded Humanity* 51; U. Banerjee, 'Aurobindo Prasanga'; Sri Aurobindo to A. B. Purani in Purani, ed., *Talks* 17. For more general remarks see Laqueur (pp. 93–5) and Avrich (p. 42).

† Barin writes in *Agnijug* (pp. 111, 106) that immediately after the parleys with Jatin, he and Aurobindo went to Deoghar to pass the *puja* holidays with their family. In 1904 (1311 Bengali era) Durga Puja began on 15 October. The principal festival day, *vijaya dashami*, was three days later (information from Pandit B. C. Bhattacharya, Government Astrologer, via Arup Mitra). Hem Das writes that the conflict occurred probably in the beginning of 1904 (H. Kanungo, *Banglay Biplab* 37).

‡ Aurobindo refers to this tour several times in his talks and writings, but never dates it exactly. In one place he says it happened 'some years' after the death of Rajnarain Bose, which took place in 1899 (*On Himself* 16); in another he says it was 'three or four years before the Swadeshi movement was born', by which presumably he meant 1905 (speech of 19 January 1908, pub. *Bande Mataram* 658). It does not seem possible that it could have taken place before 1903. Aurobindo certainly made the tour with Debavrata Bose, and it is clear from the accounts of Barin and Hem Chandra that Debavrata entered the organization in or about that year. The tour therefore must have taken place in 1903 or 1904.

visit some of the revolutionary centres already formed, but also to meet leading men of the districts and to find out the general attitude of the country and the possibilities of the revolutionary movement'. He found that 'the prevailing mood was apathy and despair'. People were so fearful that they stole away if he or Debavrata said anything the least suggestive of resistance. Aurobindo looked at those who remained and asked himself, 'These are the people who will do [it]?' For some time men 'had believed that regeneration could only come from outside, that another nation would take us by the hand and lift us up'. But lately they had come to realize that no other nation was going to help them and as a result 'apathy and despair spread everywhere'.[29]

The 'nation' that had disappointed Indian nationalists was Japan. The help that Okakura promised his Calcutta audiences never materialized. Madhavrao Jadhav is said to have been sent to Japan for military training in 1903. If he did go (and there is no indubitable evidence that he did) he stayed a very short time and learned nothing significant. Still, the hope that a foreign power would share its military knowhow with India did not die out. Towards the beginning of 1905 Tilak made contact with the Russian consul in Bombay, asking him whether an Indian candidate could be admitted to a Russian military academy. The consul was instructed by his superiors in St Petersburg to say that this could only be done through official channels. This was of course impossible.[30] Undaunted Tilak, Aurobindo and others raised some money and sent Madhavrao to England in July 1905. After a brief stay in London with Tilak's friend Shyamji Krishnavarma, the radical editor of *The Indian Sociologist*, Madhavrao got himself enrolled (apparently with Russian help) in the Swiss military academy in Bern. He passed the officers' examination at the end of 1906 and then spent a year studying the organization and observing the manoeuvres of the Swiss army.[31]

Tilak's opening of negotiations with the Russian consul was a small point of light in 'the hell of black death' that hung over the country in the beginning of 1905. Talking things over with his associates, Aurobindo noticed that those 'who were really honest with themselves were saying that there was no help for this nation and that we were doomed'.[32] Some of this defeatism seems to have rubbed off on him. In an 'open letter to those who despair of their country' he wrote around this time he gave voice to the 'dismay and weakness' of the 'sons of our mother Bharat who disclaim their sonhood':

> We are sick and broken; we are idle and cowardly; we perish every year from famine and plague; disease decimates us, with every decade poverty annihilates family after family; where there were a hundred in one house, there are now ten; where there was once a flourishing village, the leopard and the jackal will soon inhabit. . . . Worst of all we are disunited beyond hope of union and without union we must ere long perish. It may be five decades or it may be ten, but very soon this great and ancient nation will have perished from the face of the earth.

Such, he continued, was the 'Siren song' with which the despairing ones slew 'the hearts of those who have still force and courage to strive against Fate and would rescue our Mother out of the hands of destruction'. Those who succumbed to despair when action was called for were matricides. Some of them, 'the wooers of safety and ease', were contemptible; others, those who refused 'to lift her out of danger lest they defile their own spotless hands', were unworthy of contempt. But there was a third sort, 'those who love and perhaps have striven for her but having now grown themselves faint and helpless bid others to despair and cease'. It was to break the spell of this despair that Aurobindo addressed himself to his brethren. 'Come', he exhorted them, 'let us reason calmly together.' But here he broke off.[33]

PART TWO
Action

7

The Temple of the Mother

Barin accompanied his brother when Aurobindo returned to Baroda at the end of October 1904.* In the literature of the revolution, this move is referred to as the end of Barin's 'first campaign'.[1] At the time there was no reason to assume that there would be a second. The centre in Calcutta had effectively been destroyed. The leaders whose clash had brought this about were both fed up with the whole affair. Barin spent most of the next twelve months at loose ends in Baroda. In December Aurobindo asked the Gaekwar to give his brother a Rs 60 appointment. The ruler complied even though the service was 'overstocked' at that time. But Barin never reported for duty and in September 1905 the appointment was cancelled.[2] In later statements Barin represented his stay in Baroda as one of careful consideration of his future action. He says he spent much of his time studying and talking things over with Aurobindo. But Aurobindo's complaint in a letter of the period that Barin 'never sits still' and his later characterization of the young man's endeavors as 'knocking about' suggest that Barin's activities in Baroda were less purposeful than his own accounts would indicate.[3]

Jatin Banerji also left Bengal. Sometime in 1905 he put on the robes of the sannyasin and went on a pilgrimage to the Himalayas.

* See *Agnijug* 106. In 1904 Durga Puja fell on 15 October. Baroda State records show a gap in Aurobindo's official correspondence between 28 September and 28 October 1904. This suggests that he was on leave at this time. In a statement made after his arrest in May 1908 Barin said he returned to Baroda from Bengal in 1903 (GOI HPA May 1909, 112–50: 25). This obviously incorrect date was reproduced in the Rowlatt Report, par. 22, and from there has found its way into most books and articles on the period.

This typically Indian act may have been prompted in part by the recent death of his father; but according to Barin the chief motivating factor was Jatin's 'disgust and despair' over the way things had turned out in Calcutta.[4] In Naini Tal Jatin became a disciple of Soham Swami, the 'pioneer of the cult of physical strength and courage in Bengal', who had become a revered ascetic. Receiving the name Niralamba Swami from his guru, Jatin set off for Punjab and the North-West frontier where for some time he preached his religio-political doctrines. Among his converts were Ajit Singh and Kisan Singh, both of whom later helped spread revolutionary ideas in the North. Within a year of his meeting with Niralamba, Ajit became a prominent Extremist politician. Kisan was responsible for transmitting the idea to Lala Hardayal, the organizer of Sikh revolutionaries in North America, and to his son Bhagat Singh, the most famous Indian revolutionary of the 1920s. In 1907 Niralamba returned to Calcutta where he became briefly involved with the nationalist press. But he never renewed his connection with the secret society he had helped to found.[5]

This society, after Jatin and Barin's departure, virtually ceased to exist. Most of the recruits drifted away. Those like Abinash who did not lacked organization, direction, and resources. Left to itself the Bengali revolutionary movement might well have perished of inanition at this time. It was saved not so much by the renewed efforts of its originators as by a general enthusiasm that took hold of the province that year. This was roused by two unrelated events: the Russo-Japanese War and the Partition of Bengal.

Japan's success in bottling up the Russian fleet in Port Arthur in February 1904 and the subsequent land victory at Mukden were sufficiently astonishing. But the destruction of Russia's Baltic Fleet at Tsushima in May 1905 'electrified the Asiatic world'. Writing in *The Indian Review*, the Madras editor G. A. Natesan declared: 'Almost for the first time in the history of the world an Asiatic power, hitherto somewhat despised and not taken into account, has humbled a huge European power.' An English commentator saw even more significance in Russia's defeat. If Abyssinia's humbling of Italy in 1896 had been 'the first decisive victory gained by troops that might be reckoned Oriental over a European army in the open field, for at least three centuries', Japan's triumph by sea as well as by land was altogether unprecedented: 'never before in all history had an Asiatic navy won a great sea-fight against European fleets.'[6] One result of the unexpected outcome was a transformation in the attitude of other countries towards the victor. The average Westerner 'was wont to regard Japan as barbarous while she indulged in the gentle arts of peace; he calls her civilized since she began to commit wholesale slaughter on Manchurian battlefields', wrote Okakura in his classic *Book of Tea.*[7] Indians also had been in the habit of looking down on the Japanese—Natesan called them 'a race of dwarfs fed chiefly on rice'.[8] Now suddenly Indian journalists, Indian barristers and Indian schoolboys were hailing the Japanese as the champions of resurgent Asia. In Calcutta P. Mitra, Surendranath Tagore and Chittaranjan Das—all members of the moribund Bengal Council—got together to discuss the Japanese question. Saralà Devi helped coordinate a Calcutta fund-raising drive; Tilak's *Kesari* subscribed to a similar appeal in Bombay.[9] But the most conspicuous result of the Russo-Japanese War in India was the change it produced in the self-image of the Indian people. In June Surendranath Banerjea's *Bengalee* gave voice to a near-universal feeling when it declared: 'We feel that we are not the same people as we were before the Japanese successes.'[10]

Given the dissimilarity in the circumstances of the two countries and the lack of real contact between them, it might seem surprising that Indians in general and Bengalis in particular were so heartened by Japan's victory. It was to be sure a triumph of Asians over Europeans (assuming that Russians are Europeans) but what, realistically, had this to do with India? Realistically nothing, sentimentally everything. And Bengalis, perhaps more than any other Indian people, are moved by sentiment.

However much it may appear so in retrospect, there was nothing inevitable about the agitation against the Partition of Bengal. The province was certainly too large to be governed efficiently. Most of what is now West Bengal, Bangladesh, Bihar and Orissa—an area as large as modern France with a population half again as great—was under the administration of a single lieutenant-governor and his staff. Proposals to divide the province into more manageable units had been under consideration since 1866. In 1874 Assam, along with the district of Sylhet, had been made a separate province. In the years that followed the government considered various proposals to transfer other Bengali districts to

Assam. Finally at the end of 1903 a Note was published in which it was proposed to transfer Chittagong division along with Dacca and Mymensingh districts. Later other districts were added to the list. The reasons put forward in favour of the transfer were administrative efficiency, general economic uplift and the development of Dacca and Chittagong as administrative and commercial centres. But correspondence not made public at the time shows that one of the government's primary motives was its desire 'to split up and thereby weaken a solid body of opponents to our rule'.[11] These 'opponents' were the Bengali-speaking Hindus of Bengal proper, who after partition would find themselves rivalled in the west by Bihari and Oriya speakers, and in the east by Bengali-speaking Muslims.

The government, which had expected some opposition to the plan, was surprised by the vehemence of the reaction. Proponents of partition characterized the objections raised against it as 'sentimental'. Conceding this, the Liberal journalist Henry Nevinson explained that it was the 'same kind of sentiment as would set Scotland ablaze with indignation if an English Prime Minister drew a jagged line from Thurso to Dumfries, and announced that in future Scotland would consist of two separate provinces, with one government in Edinburgh and the other in Glasgow.'[12] During the early stages of the agitation most of the opposition came from Bengalis of the eastern districts, who were outraged at being grouped with the 'backward' Assamese and apprehensive about losing the administrative, judicial and commercial advantages of Calcutta. In an article written but not published at this time, Aurobindo warned that these were superficial issues. 'The true and vital side of the question', he said, was to see that 'this measure is no mere administrative proposal but a blow straight at the heart of the nation'.[13] By this he meant that it was a thrust against the integrity of the Bengali nation, which he had begun to look on as something living and divine. In the open letter cited in the last chapter he had referred to India as 'mother Bharat'. Perhaps a year later, in August 1905, he elaborated the same idea in a celebrated letter to his wife: 'While others look upon their country as an inert piece of matter—a few meadows and fields, forests and hills and rivers—I look upon Her as the Mother'.[14] It is possible to trace this idea back to Bankim Chandra's *Ananda Math*. When Mahendra says that the 'richly watered' land celebrated in the song *Bande Mataram* 'is the country [*desh*], it is not the Mother', Bhabananda replies, 'We recognise no other Mother. Mother and Motherland is more than heaven itself.'[15] But even if Aurobindo derived the idea from the novel, it is clear from many passages in his writings that from this moment he held it as his own.

As the movement against the Partition became stronger, Aurobindo realized it could be used to further his revolutionary ends. 'This is a golden opportunity', he wrote to Abinash. 'We will get many workers from this [anti-partition] movement.' Around this time a flood of anti-government pamphlets began to appear, some of which were extremely vitriolic. One of them, *No Compromise*, was written by Aurobindo. After getting this printed, Abinash took a copy to Congress leader Surendranath Banerjea, who was struck by the quality of the writing.[16] Like much of the ephemeral literature of the period, *No Compromise* has disappeared without a trace; but another pamphlet Aurobindo wrote during this period has survived. This is the famous *Bhawani Mandir*, published in Baroda sometime before August 1905, when a copy was noticed by the district magistrate of Broach.*

Although at root an exposition of the philosophical and religious bases of nationalism, *Bhawani Mandir* is cast in the form of a prospectus. 'A temple is to be erected and consecrated to Bhawani, the Mother, among the hills', the pamphlet begins. 'To all the children of the Mother the call is sent forth to help in the sacred work.' Attached to the temple (*mandir*) would be 'a new order of Brahmacharins' (religious students) 'who have renounced all in order to work for the Mother.' By choosing the name Bhawani rather than its Bengali equivalents Durga or Kali, Aurobindo evidently was alluding to the Maratha general Shivaji,

* Although *Bhawani Mandir* was unsigned, it is certain that it was written by Aurobindo. See Sri Aurobindo, *On Himself* 51 and B. Ghose, *Agnijug* 115, 124, 131. Ker (pp. 30–1) has this to say about the authorship of the pamphlet: '[Bhawani Mandir] first came to notice in August 1905, when a copy was sent anonymously from Baroda to the Head Clerk to the District Magistrate of Broach. There is nothing on the pamphlet to show who the author or the publisher is, but the Head Clerk stated at the time that he thought the author was "a Mr. Bose, a Bengali Babu who is in the employ of the Baroda Durbar and once passed for the I.C.S. but was rejected for failing to pass the test in riding." Though the name is wrong, this obviously refers to Arabindo Ghose, who was a Professor in the Gaekwar's College at Baroda at this time, and there is no doubt that he was the author.'

who worshipped the mother goddess in the form of Bhawani and felt he was acting under her inspiration.[17] But Aurobindo's Bhawani was not just a form of the mother goddess of popular Hinduism: she was 'the Infinite Energy, which streams forth from the Eternal'. This is the language of philosophical tantrism, which sees the female principle (*prakriti* or nature) as the expressive energy or *shakti* of the Absolute. The Mother had to be worshipped as Strength or Shakti, wrote Aurobindo, because this was the form in which she was chiefly manifest in the present age. 'The Shakti of war, the Shakti of wealth, the Shakti of science . . . are a thousand times more prolific in resources, weapons and instruments than ever before in recorded history.' The Western Powers and Japan embodied her strength, but India, otherwise so rich, was 'empty of strength, void of energy'. As a result India's unparalleled knowledge (*jnana*) and devotion (*bhakti*) had become ineffective and the country had fallen into decrepitude. But India could not perish, for India was the repository of something neither Japan nor the Western Powers possessed: the religion of Vedanta, which held the seed of the future religion of all mankind. If India was to give this gift to the world, the Indian people had to worship Strength or Shakti. Hence the need for a temple to Bhawani. And since 'adoration will be dead and ineffective unless it is transmuted into Karma [action]', there had to be 'a new Order of Karma Yogins [followers of the spiritual path of works] . . . who have renounced all in order to work for the Mother'. In an appendix Aurobindo enumerated seven general and eight specific rules to be followed by members of the new order.[18]

From the moment of its appearance *Bhawani Mandir* has been compared to Bankim's *Ananda Math*, and the similarities between them are obvious. In both a band of sannyasins vowed to renunciation dedicate themselves to service of the country envisaged as the Mother. This service takes the form of religious worship (in both cases recognizably Hindu) and 'work for the country'. But there are important differences between the two orders. The presiding deity of Ananda Math is Vishnu, and the santans are Vaishnavites; Bhawani Mandir clearly is of *shakta* inspiration. The santans engage themselves chiefly in military operations; the work of Bhawani's devotees is social: education, nursing, charity, industrial development, general national uplift.

This is somewhat surprising considering Aurobindo's criticism of social activism both before and after 1905, and it suggests another parallel to, if not actual influence on, the Bhawani Mandir scheme: Gopal Krishna Gokhale's Servants of India Society, which was launched in June 1905.*

There are many similarities between Gokhale's society and Aurobindo's 'order'. Both were to consist of men who pledged themselves in a religious spirit to the service of the Motherland. Members of both organizations had to give absolute obedience to the head of the order and to lead lives of moral purity. Possessing no money on their own, they would receive from the organization all they needed for a decent living. In addition to their main work of educating 'the people', they would promote industrial development and help establish good relations between different communities. Some would be sent to foreign countries to study various arts and sciences.

These remarkable similarities are more than offset by fundamental differences. *Bhawani Mandir* put forward a visionary scheme that was never realized and perhaps never intended to be realized. The Rules of Gokhale's society were practical from start to finish. But the two documents differ most strikingly in their underlying assumptions. Gokhale wrote that members of his society would 'frankly accept the British connection as ordained, in the inscrutable dispensation of Providence, for India's good'. He called for 'public life [to] be spiritualized' but was careful to avoid any appeal to sectarian sentiment. To the Hindu-turned-agnostic, religion *was* service of the people. To Aurobindo, the agnostic-turned-Hindu, service of the people was one form of a new religion of nationality. It was in *Bhawani Mandir* that his idea of India as the Mother—'not a piece of earth, not a figure of speech, nor a fiction of the mind' but 'a mighty Shakti'—was first articulated. And the mission of this Country-as-Goddess was 'to purge barbarism (Mlechchhahood) out of humanity and to Aryanize the world'. Nowhere in the pamphlet did Aurobindo write or even imply that the Mlechchhas he referred to were the

* Aurobindo did not admire Gokhale as a political thinker (*On Himself* 49); but this would not necessarily have prevented him from giving his own religio-political turn to Gokhale's notions. There is of course no way this conjecture can be proved, but a comparison of the proposed organizations of the leading Moderate and most radical Extremist of the period may be instructive in any case.

British. Rather he seemed to suggest that Aryahood and Mlechchhahood were universal conditions affecting all human endeavour. Echoing an ancient tradition he said that both were powers of the one Divine Shakti. But to India alone was 'reserved the highest and most splendid destiny, the most essential to the future of the human race', that of sending forth 'from herself the future religion of the entire world, the Eternal Religion that is to harmonise all religion, science and philosophies and make mankind one soul'.[19]

The idea that India was charged with the mission of giving its eternal religion to the modern world was of course not new to Aurobindo. It is the main burden of Vivekananda's writings, particularly the Kumbakonam speech of 1897. 'The world', said the Swami, was 'waiting' for the two grand ideas enshrined in the 'universal religion' of Vedanta: 'universal toleration' of all religious forms, and 'the spiritual oneness of the whole universe', demonstrated first by the sages of the Upanishads and lately confirmed by modern science. The same ideas, variously stated, are found also in the works of writers like Rammohan Roy, Keshub Chandra Sen, Dayananda Saraswati and B. G. Tilak. To this century-old notion of the superiority of Vedanta to Western religion, Aurobindo added the Tantric idea of the worship of Strength or Shakti.

The *Bhawani Mandir* scheme was never put into effect and Aurobindo soon lost interest in it.[20] But the pamphlet is significant as the first articulate expression of what has become known as 'religious nationalism'—a strand of the national movement that still attracts ardent critics and passionate defenders. The first and most vehement critics were the British. While there is no evidence that the district magistrate of Broach gave *Bhawani Mandir* special importance when it first appeared, once it became known that its author had conspired to overthrow the government, Raj officials claimed to find in it 'the germ of the Hindu revolutionary movement in Bengal'. These are the words of James Campbell Ker, personal assistant of the director of criminal intelligence, who reprinted the entire pamphlet in his influential report *Political Trouble in India 1907–1917*. Drawing heavily on Ker, the authors of the celebrated Rowlatt Report featured *Bhawani Mandir* as the first of three revolutionary publications 'of a mischievous or specially inflammatory kind'. Subsequently the work was given special mention in former Bengal Governor Lord Ronaldshay's *Heart of Aryavarta* and in a speech on Indian terrorism by Charles Tegart, commissioner of the Calcutta police during the revolutionary period.[21] At first sight all this attention would seem to be unmerited. The pamphlet after all said nothing seditious and was manifestly impractical. What seems to have struck the authorities was its articulateness and persuasiveness.[22] What frightened them was its appeal to 'religious' emotions. The authors of the Rowlatt Report called it 'a remarkable instance of perversion of religious ideals to political purposes'. Ronaldshay claimed that its author 'did more than anyone to breathe into the sinister spectre of anarchy the vitalising influence of religion.'[23]

To early-twentieth-century Britons, any association of religion with politics smacked of fanaticism. They themselves were beyond that sort of thing: no war of religion had been fought in Britain for a couple of hundred years. To be sure, as late as 1914 British politicians could get worked up over the issue of Welsh disestablishment. But only the benighted Irish and Asians actually *fought* in the name of religion. Faith was fine so long as it remained where it belonged, in church, mosque, or temple. If it tried to escape these confines it was a threat to the Pax Britannica.

The British in India were especially susceptible to this sort of thinking. The journalist Valentine Chirol, writing in the *Times* in 1909 on 'the literature of Indian unrest', deplored 'its appeals to the Hindu scriptures and to the Hindu deities and the exploitation of the religious sentiment for the promotion of racial hatred'. Chirol cited Aurobindo as a leading representative of this 'grave phenomenon', but was willing to acknowledge his 'sincerity'.[24] Most Britons in the government were not. F. C. Daly, the writer of a 1911 confidential police report, imputed to Aurobindo 'the sagacity to see that the surest and safest ground to proceed on would be religion'. He and other 'men of learning and ability' used their 'ingenuity' to develop 'deep religious convictions' in their less gifted followers, whom they then incited to revolutionary crime. The same note is struck in another police report of 1913: Aurobindo expounded in his newspaper articles 'the doctrines of revolution by violence under the guise of religion'. Developed over decades, this interpretation has become the standard explanation of Aurobindo's motives among one school of historians. According to one defender of the Raj, Michael Edwardes,

Aurobindo had so little success arousing 'anti-British feelings amongst the educated classes' of Bengal that he 'decided that the only way to stir up political enthusiasm was to give politics a religious bias'.[25]

A number of Indian writers, starting from a quite different set of assumptions, reached much the same conclusion. Aurobindo's old associate Hem Chandra Das blamed the ultimate failure of the movement on Aurobindo's misguided attempts to infuse it with Hindu ideas. Hem claimed that during its first two years the secret society had no connection with religion except for the ceremony of taking oaths on the Gita. Aurobindo himself showed no interest in religion at this time. It was only around 1904 that he accepted the idea, first suggested by Debavrata Bose, that the liberation of India could only be achieved through supernatural or religious means. From this point on he deliberately mixed religion with politics, with disastrous results.[26] This interpretation has also developed over the decades and became conventional wisdom to a number of Indian intellectuals. Onetime Comintern leader M. N. Roy, who started out as an Anushilan revolutionary, wrote that Aurobindo, one of the creators of 'Religious Nationalism', 'adapted the teachings of Vivekananda to political purposes'. A modern proponent of this view rebukes Aurobindo for 'appealing to religious passions' while a major historian endorses Hem's assertion that Aurobindo and his followers turned one means to achieve independence into an end in itself.[27]

It cannot be denied that from the time of *Bhawani Mandir* Aurobindo used religious terminology and imagery in his political writings. His reasons for doing so are less certain. Was he a secular politician opportunistically using religion to achieve political ends? Or was he a man of religious conviction, sincere in his expressed belief that nationalism was 'not a mere political programme' but 'a religion that has come from God'?[28]

Much of the trouble that turn-of-the-century Britons had with Aurobindo's spirituality stemmed from their knowledge that he had had the benefit of the same education as they. How could a man who had won prizes at St Paul's School and King's College, Cambridge, give any credit to the cult of Shakti, to which 'are associated... some of the most libidinous and cruel of Hindu superstitions'?[29] In fact when Aurobindo was in England he rejected all forms of religious belief, espousing the agnosticism then fashionable in university circles. But before his return to India, while reading an English translation of the Upanishads, he had what he later described as a 'mental experience' of the Atman or universal soul. This did not in itself convert him to Hinduism or any other religion; but after his return to India he gradually embraced Hindu ideas and social forms as part of his effort to recover his cultural heritage. Much of his reading at this time was of texts belonging to the Indian spiritual tradition: Bengali devotional poems, the Ramayana and Mahabharata, the Gita and Upanishads. By 1901 he took pride in regarding himself as a Hindu rather than a Brahmo, the sect of both sides of his family. His growing interest in the Indian value-system intruded into a literary article he wrote the same year. Concluding a discussion of the mediaeval poet Kalidasa, Aurobindo admonished his readers that India's 'one chance of salvation' was to shake off 'the soils and filth' of her downfall and reassert 'her peculiar individuality and national type against the callow civilization of the West'.[30] In this essay he did not mention Hinduism by name, treating India's religious tradition as part of its special cultural heritage. But in another literary article written a short while later he wrote that Hinduism—not the 'ignorant and customary Hinduism of today ... but the purer form of Vedanta'—might alone be able to prevent India from plunging 'into the vortex of scientific atheism and the breakdown of moral ideals which is engulfing Europe'.[31]

These passages make it clear that Aurobindo's interest in Indian religion was at this point closely associated with his rejection of Western values for those of his native culture. This is in itself a potentially political stance. Modern critics have emphasized that cultural imperialism is at least as damaging as the military and economic kind. If 'the imposition of foreign armies' leads justifiably to revolt, writes Terry Eagleton, the imposition of 'alien ways of experience' also creates a situation in which 'culture is so vitally bound up with one's common identity that there is no need to argue for its relation to political struggle'.[32]

If Aurobindo's interest in religion did not go beyond an intellectual recognition of its central importance to Indian life, it might be argued that his use of religious terminology was opportunistic. But Aurobindo did not just accept the philosophical underpinnings of Hinduism; he practised various methods of spiritual discipline, and according to his own testimony he attained some significant results. During his stay in Baroda he had a number of spontaneous 'spiritual experiences'.[33]* But, striking as these were, they did not induce him to take up a life of spiritual practice. Indeed he later wrote that 'he did not associate them at that time' with the yoga discipline he later adopted.[34] He was, he explained in the 1940s, too preoccupied with the idea of Indian independence to devote himself to any time-consuming spiritual practices. But when some of his friends in Baroda, among them K. G. Deshpande, told him that the spiritual discipline known as *yoga* could be used to obtain practical powers, he decided to give it a try. In 1904 or 1905 he began that form of yogic practice known as *pranayama* or breath-control. This gave him, he said, certain non-spiritual results, such as increased fluency in writing. At the same time he and Barin began to experiment with what spiritualists call 'automatic writing'. Some of the resulting communications seemed to him at the time to originate from disembodied entities, though later he attributed most of them to 'a dramatising element in the subconscious mind'.† One of the 'spirits' contacted in Baroda, who identified himself as Ramakrishna Paramahansa, told them to 'build a temple'. This was the (occult or subconscious) origin of the Bhawani Mandir idea. A short time later, in August 1905, Aurobindo began practising some of the spiritual as opposed to psycho-physical techniques of yoga. By the end of the month he could report to his wife that his preliminary experiences had convinced him that a man could have direct experience of God,

* This is not the place for an enquiry into the validity of spiritual experience. One might note in passing however that judging from Aurobindo's own poetic descriptions of his Baroda experiences (*Collected Poems* 138–9, 153–4) they were of the sort that mystics of many cultures and periods have claimed to have, and evidently were quite powerful and striking.

† In 1945 Sri Aurobindo wrote that he became interested in automatic writing after seeing some 'very extraordinary' examples done by Barin in Baroda. 'He decided to find out by practising this kind of writing himself what there was behind it.' Barin writes of these experiments in chapter 10 of *Agnijug*. There is also a detailed account of one session in a Government of India report. (The accuracy of this account, as measured against accounts by Aurobindo and one of his friends [statement of R. N. Patkar in Sri Aurobindo papers, pub. Purani, *Life* 65], is a remarkable confirmation of the efficiency of the British espionage system.) Aurobindo continued to practice automatic writing for some time after his withdrawal to Pondicherry, but eventually 'dropped these experiments altogether' (*On Himself* 65).

just as the ancient scriptures said. It was in the same letter that he told her of his conviction that India was a living goddess, 'the Mother'.

The three constituents of Aurobindo's 'religious nationalism' —his belief that India was not just a piece of earth but a living goddess; that India was charged with the mission of bringing the light of truth, in the form of the eternal religion of Vedanta, to a world in danger of succumbing to Western scientism and moral anarchy; and that India had therefore to be liberated from Western domination—were all present in his thinking by 1904 or 1905. This was just the moment that he began promoting 'religious' themes in the revolutionary movement. The attested development of these beliefs over a period of thirteen years induces one to accept Chirol's assessment that they were sincerely held. The same ideas are found consistently in Aurobindo's writings throughout his later political career and even afterwards. The philosophical conceptions that underlie *Bhawani Mandir* appear also, matured but basically unchanged, in some of the main works of Sri Aurobindo the philosopher and yogin, for example *The Synthesis of Yoga* (1914–1921) and *The Mother* (1928). These books, written after Aurobindo retired from politics, do not lay stress on the idea of India as the storehouse of spirituality and as such the destined savior of the mankind. But other works written at the same time and even later show that Sri Aurobindo never abandoned his belief that India had a divinely ordained spiritual mission.[35]

Aurobindo certainly took the religio-philosophical basis of *Bhawani Mandir* seriously, but he does not seem to have given much importance to the practical realization of the scheme. He later said that the pamphlet 'was more Barin's idea than his' and that the idea of founding a temple and starting a monastic order 'was soon dropped as far as [he] was concerned', since he knew 'it wouldn't work out'.[36] But Barin was too taken with the notion to let it drop. Besides he lacked occupation in Baroda. Sometime in the latter part of 1905 he went off in search of a holy place 'among the hills', 'far from the contamination of modern cities and as yet little trodden by man, in a high and pure air steeped in calm and energy', where the temple was to be established. Deciding that the best place would be the Amarkantak Hill where the sacred river Narmada takes its source, he went off to the highlands of central

India. After a period of wandering he was obliged to return to the contamination of modern cities when he contracted a serious fever.[37] By October he was back in Baroda, but as usual was unable to sit still. 'His energy never flags', wrote a seemingly exasperated Aurobindo to his wife. 'As soon as he gets a little better, he goes out in the service of his country.'[38]

It was probably at this time that Aurobindo, Barin and Deshpande paid a visit to Charu Chandra Dutt, an ICS officer serving in Thana, near Bombay. According to Dutt the reason for their coming was to enlist his help in establishing the Bhawani Mandir order. Barin was still anxious to build the temple; but Aurobindo assured the unreligious civilian that the order's real purpose was revolutionary. 'Look upon the ochre garb [of the sannyasins] as a uniform,' he said. Dutt was attracted by the idea and promised to help, but nothing much happened for a year or more.[39]

The Bhawani Mandir idea was kept alive in Gujarat by K. G. Deshpande, Aurobindo's Baroda friend. Deshpande had been present at the séance where the idea originated, and later decided to give it his own form. In May 1907* he and some others established a school near Chandod, a temple-town twenty-five miles from Baroda. Keshavananda Swami, the mahant of the Ganganath temple, was put in charge of the school, which became known as the Ganganath Bharatiya Vidyalaya. Moneyed men of the region contributed to its upkeep. The Gaekwar himself was said to be a patron.[40]

The Ganganath Vidyalaya was one of the first schools in India to offer what became known as 'national education'. This meant among other things instruction in the vernacular, history taught from the Indian viewpoint, and instruction in 'self-defence'. As previously in Maharashtra and Bengal, traditional games were made the basis of a quasi-military training. Some time later, when Dutt was asked to 'inspect' the school, he witnessed a rough game of 'king of the castle' that left two of the boys injured. 'But the great point was that neither of the two whined,' the inspector

* Two police sources (GOM CID report 7 (1909): 80–1; GOI HPD October 1909, 29: 2) give the date of founding as 1905, but two very detailed reports compiled by the Baroda police for the resident in 1908 and 1911 give the date as 17 May 1907 (BSR, Report from Police Commissioner's Office 4 July 1908, 'Memo on Ganganath Institution').

reported.[41] Not long afterwards the school attracted the unfriendly attention of the police and it was forced to move to Baroda. There it survived until 1911, when it was suppressed under pressure from the government.[42]

8

Revolutionary Beginnings

Barin never managed to set up his Temple to Bhawani or to establish his order of revolutionary sannyasins. But he could not get the idea out of his head and at intervals over the next two years he tried to find the right spot for the temple and the right guru for the order. During the last part of 1905 however he spent most of his time in Baroda and Deoghar recuperating from his fever.[1] By being absent from Calcutta at this time he missed out on some extraordinary events. When he returned to Bengal he found the once apathetic province in the grip of an unprecedented enthusiasm.

During the first six months of 1905 the government said little about partition and the public agitation tapered off. Then in the first week of July the rulers announced not only that the plan would be implemented but also that the area affected would be larger than expected. In the wake of the announcement hundreds of protest meetings were held and hundreds of petitions drafted. But the feelings that were roused were too powerful to be contained by the usual channels of protest. 'The publication of this murderous piece of news [about partition] does not find the Bengalis lifeless', declared the *Sanjivani*. 'Rather it finds them resolved to undertake a severer struggle than ever.' There would be more meetings, petitions with more signatures, deputations with more delegates to England. But the *Sanjivani* also suggested a form of mass response that went beyond verbal protest. As long as partition lasted the Bengali people should observe 'national mourning'. During this period 'the use of articles of foreign make will be regarded as the greatest sin'.[2] The idea of a boycott caught on quickly and soon associated itself with a drive to promote *swadeshi* or indigenous products. Resolutions in support of swadeshi and boycott were passed by numerous meetings all over the province including a gigantic one held at the Calcutta Town Hall on 7 August. The turnout and enthusiasm were 'without a parallel in the annals of Indian agitation', commented the *Indian Mirror*. 'Never were the people in such a fever of excitement', yet their mood was one of 'grim earnestness'.[3]

Resistance bred repression which generated further resistance. Men and women began shouting the opening words of Bankim's hymn—'Bande Mataram' (Hail, O Mother)—first as a patriotic slogan and then as a battle-cry. The Government of Eastern Bengal issued a circular making this illegal. The practice increased. Other circulars were issued prohibiting students from attending meetings or taking part in demonstrations. Boys endangered their prospects by defying them. Many were expelled and some schools were disaffiliated. In response to this the Anti-Circular Society was founded and leading men of the province met to consider the establishment of an alternative system of education. At one November meeting Subodh Chandra Mullick, heir to a Calcutta shipbuilding fortune, promised to donate a lakh of rupees towards the establishment of a national college. For his munificence he was hailed as 'Raja'.[4]

Mass participation in the movement reached a peak on 16 October 1905, when the partition went into effect. People all over Bengal observed the day as one of mourning. No fires were lit. Men and women walked barefoot to the Ganges for ceremonial bathing. The custom of tying *rakhi* threads around the wrists of male relatives was transformed into a ritual of national brotherhood. The swadeshi-boycott movement had by this time spread to every district of the province and to cities as far away as Lahore. At a meeting in Baroda on 24 September, Aurobindo moved a resolution stressing the need to make comprehensive efforts to ensure that the wave of popular enthusiasm did not recede.[5] He had been quick to realize the value of boycott, but unlike the leaders of the movement felt it should be used openly as a political weapon. Only British products should be boycotted, not those from Austria, America, etc. He wrote from Baroda 'asking whether it would not be possible . . . to create an organization in which men of industrial and commercial ability and experience and not politicians alone could direct operations'.[6] This proved to be a vain hope since the men of finance and commerce were for the most part on the side of the status quo.

Before the year was over Aurobindo decided to leave his job in Baroda and come to Calcutta. He was given a chance to do so when Subodh Chandra Mullick offered him a position in the national education system. In November or December Aurobindo went to Bengal to make arrangements. At this time he made his debut in Bengal politics as a 'silent listener' at a meeting preceding the Benares session of the Indian National Congress.[7] At the session even the presence of arch-Moderate G. K. Gokhale in the Chair could not prevent the passage of a resolution giving conditional support to boycott. After the Congress Aurobindo returned to Baroda and applied for leave. Red-tape kept him in Gujarat for another two months; but on 2 March he boarded the train for Calcutta. By the 7th he was busy with meetings of the Executive Committee of the National Council of Education.

His younger brother arrived in Bengal around the same time. Barin brought with him a copy of *Bhawani Mandir* and had it printed secretly at a press in Calcutta.[8] No doubt the secrecy was prudent; but really there was nothing in the pamphlet that might have endangered the printer. Many more overtly seditious pamphlets were being circulated. One of them, *Raja Ke?* (Who Is Our King?), accused the ruling power of destroying the country's commerce and industry and ruining both cultivators and land-owners by overtaxation. The people should boycott not just foreign goods but the whole edifice of the foreign government. Hindus and Muslims should stand together against their common enemy.[9] Many of the same themes were touched upon in another, more famous pamphlet: *Sonar Bangla* (Golden Bengal). 'This is the time for the Bengali to show the people of the world that [*sic*] he can do. . . . Brothers, Hindus, Mussalmans, gird up your loins for the honour of your mother. Since all must one day die, why fear?'[10]

These pamphlets were distributed 'on a very large scale' and caused much consternation among the British. But no legal action was taken until March 1906, when a sixteen-year-old boy was charged with sedition for distributing *Raja Ke?* in Midnapore. The accused, Khudiram Bose, was a recent addition to the secret society headed by Aurobindo's 'uncle' Satyendra Nath Bose. On 28 February he had been stopped by a constable while handing out copies of the pamphlet to all and sundry. When the man tried to arrest him, Khudiram gave him a blow and disappeared. A month later Satyen and two others were summoned by the magistrate for questioning. Satyen spoke what the magistrate took to be lies and as a result was dismissed from his government post. Khudiram was taken into custody the next day. His case was committed for trial but later withdrawn by the government. Perhaps the jibes of the nationalist press had told. The *Bengalee* had written: 'the spectacle of a lad of fifteen [*sic*] being prosecuted on a charge of sedition does strike the onlooker as a ridiculous one.' The only clear result of the affair was a strengthening of the resolve of the Midnapore secret society.[11]

Newspapers like the *Bengalee* and the *Amrita Bazar Patrika* sought to popularize swadeshi and boycott by publishing reports of meetings and demonstrations. Their editors, Surendranath Banerjea and Motilal Ghose, became the recognized leaders of the movement. Bitter rivals both in journalism and in politics, they nevertheless had much in common. Both were old-line Congressmen wedded to the methods of constitutional agitation: prayer, petition and protest. A new sort of political thinking was emerging, however, most clearly in the writings and speeches of Bipin Chandra Pal and Brahmabandhab Upadhyay. Pal, an early follower of Banerjea and for many years a political moderate, had started to put forward a more radical programme in the columns of his journal *New India*. Upadhyay's *Sandhya* was even more outspoken. On 8 August 1905, a day when the Indian newspapers of Calcutta were congratulating themselves on the boycott resolution, *Sandhya* asked: 'Have we become so habituated to begging that we can utter nothing but the words "give us alms" "give us alms"?'[12]

Like Upadhyay, Aurobindo considered the boycott agitation to be only a slight improvement over the usual 'mendicant' Congress tactics. To an extent it had taken politics out of the lecture-hall and into the street. But this was not an unmixed blessing, for it gave the few who were interested in revolution a safer outlet for their anti-British feelings. The thing to do now was to take advantage 'of the Swadeshi movement to popularize the idea of violent revolt in the future'.[13] The sustained propaganda required for this was more than an occasional pamphlet could provide. The party had to control a paper that would 'preach open revolt and the absolute denial of British rule'.[14] Neither of the existing radical newspapers was suitable. *New India* was written in English and therefore could not reach the masses. *Sandhya*'s editor was a difficult man to work with and his writing 'of the most rabid type'. Instead of addressing the issues, Brahmabandhab abused everyone and anyone in language that even his friends considered 'execrable'.[15]

In March Barin and three of his associates—Debavrata Bose, Abinash Bhattacharya and Bhupendranath Dutt—decided to launch their own newspaper. Barin took the plan to Aurobindo who gave his consent and helped him to find the necessary funds.[16] It was agreed to call the paper *Jugantar* (The New Age), a name borrowed from a novel by Shivanath Shastri. On 12 March *Jugantar*'s 'declaration' or statement of responsibility was filed with the government. This was done in the name of Bhupendranath, but the actual men in charge were Barin, Debavrata and Abinash.* Barin, Debavrata and later Upendranath Bannerjee were the paper's chief writers. The last two were 'masters of Bengali prose' and their scintillating articles gave the paper its characteristic stamp.[17] At their best their language was 'so lofty, so pathetic, and so stirring' that it defies translation. An Indian scholar with no sympathy for the movement was forced to admit: 'Nothing like these articles ever appeared before in Bengali literature.'[18]

From the start *Jugantar* made it clear that the swadeshi-boycott movement should be looked on as only a first step. In the issue of 18 March, apparently the first one published, the editors declared in a statement of purpose: 'Amidst all the various agitations and attempts [being made] bear it in mind—*swadesha* [one's own country] comes first and *swadeshi* [the things of one's country] after. . . . *Swadeshi* is useless without *swadesha*.'[19] Three weeks later Aurobindo set forth *Jugantar*'s credo in an article called 'Our Political Ideal'. In a time of national awakening a high and noble ideal was a pressing necessity. Without the writings of Rousseau, Jefferson or Mazzini the political life of France, America or Italy could never have been transformed. India had no political ideal because the men capable of formulating one were in a state of servitude. Like children they were content with the 'toys' the rulers gave them: telegraphs and railways, universities and municipalities, the Indian National Congress. They lived in chains

* See Appendix 1, note 7.

but were 'not ashamed to boast that these chains were of gold or silver'. But happily more and more people were becoming conscious of their debased condition. 'The idea that this all-pervading subjugation can no longer be borne, that independence in our educational, commercial and political life has to be attained by any means possible, is spreading throughout the country.' It was futile to assemble in Congress each year to beg for an increase in the number of Indian civil servants or for minor changes in an economic system that was designed to drain India's wealth to Britain. India had to become self-reliant. Every villager had to boycott British goods. The children of the motherland had to become so intoxicated with the idea of patriotic service that they would happily go to jail for the country's sake. It was time to 'cut the golden chain'. This was the road to salvation (*muktir path*); all others led only to thraldom.[20]

In subsequent issues *Jugantar* stressed, more boldly and articulately than any Indian paper before it, the fundamental need of independence (*swadhinata*). To those who said that liberty would come in the wake of all-round progress, *Jugantar* replied that it was 'lunacy to look for all-round progress in our present state of servitude'. Once independence was achieved, progress would follow. To those who harped on social reform, saying that the multitudinous problems of Indian society had to be solved before freedom was possible, *Jugantar* declared that no social progress was possible without liberty. Differences of caste and creed would not in themselves prevent the attainment of independence. If men of different castes and creeds fought together for liberty, this would produce the needed unity. The removal of poverty could only follow the acquisition of political independence. Without independence even the traditional paths of spiritual advancement could not be followed. 'In this age the field for the practice of religion is not the forest or chamber, but the bloodstained field of battle.'[21]

One of *Jugantar*'s aims was to 'preach open revolt'. It did this with such frankness that in retrospect it is hard to believe that the British allowed it to go on for as long as they did. At first the appeal was couched in rhetorical terms similar to those used in *Raja Ke?* and *Sonar Bangla*:

War or revolution is a thousand times better than that 'peace' under which mortality is fast rising in India. Would not the disappearance of fifty million men in an attempt to deliver India be a hundred times better than this impotent death under the grim shelter of peace. . . . *If you cannot be a man in life be one in death*. The foreigner has come and fixed the way in which you live, *but how you die depends entirely on yourself*.[22]

As the writers became bolder, they began dropping hints of a 'secret conspiracy' and 'bands of secret assassins'. 'Gratitude and loyalty ought not to be expected from an oppressed nation,' one writer proclaimed. 'India is oppressed, therefore the people should not be loyal but should rise.'[23]

Aurobindo wrote only a few articles for *Jugantar*. He was not sufficiently fluent in Bengali to contribute regularly to a weekly newspaper. Besides, his work at the National Council of Education was keeping him busy. But he did find time to try to piece together the fragments of the revolutionary society. It no longer seemed necessary to maintain a 'close organization of the whole movement', since the taking up of the idea by 'many separate groups led to a greater and more widespread diffusion of the revolutionary drive and its action'. P. Mitra's Anushilan group had survived the Barin-Jatin split and was now beginning to 'spread enormously', particularly in East Bengal.[24] The most active centre was Dacca, which had been visited by Mitra and Pal in November 1905. Pal, a stirring speaker, called for volunteers who were willing to sacrifice all for the motherland. Eighty young men stepped forward, one of whom was a tough twenty-eight-year-old named Pulin Bihari Das.[25]

Training under Murtaza had made Pulin one of the best lathi and sword fighters in the province, but he showed even greater aptitude in revolutionary recruitment and organization. After his initiation (according to a government report on terrorism compiled a quarter-century later) the *samiti* 'spread like wildfire'. Soon there were five hundred chapters, bound together in a 'close and detailed organization'. Inspectors sent from headquarters submitted regular reports on *mofussil* societies. 'Careful and detailed instructions' were sent from Dacca. The sturdy young men of Eastern Bengal were the sort of material that Jatin Banerji had sought in vain in Calcutta. Pulin became what Jatin had always wanted to be: 'captain-general' of a well-oiled revolutionary machine. The Dacca Anushilan 'soon overshadowed its parent society' and became the region's pre-eminent revolutionary samiti.[26] Eventually it absorbed most other East Bengal groups; but for several years local samitis flourished in the district towns. Mymensingh had two: the Suhrid Samiti and the Sadhana Samaj of Hemendra Kishore Acharyya Chaudhury. Manoranjan Guha Thakurta's Brati Samiti had branches in Khulna, Faridpur and other places.[27] Both Britons and Bengalis were struck by the 'order and method' shown by members of the various groups, a new sense of discipline in what Nirad Chaudhuri termed 'that very undisciplined people, the Bengalis'.[28] The government could hardly object to young men building up their bodies and doing community service. Nevertheless the CID began discreetly to investigate and infiltrate the new organizations.

One of the reasons for the rapid spread of samitis in Eastern Bengal was the intolerable administration of the province's lieutenant-governor, Sir Bampfylde Fuller. The disorder that persisted even after the partition became a 'settled fact' prevented this petty despot from enjoying the perquisites of his office. When Fuller arrived in his capital he was met by a few hundred men whom the loyalist Nawab of Dacca had managed to assemble. The next day five thousand people turned out to receive Bipin Chandra Pal, who convened an anti-partition meeting under the lieutenant-governor's nose. Things did not improve for Fuller when he went on tour. At Faridpur 'the railway porters refused to touch his luggage which had to be carried by police-constables.' Before going on to Barisal, one of the main centres of protest in the province, he had a hundred Gurkha military police sent ahead. When he arrived in the town he asked Aswini Kumar Dutt and other local leaders to withdraw a pro-boycott circular that they had issued. Wishing to avoid the riots he was sure would follow his arrest, Dutt complied. Fuller was satisfied but left his Gurkhas when he departed. Such 'punitive police' were supposed to prevent disturbances, for example by helping Muslims purchase non-swadeshi cloth. According to persistent reports however they took advantage of the situation to rob, rape, and generally create turmoil.[29]

Unable to rule by law, Fuller resorted to government by ordinance. It was his government that issued the infamous 'Bande Mataram' Circular and one of the circulars prohibiting student participation in the movement. When schoolboys in Serajganj refused to toe the line, Fuller sent in punitive police and demanded that the school be disaffiliated. Finding few Hindu friends he cultivated the favour of the Muslims, gaining wide notoriety for his remark that of his two wives, Hindu and Muslim, he preferred the latter. By one of his circulars he ruled that a fixed proportion of the new government's posts would be reserved for Muslims whether qualified or not—perhaps the first application of this controversial policy in India's history.[30]

The unrest in Eastern Bengal came to a head on 14 April 1906 when the Bengal Provincial Conference of the Indian National Congress was held in Barisal. Congress provincial conferences generally attracted a couple of hundred delegates and visitors. This time there were around ten thousand. All the big Calcutta nationalists attended. Aswini Dutt and other local leaders pleaded with the delegates to act discreetly. But the Calcutta men were spoiling for a fight, and when the police passed an order prohibiting processions, they decided to test its validity. Ranging themselves in columns they marched down the street chanting 'Bande Mataram'. The police let the leaders pass and then attacked the younger men with lathis. Many were injured. Banerjea courted arrest and was gratified by a fine for contempt of court.[31] The next day he found himself the most famous man in India, his position as leader of Congress in Bengal secure. As news of his arrest spread, indignation meetings were held in every part of the country. Most nationalist papers were satisfied with the way things had turned out, but *Sandhya* wrote that it was 'a mistake to offer one's head to be broken by the Feringhi [hated European]'. *Jugantar* commented: 'Force must be opposed by force, deceit by deceit.'[32]

Bipin Pal, Aurobindo and Subodh Mullick had been present at the Barisal conference. Afterwards, wishing 'to know first hand what sort of people' were ruled by Bampfylde Fuller, they toured the districts of East Bengal. Pal spoke to large and enthusiastic audiences. In Comilla he 'gave a fiery speech—hinting at bullets and cannons and so forth'. Aurobindo and Mullick, both unable to address meetings in Bengali, held 'closed-door discussions' with local leaders. In Mymensingh and other places they made contact with revolutionary societies such as the Sadhana Samaj. In all the three men spent a month and a half on the road, returning to Calcutta by the end of May.[33]

Barin Ghose left the capital for eastern Bengal just around the time his brother arrived home. After three months as editor of *Jugantar* he was beginning to get restless. The paper was attracting some attention, but most readers still preferred *Hitavadi*, *Sanjivani* and *Sandhya*. Sometimes Barin and Abinash had to go out on the streets to hawk copies.[34] This was not the sort of work Barin had in mind when he came to Bengal and in May he got a chance to do something more substantial.* Nirode Mullick, Subodh's cousin, offered him a thousand rupees to kill Bampfylde Fuller.[35] Barin accepted the commission. Taking a couple of revolvers and a crude homemade bomb he went to Shillong, the summer capital of the province. It was agreed that he would complete certain preparations and then wire Hem Chandra Das of Midnapore, who had been selected as the hit-man.† After receiving Barin's telegram Hem started for Shillong, only to meet Barin on his way back to the plains. The leader had decided it would be better to do the job in Gauhati. When they arrived in that town Barin decided it would be preferable to do it in Barisal. Wherever they stopped Hem was astonished to see the alacrity with which Barin took people into his confidence and told them the whole story. 'This circumstance,' he later wrote, 'made me wonder whether my evaluation of Barin as a first-class revolutionary worker was correct.' He concluded that Barin's main object was not killing the lieutenant-governor but carrying out 'revolutionary propaganda and self-advertisement'.[36]

At Barisal the would-be assassins received a cordial reception from the local people, many of whom expressed pleasure on hearing their plans. But none of them were willing to assist the

* The events recounted in this and subsequent paragraphs took place, according to Hem Chandra Das, after the first week of May and before the end of July 1906 (*Banglay Biplab*, chapters 9–11). Aurobindo mentioned Barin's desire to go to Shillong in a letter to his father-in-law dated 8 June 1906 (*A&R* 1 (December 1977): 85).

† In his account (*Banglay Biplab*, chapter 9) Hem does not mention the name of the individual selected but it is sufficiently evident that it was he. In a statement to the police in 1910 Upen Banerjee said that the attempt on Fuller in Rangpur was made by Hem Das and Barin, assisted by Prafulla Chaki and Mani Lahiri (GOI HPD August 1911, 9: 13). (In his account Hem also mentioned the then dead Chaki by name.) Upen was not directly connected with this attempt but there is no reason to doubt his testimony on this point. Arun Guha also wrote that Hem was involved in the Fuller attempt (*First Spark* 210).

assassins and the lieutenant-governor left the town unharmed. Learning that he was planning to go to Rangpur, Barin and Hem went there to await his arrival. But by this time they were running low on money and Barin sent Hem to Calcutta to get some from Aurobindo. Aurobindo had only Rs 25 to spare and, according to Hem, suggested they rob someone to get the needed funds. Aurobindo sent a new man named Narendra Nath Goswami to help them do this.[37] Narendra, the son of a Serampore landowner, had decided to dedicate himself to the cause after being moved by what he read in *Jugantar*. After his admission he was informed that the society would get money for arms and ammunition by looting. Charu Dutt referred to this as the 'Mahratta' method, an allusion to the plundering raids of the eighteenth-century Maratha freebooters.[38]

According to Naren, Aurobindo gave him twelve rupees and some cartridges and sent him to Rangpur. The cartridges, it turned out, did not fit the gun Naren had been given by Abinash, and he had to be re-equipped.[39] In Rangpur Naren met Barin, Hem and the local revolutionaries. Since Fuller was still delayed they decided to go ahead with the dacoity. The intended victim was a widow who lived alone. Barin organized two parties and sent them on their mission, himself staying in Rangpur in order, he said, to direct the operation. The dacoits got close to the widow's village when they learned that a police sub-inspector was there. They returned to Rangpur, not at all unhappy about their failure. Barin was disappointed but glad his men had made an 'honest attempt'.[40]

When it became clear that Fuller was not coming to Rangpur, Hem and Prafulla Chaki, a new recruit from that town, went south to Naihati Junction. Guns in hand, they waited for the lieutenant-governor's train, intent to board it, break into his compartment and open fire. Fortunately for Fuller (and the young desperados) his special did not take its expected route. Disappointed, Hem and Prafulla went to Calcutta, where they told the whole story to Aurobindo. 'He listened to it calmly and told [them] to go home.'[41]

The unsuccessful attempt to kill Fuller was probably the first serious effort to commit a political murder in Bengal's modern history. As such it was the predecessor of dozens of attempts, some of them successful, in the decades that followed. The laughable bid to rob the widow of Rangpur was similarly the predecessor of scores of political dacoities. According to Hem the idea of political murder and dacoity had first been put forward at a meeting convened by Aurobindo shortly after his arrival in Calcutta. Besides resolving to bring out *Jugantar* and to establish Bhawani Mandirs, the participants decided it was time to carry out 'actions'. In the vocabulary of the revolution, 'action' meant a terrorist attempt, in particular the murder of officials or the robbery of rich men or government treasuries. The reasons advanced in favour of these activities were, first, that successful attempts would catch the attention of the public and facilitate the spread of the revolutionary idea; and second, that the performance of daring deeds would help the young men of Bengal throw off their perennial faint-heartedness and develop manly qualities. There were also financial considerations. Robberies would fill the society's coffers directly, assassinations indirectly; for there were plenty of nationalist sympathizers ready to pay for the death of someone like Bampfylde Fuller.[42] Hem says that the idea of raising funds by means of dacoities was taken right from the pages of *Ananda Math*. It was also supposed to be practiced by Russian revolutionaries, though no one knew quite exactly how.[43] In fact 'expropriation' (as the Russians euphemistically termed it) has been practiced by most revolutionary terrorists. By undertaking political assassinations and robberies the revolutionaries of Bengal were simply adopting the universal tactics of terrorism.[44]

By his own (retrospective) account, Aurobindo was opposed to terrorist methods, preferring rather a steady preparation for a general uprising. 'My idea', he said in 1938, 'was for an open armed revolution in the whole of India.' Assassination and dacoities 'were not at all my idea or intention'. Nevertheless he did nothing to stop the society's turn to terrorism. Asked why years later he replied: 'It is not wise to check things' like this, particularly when they have taken a 'strong shape', 'for something good may come out of them'.[45]

The exact nature of Aurobindo's connection with Barin and his terrorists remains a controversial question.* It is complicated by the fact that later in life Aurobindo became a revered spiritual leader whose disciples find it difficult to picture him as an advocate

* I have discussed this question at greater length in 'Aurobindo Ghose as Revolutionary' (*South Asia* 15 [1992]).

of robbery and murder. Some statements of Aurobindo's lend support to the belief that he had no direct connection with the terrorists. 'The whole movement was in [Barin's] hands,' he said in 1938, 'I had no time for it. . . . If I had been the head, I would have been much more cautious.'[46] But Barin himself declared that while Aurobindo 'had never taken part in any overt act of revolutionary or terrorist nature', he yet was 'the very soul of the [revolutionary] movement'. Barin also claimed that Aurobindo was behind certain specific actions including the attempt to kill Fuller.[47]

There can be no doubt in any case that Aurobindo was cognizant of Barin's activities. Among those who affirmed this was C. C. Dutt who, writing in the context of the attempt on Fuller, said that Aurobindo 'knew everything' about the revolutionary work, either before the attempt was made or after.[48] Whether Aurobindo actually initiated or helped plan any specific action is more difficult to determine. Hem Das and Narendra Nath Goswami both claimed that Aurobindo initiated the Rangpur attempt. But Aurobindo said that Barin and his associates 'wanted to do it but did not'.[49]

Some of the apparent disparity between such assertions may be due to Aurobindo's style of leadership. Bhupen Dutt wrote of him, 'He didn't say, "Do this, do that"; but for any action his sanction was necessary.'[50] This accords with Barin's claims that Aurobindo gave his counsel (*paramarsh*) or sanction (*anumati*) in connection with certain actions. What exactly Aurobindo's 'counsel' consisted of is unclear. In certain instances discussed in later chapters Barin seems to have received a general approval from his brother and then presented it to his associates as Aurobindo's 'order'.

Barin himself admitted that Aurobindo was 'seldom [the movement's] active leader . . . but rather the inspirer and the soul behind it, I being at the helm of things in working its secret and inner details'.[51] This agrees in general terms with Aurobindo's statements. He never denied being a revolutionary; indeed he wrote a long note giving the lie to the notion that 'he was opposed in principle and in practice to all violence and that he denounced terrorism, insurrection, etc., as entirely forbidden by the spirit and letter of the Hindu religion.' The notion that he was opposed to these things was 'quite incorrect', he said, adding with obvious reference to the Gandhian cult of non-violence that he was 'neither an impotent moralist nor a weak pacifist'.[52]

9

Tribulations and Trials

The abortive attempts at assassination and dacoity in the summer of 1906 were the society's last 'actions' for almost a year. Barin's health was still precarious and he spent much of this period in Deoghar trying to shake off his fever.[1] Hem Das, after his month-long wild-goose chase, had become disgusted with Barin and the society in general. When he got back to Midnapore he sold part of his property and bought a ticket for Marseilles. If nobody else knew how to run a revolution he would find out how to do so himself. Before leaving India he obtained letters of introduction to three radical editors working in Europe. One of them was Tilak's friend Shyamji Krishnavarma, who had helped Madhavrao Jadhav on his way to Bern.[2]

After spending several unproductive months in Switzerland and Paris, Hem went to London where he met Krishnavarma. The two men did not hit it off. Despite his strident advocacy of Indian Home Rule, Krishnavarma was opposed to the use of force. When he learned that Hem was interested in bombs, he refused to offer him any assistance. Some of the young men at 'India House', Krishnavarma's student hostel, had interests similar to Hem's; but when Hem applied for a job at the hostel, Krishnavarma drove him out.[3] He returned to Paris, where he was taken up by S. R. Rana, a Kathiawari Rajput who was in the jewelry business. Rana gave Hem and his friend P. M. Bapat, a Maharashtrian who had just come over from England, enough money to start studying chemistry.[4]

At this point—apparently in July 1907—Hem and Bapat got in touch with 'Libertad', a prominent French anarchist.[5] Libertad gave the young Indians work on his newspaper and encouraged them to attend anarchist meetings.* Before this Hem had thought that anarchism was just another word for revolution. When he learned what anarchists actually believed, he stopped attending the meetings. But by this time he had met some people who were interested in his plans, among them an American anarchist who may have been Emma Goldman.† She introduced Hem and Bapat to the leader of a French socialist organization, a reclusive figure they knew only as 'Ph.D.' After obtaining the necessary recommendations, the two Bengalis were admitted to Ph.D's party. Badly in need of money, they decided to approach Krishnavarma, who had recently shifted to Paris after a question was put in Parliament about his activities. With the help of Ph.D., Hem and Bapat were able to win Krishnavarma over, in part because he was impressed by the growing maturity of the nationalist movement as shown by the writings of *Jugantar* and other Calcutta papers.[6]

Ph.D. and another man, identified by Hem as 'a former officer belonging to his party', taught him and Bapat history, geography and economics, along with socialism, communism, etc. Finally they began to instruct them on the organization of secret societies —information the students eagerly jotted down in their notebooks. The teachers were at first hesitant about giving information on bomb-making; but finally they relented and got a member of their party to instruct Hem and Bapat in explosive chemistry and demolition.[7]

One of Hem and Bapat's teachers was the Russian revolutionary Nicolas Safranski. During this period of revolutionary upheaval in Russia, many activists had emigrated to the West. According to Paris police, by 1907 there were some 1500 Russian 'terrorists' in

* Libertad (real name Joseph Albert) was born in Bordeaux in 1875. He went to Paris at the age of twenty-one and soon became one of the principal figures in the individualistic school of anarchism, which was opposed to the syndicalism that at that time dominated the French workers movement. In 1905 Libertad launched the newspaper *L'Anarchie*. He was sent to jail more than once for various offences, the last time in June 1907. It was apparently a report of his sentencing on the 30th of this month that brought Hem Chandra Das to his door. Libertad died in November 1908 (Maitron, *Dictionnaire*, vol. 13, 293; Maitron, *Histoire*, 277–8; AN F/7/13050, 'L'anarchisme en France' 23; F/7/12723 passim).

† Hem (who mentioned few names in his account) spoke of this person as a female anarchist who lived in America. Paris police reported that Emma Goldman, the Russian-born anarchist resident since her childhood in America, was active in Paris in September 1907 (AN F/7/12894, nº 1, 33).

the city. Safranski was regarded as the leader of the 'maximalist' faction of the socialist revolutionary party and he was kept under close surveillance.[8]* When the police came to know that he was in contact with Indian students they decided to inform their counterparts in London. Sometime in December they sent a note through the French embassy, the contents of which were transmitted to the India Office. On 30 December Lord Morley wired to the viceroy, Lord Minto: 'The French Government has furnished a Memorandum by the Paris Police in which it says that Nicolas Şafranski, Russian Anarchist, has been instructing natives of India at Paris in manufacture of explosives.'[9] In January British detectives tried to gather further information in Paris. They were unable to learn anything about Hem, however, for he had left Europe around the middle of December.[10]

During the year and a half of Hem's absence in Europe the advanced nationalists became a force to be reckoned with in India. In June 1906 Tilak came to Calcutta to preside over a celebration of the Shivaji festival. His lieutenant G. K. Khaparde noted that at the time there were three parties in the city: 'the Moderate party' led by Surendranath Banerjea, a middle-of-the-road group led by Motilal Ghose, and 'the party led by Bepin Babu [Bipin Chandra

* Hem Chandra does not give the names of any of the socialists. In a file in the French National Archives (AN F/7/12894, nº 1) there is an eight-page dossier on Nicolas Safranski, in which it is stated that in November 1907, 'very precisely' on the sixth of the month, Safranski met certain Indians, apparently Bengalis, to whom he gave lessons in bomb-making. According to this report, Safranski was born in Poltava (in the present Ukraine) in 1878, was 'formerly a brilliant officer in the Russian army', had come to Paris in January 1907, and was considered 'the real head of the maximalist party' of the Russian 'socialist revolutionaries'. I think there is no doubt that the man known to the Paris police as Safranski was one of Hem Chandra's teachers—probably the former officer but possibly Ph.D. It is certain that Safranski was a former military officer; on the other hand Hem Chandra describes Ph.D. as 'a student of Hindu philosophy in a European university' and the Paris police report that Safranski was enrolled in l'Ecole des Langues Orientales, a fact that was confirmed by British police later (Ker 131). Gharpurey (p. 412), who claims Bapat as an informant, says that the teacher of Hem and Bapat was 'a young Russian revolutionary in Paris'. Birendra Chandra Sen, imprisoned with Hem in 1908, says that the man Hem contacted in Paris was 'the Russian revolutionary Mironow—an exiled military engineer and a Sanskrit scholar' ('Sri Aurobindo as I Remember Him' 21). It may be that Bapat told Gharpurey about Safranski, and that Hem Chandra told Sen about Ph.D. That one or both of the men were Russian seems certain.

Pal]' which was 'the real popular party' corresponding 'to Tilak's party in Poona'.[11] During and after Tilak's visit his followers and Pal's began to regard themselves as parts of a single entity. This was the origin of the party that soon became known as the Extremists.*

After Tilak left Calcutta the conflict between the Banerjea and Pal factions assumed 'alarming proportions'.[12] The clash centred round the selection of the Reception Committee for the 1906 session of Congress, which was scheduled to be held in Calcutta in December. Unlike most Congress bodies the Reception Committee was of more than ceremonial importance since it was empowered to chose the president of the session. The Extremists were hampered in their efforts to promote their programme by their lack of a newspaper with the clout of Banerjea's *Bengalee* and Ghose's *Patrika*. At the end of July Bipin Pal decided to launch a new English daily, to be called, provocatively, *Bande Mataram*. After seeing the first issue through the press on 6 August, he dashed off on a speaking tour of East Bengal. Before leaving he extracted a promise from Aurobindo to contribute an article every day.[13]

Since his return to Calcutta in June, Aurobindo had had little time for political, much less revolutionary work. His chief preoccupation was the Bengal National College, which opened its doors on 15 August with him as its first principal. During the last part of the year Aurobindo gave much of his time to administrative work and teaching. But the College proved to be a disappointment. Most members of the National Council of Education were reluctant to do anything to offend the government. They went so far as to prohibit students from taking part in political meetings, forgetting that a primary reason for the establishment of the system was to assist students whose political activism had got them expelled. Under such stewardship 'national' education became little better than a second-rate copy of the British variety. Whatever its merits, it no longer could be considered a part of the national movement as a whole.

* This name was first applied to the party by the London *Times* and later picked up by the rival party, who were called the 'Moderates' by the 'Extremists'. The originally pejorative nicknames eventually became established as the parties' names, but neither of them was current until 1907. I use them here to avoid confusion.

Long before this failure became apparent, Aurobindo's interest had shifted from the College to *Bande Mataram*. His writing, a blend of lucid thinking and subdued passion, attracted the attention of nationalists across the country. As the journal grew in stature it became the object of a power struggle between the supporters of Bipin Pal and a more radical group that favoured Aurobindo. The most acute differences of opinion were over the attitude to be taken towards 'secret revolutionary action'. 'Bipin Pal was opposed' to this, Aurobindo explained later, while 'others sympathized'. In October, while Aurobindo was bedridden with fever, his supporters managed to oust Pal and have Aurobindo declared editor. Aurobindo regretted this move 'as he regarded the qualities of Pal as a great asset to the *Bande Mataram*'. On the other hand Aurobindo's position as unchallenged head of the paper enabled him to transform its editorial policy and financial structure.[14] Reorganized as a joint-stock company, *Bande Mataram* was taken up by the Bengal Extremists as their official organ.

With the Congress session less than two months away the issue of the moment was the selection of the president. Aurobindo and his associates supported Tilak. To block the Maharashtrian's election Surendranath Banerjea offered the post to Dadabhai Naoroji, misleading the elder statesman by declaring that even the Extremists wanted him in the chair.[15] When India's 'Grand Old Man' accepted, the supporters of Tilak were obliged to withdraw his name. Realizing the need for more organized political action, Aurobindo called a meeting of the Bengal Extremists and insisted that they 'give up the behind-the-scenes jostling with the Moderates, and declare an open war on Moderatism', placing before the country 'what was practically a revolutionary propaganda'.[16] The others agreed and the radicalized *Bande Mataram* soon won an enormous following.

Unlike *Jugantar*, which as a 'vernacular' paper escaped to some extent the scrutiny of the government, *Bande Mataram* never spoke openly of revolutionary action. But it was just as forthright as *Jugantar* in putting forward independence as the goal of the national movement. In an article that was reproduced by the London *Times* as an example of how things had got out of hand in Calcutta, *Bande Mataram* declared:

The time has come when . . . our British friends should be distinctly told that . . . we cannot any longer suffer ourselves to be guided by them in our attempts at political progress and emancipation. Their point of view is not ours; they desire to make the Government of India popular, without ceasing in any sense to be essentially British. We desire to make it autonomous and absolutely free from British control.[17]

As Aurobindo's activities 'turned more and more' in the direction of politics and journalism, his 'secret [revolutionary] action became a secondary and subordinate element'.[18] But it never ceased altogether. From time to time he went on inspection tours to revolutionary centres. Once, for example, he visited the Sibpur (Howrah) branch of the Anushilan Samiti, encouraging new recruits and attempting to resolve the inevitable differences between local leaders.[19] Anushilan was prospering in western Bengal in its original incarnation as a society for physical and moral training. Under P. Mitra's guidance, Satish Bose had continued to set up akharas even after Jatin and Barin's quarrel. When Barin returned to Bengal he got in touch with his old associates and established a loose connection between his group and Anushilan; but fundamental differences of approach kept the organizations apart. Mitra was against premature forays into terrorist activity; Barin 'believed in the sword alone'. Mitra encouraged young men to take part in the boycott movement; Barin referred to this contemptuously as the *bania* (shopkeeper) movement.[20] But as the movement gained in intensity the boundaries between the Moderate-led boycott, the more radical approach of Mitra and Barin's revolutionary action began to wear thin. The 'national volunteers', who used picketing and intimidation to keep people from buying foreign goods, were gradually absorbed by Anushilan.[21] A similar process of radicalization transformed Chhatra Bhandar, the 'Students Store', into the revolutionaries' commercial front. The declared aim of this enterprise was to engage in wholesale and retail commerce, a share of the profits to be donated to philanthropic causes. Its actual activities were spreading propaganda, training workers, and opening branches in every part of the province. Eventually it became the 'material centre' of the samitis. Among its functions were the supply of funds to revolutionaries in the guise of philanthropic contributions and the purchase and distribution of arms and ammunition.[22] A 'fairly extensive' arms traffic had begun to develop and 'the possession of revolvers and guns' became 'a sort of elementary symbol of membership to the revolutionary societies'. Calcutta was the focus of these activities but *mofussil* groups did not lag behind. Branches of Anushilan were opened in several towns of Howrah and Hooghly districts while established groups like those in Chandernagore and Midnapore were becoming more and more active.[23]

Late in December, when men from all over India converged on Calcutta for the Congress session, the Bengal revolutionary party held its first 'provincial convention' in the house of Subodh Chandra Mullick. District representatives described the activities in their territories. Aurobindo and other leaders 'addressed the workers as to the programme of work and the method of organization'. From the chair P. Mitra called for increased support for *Jugantar* and related projects.[24] Meanwhile, and with less secrecy, the leaders of the Extremist Party were working out their strategy for the session. The Bengal and Maharashtra parties put together a joint fourfold programme: swadeshi, boycott, national education and, most important, *swarajya*. This word, used in the days of Shivaji to mean territory under the Marathas' direct rule, had been revived by Tilak and popularized by Deuskar in the sense of political 'self-government'. The more advanced Extremists had begun to use it (usually in its clipped form *swaraj*) as a code-word for 'independence'.[25]

The only real action at national Congress sessions took place at the closed meetings of the Subjects Committee. It was here that the resolutions to be passed without debate by the assembly were hammered out. Up to 1906 the Congress oligarchy made up of the Bombay group of Pherozshah Mehta and like-minded men from other provinces had dominated the Committee and so controlled the Congress. At Calcutta the Extremists made the first successful challenge to this power monopoly. The principal point of discussion was the boycott resolution, which the Extremists wanted to strengthen and the Moderates to tone down. During the deliberations Pal, Aurobindo, Khaparde and two hundred of their followers walked out, forcing the Moderates to seek a compromise. The next day, Madan Mohan Malaviya, the Moderates' spokesman, met Tilak, Pal, Aurobindo and Lala Lajpat Rai of Lahore. The resolution that they agreed on incorporated most of the Extremists' demands.[26] Pal's speech to the assembly victoriously seconding the resolution was looked on by many 'as the speech of the Session'.[27] To the Moderates it was salt rubbed in their wounds.

The Extremist press expressed cautious optimism about the outcome of the Congress, but *Jugantar* was unimpressed. Passing resolutions in the hope that the government would reform itself was as profitable as milking bulls, it said. What the people really needed was not 'amateur conferences' but propaganda that would 'excite in them a desire for freedom'.[28] During its first year of publication *Jugantar* had been spreading this sort of propaganda with increasing boldness. It spoke regularly of the need for 'complete independence' and declared that active, not passive resistance was the way to achieve it. Where the rulers used brute force to oppress the people, moral force was not enough to bring about a change. But when 'oppression attains its fullest measure', the people would rise and the ruling power would be 'exterminated to its root'.[29]

Jugantar's most daring enunciation of its revolutionary programme was an article called 'The Formation of Bands'. 'If only a thousand out of the eighty million people in Bengal cherish the desire for liberty in their hearts,' the piece begins, 'these thousand, united in a common determination, can bring about a change in the thoughts and efforts of the whole country, directing them towards one great goal. But first of all these thousand must form themselves into a band.' The writer went on to speak of the formation of 'district bands' whose aim was 'to direct local thought and effort towards independence'. Once established, district bands would attempt to expand, capitalizing on contemporary events and local disturbances. Discipline, order and above all secrecy were essential. New members would be admitted only if they could prove they possessed six qualities: loyalty, energy, selflessness, perseverance, reliability and obedience. Once admitted, members would 'stake their lives on increasing the scope of the bands', at the same time seeking out opportunities to use various 'undertakings and agitations' to keep the country in a state of excitement. At the close of this do-it-yourself guide to agitprop, *Jugantar* told its readers that if informed of the formation of a band, it would do its best 'to give council and to connect it with other bands'. Persons having communications on this subject should of course not trust the post, but bring them to the office in person.[30]

This audacious announcement did not go unheeded. Scores of young men, many of them still in their teens, wandered in from the districts and found their way to the *Jugantar* office. One of them was Upendranath Bannerjee of Chandernagore. After passing his F. A. examination and winning a gold medal in French, Upen became a medical student and then a sannyasin. Two years in a Himalayan ashram were enough for him however and he came back to Bengal and found work as a schoolteacher. Then in a copy of *Bande Mataram* he read Pal's demand for 'absolute autonomy free from British control'. Electrified, he rushed to Calcutta and volunteered his services. He had heard that the *Jugantar* office was a very 'den of revolutionaries'. The words 'made his blood sing'. 'The long procession of revolutionary heroes from Robespierre down to the latest firebrand flashed across' his mind. Stopping in at the office he found a few young men sitting around doing nothing. His disappointment was intense but short lived for 'the young hopefuls soon supplied with tall talk what they lacked in the way of war equipment'. There was diversity of opinion on many subjects, but about one thing all were agreed: they would have no trouble kicking the British out of India. In a year or two the *Jugantar* office would move to Government House where there would be more room for its activities.[31]

It is easy to laugh at the presumption of the young insurrectionists; but overconfidence in the face of overwhelming odds is a recurrent if not inevitable feature of the early stages of revolutions. One is reminded of the member of the Black Hand who said of his youthful efforts to free the south Slavs from Austrian domination: 'In those days all of us were mad.'[32] Wordsworth's lines on 1789, so often quoted by Indian revolutionaries (who were obliged to read the poet in their classrooms), are even more appropriate: 'Bliss was it in that dawn to be alive, But to be young was very heaven!'

Barin was still in Deoghar when Upen came to Calcutta; but some time later he returned and met the new man in the *Jugantar* office. After his bout with malaria the always lean Barin was 'all bones with a bare covering of skin'. But through this unprepossessing exterior radiated a 'strength of imagination and intensity of feeling' that seemed to Upen sufficient to 'break down all barriers'. In little more than a minute Barin had convinced him that India would be free within ten years.[33]

Upen became one of *Jugantar*'s principal writers, sharing the responsibility with Debavrata and Barin. The journal continued to test the limits of the government's toleration. On 3 February 1907 it began a series of articles entitled 'Principles of Revolution'. The first instalment dealt with the moulding of public opinion. Five means of propaganda were listed: newspapers, which had to be 'filled with discussions of independence and the necessity of revolution'; musical performances similar to the *charana* songs beloved of the Chapekars; high literature such as Bankim's novels; popular entertainments like *jatra* parties; and secret meetings and associations. The writer reminded his readers of the nocturnal gatherings at which the santans of *Ananda Math* collected arms to use in their righteous battle. This thought was taken up in the next instalment, which spoke of the three main methods for obtaining weapons: secret manufacture, importation from abroad, and raids on armouries. The third instalment discussed the collection of funds. In the beginning volunteer donations would be enough to defray the society's expenses. But at a later stage increasing expenses would make it necessary to resort to theft and dacoity. Since the government was itself nothing but a thief, it was perfectly legitimate to loot government property.[34] In another article published the same day, the paper took up the question 'of how, being weak, we can enter on a trial of strength with the powerful English'. 'Be not afraid,' the writer began,

> The number of Englishmen in the entire country is not more than a lakh and a half. And what is the number of English officials in each district? With a firm resolve you can bring English rule to an end in a single day. The time has come to make the Englishmen understand that enjoyment of the sweets of dominion in the country of another, after wrongfully taking possession of it, will not be permitted to continue for ever. Let him now fully realize that the life of a thief who steals the property of another is no longer an easy one in this country. Begin yielding up a life for a life.. Dedicate your life as an offering at the temple of liberty. Without bloodshed worship of the goddess will not be accomplished.[35]

The government was not unaware of what *Jugantar* and other 'vernacular' journals were publishing. Week after week translated transcripts were reproduced in the *Report on Native Newspapers*, which was distributed to provincial officials. Why, one might ask, did the British put up with such an open challenge to their authority? Barin himself wrote decades later, 'It was strange indeed how the Government gave so much latitude for the movement to grow.' The *Indian Nation*, a Moderate English-language newspaper of Calcutta, was probably right when it wrote in April 1907 that the sort of provocation that appeared in *Jugantar* 'would not be tolerated by any [colonial] Government but the English'.[36] In part the government countenanced *Jugantar* because of Britain's traditional defence of press freedom; but a more significant factor was that the paper 'was not at first taken seriously'.[37] By the beginning of 1907 however the government's indulgence was getting strained. It had at its disposal a number of laws that empowered it to suppress sedition. It was under one of these that Tilak had been tried and convicted ten years earlier. In 1906 and 1907 the governments of Punjab and Bombay had instituted cases against newspapers in those provinces. Now it was the turn of Bengal. In the beginning of June Calcutta was rife with rumours that the government was getting ready to act. It did—but not in the way expected.

On 7 June notices were sent to the editors of *Jugantar*, *Sandhya* and *Bande Mataram* warning them that they would be prosecuted if they again published articles that were 'a direct incentive to violence and lawlessness'.[38] None of the papers changed their tone and the government resolved to proceed against *Jugantar*. Earlier in the year police inspector Purna Chandra Lahiri had gone to the paper's office to find out the responsible persons: editor, printer, publisher, proprietor. Bhupendra Nath Dutt, who was among those present, replied: 'I am everything'. On 1 July Lahiri returned with a search warrant. He found Bhupendra Nath, Abinash Bhattacharya, Bibhuti Bhusan Sarkar, Upendranath Bannerjee and several others. Again he asked who was responsible. Bhupen answered that he was the editor, Abinash the manager and Sailen the sub-manager. Lahiri made a note of this, seized some papers, and departed.[39] Four days later he returned with a warrant for Bhupen's arrest. The young man surrendered himself and was taken to Police Court where he was charged with sedition under Section 124A of the Indian Penal Code. This was the most serious charge that could have been brought against him. Conviction would mean transportation or imprisonment 'for life or any shorter period'.[40] During a night spent in jail while his bail was being arranged Bhupen had occasion to repent of his rashness. On the first opportunity, according to a government report, he 'sent to the commissioner of police a petition to the effect that he was young and inexperienced (his age being in fact about 28) and had been misled by the swadeshi agitators'.[41] When this backsliding became known to the party 'it was decided that the Yugantar, a paper ostentatiously revolutionary advocating armed insurrection, could not do that [defend itself] and must refuse to plead in a British court.' On Bhupen's behalf Aurobindo wrote a statement in which the accused declared that he was 'solely responsible for all articles in question' but declined to 'take any further action in the trial'. He would not deny his involvement, for he had acted 'in what I have considered in good faith to be my duty to my country'. The statement was a master stroke that 'immensely increased the prestige and influence of the paper'.[42]

On 24 July Bhupen, his composure restored, was sentenced by chief presidency magistrate Douglas H. Kingsford to one year's rigorous imprisonment. Across the country nationalist newspapers sang his praises. Even the loyalist *Indian Empire* called Bhupen's stance 'bold and unequivocal' and 'without a parallel in this country'. The women of Calcutta showed their appreciation by presenting Bhupen's mother 'with an address imprinted on a silken cloth put on a silver tray'. Whereupon, as Ramsay Macdonald commented, 'the old lady made an aggressive reply'. Bhupen's mentor Sister Nivedita wrote proudly to a friend: 'He is manly and heroic and went to prison, entirely in order to screen others.' Bhupen served his time but after his release left the country when he learned that he might become embroiled in an even more serious prosecution.[43]

The government was nonplussed by the result of the *Jugantar* trial. 'Counsel for accused did not even address court', wired the viceroy to the secretary of state in London.[44] But the Bengal authorities were committed to rooting out sedition and now they had to go ahead. The next newspaper on their list was *Bande Mataram*. Six days after Bhupen's conviction the police searched the paper's office, hauling away numerous documents and account books. They had come with a warrant for the arrest of Aurobindo, whom they had been told was *Bande Mataram*'s editor. In fact the paper had no declared editor and this time no one stepped forward to claim the honour. The confiscated documents were not much help: all entries showing that Aurobindo was the editor had been 'erased by the knife'.[45] In addition the government had trouble finding material published in *Bande Mataram* that clearly was seditious. 'The paper reeked with sedition patently visible between every line', complained the Anglo-Indian newspaper *The Statesman*, 'but it was so skilfully written that no legal action could be taken.'[46] In the end the authorities decided to take action on two non-editorial features: a letter to the editor and reprints of the official translations of the articles in *Jugantar* that had been found seditious. Informed by the advocate-general 'that it would be inadvisable to proceed against the manager and the printer, leaving out the editor, who was the most responsible person', the police made 'strenuous efforts' to determine the editor's identity and finally arrested Aurobindo on 16 August.[47] Considering this case different from that of Bhupen, who was neither a writer nor a politician, the staff of *Bande Mataram* made arrangements for Aurobindo's defence, instructing the witnesses to give evidence 'that was all false'.[48] One former employee was induced to testify that Aurobindo was the editor, but his evidence was not considered conclusive. When the government subpoenaed Bipin Pal, who evidently was in a position to name the editor, he refused to take the oath or to answer questions. Charged with contempt, he was found guilty by the chief presidency magistrate and sentenced to six months' imprisonment. The same magistrate found Aurobindo not guilty. 'Meetings were . . . held in many places in India to rejoice over his acquittal,' noted a disappointed government.[49]

Even before the conclusion of the *Bande Mataram* trial the government took further action against *Jugantar* and also initiated proceedings against *Sandhya*. In July, at the same time that Bhupen was sentenced, magistrate Kingsford had ordered the confiscation of the press where *Jugantar* was printed. This order was contested by Abinash Bhattacharya and ultimately overturned by the Calcutta High Court. In the meantime, after only a week's gap, the paper began appearing again 'a little improved in size and get-up'.[50] Sympathetic editors of other papers such as the *Hitavadi* and *Sandhya* allowed Abinash to use their presses at night. On 7 August police searched the *Sandhya* office and seized *Jugantar* material. A week later Basanta Kumar Bhattacharjee, the paper's registered printer, was arrested. Like Bhupen, Basanta offered no defence and on 2 September he was sentenced to a fine and two years' imprisonment. Kingsford observed that the offending articles seemed even more inflammatory than those that had brought about the first prosecution.[51] The next week a boy named Purna Chandra Sen came forward to register himself as *Jugantar*'s printer and publisher. He gave his age as seventeen. Declaring that he looked more like thirteen, Kingsford denied the application. For two months *Jugantar* did not appear while Abinash looked around for another 'jail-editor'. Meanwhile the authorities proceeded against *Sandhya*, arresting the editor Brahmabandhab Upadhyay on 3 September. The case came up for hearing on the 23rd, immediately after the judgment in the *Bande Mataram* case. Brahmabandhab took responsibility for the article in question, one in which he had written: 'Arm, brothers, arm! The day of deliverance is near.' Following the precedent established by the two *Jugantar* trials he declared he would take no part in the hearing since in carrying out 'my humble share of this God-appointed mission of Swaraj' he was not 'in any way accountable to the alien people who happen to rule over us'. A month later he died in hospital while his case was pending.[52]

Before its final suppression in 1908, *Jugantar* was prosecuted no less than six times. Needless to say it is difficult to run a newspaper when every month or so the printer is arrested and the plant confiscated. After the first two arrests Barin decided that he had had enough. 'No use wasting strength like this', he told his friends, 'the British are not going to be moved by big talk. What we need is action.' Behind this bluster was the fear that the paper was attracting too much attention. If the police continued to make searches they were bound someday to make an unfortunate discovery. Barin accordingly recommended that the party abandon *Jugantar*. But the Chhatra Bhandar group led by Nikhileswar Roy Maulick thought the paper too important and too profitable to be allowed to lapse.[53] It was now the most popular journal in the country. In a few months its circulation had soared from 200 to 7000 and would soon reach, and then exceed, the unprecedented figure of 20,000.[54] Both as a propaganda organ and a generator of funds it was indispensable. Nikhileswar and Barin could not come to an agreement and the matter was referred to Aurobindo. It was decided that the Chhatra Bhandar group would continue to publish *Jugantar* while Barin and those who shared his interests would embark in a new direction.[55] With characteristic boldness (that, just as characteristically, was at cross purposes with his desire for secrecy) Barin published what amounted to a notice of his intentions.[56] In an article called 'Our Hope', published on 19 August, the writer declared: 'If only a few determined men can, by their example, implant' in the mind of the people the idea that 'the English are not superior to us in strength', then the 'diadem of the English shall roll in the dust'. So far this message had been given by words alone; 'but the time has at last come to show this by our actions. Now will begin the trial as to who is the stronger.' To those who said, 'Hush, hush, the police will at once arrest you,' he replied that power was not 'a monopoly of the police'. It was time 'to take a life for a life'. The writer concluded: those who read *Jugantar* should bear in mind that the paper was 'not meant for perusal only; we are looking to every youth of Bengal to take up the worship of the Mother in this manner. It is with our eyes towards you that we are rushing forward on the path of death. It is you who are our hope.'[57]

10

The Garden

Since the beginning of 1907 Barin had been spending part of his time on a piece of land in the Calcutta suburb of Maniktola that belonged to him and his brothers. On this two-acre plot stood an abandoned 'garden house' of the kind that the well-to-do of the city used to retire to for brief holidays. The suburb, once verdant, had lost much of its charm when factories began to appear. No one in the family visited the place any more and it had gradually gone to ruin. But in remembrance of better days they still referred to it as the *bagan* or 'Garden'.

To get to the Garden from North Calcutta you had to cross the Circular Canal, make a sharp turn to the east and almost immediately another turn onto Muraripukur Road. After following this winding lane for about half a mile you had to look out for a narrow unmarked drive. Taking this to its end you reached a pair of masonry pillars marking the entrance to the Ghose's property: 32 Muraripukur Road. Unenclosed by walls it was bounded on three sides by other 'gardens' and on the fourth by an open field. A path ran through it that people of the neighbourhood sometimes used. But the spot was still quite secluded. There were a number of fruit-trees in the grounds—mango, jackfruit, coconut and betelnut—and these together with the bamboos and underbrush made it hard for passers-by to see the house. Situated in the centre of the plot, the dilapidated one-storied building consisted of a single large room with two verandas and an attached shed. Another separate shed stood nearby. In the grounds were a couple of ponds filled with slimy water. [1] It was just the sort of place that a bunch of young men could feel at home in. Habitués of the *Jugantar* office began visiting the Garden from the early part of the year. But it was not until after the party split up in August that Barin really decided to put the property to use.

Barin had not forgotten his dream of establishing an *Ananda Math*-style temple as the headquarters of a band of sannyasin-revolutionaries. The idea also appealed to Upen, himself a lapsed sannyasin. When the two left *Jugantar* they resolved to make the Garden their centre of operations. To be sure an industrial suburb was less desirable a location for an ashram than the source of the holy Narmada. On the other hand it was more accessible. Among the first to join them here were Prafulla Chaki, a veteran of the attempt to kill Fuller, and Bibhuti Bhusan Sarkar, a student of the National College who was eager to take part in something similar. Abinash Bhattacharya was obliged to spend most of his time in Calcutta looking after Aurobindo's household; but he occasionally found time to make the trip to the Garden, as did Upen's friend Hrishikesh Kanjilal. Other trustworthy mofussil men like Narendra Nath Goswami were also occasional visitors. And the arrival of fifteen-year-old Bijoy Nag of Khulna was a sign that new recruits would not be wanting.

As a year of social and political turmoil, 1907 was an excellent time for recruitment. In East Bengal deteriorating relations between Hindus and Muslims led to a number of serious riots. For as long as anyone could remember the two communities had lived their separate lives in peace. But the swadeshi-boycott movement had polarized them. Many Muslims had opposed the partition when it was first announced; but they soon realized they had much to gain from the new arrangement. The Nawab of Dacca, an early supporter of the anti-partition movement, had been seduced to the opposite view by a timely British loan. Since then he had done his best to convert his co-religionists, encouraging them to ignore the boycott and to organize anti-swadeshi demonstrations. Few arguments were needed to convince the Muslim majority of East Bengal that the boycott was not in their interests. Most of them were landless cultivators who felt little incentive to pay high prices for second-rate goods in the name of a cause they did not believe in. In order to enforce the boycott Hindu volunteers lectured their Muslim 'brothers' on their duty to the motherland; but they often had to resort to veiled or unveiled threats to get their point across. Smouldering resentment was kindled to flame by the infamous *Red Pamphlet*, which persuaded the sons of Islam that no penalties would be exacted for crimes against kafirs. Itinerant *mullahs* spread equally fantastic stories. In March, when the situation was becoming volatile, the nawab of Dacca went to Comilla to address local Muslims. Riots broke out that were only suppressed with difficulty.[2] The next month more serious disturbances erupted in Jamalpur. Here Muslim rowdies attacked Hindu volunteers who were destroying foreign-made goods at a fair. Then they went on a rampage, burning down shops where swadeshi products were sold. The breakdown of law and order encouraged Muslims to settle old scores with Hindu landlords, moneylenders and collectors of the temple-cess (*iswar-britti*).[3] Mobs attacked landlords' houses, destroyed debt bonds, and smashed an image of Durga. This act of desecration outraged Hindus in every part of the country. *Bande Mataram* fanned the flames by publishing an etching of the broken image along with headlines like 'Hindu Women Wait with Knives in Their Hands./ Rather Death than Dishonour.' The picture of the broken image was, it said, 'a picture of our own shame, of demoralization under long subjection, of our loss of manhood and even the semblance of a great and religious people'.[4] The cry of religion in danger and womankind in danger had predictable results. *Bande Mataram*'s sub-editor Hemendra Prasad Ghose spoke for hundreds when he wrote: 'It makes one's blood boil to think of it. . . . Revenge is the word that escapes one's lips.' Others were not content just to utter the word. A band of five youths went to Jamalpur from Calcutta and in a confrontation with local Muslims shot and wounded one of them.[5] Not surprisingly this led to increased tension. In the metropolis 'wild rumours' circulated that Muslim hooligans were making plans 'to teach a lesson to the swadeshists'.[6]

The five Hindus who took part in the Jamalpur shooting—Indra Nandi, Sudhir Sarkar, Naren Bose, Sisir Ghose and Bipin Ganguli—were all connected with the revolutionary network. Indra later disclosed that they had been sent to East Bengal by Aurobindo, who gave them money for their passage and instructions to help victims of Muslim violence.[7] The attack was presumably their own idea. Aurobindo and other Extremists believed in a policy of 'masculine courage in speech and action', but did not propose that this be directed particularly against Muslims.[8] In fact Extremists and revolutionaries had made efforts to elicit Muslim support. The pamphlets *Sonar Bangla* and *Raja*

Ke? both contained pleas for united action against the common enemy. *Jugantar*'s emblem incorporated symbols of both faiths: crossed trident and sword, with the crescent above and chakra below. Few Muslims were won over by such gestures, however, and as communal disharmony increased some of the samitis, including the Dacca Anushilan, excluded Muslims from membership. This cut the revolutionaries off from a potential source of strength.

Contemporary Hindus found it convenient to put the blame for the riots on the British. A diary entry of Hemendra Prasad Ghose is typical: 'Mahomedans, encouraged if not instigated by [the British] Authorities, looted Hindu Swadeshi shops, broke image of Basanti Durga.'[9] There is no actual evidence of such encouragement or instigation, though it is probable that the British dragged their heels when called on to protect 'seditious' Hindus.* The government viewed the riots as by-products of a widespread movement of protest that was entering its third year. They did not yet consider the Bengalis as serious adversaries, and so were not unduly concerned about the situation. They had reacted quite differently when disturbances rocked Punjab, as Sikhs from that province formed the core of the Indian army. Changes in Punjab's agricultural policies had caused widespread disaffection. Speakers like Ajit Singh (Jatin Banerji's disciple) and Congress leader Lala Lajpat Rai took advantage of the situation to spread nationalist ideas. On 21 April, after a particularly inflammatory speech by Ajit, riots broke out in the garrison city of Rawalpindi. The Punjab Governor, Sir Denzil Ibbetson, flew into a panic and asked Lord Minto to deport the two 'agitators'. Minto consented and in May Lajpat Rai and Ajit Singh were sent to Burma without arrest or trial. The nationalist press erupted in a chorus of protest.[10] Aurobindo wrote in *Bande Mataram*: 'Men of the Punjab! Race of the lion! Show these men who would stamp you into the dust that for one Lajpat they have taken away, a hundred Lajpats will arise in his place.' *Jugantar* drew a bitter comparison between the unresponsiveness of the Government of Bengal to the swadeshi agitation and the quick steps taken by the Government of Punjab to mollify public opinion after the Rawalpindi riots and deportations:

* See Appendix 1, note 8.

In Bengal we have cried ourselves hoarse during the last two years and sent up the price of paper in the bazar by using up quires upon quires submitting petitions couched in the most correct and elegant language. But as the result of all this we have been fortunate enough to get nothing but thrusts of lathis, and partitioned Bengal remains parted. In the Punjab a hue and cry was raised as soon as the water-rate was enhanced. The period of making representations and submitting petitions did not last for more than two weeks. The people then applied the remedy which is always applied to fools. There were a few broken heads and a few houses were burnt down and the authorities gave up the idea of enhancing the water-rates.[11]

Goaded by the gibes of the radical press, young Bengalis began to shed their traditional faintheartedness. When the police came to search the *Jugantar* office on 7 August, Sailendra Nath Bose, the acting manager, went to the door and alerted some passing students. In the scuffle that followed two European inspectors were injured. This act of aggression was 'the first of its kind', wrote Hemendra Prasad Ghose. As the authorities grew aware of the Bengalis' changed mood they began to increase the strength of police stations, attempting 'to overawe people by a show of force'. They found to their surprise that people had 'grown bold enough to defy power and ridicule a show of it'.[12] On 27 August, during the trial of Bipin Pal by magistrate Kingsford, a crowd gathered outside the building where the trial was being held. One of them was Sushil Kumar Sen, a fourteen-year-old student of the Bengal National School, who happened to be passing by. As he mingled with the crowd the police began driving it away. A European sub-inspector gave Sushil a blow, who immediately returned it. Overpowered by several policemen, he was placed under arrest and the next day produced before Kingsford. The magistrate, not wishing to send the boy to jail, 'let him off with 15 stripes'. This was a harsh but common punishment for juvenile offenders —strokes of a rattan cane delivered to the bare buttocks. In August 1907, however, the 'monstrous sentence' was ready-made for nationalist propagandists. The magistrate's 'brutality', hyperbolized *Bande Mataram*, had 'unnerved the whole city of Calcutta.' The day after his ordeal Sushil was brought in procession to College Square, where thousands were gathered 'to do honour to the brave boy'. He was garlanded, 'given a unique ovation', and proclaimed a martyr by nationalist orators. A short while later he disappeared from view and after a few months turned up at the Garden.[13]

Revolutionary recruitment was now in full swing in Calcutta. It was at this moment that *Jugantar* announced that it was time 'to show by our actions' that 'the English are not superior to us in strength'. Enough would-be revolutionaries got the message that Barin began thinking about expanding the operations of his suburban *Ananda Math*. But first he had to find his Satyananda: a guru who could instruct his revolutionary sannyasins in the subtleties of Vedanta philosophy while they learned the use of firearms. He and Upen were convinced that without a solid grounding in spirituality their efforts at revolution would come to nothing.[14] Barin had received promising reports from the Ganganath Vidyalaya, K. G. Deshpande's national school near Baroda. Perhaps, he thought, the *mahant* in charge of the school would be the guru they were looking for. Caught up in one of his enthusiasms he made a trip across the country, accompanied by a rather reluctant Upen. In Gujarat they found the Bhawani Mandir idea still 'in the air' but nothing being done about it.[15] The *mahant*, Swami Keshavananda, was in Barin's opinion 'a dry as dust pedant . . . knowing no higher yoga at all'. Upen, equally disappointed, returned to Bengal. Barin stayed in Gujarat and soon met a more interesting prospect. Sakharia Baba, besides being renowned as a holy man, was said to have fought on the rebel side in 1857. He gave Barin a mantra of initiation, which the young man promptly forgot. A few days later Barin came across yet another yogi, a man of undoubted spiritual realization named Vishnu Bhaskar Lele. After sitting with Lele in meditation Barin had his first 'psychic experience'. Soon afterwards he returned to Calcutta. He had not succeeded in bagging a guru; but he was confident that he and Upen would now be able to give their group the needed spiritual orientation.[16]

It was now October 1907. A new, nameless samiti began taking shape at the Garden. Charter members Prafulla and Bibhuti Bhusan were soon joined by a self-taught chemist named Ullaskar Dutt, of whom more in the next chapter. In the months that followed another dozen came to stay: Prafulla Chakrabarti, Nolini Kanta Gupta, Paresh Mallick, Sisir Kumar Ghose, Indu Bhusan Roy, Bijoy Kumar Nag, Sachin Sen, Narendra Nath Bakshi, Purna Chandra Sen, Birendranath Ghose, Nirapada Roy and

Sushil Kumar Sen. A number of others—Sudhir Sarkar, Bhababhusan Mitra and Sushil's brothers Biren and Hem—used to come and go.

Nolini Kanta Gupta was in many respects a typical recruit. A bright student from politically active Rangpur, he had taken part in the swadeshi and national education movements from the age of sixteen. While a student of literature and philosophy at Presidency College he was introduced to Barin by his fellow-townsman Prafulla Chandra Chakrabarti. Prafulla had been a gold medalist at the Bengal National College when he decided to continue his studies at Maniktola. Nolini too spent some time at the National College, at least partly with the idea of studying chemistry. Eager to master the art of bomb-making, he approached Sister Nivedita and asked her to persuade her friend Jagadis Chandra Bose, the famous physicist, to let him use his laboratory. Jagadis Chandra was sympathetic and made arrangements for Nolini to work in the laboratory of the prominent chemist Prafulla Chandra Roy. But before the eager student had a chance to start his experiments he got caught up in the life of the Garden. Early on he learned that there were two sides to the work: 'civil' and 'military'. The civil section was concerned with recruitment and publicity: *Jugantar* and so forth. Nolini opted rather for the military line, proving his mettle by successfully delivering an unlicensed revolver. But he never lost his thirst for knowledge, reading instead of *Paradise Lost* and *The Prelude* works like Clausewitz's *On War*, Frost's *Secret Societies of the European Revolution*, and Gibbon's *Decline and Fall of the Roman Empire*. He found Gibbon's book fascinating but regretted that it gave few hints on how to undermine empires.[17]

Like all other members of the secret society, Nolini was a Bengali Hindu. Almost all of them belonged to the three castes—Brahmin, Kayastha and Baidya—that make up Bengal's bhadralok, the respectable class. Nolini was something of an exception in coming from East Bengal. The majority of the members came from the districts around Calcutta. The senior men were over twenty-five, most of the recruits under twenty, some as young as fifteen. All of them were fairly well educated. A few had failed their examinations, but others like Nolini and Prafulla were unusually intelligent. But all, whether good students or not, were 'animated by something uncommon'—to use a phrase of Upen's.

In other words they had 'more stuff' than ordinary steady students even though for the most part they were 'bad boys': inattentive in class, unconcerned about their prospects, ready to pick a fight. As heroes and martyrs of the revolution they have been canonized by a grateful motherland; but it is worth remembering that at the time they were the despair of their parents and teachers and, needless to say, on the wrong side of the law.[18]

As recruits drifted in, a rough distinction was made between newcomers or 'students' and old hands or 'workers'. The students actually did spend a fair amount of time studying. As might be expected at an ashram, there was a special emphasis on religious texts, in particular the Gita and Upanishads. Upen and Barin expounded these scriptures in the traditional way, even going to the trouble of seeing that their charges pronounced Sanskrit without a Bengali accent. But they let it be known that the real object of the study was to become 'spiritually advanced to such an extent' that they would be able to serve the motherland and in the end 'to secure its independence'. After a full year's training, which would prepare the students 'to undergo all sorts of hardships and privations', they would be fit to dedicate themselves to this great work.[19]

Successful neophytes had to take two oaths, one in Sanskrit and the other in Bengali. The Sanskrit oath, probably written by Aurobindo,* took the form of a Vedic sacrificial hymn. Invoking Varuna, Agni and other deities as well as the divinized ancestors, bowing down to 'the ideal heroes of India that sacrificed their lives to save mother-land from the grip of foreigners', the oath-takers poured their hatred and shame like ghee into 'the fire of our resolve to save the mother-country'. Renouncing all life's pleasures, they vowed to dedicate themselves to the establishment of the Dharma rajya (the kingdom of Righteousness). Then bowing to a sword, 'crown of all weapons, the symbol of death', they lifted it up in the name of the Adya Shakti (original Energy, conceived as the goddess Kali). The Bengali oath continued with praise of the sword and of the Gita, 'source of all, pregnant with all truths'.

* Aurobindo wrote Sanskrit poetry and prose. It is unlikely that any other member of the society had an equal command of the language. There are many similarities between the oath and *Bhawani Mandir*. The text of the oath has been lost; it exists only in the form of a clumsy English translation preserved in a Government document (GOI HPD May 1908, 17: 6).

Holding these objects in his hands, the aspirant took six specific pledges binding himself to the duty of establishing Dharma rajya, obedience to the community, etc. The oath concluded: 'If any way I dishonour or break this vow, let the curses of the great patriots, ancestors, and of God that knows the heart soon overtake and destroy me.'[20] It appears that when some aspirants reached the Bengali oath, which they could understand, they rather unceremoniously took to their heels.[21]

In the Garden school 'religious training' constituted one of three main sections of the junior curriculum. The other two were 'political training' and 'physical training'. According to a handwritten syllabus that was apparently the work of Upen, the political training consisted of Economics, History and Geography. There was also a special course in the Philosophy of Revolution and a critique of the methods of the Moderates. The main textbook in Economics was of course Sakharam Ganesh Deuskar's *Desher Katha*. Popular historical books included Mazzini's autobiography and *Sikher Balidan* (The Self-Sacrifice of the Sikh), a collection of stories by Barin's cousin Kumudini Mitra showing how the Sikhs 'gave up their lives but did not forsake God'.[22] Required reading in military science was *Bartaman Rananiti* (Modern Warfare), an adaptation in Bengali of J. S. Bloch's *Modern Weapons and Modern War*. The Bengali text covered the organization and operations of modern armies and drew heavily on the lessons of the Boer War. It discussed the latest weapons —'On bursting, a shrapnel is reduced to 340 fragments, which fall like a shower upon an area 880 yards in length and 440 yards in breadth'—and evaluated the latest tactics, particularly those of guerrilla warfare. *Bartaman Rananiti* was published by Abinash Bhattacharya in October 1907—just in time for use at the Garden.[23] A month later Abinash issued a second edition of the school's most popular title: *Mukti Kon Pathe?* (Which Way Freedom?). This reprint of some of the most incendiary *Jugantar* articles was used for indoctrination not only at the Garden but by other groups as well.[24] The teaching of geography at the Garden was largely empirical. Besides giving a 'thorough knowledge of Bengal and general knowledge of India', the teachers showed the boys how to read maps of Bengal and its districts, sections of railway lines and plans of magistrate's houses.[25] The medium of instruction for all courses was Bengali, but students were also required to learn Hindi and Sanskrit. English, which most of them spoke, was an optional subject.

Technical training was to be given by 'other departments', for example the department referred to in one of Upen's notebooks as 'Ex+Mech+An', which may have meant 'explosives, mechanics and anarchism'. Theoretically at least students had to pass through several stages of training before being initiated in the mysteries of 'action'. But in fact even neophytes received practical as well as academic instruction. Fifteen-year-old Kristo Jiban Sanyal said that 'in the garden Upen Babu used to teach us *Upanishads* and politics and Barindra Babu [taught] Gita and History of Russo-Japanese war and Ullas Babu delivered lectures on explosives'. Indu Bhusan Roy spent his time 'studying Gita and preparing shells' while Biren Ghose, attracted to the Garden because he 'had a religious turn of mind', was assigned the task of arranging for the supply of dynamite.[26]

As in many educational institutions, finance was a constant source of worry. Most of the students had left home without their parents' permission and as a result had no money of their own. The establishment's expenses were met mostly by donations from rich men like Nirode Chandra Mullick and Manoranjan Guha Thakurta. C. C. Dutt contributed thirty rupees a month.[27] Attempts to supplement this meagre income with the earnings of a vegetable garden and a chicken flock did not come to much. The boys were obliged to lead ascetic lives as much from necessity as conviction. The vegetarian diet they were sworn to as monks was as economical as it was purifying. Lacking servants these sons of respectable houses had perforce to do the kitchen-work themselves. Every day a new pair of cooks whipped up an almost identical pot of *khichri*. After meals they washed the exiguous vessels—a crockery plate and coconut-shell cup for each—in the dubious waters of the pond.[28]

The school's timetable was as demanding as that of a training camp or monastery. It may be doubted whether the young men actually followed it; but it gives some indication of their preceptors' intentions. The students had to rise at 4 o'clock. Before their first class two hours later they had to wash, meditate, and do their physical exercises. After class there was cooking and shikar, which generally means big-game hunting but here apparently connoted taking shots at crows or at a target painted on a tree.

After bath and meditation came the main meal of the day, after which the students could rest until three. Later in the afternoon they had to attend more classes, followed by exercise, meditation, study, cooking and supper. Before lights out at ten there was a period set aside for conversation and singing. A favourite topic was how they were going to assassinate the viceroy, the commander-in-chief and other high officials.[29]

These adolescent revolutionaries had a remarkably insouciant attitude towards the dangers of their situation. No doubt they avoided leaving bombs and rifles lying about; but they made no effort to hide their names or those of their comrades, leaving letters, inscribed books, library cards and other personal effects scattered about the Garden. Seventeen-year-old Narendra Nath Bakshi used an old school notebook, with his name written neatly on the cover, to copy out an explosives manual.[30] The adults showed little more caution. When Upen drew a chart of the society's structure the only effort he made to conceal the names was the transparent use of initials. In the case of the recruits such carelessness may be excused as youthful folly. In the case of Barin and Upen one is inclined to set it down to plain stupidity. Although sworn to secrecy and silence, Barin seemed to enjoy dropping hints that he and his friends were on to something big. Pretty soon the word got around. From as early as March 1907 detectives began hearing reports of a 'mysterious garden somewhere in the suburbs of Calcutta where arms were being collected'. In October this vague information was confirmed and the Criminal Investigation Department started to make inquiries. They did this through their own channels without bothering to inform the local police. All that the Maniktola beat cops knew about the Garden was that a *sadhu* was teaching the Gita there. One unsuspecting inspector was so intrigued by this sign of culture in his neighbourhood that he occasionally dropped by to listen. The boys always made him feel at home.[31]

As overall head of the Garden, Barin must take most of the blame for its failings along with most of the credit for its achievements. It was he who made the group's day-to-day decisions, often in consultation with Upen and Ullaskar. Barin was able, unlike 'Military' Jatin Banerji, to win respect and command obedience without acting the tyrant. Despite his easy-going ways the younger members regarded him as 'the chief whose orders had to be implicitly obeyed'.[32] His authority was not unqualified, however. He was responsible to the financial backers of the society—notably Subodh and Nirode Mullick and C. C. Dutt —and of course to his brother Aurobindo. In the argot of the Garden, Barin was *chhota karta*, 'little boss'. The big boss, *bara karta*, was Aurobindo.

At the time the Garden was taking shape Aurobindo was preoccupied with the *Bande Mataram* case. He had little detailed knowledge of what was going on at Maniktola, but he certainly knew the essentials of Barin's activities. The Garden was after all the culmination of his efforts since 1902. Before coming to Bengal he had looked on revolutionary action as the principal means by which India would attain independence. If he had given most of his time since 1906 to politics and journalism, it was because he regarded these activities as essential for the necessary 'organization of all forces in the nation for revolutionary action'. He joined *Bande Mataram* because he saw the launching of the journal as 'an opportunity for starting the public propaganda necessary for his revolutionary purposes', of which the 'central' one was 'the preparation of an armed insurrection'.[33]

In Aurobindo's view rebellion could come about only when the minds of the people had been prepared by radical propaganda. The youth of the country had to be willing to devote themselves to the cause, scorning hardships, imprisonment, even death. *Jugantar*, *Bande Mataram* and other publications had done much to bring about the needed change; but it was still confined to a comparatively small segment of the population. Another side of Aurobindo's long-term programme was the sowing of disaffection in the Indian army. Before coming to Bengal he had made a start in this direction with the help of the West Indian leader Thakur Saheb. But these efforts were cut short by the Thakur's death, apparently in Manchuria during the Russo-Japanese War.[34] Bengal offered few opportunities for troop subversion, since its own men were not permitted to enlist. Rangpur revolutionaries had had some success in winning over the commander of a corps of military police,[35] but isolated efforts like this could only have made a difference only if they had been sedulously followed up and organized. Barin and his friends had neither the time nor the temperament for this sort of work. They and their backers wanted spectacular results and they wanted them fast. The only way to produce them was by an increasing resort to terrorism.

In a statement given to the police in 1908, Barin said that he never thought political murders would bring about the regeneration of the motherland. But he felt that they were an important 'means to educate the people up [*sic*] for facing death and doing anything for their country's sake'. There was, he said, 'a wide and persistent demand all over India for one successful political murder in order to stiffen the back of the people and satisfy their spirit of vengeance'. Or as Upen more graphically put it: the jailing of the editors of *Jugantar* and *Sandhya* and the outrages done by the police so enraged people that everyone seemed to be saying, 'No. This can't go on. We'll have to blow the head off one of these bastards.' Since no one else was up to it, Barin and his friends were 'compelled, unwillingly, to take up the task as slaves of the nation'.[36]

In later statements Barin and Upen dealt with the subject less rhetorically. If they and their friends were slaves, the real masters were the society's supporters. These men demanded assassinations, advancing specific amounts towards the death of specified officials. After the resignation of Fuller the target of choice became Sir Andrew Fraser, the lieutenant-governor who had helped to partition Bengal. Towards the end of 1907 a meeting was held at which it was decided that Fraser must be killed.[37]

ORGANIZERS AND INSPIRERS

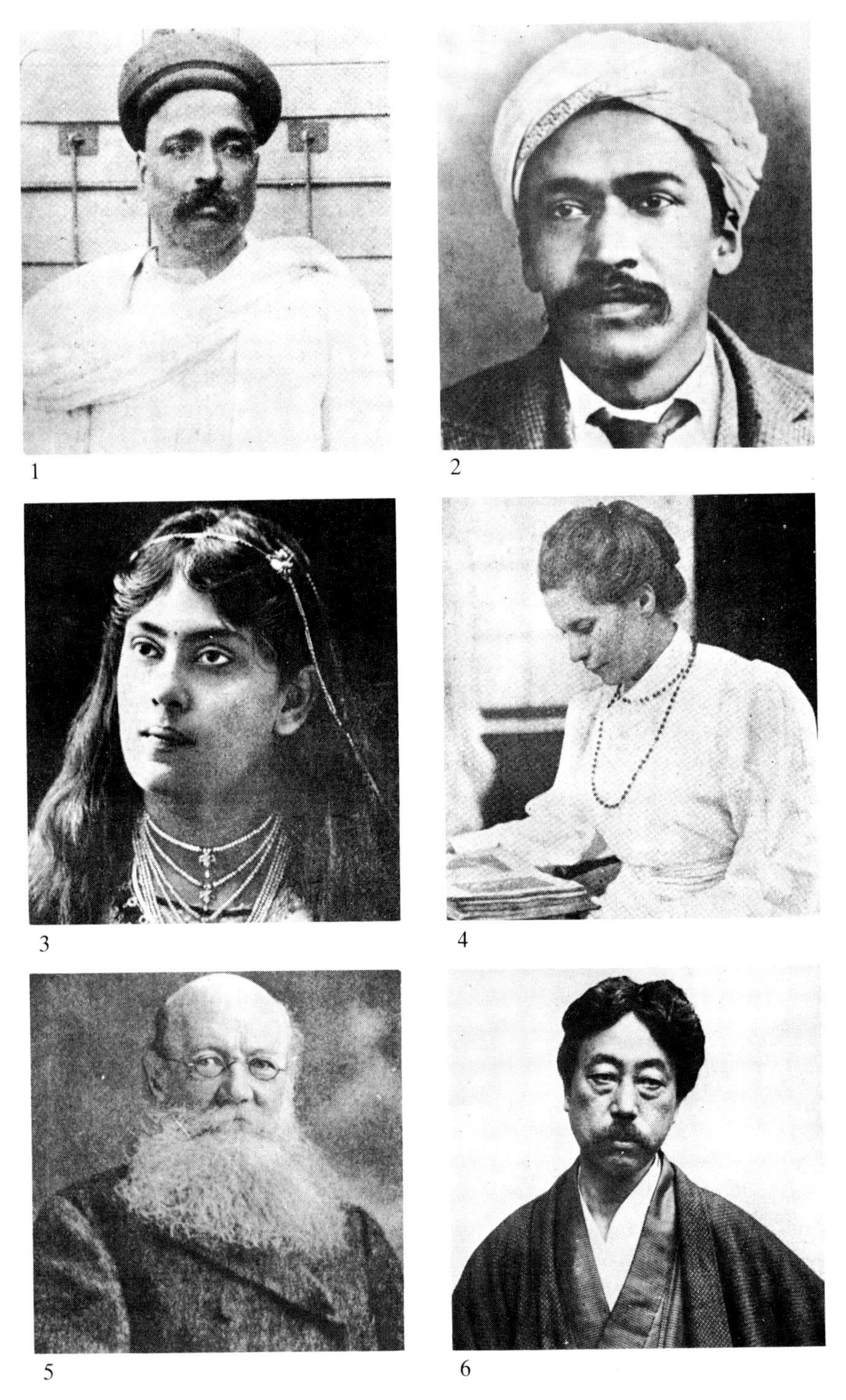

(1) Bal Gangadhar Tilak. (2) Aurobindo Ghose. (3) Sarala Ghosal. (4) Sister Nivedita. (5) Peter Kropotkin. (6) Kakuzo Okakura.

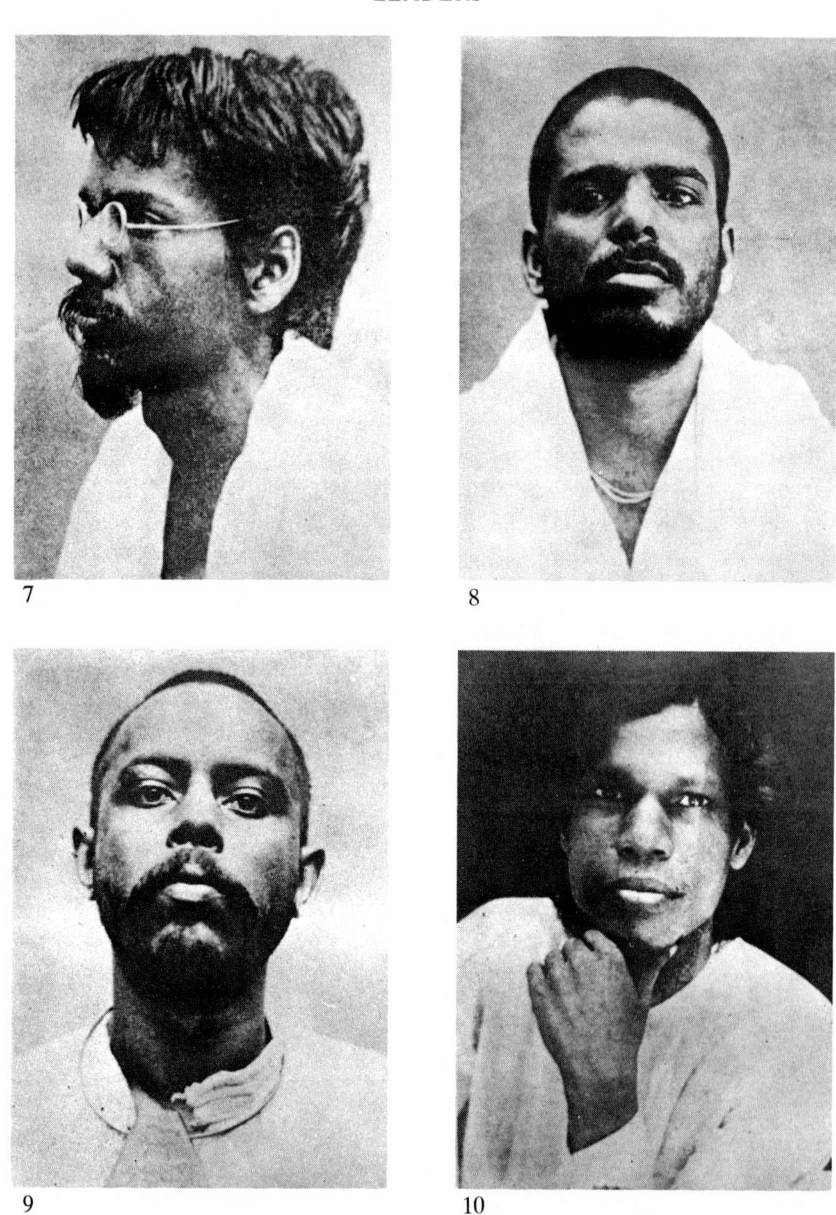

7 8

9 10

(7) Barindra Kumar Ghose, brother of Aurobindo, became leader of a revolutionary secret society in 1906. (8) Upendranath Bannerjee was responsible for the society's religious instruction. (9) Ullaskar Dutt was the group's principal bomb maker until Hem Chandra Das (10), returned from Paris, where he had learned political theory and explosive chemistry from the Russian Nicolas Safranski and others.

RANK AND FILE

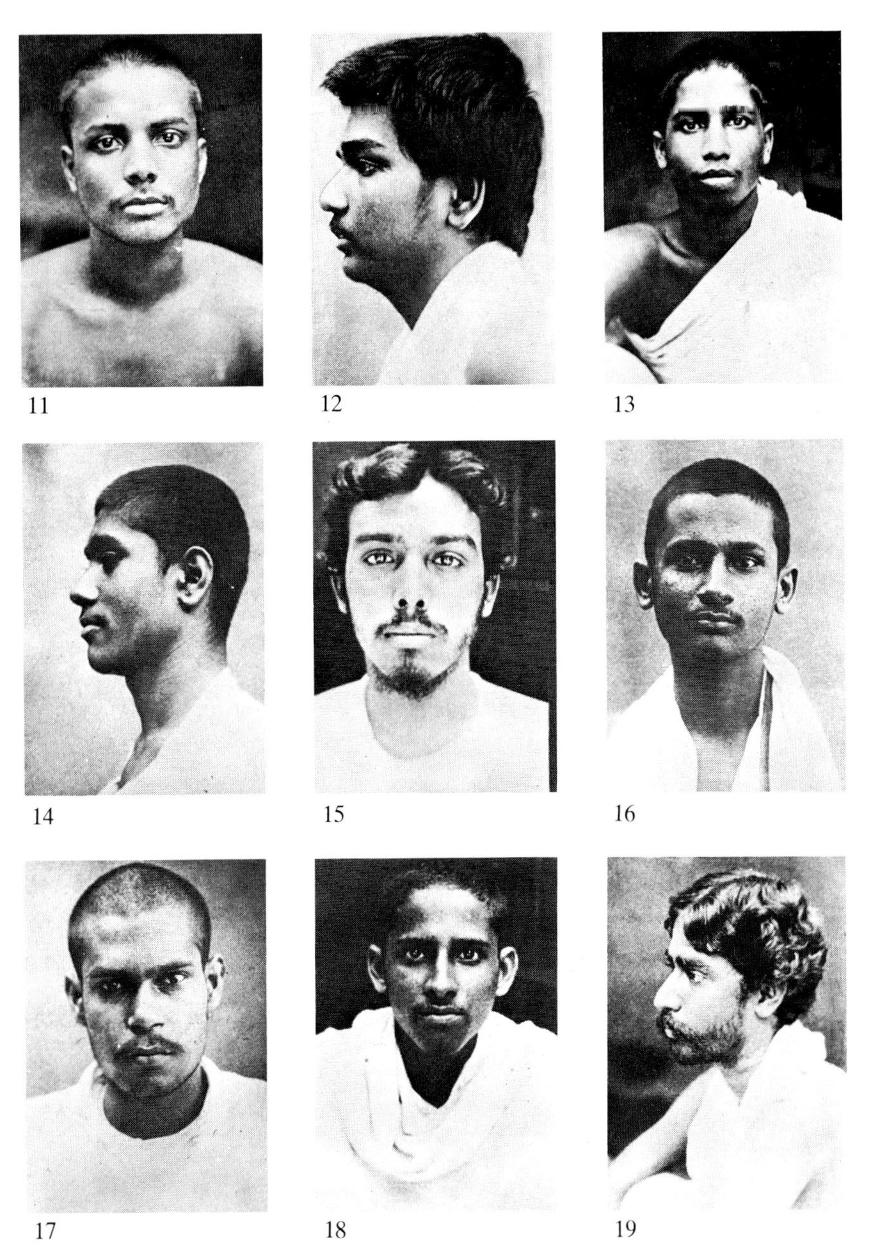

Members of the secret society started by Barindra Kumar Ghose: (11) Indu Bhusan Roy; (12) Birendra Nath Ghose; (13) Bibhuti Bhusan Sarkar; (14) Sudhir Kumar Sarkar; (15) Indra Nath Nandi; (16) Bijoy Kumar Nag; (17) Sailendra Nath Bose; (18) Kristo Jiban Sanyal; (19) Abinash Chandra Bhattacharya.

20

21

22

(20) The Maniktola Garden, showing part of the house that was the headquarters of the secret society. (21) A shed in the Garden used for making bombs. (22) A mango tree used for target practice.

23 24 25 26

(23) Sir Andrew Fraser, Lieutenant-Governor of Bengal, escaped unscathed from several assassination attempts. (24) Douglas Kingsford, an unpopular magistrate, was the target in the Muzaffarpur bombing. (25) Sir Bampfylde Fuller, Lieutenant-Governor of Eastern Bengal and Assam; several attempts were made on his life. (26) Ashutosh Biswas, public prosecutor in the Alipore case, was shot dead in the courthouse.

DOWN WITH THE MONSTER!

[An Anarchist Society of some mad Bengalee Babus has been unearthed by the Calcutta Police, and a number of arrests have been made, a bomb factory has been discovered and a quantity of weapons, powder, dynamite, &c. found in the Maniktolah garden in Calcutta. The killing of two innocent European ladies at Mozufferpore, the wife and daughter of Mr. Pringle Kennedy, a Congressman and once the President of the Bengal Provincial Conference held in 1891, also a brilliant alumnus of the Calcutta University who carried off its blue ribbon, the Premchand Roychand scholarship, has led to the unearthing of the whole thing. A bomb intended for killing Mr. Kingsford, late Chief Presidency Magistrate of Calcutta, was thrown by mistake towards the carriage of the poor ladies with direful results. The Indian public has expressed its horror at the foul deed.]

[*Hindi Punch, May, 1908.*]

(27) Lord Minto as Hercules killing the hydra of 'anarchism'. As in the legend, the beast proved difficult to dispatch. Cartoon published in *Hindi Punch* in May 1908.

28

29

30

(28) Gilbert Elliot, 4th Earl of Minto, Viceroy of India 1905-10; (29) F. L. Halliday, Commissioner of Police, Calcutta, in 1908-9; (30) Policeman near a pit in the grounds of the Maniktola Garden where a case of firearms was unearthed.

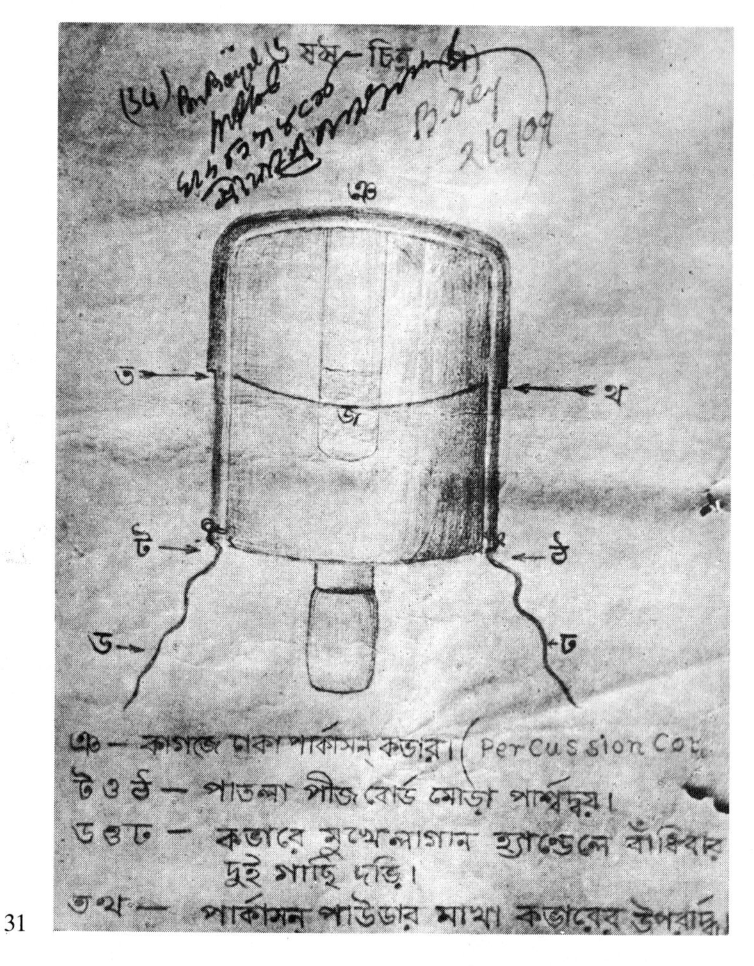

31

32

33

(31) Diagram of a simple bomb, with markings in Bengali. (32) Four bombshells found at 134 Harrison Road, one is the brass knob of a bedpost, another the ball cock from a cistern. (33) The book-bomb sent to Douglas Kingsford, consisting of a law commentary hollowed out to receive a cocoa-tin filled with picric acid.

34

35

(34) Khudiram Bose after his arrest; (35) The Maniktola garden house under guard.

36

37

38

(36) C. R. Das, leader of the defence; (37) Eardley Norton, leader of the prosecution; (38) Courtroom in Alipore where the sessions trial was held.

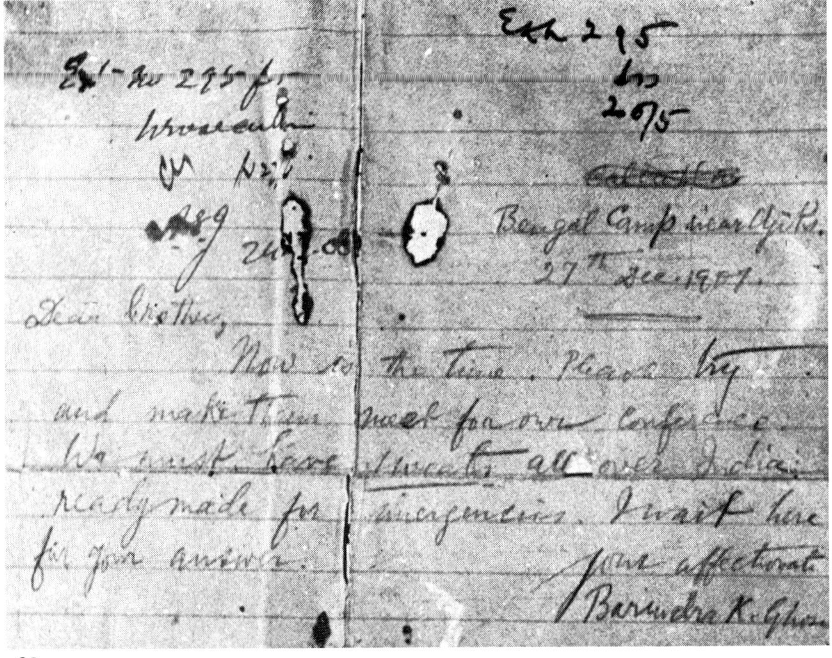

Ext. 295

Bengal Camp near [illegible]
27th Dec. 1907.

Dear Brother,

Now is the time. Please try and make them meet for our conference. We must have sweets all over India ready made for emergencies. I wait here for your answer.

Your affectionate
Barindra K. Ghose

39

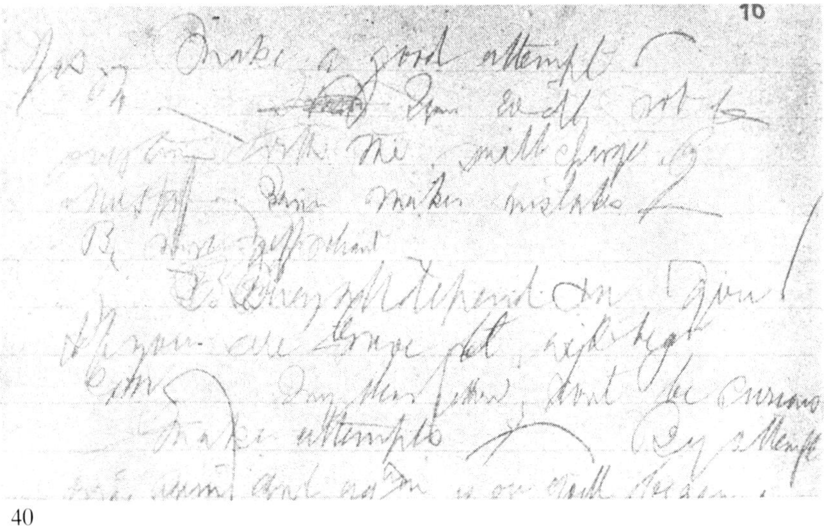

40

(39) The 'Sweets letter' sent by Barin Ghose to his brother Aurobindo: 'Now is the time for *sweets* all over India.' (40) A page of the 'Scribblings', found in one of Aurobindo's notebooks, mentioning 'the small charge of the stuff'.

41

42

43

Views from the outside (41) and inside (42) of the solitary cell in Alipore jail where Aurobindo Ghose was imprisoned. (43) Part of the '44 degrees' where most of the other prisoners were kept.

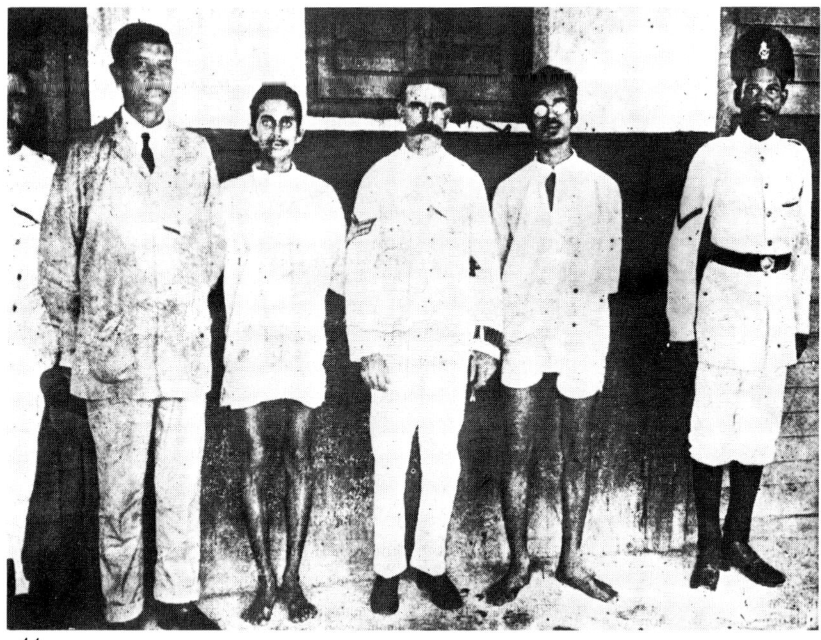

44

45

(44) Kanailal Dutt (right, with spectacles) and Satyendra Nath Bose, after shooting Narendra Nath Goswami in Alipore jail. (45) The two revolvers used to kill Goswami: on the left the Osborne .38-calibre pistol held by Satyen, on the right the Webley .45 used by Kanailal.

46

47

48

(46) F. W. Duke, Chief Secretary, Government of Bengal (left), and Sir Edward Baker, Lieutenant-Governor of Bengal 1908-11; they considered Aurobindo Ghose the most dangerous man in India after his release in 1909. (47) Aurobindo preaching 'militant swadeshism': cartoon published in *Hindi Punch* on 20 June 1909. (48) Aurobindo speaking in Beadon Square, Calcutta.

49

50

(49) A block of Cellular Jail in the Andamans, where many revolutionaries were imprisoned.
(50) Lord Hardinge (Viceroy 1910-16) on the back of an elephant at the time of his ceremonial entrance into Delhi on 23 December 1912. Shortly after this photograph was taken, Basanta Kumar Biswas threw a bomb at Hardinge, seriously wounding him.

51

(51) Arbind Mandir ('The Temple of Aurobindo'), a poster printed in Kanpur during the 1930s, showing Aurobindo Ghose surrounded by north Indian revolutionary heros such as Bhagat Singh.

11

Mother Kali's Bomb

In the autumn of 1907 Sir Andrew Fraser went to Darjeeling, the summer capital of Bengal, to pass the *puja* holidays. Charu Chandra Dutt, the revolutionary civil servant, also was there. Convinced that the 'Queen of Hill-Stations' offered excellent opportunities for assassination, Dutt summoned Prafulla Chaki from Calcutta. After studying Fraser's movements, Dutt decided the best time to kill him would be while he was walking to church. The plan was for Prafulla to wait on the road with a bomb that Dutt had brought from Calcutta. When Fraser came by Prafulla would throw the bomb and disappear in the confusion. Dutt would be waiting on the railway platform. That Sunday, Divine Providence smiled on Sir Andrew, sending him to church with a police escort. Dutt and Prafulla put off the attempt until a later cricket match—which Fraser did not attend.[1]

As the weapon of choice of European anarchists, the hand-held bomb had come to symbolize violent revolution. Months before real bombs were used against real victims in India, Brahmabandhab Upadhyay had written in *Sandhya*:

> It is a matter for great rejoicing that an excellent kind of bomb is being manufactured. This bomb is called *Kali Mai's boma* (the bomb of Mother Kali). It is being experimented on, and if it comes out of the test successfully it must be kept in every house. This bomb is so light that one can walk with it in one's hand. It has not to be set fire to: it explodes with a loud noise and shakes the earth if it is thrown on the ground with some little force. . . . A son is wanted from every family who must practice the virtues of the *Khatriya* (Warrior). Let them play with *Kali Mai's boma*.[2]

The purpose of this passage was intimidation. It is unlikely that it was taken seriously either by *Sandhya*'s readers or by the British police. But it is true that revolutionary groups in Bengal had been experimenting with bombs for a year or so before the article was written. The first attempts used crude mixtures of amorphous phosphorus and chlorate of potassium—the ingredients of safety matches. The results were not deadly; at best such bombs were 'sufficiently powerful to scare away mobs'. It was a show bomb of this variety that Hem and Barin lugged around East Bengal in pursuit of Bampfylde Fuller.[3]

A desire for more powerful explosives drove a number of young Bengalis to clandestine experiment. The first to succeed was Ullaskar Dutt. While a student of Presidency College, Ullaskar had won renown for slapping an arrogant British professor with his slipper.[4] Thinking it best to leave the college after the incident, he went to Bombay to study textile manufacture. But after reading a few copies of *Jugantar* he decided he would rather learn bomb-making instead. With such a skill he might be able to join one of the secret societies whose existence the paper had hinted at. Returning to Bengal Ullaskar taught himself chemistry and performed experiments in the laboratory of his father, a professor at Sibpur's Civil Engineering College. Having mastered the rudiments of his trade, he 'approached the secret societies, and was readily taken in'.[5]

One evening late in 1907 Ullaskar invited Biren Sen and other student-revolutionaries to his Sibpur laboratory. After treating them to *khichri* (he was an excellent cook) Ullaskar showed his guests a phial containing nitroglycerine, the basis of dynamite, and another containing fulminate of mercury. The fulminate was used as a detonator in bombs made of picric acid, which was considered better than dynamite for do-it-yourself terrorists.[6] In those days picric acid could be bought across the counter since it had a number of legitimate uses, in the tanning industry for instance. Of course one had to be careful melting its honey-coloured crystals, for if heated too fast they explode. But once successfully melted, the compound could be poured into a shell or other object that suited the purpose. The fulminate was more difficult to prepare, since it 'has a property of exploding on slight friction'. Ullaskar was a competent chemist, but to the end of his life he had a scar on his forehead that was produced by a bomb that went off unexpectedly.[7]

High spirited and an excellent singer, Ullaskar was a favourite of the Garden boys. He became the head of the bomb section, operating a small forge and maintaining stockpiles of dynamite, picric acid and other explosives. Commercially made dynamite was more reliable than home-made stuff but it was very difficult to obtain. Still, Barin managed to get three-quarters of a bucketful. Some of this was purchased from a trading company in Gauhati, the rest supplied by nationalist leader Manoranjan Guha Thakurta, who owned a mine in Giridih.[8] The revolutionaries also stocked up on sulphuric acid and other chemicals used in making explosives, buying reasonable amounts from different suppliers in Calcutta. At the same time they were making efforts to obtain firearms and ammunition. In time they accumulated two guns, six rifles, and a dozen revolvers. Many of these came from the French enclave of Chandernagore, where the Arms Act was not in force. Others were obtained through the intermediary of Indra Nandi, whose father, Lieutenant-Colonel Nandi, IMS, was exempted from the Act.[9]

A week or two after his Sibpur demonstration, Ullaskar announced that he was ready to put together a mine to blow up Andrew Fraser's train. Barin learned from the newspaper that Fraser would leave Darjeeling on 1 November and, after spending the weekend in Calcutta, would begin a tour of Bihar four days later.[10] A friend in Burdwan who worked in the telegraph office gave them the timetable of the lieutenant-governor's special. Deciding that the best place for the attempt was Mankundu, a town just south of Chandernagore, Barin made a number of journeys to the French enclave to work things out with the local revolutionaries. Their leader, Charu Chandra Roy, did not want an attempt in his own backyard; but Barin had made up his mind and could not be talked out of it. A son of Manoranjan Guha Thakurta brought some dynamite from Giridih, which Ullaskar charged in a hefty iron cylinder. On the 5th he, Barin, Upen, Narendra Nath Goswami and Hrishikesh Kanjilal went to Howrah and caught the train to Chandernagore. From there Ullaskar walked back towards Mankundu, keeping his eye out for a place to lay the mine. Disturbed by passers-by, he selected his spot just minutes before the train approached. Unable to set the mine, he tossed a couple of sticks of dynamite on the tracks. The detonators exploded harmlessly as the train passed over.[11]

Undaunted, Barin decided to try again when Fraser returned from Bihar ten days later. Taking a mine made by Ullaskar, he, Bibhuti Bhusan and Prafulla Chaki went to Mankundu. Choosing a spot near a bridge, Barin asked Bibhuti to dig a hole. Then, on the night the special was expected, they lay in wait, ready to place the mine before the train arrived. It never did. Once again Barin and his companions had to return to Calcutta disappointed.[12]

Clearly a good deal of planning was necessary if one wanted to blow up a train, particularly a train carrying Bengal's highest official. But the scheme was still attractive, not least because C. C. Dutt had persuaded Surendranath Tagore to give a thousand rupees for a successful attempt.[13] Learning that the peripatetic lieutenant-governor was planning to visit Orissa, Barin decided to lay a mine near Kharagpur, a rail-junction on the way to that region. Close by was Midnapore, the town where Satyendra Nath Bose—Aurobindo and Barin's 'uncle'—ran an active branch of the secret society. Ullaskar made the mine, charging six pounds of dynamite in a iron vessel purchased in the bazar. He also made a detonator and fuse of a picric compound.[14] Bibhuti Bhusan and Prafulla Chaki, both veterans of previous attempts, were selected to do the spade-work. Towards the end of November or the beginning of December they took the Puri Passenger to Benapur, ten miles south of Kharagpur. From here they walked another four miles south in the direction of Narayangarh. The stretch between the two towns was desolate and rail traffic infrequent. If the timetable supplied by a Kharagpur signaller was adhered to, the lieutenant-governor's special would reach it in the dead of night.[15] Having found a suitable spot the men waited out the evening under a tree. Around nine they began digging a hole, partly under the rail and partly under a pot-sleeper, the metal bowl filled with ballast that supports the rail. After five hours' work the hole was finished. Filling it loosely with soil, they returned to Calcutta.[16]

On the 3rd of December Barin, Prafulla and Bibhuti went by train to Kharagpur and thence to Narayangarh. One of them carried a bag containing the vessel charged with the dynamite and the detonator. Another brought the fuse, wrapped carefully in cotton-wool and placed in a shoe-box. From Narayangarh they walked to the spot where they previously had dug the hole. There they set the mine and waited—but again the train did not come. Before dawn they returned to Kharagpur, carrying the explosives with them. Prafulla and Bibhuti waited at the station while Barin hurried back to Calcutta. He returned the next day with a copy of the *Englishman* containing an announcement that Fraser was due to depart from Orissa on the 5th. On the afternoon of that day the three men went to Narayangarh and walked to their hole. Under Barin's supervision Prafulla and Bibhuti laid the mine, finishing the job around eleven. After sharing a snack of sweetmeats with the others, Barin walked to Narayangarh to catch the last train to Calcutta. After his train passed the spot where Prafulla and Bibhuti were waiting, they carefully set the fuse and started for Kharagpur.[17]

Having finished his tour of the government relief works in famine-stricken Orissa, Sir Andrew Fraser boarded the special that would carry him back to Calcutta on the evening of the 5th. Sometime between two and three in the morning his train passed through Narayangarh. When the engine hit the mine there was a tremendous explosion. It seemed to the driver that the engine was being thrown upward. But incredibly the train was not derailed. When the passengers got down, they saw that one of the rails had been twisted up like wire. Several sleepers had been broken and others blown to pieces. Where the mine had been was a crater five feet deep and five feet across. Later investigators declared that 'a considerable amount of knowledge and ingenuity was displayed' in the laying of the mine. Sir Andrew's train, they said, had 'had a miraculous escape'.[18]

The government began an investigation immediately. The local police, under pressure to make an arrest, managed to find a coolie that did spade-work for the railways, who 'was induced to make a statement' implicating himself and seven other coolies. Soon the whole lot had entangled themselves in a web of accusation and counter-accusation. All eight were put on trial and on 9 April 1908 six of them were convicted and sent to jail. There they remained for two years, after which an official 'surmised' that their 'incredible' statements 'must have been taught' them while they were in jail 'in the interests of the police who held the enquiry'. Belatedly deciding that all the coolies were 'entirely innocent' the government released them in 1910.[19]

Although happy to believe that the coolies had done the spade-work, the Criminal Investigation Department was from the beginning convinced 'that the coolies were the tools of better educated people', presumably some influential Calcutta men.[20] Using their own methods the CID began assembling data. The information that there was a 'garden' in the suburbs of the city where arms were being collected now seemed more interesting than it had before. Investigations also were set afoot in Midnapore, headquarters of the district where the outrage had taken place. It was here that the CID got their break. In course of his enquiries into the bombing incident, Maulvi Mazharul Haq, the district's deputy superintendent of police, obtained clues leading him to 'suspect the existence of an anarchist party in the town'. Needing an informer to provide him with further information, Haq approached a former tenant of his named Abdur Rahman. Until recently Rahman had taught lathi-play and wrestling in various Midnapore akharas including the one run by Satyendra Nath Bose. 'Being a Muhammadan', as a candid Briton later put it, Rahman 'was likely to give trustworthy information on the doings of the Hindu Extremists, towards whom he stood in a unique position'. On 19 January 1908 Rahman entered the employment of the police and two days later began supplying them with information. He quickly won the 'fullest confidence' of Satyen, who told him all about the Narayangarh incident and also about a certain bomb factory in Calcutta. Prompted by Huq, Rahman asked Satyen for a revolver. When Satyen complied, Rahman asked him for a bomb. Pleased with his zeal (Rahman had volunteered to kill the district magistrate) Satyen gave him a letter introducing him as a 'known Muhammadan brother of Midnapore' and sent him to Calcutta. There Rahman met members of the Atmonnati, Anushilan and other samitis. His wish to see the bomb factory was not granted, but he learned a great deal about the organization and operation of the secret society, including the role of Aurobindo. Back in Midnapore Rahman reported his findings to Huq, who communicated them to his superiors.[21] The Bengal government was glad to have the information but considered it 'so scanty and uncertain that it seemed dangerous to risk losing touch altogether with the criminals by too great haste in attempting to capture them'. After high-level consultations, the chief secretary of the government urged Calcutta's commissioner of police, F. L. Halliday, 'to take no action in Calcutta as it was feared that the conspirators might take alarm and re-form at another centre which would not be known, and would therefore presumably be the more dangerous'. Halliday consented 'in the public interest' and assigned detective policemen to watch a number of places frequented by members of the society in Calcutta and elsewhere.[22]

In one of its reports to the Government of India, the Government of Bengal complained that the 'conspirators showed great caution'.[23] Given the rapidity with which the society was penetrated this may safely be called an overstatement, evidently intended by Bengal to absolve itself from responsibility for the 'outrages' that continued to occur. It is however true that after the Narayangarh attempt the terrorists decided to play it cool for a while. Over tea one afternoon a relative of Upen's told him that some Russian Nihilists had come to India. The authorities, it seemed, were well informed about the whole affair. Concerned about this and other reports, Upen made up his mind to go on a pilgrimage. As often his motives were mixed. On the one hand he still longed to find a guru, revolutionary or otherwise. On the other he thought he might locate a good place for the society to experiment with bombs. Sometime around the middle of December he, Ullaskar, Prafulla, Bibhuti and another man went to Bihar and visited Deoghar and other places. In Patna they fell in with a band of *ganja*-smoking sannyasins bound for Dhuni Saheb in Nepal. Besides being eager to visit this sacred spot, Upen thought (as Tilak had thought before him) that the independent Himalayan kingdom might be a good place for the manufacture of munitions. Standing on the free soil of Nepal, the pilgrims' minds were filled with 'a gay flutter of excitement'; but soon the magnetic attraction of Bengal drew them back to Calcutta. They found the Garden practically deserted. Many of the boys had disappeared, and Barin had gone with Aurobindo to western India.[24]

12

Upheavals

On 7 December 1907, the day after the Narayangarh bombing, the Midnapore District Conference was held in Midnapore town, twelve miles from the scene of the attempt. District-level Congress meetings generally attracted little attention outside the immediate area. But in the charged atmosphere of the time, the Midnapore District Conference became the most important political event in Bengal since the Calcutta Congress. During 1907 Extremists and Moderates had become increasingly polarized and hostile. Members of the national Moderate oligarchy strove to recover their old monopoly. But Extremism was on the rise. The writings of Aurobindo, Tilak and other Extremist spokesmen were being devoured in every part of the country. Readers were stirred by accounts of the Punjab deportations, the press trials in Calcutta and the continuing repression in East Bengal. The Swadeshi movement, though actually levelling off, was still able to generate enthusiasm, allowing people from Peshawar to Madras to make gestures of solidarity with the Bengalis.

The progress of Extremism had been especially significant in the Central Provinces, whose capital, Nagpur, had been chosen as the host of the 1907 annual session of Congress. The Moderates had settled on Nagpur 'on purpose to exclude Tilak from the presidency'.[1] But as the time for the session drew near, Nagpur's Moderates found themselves locked in a struggle with Extremists for control of the Reception Committee. Still in the minority, the Extremists, led by B. S. Moonje, resorted to tactics of intimidation and obstruction. Realizing that the situation was slipping out of their control, Nagpur Moderates announced that the city would not be able to host the session. On 10 November a cabal of

Moderates meeting in Pherozshah Mehta's residence shifted the venue to Surat, an ultra-Moderate town in politically inactive Gujarat.

The Nagpur imbroglio had been followed with interest by Moderates and Extremists throughout the country and by the Government of India as well. After Mehta's magisterial manoeuvre, Aurobindo and other Extremists wanted to break with the other party, boycott the Congress and hold a separate Conference in Nagpur. Tilak however wished the party to make a strong showing in Surat and his view prevailed. Nevertheless it was decided to hold separate Extremists conferences before and after the session.[2]

This was the position when the Midnapore Conference was held. The organizers had invited the principal leaders of both parties—Surendranath Banerjea and his associates for the Moderates, Aurobindo and his allies for the Extremists. Not surprisingly the conference turned into a struggle for power. The Extremists packed the meeting place with National Volunteers wearing showy turbans and badges and carrying lathis. They were led by Satyendra Nath Bose, captain-general of the Midnapore secret society.[3] The Extremists demanded that the Chairman, Moderate barrister K. B. Dutt, speak out in favour of *swaraj*. When he refused to go along the National Volunteers created an uproar. The Moderates appealed to Aurobindo to restore order. Aurobindo said and did nothing. The next day the Extremists held a separate meeting instead of attending the Conference. 'The inevitable schism has taken place,' wrote Hemendra Prasad Ghose, adding prophetically: 'This is the beginning only.'[4]

With Bipin Pal in jail, Aurobindo had become the leader of the Bengal Extremists. This put him under considerable mental stress. It was, he wrote to his wife before departing for Midnapore, 'a time of great anxiety for me. There are pulls from every side that are enough to drive one mad.' In Calcutta he did 'not have a minute to spare. I am in charge of the writing; I am in charge of the Congress work; I have to settle the *Bande Mataram* affair. I am finding it difficult to cope with it all. Besides, I have my own work to do; that too cannot be neglected.'[5] Aurobindo's 'own work' was his practice of yoga, which was becoming increasingly important to him. It will be recalled that he had taken it up to get power for action, specifically political and revolutionary action. Far from pulling him away from the movement, yoga had opened up to him sources of guidance and energy that he had never known. Occasionally he sought guidance by means of 'automatic writing'. One of his experiments from this period has survived. The 'spirit' behind the writing addressed him as 'you':

> Bengalis are a timid race but they are very desirous of being brave —Many make attempts but few can succeed You do a lot of work but not properly Because you do not see to the execution
>
> Barin may try but he will not succeed when you cannot help him— ... Sudhir will be a good man for the next attempt. Prafulla has lost confidence in himself. Because he will not do it. Many will try but fail ...
>
> Yes, make a good attempt—[*illegible*]—You will not be [*illegible*] with the small charge of the stuff. Barin makes mistakes—Be more self-reliant.[6]

Aurobindo kept an open mind about 'automatic writing' but did not believe that all such 'communications' were valid. Nevertheless he did think some of them were remarkable or even prophetic.[7] It is not known what he thought of the above example; but it shows, besides the obvious fact that he knew what his brother was doing, that his interest in 'spiritual' matters extended even to the down-to-earth business of revolutionary action.

After returning from Midnapore, Aurobindo was swept up in the preparations for the Surat Congress. At a meeting on 11 December, he and other Extremists 'decided to attend the Congress in large numbers.'[8] As in 1906 the most contentious pre-Congress issue was the selection of the president. The Bombay Moderates had given the post to Rash Behari Ghose, a Calcutta lawyer who was acquainted with the viceroy. The Extremists wanted Rash Behari to step down in favour of Lala Lajpat Rai, who had been released from Mandalay jail in November. On 14 and 15 December two meetings were held in Calcutta 'to support the claims of Lajpat Rai'. Aurobindo spoke at both—his first public addresses. On the 15th stones were thrown at the police, as a result of which further meetings were banned.[9] Six days later the Congress delegates left for Surat by train. Among them was Barin Ghose. Although uninterested in Congress politics, he had accepted an invitation to go in order to meet Extremists from other provinces to sound them on his revolutionary programme.[10]

Barin's society was not the only group in Bengal that was in favour of revolutionary action. On 6 December, coincidentally the same day as the Narayangarh attempt, a group of men led by Narendra Nath Bhattacharya (later famous as M. N. Roy) carried out a successful dacoity in Chingripota, a town twelve miles south of Calcutta. Two weeks later, while the delegates were on their way to Surat, three members of the Dacca Anushilan shot and wounded Dacca's district magistrate, B. C. Allen. News of the attack created a sensation. From the comfortable distance of Whitehall, Secretary of State Morley wrote in a philosophic vein to Lord Minto: 'It has long been evident that Indian antagonism to Government would run slowly into the usual grooves, including assassination.'[11] Delegates arriving in Surat learned that Allen's life was despaired of. 'The news,' wrote *Guardian* correspondent H. W. Nevinson, 'threw the same gloom and consternation over the Indian party of reform [the Moderates] as struck the Irish Home Rulers on the news of the Phoenix Park murders'.[12] Many Extremists were anything but gloomy.

In Surat the parties stayed in separate camps, a physical sign of the clear-cut separation between them. They differed not only in their stance on major issues—swaraj, swadeshi, boycott—but also in their approach, methods and aim. For the Extremists the Calcutta swaraj resolution had not gone far enough; the Moderates believed that it had gone much too far. They were anxious, in the words of A. Chaudhuri, 'to regain what we have lost', that is, to overturn the 1906 resolutions. Surat looked to be the place where they could do this. There were, wrote Moderate leader R. N. Mudholkar to Gokhale, 'no extremists' in the town 'beyond the half a dozen cranks'. Mudholkar was confident that at Surat 'neither Sj. [*Srijukta*] Arabinda Ghose or Lalit Mohan Ghosal or Lokmanya Tilak & Khaparde can do *much* mischief'. Nevertheless some trouble was anticipated. In the middle of December Surendranath Banerjea had written to Gokhale, 'I fear Tilak & his party mean mischief about the election of the president.'[13] Tilak in fact did want Rash Bihari 'to retire in Lala's favour'. This would be 'not only honouring Lala' but also 'effectively protest[ing] against the high handedness of Government' in deporting him. The Extremists intended to press this point. But there was widespread speculation that if they pressed too hard the Congress would 'be split into two institutions'. This might mean the end of the organization.[14]

Tilak was aware of the danger, but he assured a correspondent that 'I or the new party so far as I can control it will not allow Congress to die.' He repeated this conviction in a speech made at the Extremist Conference on 24 December, two days before the session. The party he said, 'had not come to Surat to wreck the Congress but to strengthen it'.[15] His idea was to establish the Extremists as a second force within Congress and then to capture the organization from within. But for the moment compromise was necessary. On this point Aurobindo and other irreconcilables bowed to Tilak's authority. But all were agreed that there could be no backpedalling on issues like swaraj and boycott. A negotiating committee consisting of Tilak, Aurobindo and Khaparde was constituted to carry on parlays with the Moderates. There was much coming and going between the two camps. Tilak paid a call on some of the leading Moderates but was treated contemptuously. Lajpat Rai, who had angered the Extremists by refusing to stand as their candidate, held talks with Tilak, Aurobindo and Khaparde. He pleaded with Aurobindo to work for unity. Aurobindo replied, 'You cannot fill the cup till you have first emptied it,' emphasizing his point with an appropriate gesture.[16]

No agreement could be reached before the 26th, the first day of the session. That morning a delegation of Extremists called on Surendranath Banerjea. They said they would raise no objection to the election of the president if the Calcutta resolutions were not changed and some 'graceful allusion' made to 'the desire of the public to have Lajpat Rai in the Chair'.[17] Banerjea said they would have to speak with Tribhovandas Malvi, a Surat bigwig who was head of the Reception Committee. Malvi, engaged in his devotions, declined to see them. At two in the afternoon the delegates assembled in the pavilion. The Moderates outnumbered their rivals, but the Extremists were conscious of their strength. During Malvi's welcoming address Tilak was given a copy of the resolutions the Moderates planned to propose. This made it clear that they planned to alter the Calcutta resolutions.

The delegates sat through Malvi's speech in silence and raised no objection when Ambalal Desai proposed Rash Behari Ghose to the chair. But when Surendranath rose to second the motion, he could speak only a half-dozen words before pandemonium broke loose. 'Remember Midnapore' cried Extremists from Bengal. 'Remember Nagpur' cried Extremists from the Central Provinces. Soon ten thousand men were on their feet 'shouting for order, shouting for tumult'.[18] After some unavailing attempts to silence the assembly the sitting was suspended.

That afternoon Surendranath invited the Bengal Extremists to his quarters and pleaded for unity. Producing a compromise agreement, he asked for signatures. The paper was passed from one man to another, no one signing. Finally Satyen Bose said, 'Wait, sir, give it to me.' Still incensed over Surendranath's Midnapore betrayal, Satyen tore the paper to pieces. This was more than the old guard could bear. As the Extremists filed out, a distinguished Moderate raised his fist and abused Aurobindo in the most vulgar terms. This did little to calm Extremist tempers.[19]

Tilak meanwhile was trying to mend things as best he could. The 'whole thing', he explained, 'had been a mistake'. When the session reconvened the Extremists would give the speakers a hearing, so long as the Calcutta resolutions were 'replaced in the original form'.[20] Negotiations went on through the evening and night. By the morning of the 27th there was some hope that the session would go forward as planned. Before the speeches began, Tilak sent Malvi a note asking for a chance to say something about the election after the seconding address had been delivered. But after Banerjea finished his speech and Motilal Nehru said a few words, Malvi declared Rash Behari elected without calling Tilak to the platform. As the president launched into his address, Tilak approached the chair and demanded to be heard. Rash Behari declared him out of order. Tilak stood his place. Even as bedlam broke loose he remained firm, arms folded across his chest, facing the hostile delegates. Rash Behari stood on the table and rang the bell as Moderates threatened Tilak with bodily harm. A shoe flew through the air, apparently meant for Tilak but striking Banerjea and Mehta instead. Maharashtrian volunteers streamed on the platform swinging lathis. After a free-for-all the pavilion was cleared by the police.

Politics had failed. Revolution was on the rise. Barin, Satyen and their associates had not come to Surat to take part in the debates. They wanted 'action' and were ready for it at any moment. At one point during the session Satyen went up to Aurobindo and told him that he was carrying a pistol. Did he want him to shoot Surendranath Banerjea? Horrified, Aurobindo answered that this would not be necessary.[21] Barin's plans for assassination were less impulsive. While others in the Extremist camp were talking over the issues, he had been trying to organize a meeting of revolutionaries. On the 27th (the day of the melee) he wrote to Aurobindo: 'Dear Brother, Now is the time. Please try to make them meet for [our] own conference. We must have *sweets* all over India readymade for imergencies [*sic*]. I wait here for your answer.'[22] By 'them' Barin meant leaders like Tilak. By 'sweets' he meant bombs.

What answer if any Aurobindo gave to this indiscreet letter is not known. At any rate neither he nor Tilak attended the 'conference'. Most other Marathis also begged off, Khaparde and Moonje included. These two, it transpired, suspected that one of the men invited, a certain Punjabi Muslim, was an informer. In the end the only persons to attend were some Punjabis, including Sufi Amba Prasad, Ajit Singh and the dubious Muslim; a few lesser-known Maharashtrians, including Dr. V. M. Bhat; and Barin and his associates.[23] Barin told them of his plan for a countrywide uprising. The Punjabi Muslim was enthusiastic, saying that when the country was in turmoil the Amir of Afghanistan would thunder down to the plains. This idea met with a cold reception and the meeting ended inconclusively.

Barin was acutely disappointed by the lack of Maharashtrian participation. Since the time of his initiation into Thakur Saheb's society, he had been sure that the race of Shivaji would be India's salvation. More recently a prominent Marathi leader, apparently Khaparde, had informed Barin that when he gave the order his men would blow up bridges, capture districts, and so forth.* Seeking out Khaparde and Moonje after the meeting, Barin learned that Thakur Saheb's secret society no longer existed. Despondent, he asked Tilak for an interview. Tilak sent word that he was sympathetic, but that his own path was chalked out before him and he was too old to change.[24]

The failure of the conference had a decisive effect on Barin. All along he had been hearing that every province except Bengal was ready for revolution. Now he discovered that Bengal was in the

* Barin did not mention the Maharashtrian's name in *Atmakahini* but spoke of a well-known Marathi leader involved both in Extremist politics and revolution. In a letter of 1955 (HFMP IV & V 41/2) he wrote of Khaparde as being especially knowledgeable about Thakur Sahib's society. His gibe in *Atmakahini* that the 'Marathi leader' fled across the seas when things became difficult may be a reference to Khaparde's going to England in August 1908.

vanguard. It became clear to him that 'we had to walk our lone path and somehow convince and initiate the whole of Congress-minded India into this new creed of violent and armed revolution'.[25]

Meanwhile 'Congress-minded India' was undergoing changes as decisive as those affecting the terrorists. After the break-up of the session on the 27th, the two parties had withdrawn to their separate camps. Both of them issued statements that blamed the break-up on the other party. Both held conferences from which members of the other party were excluded. Before entering the Moderate Conference delegates had to sign a 'creed' affirming their adherence to the party's tenets. Seeing that the Moderates were in a position to take control of the machinery of Congress, Tilak expressed his willingness to sign. He thought if the Extremists were admitted to the conference they would eventually be able to wrest power from their opponents. Moreover he had been warned by Lajpat Rai that 'the Government had decided, if the Congress split, to crush the Extremists by the most ruthless repression.' Tilak thought, correctly as it turned out, 'that the country was not yet ready to face successfully such a repression'. In order to circumvent this, and to beat the Moderates at their own game, he proposed that the Extremists enter the convention. Aurobindo and others were vehemently opposed to this and predicted besides that no Extremists would be permitted to enter. In fact no known Extremists were. Following a proposal of Aurobindo's, the party held a conference on the 29th in order to set up a separate Extremist organization to rival the Moderate Convention.[26] On the last day of 1907 the Extremists finished their Congress business and went their separate ways.

Aurobindo was bound for Baroda. There, besides seeing some old friends, he planned to meet Vishnu Bhaskar Lele, the yogi who had impressed Barin in September. In response to a wire from Barin, Lele came from Gwalior and met Aurobindo in Khaserao Jadhav's house. Needing to escape from the crowds that thronged to see the leader, the men retired to another house where for ten days Aurobindo meditated with Lele. He proved to be an apt disciple. Within three days, he later said, he was able to reach the state of consciousness known to yogis as the 'silent Brahman' or Nirvana. The latter term means 'extinction', the idea being that the individual ego-personality is abolished. When Aurobindo resumed work—meeting people, delivering speeches, even visiting a Poona bomb-factory—it appeared to him that his actions were being performed by someone else.[27] From this point on Aurobindo was primarily a yogi. He regarded his work and writings as the expressions of a higher will. When he returned to Calcutta, he explained this new mental state to his wife:

I was to have come on the 8th January, but I could not. This did not happen of my own accord. I had to go where God took me. . . . The state of my mind has undergone a change. . . . I no longer am the master of my own will. Like a puppet I must go wherever God takes me; like a puppet I must do whatever he makes me do. . . . I am no longer free. From now on you will have to understand that all I do depends not on my will but is done at the command [*adesh*] of God.[28]

13

Bombs and Monkeys

Barin had accompanied Aurobindo to Baroda and while there he also passed some time with Lele. Not nearly so proficient in meditation as his brother, he soon went back to his ordinary pursuits. During his stay in Baroda he made a bomb using a formula Ullaskar had given him. Before leaving town he passed the formula on to Chhotalal Purani, a local revolutionary.[1] Returning to Calcutta by mid-January, Barin found things at the Garden in high gear. Upen, Ullaskar and company were back from Nepal and recruitment was going on apace. During February and March around eight new men began staying at the centre, more than doubling its strength.[2] The growing numbers made the leaders uneasy. What if the Garden was under police surveillance? They decided nothing risky should be done there any more; the Garden would be an ashram and nothing else. The anonymity of the city seemed to offer more security than the seclusion of the suburbs. While they set about acquiring safe houses in Calcutta, some of the boys started spending time at Hem Das's place on Russa Road.

After more than a year in Europe, Hem had returned to India in the first week of January. His stay on free soil had made him sufficiently confident to send a collection of revolutionary literature ahead of him in a sea parcel. As his ship neared Bombay he 'was overpowered by a strange feeling of fear'. 'With much trepidation he cleared the parcel and then made contact with some Maharashtrian revolutionaries known to his friends in London. After meetings in Bombay, Nasik and Nagpur, Hem reached the same conclusion that Barin had in Surat: the Maharashtrians talked big but were too cautious to act. If anyone was going to start a revolution it would have to be the Bengalis. Before returning to Bengal at the end of the month, Hem arranged for one or two of the more spirited Marathis to study at the Garden.[3]

Before leaving for France in 1906 Hem had grown disenchanted with Barin and Aurobindo—the latter because of his religious ideas, the former 'because whatever he did was revealed either to the public or to the police'. With encouragement from Charu Chandra Dutt, Hem decided to start his own party. But soon he ran into financial difficulties. His backer supplied him with plenty of talk but no cash. When Aurobindo came to Calcutta from Surat Hem again fell under his spell. Aurobindo sent him to Barin who advised him to set up a separate establishment in the city. Hem passed on to Barin the material on revolutionary organization and bomb-making he had brought from Europe. Barin thought that a Western-style set-up would never work in a spiritual country like India.[4] He was glad however to have Hem's bomb-making manual and soon had his charges copying it out. A translation of a Russian work acquired by Hem in Paris, the manual provided first-rate instructions on the manufacture of explosives, the fabrication of shells and the techniques of blowing up buildings, bridges and so forth. It was, an expert later testified, 'the best guide to explosives I have ever seen.' Written in simple non-technical language, it permitted a layman to 'use the contents of a Chemist's shop for the manufacture of explosives'. Its general purpose was described in its opening sentence: 'The aim of the present work is to place in the hands of a revolutionary people such a powerful weapon as explosive matter is.'[5]

Once he resolved to join up with Barin, Hem lost no time getting started. The publicity generated by the attempt to blow up the lieutenant-governors's train made it necessary to choose a new target. The obvious choice was Douglas H. Kingsford, who as chief presidency magistrate had sent Bhupen Dutt to jail and ordered the caning of Sushil Sen. Kingsford was living closely guarded in Garden Reach, Calcutta. Hem thought the best way to penetrate his defences would be to deliver a bomb to his door. He got hold of a copy of *A Commentary on the Common Law designed as Introductory to its Study*, a 1075-page tome by Herbert Broom, LLD, and cut a square hole out of its middle. In this he inserted a Cadbury's Cocoa tin containing a pound of picric acid, three detonators and a mechanical device meant to set off the charge when the parcel was opened. Hem was by now an excellent bomb-maker and his infernal machine was well made. Wrapping it up in brown paper he entrusted it to Paresh Mallick, one of the new recruits. Dressed up as a postal peon, Paresh delivered the bomb to Kingsford's servant, who took it to his master. Kingsford looked at the package, decided it was a book being returned by a friend, and put it on a shelf. The revolutionaries waited in vain for news of the explosion. When none came some suspected that Paresh had got cold feet and thrown the bomb in a rubbish pile.[6]

Around this time Barin and Ullaskar decided to shift the society's bomb-making activities to Deoghar. Ullaskar, Upendranath and some of the others had spent some time in this hill resort, Barin's childhood home, during their recent wanderings. In January Barin, Ullaskar, Bibhuti, Nolini and Prafulla Chakrabarti went to stay in Raidi, a village close to Deoghar, in a place called Sil's Lodge.[7] Green fields stretched from the door to the distant hills where Santal tribals lived. Rising before dawn the sadhu-revolutionaries chanted verses from the Upanishads in the silence of that lonely country. After breakfast they got down to business. For experimental purposes, Ullaskar made a small picric-acid bomb. Nolini and the others helped out. When they were finished they carried their creation to the top of a hill on the other side of the tracks. Here among the rocks they found a place that offered a good surface for impact as well as shelter from the explosion. To Prafulla was given the honour of throwing the bomb. Ullas stood near him while Barin and Bibhuti hid behind the rocks and Nolini climbed a tree to get a better view. From his perch the youngster saw a flash of light and a puff of smoke and heard a sound like 'a hundred simultaneous claps of thunder'. Thrilled, he clambered down his tree and ran towards the others, crying out 'Success, success!' But as he drew near he saw Prafulla hanging in Ullaskar's arms, his head mutilated and bloody. Instead of exploding on impact the bomb had gone off in the air. Prafulla had not had time to duck and a splinter had pierced his skull, killing him instantly. Ullaskar also had been hit, but his wounds were relatively minor. Taking stock of the situation, Barin decided the first priority was getting Ullaskar to a doctor. The only person they could trust was in Calcutta. They had to depart at once. Leaving Prafulla's motionless body where it lay, the men climbed silently down the hill. At one point Nolini blurted out, 'We were five when we went up, but now we're only four.' 'No sentimentality, please,' Barin answered.[8]

The leader took Ullaskar to Calcutta and was relieved to learn that his wounds were not dangerous. He then picked up Upendranath and returned to Deoghar, where the others were waiting. After a day or two they decided to strike camp and go back to the Garden. Needless to say the death of one of their number, a youth considered by some to be 'the best of the whole lot', was a terrible blow to the group. But at the same time it 'filled them with the resolve to finish what they had started'. Back in Calcutta Upen noticed that Barin seemed to be 'looking anxiously into his heart in search of something he could rely on'. Not long afterwards Barin wrote to Lele, the yogi who had initiated him and Aurobindo, asking him to come to Bengal.[9] Lele came and passed some time with the young men, both at the Garden and at Deoghar. Barin had finally succeeded in obtaining a Satyananda for his Ananda Math; but Lele declined to play the role. When he found out what the revolutionaries were up to he told them that they were bound to fail. 'A work like this,' he said, 'demands clean hearts; otherwise it will end in useless bloodshed.' What was needed was a group of men who knew 'God's mandate'. Only such could be trusted to lead the country. Lele assured them: 'India will have her freedom; but not by these means. I have found this out through twenty long years of meditation. Believe me, a time will come when all power will simply pass into your hands. You will only have to work out the administration.' He asked them to come with him to practise yoga. If they obtained no results they were free to go back. Upen and some of the others seemed interested, but most thought Lele was telling a fairy story. 'This is nonsense,' cried Barin, convinced that India could never achieve freedom without violence. Besides, he had his backers to consider. They had given him thousands and were clamouring for results. Lele warned him that if he persisted he would regret it. 'If you mean they'll make me dance at the end of a rope, I'm not worried!' Barin declared. The yogi told him that what would happen would be more terrible than death. Barin stuck to his guns, however, and by the time of Lele's departure Upen too had made up his mind to stay. But Prafulla Chaki, to whom Lele had taken a liking, decided to follow the guru. It was only Upen's last-minute pleading that convinced the boy to stay.[10]

Lele also spent some time with Aurobindo at his new Calcutta residence. The yogi asked him how his yogic practice was going. Aurobindo replied that he had stopped regular meditation, not adding that he found himself in a state of constant inner concentration. Lele told him he had taken a wrong turn. Aurobindo was not concerned. It was around this time that he wrote to his wife: 'All I do depends not on my will but is done at the command of God.' There can be no doubt that he felt himself in contact with a supernatural power that was guiding his footsteps. He was apparently convinced that this power would protect him and those who accepted his leadership. Despite appearances to the contrary, he was not unaware of the danger that he, Barin and their followers were getting into. On 11 March he told Sudhir Sarkar to write to Sil's Lodge to inform Upen and the others to return to Calcutta. In a postscript Sudhir added: 'The condition of the garden is bad. Monkeys are entering'.[11] By 'monkeys' Sudhir meant the police. The friendly visits from the local sub-inspector (who in fact knew nothing) were making the boys nervous. Besides they sometimes seemed to be followed—as in fact they were. On 8 February, after the first reports from Midnapore arrived, the CID put a dozen men on the case. For some time they were without specific information. Then Abdur Rahman made his visit to Calcutta. Ironically his success in penetrating the society came just at the time that Barin and Upen were trying to promote greater security. But once the centre and its inhabitants had been identified, the shift to new locations in the city just meant that there were more places for the CID to watch. In the middle of March Inspector Purna Chandra Biswas went to see the Garden himself. Throughout March and April his men shadowed the revolutionaries wherever they went. Boys from the Garden led detectives to Hem's new house on Raja Naba Krishna Street, which after that was kept under close surveillance. As it happened there was a brothel across the street. An enterprising detective 'used to go there and stay some time and pay something to the woman'—presumably for the privilege of looking out of the window.[12] Other detectives kept watch over the society's bookshop at 4 Harrison Road, its 'post office' at 30/2 Harrison Road, and other places as well. Before long the CID had pieced together a fairly complete picture of the society's activities. But the government asked the department not to make any arrests since 'definite evidence alone was wanting to connect their operations with one or other of the specific outrages'.[13]

One of the places the detectives kept under observation was 23 Scott's Lane, where Aurobindo was living with his wife and sister. Abinash Bhattacharya also stayed there, as did Sailen Bose. After serving his three months' imprisonment for the *Jugantar* office assault, Sailen had gone home to the 24 Parganas, where he took part in the Chingripota dacoity. Afterwards he came to Calcutta and started living with his fellow-townsman Abinash. Sudhir Sarkar, another revolutionary, also occasionally stayed at Scott's Lane, and many members of the society visited: Barin and Bijoy Nag frequently, Narendra Nath Goswami, Purna Chandra Sen and others more rarely. Detectives made copious and detailed notes of their comings and goings.[14]

On 5 April a particularly important meeting took place at Scott's Lane. Barin and Upen wanted to talk over the situation in Chandernagore with Aurobindo. The town's mayor, L. Tardivel, had recently taken steps to control the arms traffic between French and British India. He had also begun to interfere with the activities of local Extremists. On 3 April he banned a meeting that was to be addressed by Bipin Chandra Pal. For these reasons Charu Chandra Roy, the leader of the Chandernagore secret society, decided that Tardivel must be eliminated. Misri Babu, a zamindar of neighbouring Uttarpara, put up the money for the job. Upen, a former member of the Chandernagore group, wanted the Garden society to take part. Barin also thought it would make a good 'action'. The two came to Scott's Lane to get Aurobindo's approval.[15] According to Abinash, who was present, the conversation ran something like this:

BARIN: Sejda [older brother], I want to kill the mayor of Chandernagore.
AUROBINDO: Why?
BARIN: He broke up a swadeshi meeting and oppressed the local people.
AUROBINDO: So he ought to be killed? How many people will you kill in this way? I cannot give my consent. Nothing will come of it.
BARIN: No, Sejda, if this isn't done, these oppressors will never learn the lesson we have to teach them.
AUROBINDO: Very well. If that's what you think, do it.[16]

Aurobindo's passive consent seems typical of his attitude towards Barin's activities. He was too busy with his political work and *Bande Mataram* writing to play a more active role. Besides contributing most of the paper's editorials he had to struggle against its mounting deficit. He sometimes spent the morning trying to sell some company shares so that the paper could survive another day.[17] At the same time he was, until Pal's return in March, the most prominent Extremist in Bengal. In February he led the party at the Provincial Conference at Pabna, East Bengal. In the weeks that followed he attended dozens of public and private meetings, often acting as the principal speaker. If he had any free time he devoted it to his yogic practice. When there was a lull at work he often passed into meditation. If someone came to see him he at once began to speak or write a needed article; but as soon as the visitor departed he went back to his meditation.[18]

After his 5 April meeting with Aurobindo, Barin told the revolutionaries that *bara karta* had consented to his plan.[19] A week was spent preparing for the attempt. Around this time P. M. Bapat, Hem's chemistry classmate from Paris, came to Calcutta with a message from the Indian revolutionaries in London. They advised the Bengalis to go slow. It was time for quiet preparation, not attention-getting action. Hem and Barin heard Bapat out and went back to their preparations. They both had had their fill of Marathi circumspection.[20]

On 10 April Barin, Narendra Nath and Indu Bhusan Roy met at the Garden. Naren had taken part in some of the group's earliest actions, including the Rangpur dacoity. Eighteen-year-old Indu had joined them only in February but was eager to prove himself. From the Garden the three went to Hem's house on Raja Naba Krishna Street. They were followed by two CID detectives and on arrival noticed by the private agent assigned to watch the house. He immediately informed Inspector Purna Chandra Biswas, who was stationed nearby. While the four detectives talked the situation over, the four revolutionaries discussed their plans. Hem gave the assassination-team a picric-acid bomb packed in a shell that looked like a carriage lamp. Taking this along, Barin, Naren and Indu, followed by the four detectives, went to Howrah station. There another private agent joined the parade. The three terrorists, followed by the five detectives, got into a north suburban train. At Mankundu, the station before Chandernagore, all eight got down. The detectives formed two parties, only one of which followed Barin and the others into Chandernagore. In the crowded bazar the detectives lost Naren and Indu but managed to trail Barin to the house of a Chandernagore revolutionary. While Barin was inside the detectives went to report to Purna Chandra. Apparently during their absence Barin left the house, went to the bazar and met Naren and Indu. It was now 8.30. Barin took his comrades to the house of the mayor, but found the gate locked.[21]

The three passed the night in an open space near the railway station. In the morning Barin returned to Calcutta while Naren and Indu went to Naren's house in Serampore, where they passed the day. (Two detectives followed them there from Mankundu, then went back to Calcutta. Purna Chandra Biswas spent the morning looking for Barin in Chandernagore. Then he too went home.) Returning to Chandernagore in the evening Naren and Indu met Barin in the bazar. Again they went to the mayor's house. This time His Honour was at home. Through a window the would-be assassins saw the Frenchman eating dinner with his wife. Barin gave Indu the bomb along with some last-minute tips. Then he and Naren hid in a lane. Climbing up on a ledge Indu tossed the bomb through the lattices of the window and ran as it exploded. Tardivel's luck was as good as Fraser's and Kingsford's. The detonator went off but the picric acid did not explode. If it had it would have caused great damage; an expert later reported that the bomb was 'powerful enough to wreck a large room and kill everyone in it'. As it was 'the lady fainted and her husband received certain slight injuries'. Unaware of the failure of their mission, the terrorists hotfooted it to the bank of the Hooghly, which they crossed by boat. An hour later they took a train to Calcutta, reaching the Garden on the morning of the 12th. That afternoon Barin met Abinash at Sealdah Station and later went with him to 23 Scott's Lane, the place (as the detective following them reported) 'where Aurobindo Ghose was then living'.[22]

The detective submitted his report to CID inspector Soshy Bhusan De. Soshy Bhusan had been on the case since October. Now he felt he was really getting somewhere. On the 14th the CID deputed a number of men to keep close watch on the houses frequented by the suspects. The next day the Chandernagore police reported the attempt on Tardivel to their counterparts in Calcutta. F. L. Halliday, the commissioner of police, sent two officers to Chandernagore to take part in the investigation. Shortly afterwards these men were withdrawn and the case was taken up by the Bengal CID. On the 20th Halliday met with L. F. Morshead, officiating inspector-general of police, Bengal, and C. W. C. Plowden, head of the Bengal CID. Morshead and Plowden 'still pressed the fact that they were not prepared to search houses' in Calcutta or elsewhere for fear that the culprits would escape and regroup. The following day Halliday and Plowden met with the governor of French India, the administrator of Chandernagore, and Mayor Tardivel. They promised the Frenchmen all the help they could give them. The bomb that had failed to kill Tardivel was sent to Calcutta for analysis.[23]

In the weeks that followed information flowed in from Soshy Bhusan's detectives. Inspector Satish Chandra Banerjea was a particularly copious and daring source: he 'sometimes passed within a cubit' of his quarry as he shadowed first one and then another of them around Calcutta. On the 20th Satish Chandra followed Upen, Nirapada and Kristo Jiban from the Garden into Calcutta. Kristo Jiban turned off towards Bagmari while the others proceeded to 4 Harrison Road. On the way they stopped and spoke with their new friend Balkrishna Hari Kane, one of the Marathis sent to Calcutta by G. S. Khaparde. On the 21st another detective trailed Nirapada and a friend when they went to D. Waldie & Co. to purchase chemicals. Two days later plain-clothesmen followed Barin, Upen, Bibhuti and Kane when they paid a visit to Hem Das at 15 Gopi Mohan Dutt's Lane. On the 24th Barin went alone to 23 Scott's Lane and the day after that to Hem's house, to the workshop at 15 Gopi Mohan Dutt's Lane and to 48 Grey Street. The last address was the office and plant of the *Nabashakti*, a Bengali paper that Aurobindo recently had agreed to take up. He was planning to move his household from Scott's Lane to the upper floor of the *Nabashakti* office.[24]

At the same time that the CID's detectives were following each member of the secret society each time they went to Calcutta, the Maniktola beat cops continued to pay friendly visits to the Garden. They 'had no suspicion about the place', one later reported, they simply liked the boys. One day in April Sub-Inspector Dinabandhu Bhattacharya had a nice chat with Sachin Sen, who told him he was studying the Gita with Upen. Dinabandhu also talked with Upen and found his conversation stimulating. He could well imagine 'that he would interest young people'. When Dinabandhu went out he took no notice of the

CID plainclothesmen stationed around the Garden.[25]

The boys were not so unobservant. By the end of April it was obvious that they were being watched. Clearly they had to do something about the incriminating material that they had accumulated. On the 21st everything in Hem's house on Raja Naba Krishna Street was taken to the new place on Gopi Mohan Dutt's Lane. Five days later, apprehensive that this too was being watched (as indeed it was) Ullaskar took a basket containing a bomb and three trunks filled with an assortment of chemicals, explosives, detonators, etc. from Gopi Mohan Dutt's Lane to 134 Harrison Road, where his friend Nagendra Nath Gupta had a pharmacy. Ullas told Nagendra that he meant to leave some things with him for a while. Nagendra had no objections. Detectives followed the move carefully and reported it to their superiors.[26]

14

To Kill Kingsford

Since the summer of 1907 Barin had been 'obsessed with the idea of killing' Douglas Kingsford. For finding various men guilty of sedition and for sentencing a teenage boy to be flogged, the magistrate had become an unpopular man. Barin was informed that the thousand rupees promised for the assassination of Fraser would also be paid if 'Kingsford could be killed'.[1] He and his friends had tried to get him by means of Hem's book bomb. Before another attempt could be made, Kingsford was given a judgeship and transferred to Muzaffarpur. This unimportant town was headquarters of a district famous chiefly for its mangoes and litchis. It was also—and this was the deciding factor—as far away from the capital as any judicature in the province. Kingsford's life had been threatened in Calcutta and the government thought it better not to take chances. The new judge reached Muzaffarpur on 26 March 1908.[2] When his library was shifted, Broom's *Commentary on the Common Law*, still wrapped in brown paper and still containing a live bomb, accompanied his other books.

The fact that the hated Kingsford was three hundred miles away did not diminish the terrorists' interest in him. Less than a week after his transfer it was decided to send someone to Muzaffarpur to kill him. According to Barin, this decision was taken by Aurobindo, Subodh Mullick and Charu Chandra Dutt.[3] Later writers have transmogrified the 'order' of the leaders into a 'death sentence' passed by a 'revolutionary tribunal'.[4] This detail was certainly a later addition, apparently borrowed from accounts of the tribunal that sentenced Czar Alexander II to death. Whether the rest of the story is fictitious is more difficult to determine. Aurobindo, as we have seen, denied playing an active part in the terrorists' affairs, although he did admit that Barin sometimes came to him and Mullick for advice.[5] But Barin was not the only insider to say that Aurobindo helped to plan terrorist 'actions'.[6] In regard to the Kingsford attempt, Aurobindo's friend Abinash Bhattacharya said: 'It is true that Charu Dutt, Subodh Mullick and Aurobindo gave their consent to the murder of Kingsford.' But Abinash was quick to add: 'It is difficult to say just how far Aurobindo really consented'.[7] Perhaps not very far, particularly if his 'consent' was similar to his reaction to Barin's plan to kill Tardivel. In that instance, pressed by his brother, Aurobindo at last said 'very well'. Barin reported this to others as 'Aurobindo approves'. He may have done the same in the Kingsford affair.[8]

At any rate, once the decision had been taken it was up to Barin to select the assassins. His first choice was Sushil Kumar Sen, the boy Kingsford had sentenced to fifteen stripes. Sushil certainly bore no love for the man who had humiliated him and this easily explained resentment would prove advantageous if he was captured. He could simply tell the police that he wanted to kill Kingsford out of revenge. This might keep the authorities off the track of the secret society.[9]

However eager he may have been to take part in an important action, Sushil was still a neophyte and lacked experience. Someone else was needed to support him. Barin's choice fell on Prafulla Chaki. Only nineteen, Prafulla had been a member of the society since 1906 and already had taken part in four attempts. Remembered by his neighbours as a 'meek and docile' lad with a 'meditative and thoughtful' temperament, he was spirited enough to join the swadeshi demonstrations in Rangpur. Expelled from school, he and his classmates became members of Bengal's first institute of national education, the Rangpur National School. But by this time he had lost his interest in conventional education. When Barin and Hem came to Rangpur in 1906 in pursuit of Bampfylde Fuller, Prafulla leapt at the chance to join them. From this moment he was one of the most ardent members of Barin's society; but in many ways he remained a typical Indian schoolboy. He 'could not forget his mother' and occasionally wrote letters to her—without a return address. In one of them he informed her that he 'had espoused the order of Brahmacharya [i. e. become a religious student] and was making fair progress in religion, and in the study of other subjects'.[10] One of these was the chemistry of explosives. After four failed attempts to put bombs or bullets to use, Prafulla was more eager than ever to kill a British official. If Aurobindo's automatic writing was right in saying 'Prafulla has lost confidence in himself', he had not lost his remarkable sang-froid. More than once at the Garden he took an unloaded pistol and announced: 'If they ever get hold of me I for one won't stay alive. The police won't get a chance to torture me or to tempt me into confession. Look, this is the way I'll finish myself off.' Shoving the barrel into his mouth he pulled the trigger. 'This is the only sure way,' he explained. 'Any other way and most of the time you just wound yourself.'[11]

Sushil and Prafulla left Calcutta for Bihar around 4 April.* In Muzaffarpur they took a room in a *dharmasala* run by a Bengali named Kishori Mohan Banerjee. On the way Sushil, now known as Durga Das Sen, lost most of the money they had been given. This obliged Prafulla, renamed Dinesh Chandra Roy, to write to the Garden for more. After explaining the situation and appealing (like other adolescents) 'please send money soon', he added: 'I have seen many places here. Nice, not bad. We have not seen the bridegroom even now.' They had however seen the bridegroom's house, which was also 'not bad'. Prafulla closed his note: 'In sending the money, please do not put any address of our place there. Put a wrong address.' This was a good piece of advice from one terrorist to another. An even better one would have been to tell his friends to destroy his letter with its Muzaffarpur post-mark.[12]

The young assassins' financial difficulties were solved on 9 April when they received a money order for twenty rupees sent by Bibhuti Bhusan. They remained in Muzaffarpur a day or two longer to observe the lie of the land and to watch the bridegroom's movements. Then they went to Calcutta to talk things over with the others. After another reconnaissance mission to Muzaffarpur

* I assume that Prafulla wrote his letter to the Garden the day he arrived, that the letter arrived in Calcutta one or two days later, and that the money order was sent the day the letter was received or the day after. The money order was in fact sent from Calcutta on April 8th and received on the 9th (ABT records XV: 1505–8). Kishori Mohan Banerjee testified in court that Prafulla came to the dharmasala at the end of March (*Bande Mataram* weekly 31 May 1908: 15). He seems to have been relying on his memory and not on a register. Kingsford did not arrive in Muzaffarpur until 26 March.

they returned to the Garden to make the final arrangements.[13] At this point Sushil learned that his father was close to death in Sylhet. Torn between duty to the motherland and duty to his family, Sushil chose to go to his father's bedside.[14]*

A replacement had to be found. Hem Das suggested Khudiram Bose. A year younger than Prafulla, Khudiram had been involved in the revolutionary movement for as long or longer. Recruited in his native Midnapore by Satyendra Nath Bose, he had undergone the society's political and religious training and also had learned how to shoot a gun. Active in the boycott movement, he took pleasure in burning British cloth and sinking boats loaded with British salt. Then in February 1906 he was arrested in the *Sonar Bangla* sedition case. After his release he became one of the most active members of the Midnapore society. In December 1907 he was one of the tumultuous National Volunteers at the Midnapore Conference. Early the next year he went to Calcutta where he put up with his fellow-townsman Hem. He was delighted when he learned he had been selected for a major action.

Sometime towards the end of April Barin took Prafulla from the Garden to 15 Gopi Mohan Dutt's Lane. Here they picked up the bomb that Hem and Ullaskar had made for Kingsford. In a tin sphere smaller than a tennis ball the two had packed six ounces of dynamite, a detonator and a black-powder fuse.[15] From Gopi Mohan Dutt's Lane Barin and Prafulla went to Hem's house on Raja Naba Krishna's Street, where they met Hem and Khudiram. Barin introduced Prafulla as Dinesh Chandra Roy; Khudiram apparently never knew him as anything else. A short while later the two went by train to Muzaffarpur. There they took a room in

* Khewan Kakar, the *chowkidar* at Kishori Mohan's *dharmasala*, stated in the sessions court that Prafulla's companion on his early visit(s) was Khudiram Bose. But Kishori Mohan said in the same court that Khudiram was 'not the same as Durga Das who came in March' (ABT records XV: 1505–8). G. C. Denham, who piloted the government's case at Alipore, was told by an unidentified Alipore Bomb Trial convict that it was Sushil who accompanied Prafulla on the early visits. The CID officer believed this 'to be true, as I had always thought the Muzaffarpur witnesses had been shaky over the identification of Khudiram as the boy who had stopped with Prafulla Chaki at the Dharmasala sometime previous to the murder' (GOB pol. conf. 265 of 1910, report dated 22 July 1910). Sushil Sen's brother Biren, in his retrospective memoir, also affirmed that Sushil was Prafulla's original companion. Note also that Khudiram Bose was seen in Midnapore on 19 April (Midnapore report 6).

Kishori Mohan's dharmasala. Their only luggage was a Gladstone bag containing their clothing, three revolvers and the bomb.[16]

Abinash later claimed that it was he who gave Prafulla and Khudiram their revolvers. This may or may not be true. What is certain is that it was Abinash who gave the plan away to the police.[17] Sometime around the middle of April he bragged of the scheme to an acquaintance named Rajani Sarkar. This man was in the pay of the CID.[18]* Rajani gave his information to his contact who communicated it to Deputy Superintendent Ramsaday Mukherjee. On 20 April, while the investigation of the Chandernagore bombing was gathering momentum, Ramsaday informed Police Commissioner Halliday that 'two unidentified persons had left Calcutta for the purpose of killing Kingsford at Muzaffarpur'. This was apparently Sushil and Prafulla on their second reconnaissance mission. The same day Halliday wrote a letter to J. E. Armstrong, the Muzaffarpur superintendent of police, informing him that the CID had heard a 'pretty strong rumour' that a Bengali man accompanied probably by a Bengali youth had left Calcutta three days earlier in order to 'make an attempt on Kingsford's life'. The information was 'so shadowy' that Halliday did not wish to write direct to Kingsford. He asked Armstrong to 'make enquiries (very quietly)' and to warn the judge. Kingsford attached no importance to the report. Nevertheless Armstrong assigned two constables to watch his house and two to follow him when he went to the club, the only outing he was permitted.[19]

Back in Calcutta Aurobindo was preparing to take over the editing of the *Nabashakti* as planned. Abinash went to Giridih to speak to Manoranjan Guha Thakurta about the fate of the paper, which had not come out since a sedition conviction two months earlier. Delighted that *Nabashakti* would not have to fold, Manoranjan gave Abinash the last of his capital.[20] On 28 April Aurobindo, his wife, his sister, Abinash and Sailen shifted from Scott's Lane to the *Nabashakti* office at 48 Grey Street. Detectives took note of the removal and also of the visits that various members of the society, among them Narendra Nath Goswami, paid to the office.[21]

* Sarkar was a friend of CID inspector Purna Chandra Biswas. In his deposition in the sessions court Biswas claimed that he had not heard Rajani's name for a number of years. This evidently was to protect him from reprisals (ABT records X: 234).

Once settled in at Grey Street Aurobindo began a new routine of going daily to the *Bande Mataram* office. He was still writing most of the paper's editorials, which at the time were principally concerned with the Extremist-Moderate conflict. At a meeting at Allahabad on 19 April, the Moderate leadership had adopted the four tenets drafted at Surat as the official Congress creed. This effectively shut out the Extremists. In a comment published on 29 April, Aurobindo wrote of this exclusion in almost apocalyptic terms. 'The times are thickening already with the shadow of a great darkness. The destruction of the Congress, begun at Surat and accomplished at Allahabad, is the prelude for the outburst of the storm that had long been brewing.' In the sequel he suggested that the destruction he foresaw would extend far beyond the field of politics:

> The grim forces that have been moving under the surface will now find the field open to them by the shattering of the keystone of the old political edifice. . . . The fair hopes of an orderly and peaceful evolution of self-government, which the first energies of the new movement had fostered, are gone for ever. Revolution, bare and grim, is preparing her battle-field, mowing down the centres of order which were evolving a new cosmos and building up the materials of a gigantic downfall and a mighty new-creation. We could have wished it otherwise, but God's will be done.[22]

The day Aurobindo's article appeared, Khudiram and Prafulla passed the evening in the *maidan* opposite the Muzaffarpur Club. A boy playing football asked if they wanted to join the game. They told him that they had to meet someone. Fayazuddin, one of the plain-clothes policemen deputed to watch Kingsford, saw the two Bengalis walking back and forth. In this he showed more alertness than the detective who had brought Halliday's letter to Armstrong. After looking around for a week this man decided there were no 'suspicious Bengalis' in the town and on the afternoon of the 30th he boarded the train for Calcutta.[23]

That evening Khudiram and Prafulla returned to the maidan. This time they carried a small tin box. Around seven, as they were walking down the road near the club, they were accosted by two men—Fayazuddin and another plain-clothes constable—who asked them who they were. They answered in bad Hindi that they were schoolboys staying at Kishori Mohan's place. The men answered, 'The sahebs pass by this road, move on.' One of them escorted the Bengalis (their province was obvious from their accent) to the boundary of the club. They walked twenty yards down the road, then turned into the maidan. Nobody was playing football, so they went near the goalpost and took out the bomb. Leaving the box behind, they walked to a place across from Kingsford's house where the road was bordered with trees. Here they hid, took off their shoes, and waited. It grew very dark, for it was Amavasya, the night of the new moon.[24]

Kingsford was playing bridge in the club with his wife and the wife and daughter of his friend Pringle-Kennedy. A pleader at the Muzaffarpur Bar, Pringle-Kennedy was a graduate of Calcutta University. No typical Anglo-Indian, he had taken part in several sessions of the Indian National Congress. His wife and daughter Grace, a 'tall, good-looking young lady', were popular with the local English society. Around eight-thirty the foursome finished their last rubber. Bidding the Kingsfords good-night, Mrs and Miss Kennedy got into their carriage and started for home. The Kingsfords followed in an almost identical carriage, drawn like the Kennedys' by a single bay horse.[25]

As the first carriage passed Kingsford's driveway, Khudiram and Prafulla ran out from under the trees. The coachman and the syce saw them coming. The syce cried out 'aie aie'; but it was too late. Khudiram ran up to the carriage and threw the missile inside.* There was a 'terrific report and blinding flash'. Young Miss Kennedy, who absorbed most of the blast, suffered terrible injuries. Her mother's wounds were almost as severe. The syce was hurled across the road as the back of the carriage was blown away. The horse bolted. Miss Kennedy fell backwards and was dragged behind the carriage, her long hair trailing in the dust.

* After his arrest Khudiram admitted to throwing the bomb. He did not retract his statement even after learning that Prafulla was dead. The coachman identified Khudiram as the one who threw the bomb that caused the deaths. Khudiram did not dispute this in court but rather argued with the coachman over the manner in which he had hurled the missile. The sessions judge ruled that Khudiram alone was the assassin. In the High Court, Khudiram, acting on legal advice, claimed that he had nothing to do with the throwing of the bomb. His new story was altogether unconvincing and the judge rejected it. Wilson, the neighbour who came to the aid of the ladies, said that he had heard two explosions. The coachman also claimed (some time after the event) that two men had thrown objects that caused explosions. But the two-assassin theory was not accepted by the High Court (High Court judgment, reported in *Bande Mataram* weekly 19 July 1908: 16).

When the horse stopped a man named Wilson ran up and extinguished the fire that was burning the upholstery and the ladies' clothing. Then he had some men drag the carriage to Kingsford's bungalow where he and the judge, who had reached home without realizing what had happened, carried the ladies into the house. Grace Kennedy died within the hour, her mother two days later.[26]

Kingsford reported the attack to the magistrate, who came and took statements from the coachman and the syce, despite the fact that the latter was in 'pretty bad shape'. Kingsford then spoke to Superintendent Armstrong, after which he remembered he had important business in Motihari and left town precipitously. Armstrong sent sub-inspectors down both rail lines leading south with orders to drop off plainclothesmen at every station. They were to look for two Bengalis, young, barefooted and bareheaded. A reward of five thousand rupees was offered for information.[27]

The moment the bomb exploded Khudiram and Prafulla started to run. The constables standing near the Club gave chase but soon lost the fugitives in the darkness. Another constable passed them on the road and called out but they ran on. When they reached the *dharmasala* they decided to split up. Khudiram covered twenty-four miles during the night, reaching the small town of Waini, eight miles from Samastipur Junction, the next morning. Entering a grocer's shop near the station he asked for parched rice and water. While he was eating two men approached him and started asking questions. Flustered, he mixed up his story. Noticing that one of the men was wearing boots, he guessed the worst and fled. One of the constables tackled him from behind. In the tussle that followed a revolver fell from the bundle under Khudiram's arm. He drew another but before he could fire he was overpowered. That afternoon he was taken to Muzaffarpur where he made a statement mentioning 'Dinesh' but taking full responsibility for the attack. He had done it himself, he said, because he had 'the greater zeal (*beshi iccha*) for the work'. He regretted that he had killed two memsahibs instead of Kingsford but otherwise showed no repentance.[28]

Prafulla also managed to get out of Muzaffarpur. On the afternoon of the first he appeared at Samastipur Junction station dressed in a clean white dhoti and new pair of shoes. After purchasing a ticket for Mokameh, where the line to Calcutta branches south, he waited on the platform for the evening train. It pulled in around six o'clock. During the half-hour halt he got to talking with a Bengali passenger who had stepped down to take a stroll. When they found they both were going to Mokameh, they decided to travel together.[29*]

Prafulla had chosen a bad companion. The man was Nandalal Banerjee, an off-duty sub-inspector who had just passed his leave in Muzaffarpur. Before leaving the town he had heard about the bombing and about the five-thousand-rupee reward. His suspicions about Prafulla grew stronger when he recognized his accent as that of East Bengal. Excusing himself Nandalal went to the station and sent a telegram to his grandfather, a government pleader in Muzaffarpur. He told him to go to the police superintendent or magistrate to ask 'whether I shall arrest [on] suspicion'. The reply should be sent to Mokameh. When Nandalal rejoined Prafulla they again got into the same compartment. On their way south they talked of many things: Swadeshi (which Prafulla supported); the Muzaffarpur outrage (which interested him greatly); and ammunition (he preferred the German kind). Nandalal also asked Prafulla about his studies. He said he was attending school in Burdwan (in West Bengal). Finally, annoyed by the man's incessant questioning, Prafulla went into another compartment. Soon he fell asleep, as did Nandalal.

The next morning Nandalal asked Prafulla how he had passed the night. Prafulla said he felt 'rather jaded'. Nandalal said that he would treat him to breakfast when they reached Samaria Ghat, where they would cross the Ganges. At the ghat Prafulla went down to drink from the sacred river. Then the two boarded the steamer, where Nandalal ordered breakfast for both. By the time they reached Mokameh their differences of the night before had been forgotten. As they stepped off the train a plain-clothes

* This and the next paragraphs are based the statement made by Nandalal Banerjee after Prafulla's suicide and the depositions he made before the Muzaffarpur magistrate and sessions judge (ABT records XIX). There are some inconsistencies between the statement, which is quite detailed, and the depositions. I have left out some of the more incredible details, such as Prafulla's declaration upon learning that Khudiram had been arrested that 'the man who had been arrested would be a fool if he disclosed the names of the party to which he belonged'. But even this is not altogether unbelievable. Nandalal repeated the detail about the German ammunition before the sessions judge.

policeman handed Nandalal a telegram.* It read 'Arrest and bring the man here.' Nandalal turned to Prafulla and told him he was placing him under arrest. Prafulla broke away and dashed down the platform, pursued by a constable and the plainclothesman. They called to a local constable to cut him off. Prafulla drew his pistol and fired at his pursuers. Then, seeing that he was trapped, he raised the barrel to his throat and, just as he always said he would, pulled the trigger twice.[30]†

Prafulla's corpse was taken to Muzaffarpur where it was shown to Khudiram. He identified it as that of Dinesh Chandra Roy. Later Prafulla's head, which had been almost blown from his trunk, was cut off, kept in spirits and sent to Calcutta for identification.[31]

Khudiram was charged with murder and committed for trial by the additional sessions judge of Muzaffarpur. He pleaded guilty to the charge and took little interest in the trial. About the only witness he cross-examined was the Kennedys' coachman, whom he tried to set straight as to precisely how he had thrown the bomb. The judge was obliged to advise him that 'the object of cross-examination is not to incriminate [oneself] but to discredit the witness'. After hearing the evidence the judge found Khudiram guilty and sentenced him to death.[32] The High Court upheld the verdict and on 11 August 1908 Khudiram Bose was hanged. The day before his execution he told his pleader that he 'would die as fearlessly as the Rajput women of old'. He mounted the scaffold with erect body, 'cheerful and smiling'. Reporting the event, *Bande Mataram* commented: 'He not only read the Gita but also acted it.'[33]

* This part of Nandalal's story differs in each of his three statements. It would appear that in the earlier versions he tried to make his own cleverness and initiative seem greater than they were in order to qualify for the Rs 5000 reward and perhaps a medal as well. Compare his statement and depositions with the deposition of the other sub-inspector, Public Witness 20 in the sessions court. (This man said the suicide took place at Mokameh Ghat, a statement that certainly is wrong. The telegrams to and from the place of the suicide all have 'Mokameh'.)

† Legend has it that when Nandalal went to arrest Prafulla, the latter cried out, 'You are a Bengali, how dare you arrest me, your countryman?' or something to that effect. This attractive piece of dialogue does not form part of any of the accounts of Nandalal Banerjee or the other sub-inspector. In his first statement Nandalal was quite forthcoming about other things that Prafulla said at various times. The 'last words' first appeared in the newspapers some time after the event (e.g. *Bengalee* 5 June 1908). They almost certainly were the creation of a journalist with literary ambitions. It is highly unlikely that anyone in Prafulla's position would have wasted his time making such a quotable declaration.

PART THREE
The Trial

15

A Rude Awakening

When news of the Muzaffarpur bombing reached Darjeeling and Calcutta, the Bengal Government, the Criminal Investigation Department and the city police swung into action. In the summer capital Andrew Fraser had his chief secretary draft a request to the Government of India for permission to deport five men—Aurobindo Ghose, Barin Ghose, Satyen Bose, Abinash Bhattacharya and Hem Das—who were believed to be the 'the prime movers and principal culprits' of the recent 'outrages'.* Fraser informed the imperial government that the police had proof of the existence of a secret society that undoubtedly was behind all these crimes. But owing to the lack of an adequate law of conspiracy, it would be 'impossible to proceed against the society as such' since 'some specific offence must be charged and proved'. This, he

* The term 'deportation', used in contemporary documents and newspapers and by modern historians, is somewhat misleading. Prisoners detained under Bengal's Regulation III of 1818 (and corresponding regulations in Bombay and Madras) were sent outside their home province but not outside British India. (Burma, a frequent destination, was of course part of British India until 1935.) The regulation permitted the governor-general in council 'to place under personal restraint individuals against whom there may not be sufficient grounds to institute any judicial proceedings'. It amounted, as a member of Minto's council observed while the case against Aurobindo was under consideration, 'to a suspension of Habeas Corpus' since the detained person was not given the benefit of legal arrest or trial. Liberal MPs spoke of the Regulation as being 'the principle of the *lettre de cachet* under Louis XIV' and 'clearly unconstitutional if the Magna Carta had any meaning'. Even an imperialistic *Times* journalist admitted that 'such a measure' was 'very repugnant to British traditions and British sentiment' (GOI HPA May 1908, 104–11: 9, 18; Wedgewood and Mackarness in *Debates on Indian Affairs: House of Commons*, q. S. Ghose 107; Chirol 99).

feared, was 'not practicable at present'. Even if the Muzaffarpur murderers were captured (as they soon were), it was probable that they, like the Narayangarh coolies (who were still believed guilty), would not implicate the others. Deliberately understating the facts, Fraser claimed that the police's connection with the society 'was very slight, and any mischance or leakage might destroy it altogether'. Since there was 'no present hope of getting conclusive evidence regarding any of the offences already committed' the 'only course' was 'to resort to the special provisions of the State Prisoners Regulation III of 1818'—the notorious measure that permitted the government to deport any person without arrest or trial.[1] Fraser was not the first administrator, nor would he be the last, to assert that British law, with its insistence on the right of habeas corpus, was inappropriate in a country like India.

Meanwhile in Calcutta the police were deciding how to deal with the situation in the city. They had been waiting for the society to commit an overt act. The Muzaffarpur bombing was certainly that. Commissioner Halliday wanted to search the Garden and other centres immediately. CID Deputy Superintendent Plowden was still hesitant. He wanted to wait three more days until searches in Calcutta and Midnapore could be co-ordinated. At this point Halliday was interviewed by a reporter from *The Empire*, a British-run evening newspaper. The *Empire*'s Bihar correspondent had wired details of the outrage that morning. The story included a statement by Kingsford that he had been warned by the police that two men had been sent from Calcutta to kill him. This was a grave indiscretion on Kingsford's part and Halliday asked the paper not to publish the statement. But it was obvious now that action had to be taken promptly. Halliday telephoned Mr Thornhill, the officiating chief presidency magistrate, and requested him to remain in court in order to hear an important application. At five o'clock Halliday, Plowden and Purna Chandra Biswas, the CID inspector who had been in charge of the shadowing operation, drove to Thornhill's court to obtain legal sanction to search and make arrests. Complaining against the activities of 'Arabindo's gang of outlaws', Biswas asked for and received warrants to search eight places frequented by members of the society. Two hours later a meeting was held at Halliday's residence at which officers of both town and provincial police were present. Elaborate arrangements were made for the next day's operation. Several European officers, numerous inspectors and sub-inspectors and at least a hundred constables were mustered. Eight posses were formed for searching the Garden and seven sites in Calcutta including 134 Harrison Road, the *Nabashakti* office, and 15 Gopi Mohan Dutt's Lane. The searches and arrests would be carried out simultaneously early the next morning.[2] A cipher telegram was sent to Midnapore asking the Superintendent of Police to search the house of Satyen Bose and other places and to arrest suspicious persons.

'BOMB OUTRAGE IN BEHAR./EUROPEAN LADY KILLED./ATTEMPT TO ASSASSINATE MR. KINGSFORD.' cried a headline in the issue of *Empire* that hit the street that evening. After giving some details of the event, the paper reported that Police Commissioner Halliday had 'confirmed the tragic intelligence, but was reticent as to particulars'. It added however, 'The perpetrators are believed to be well-known.'[3] When Aurobindo read this article at the *Bande Mataram* office, he took special note of that sentence.[4]

At the Garden Barin and the others had been anxiously awaiting news from Muzaffarpur for several days. Around eight that evening Abinash rushed over with a copy of the *Empire*. Finding the article on the bombing of more than usual interest Barin marked it in blue pencil.[5] It was now apparent—if it had not been before—that the police were closing in. That very evening the local constable paid one of his friendly visits. This did not bother the boys very much; but later on there were movements and voices in the dark.[6] Clearly they had to abandon the Garden. This they would do before daybreak; but first they had to conceal or destroy the incriminating material that was lying about.[7] Besides the arms, ammunition, and explosives at the Garden there were some guns at the *Nabashakti* office, the explosives and apparatus in the boxes at Harrison Road, and various materials at Gopi Mohan Dutt's Lane and elsewhere. Priority was given to the *Nabashakti* office. A group sent from the Garden removed the guns and brought them to Maniktola, where they were put in boxes together with the materials stockpiled there.* The boxes were placed in shallow

* The four accounts that mention this incident all disagree with one another. The most complete and detailed version is that of Abinash Bhattacharya, who wrote in 1950 that at around eight o'clock in the evening he brought five rifles and five bags of cartridges to Grey Street and kept them in a room on the ground floor, where someone was to come and pick them up. When Aurobindo learned of this he

holes in the garden and covered over. For Barin it was a trauma to do even this. Those arms 'were our lifeblood, terribly difficult to obtain in our disarmed country', he later wrote.[8] While the arms were being buried some of the boys gathered up papers and burned them. Their work accomplished, they put a pot on the fire and started boiling rice. The pot cracked, causing much laughter. Only Upen saw the incident as a bad omen. He had returned to the Garden dead tired after a day of walking the streets. When he read the news from Muzaffarpur he had wanted to flee at once, but agreed to leave with the others in the morning. At around ten the young men finished their dinner and an hour or two later, quite exhausted, went to sleep on a platform in the enclosed veranda of the house.[9]

About four the next morning those who slept fitfully were awakened by noises outside—the snapping of branches and creaking of boots. Peering through a crack in the door, Barin and Upen saw men standing in the darkness. Realizing that 'the first chapter of the history of Indian independence was over', Upen slipped through a side door into a lumber room, where he hid behind a screen of burlap. Meanwhile, filled with 'desperate courage', Barin pulled the door open and found himself facing a European holding a revolver. 'Your name?' Inspector Frizonni demanded in Hindustani. 'Barindra Kumar Ghose,' came the answer. '*Bandho isko*!' (Tie him up!), the inspector cried. While three or four constables were engaged in this task a dozen more rushed in and laid hold on the men and boys inside. Nolini Kanta

---

told Abinash to get rid of the things immediately and to tell Barin to do the same at the Garden. Abinash went to the Garden and brought back Barin and half a dozen others, who cleared out the building (A. Bhattacharya, 'Aurobindo' 844–5). In a talk of 1940, Aurobindo said that on the eve of the search Barin brought two bombs to his residence. Aurobindo told him: 'Take them away. Don't you know that the house is going to be searched? And remove the things from Maniktala' (Sri Aurobindo, talk 28 February 1940, pub. Nirodbaran, *Talks* 2 & 3: 258). Nolini Kanta Gupta wrote that the men at the Garden realized that the guns had to be removed from the Grey Street office. A party of them went over, took away the guns and brought them back to the Garden where they buried them along with the other things (N. Gupta, *Smritir Pata* 52). Hem Chandra Das wrote that he and others had been telling Barin for some time that he ought to get rid of the things at the Garden, but that Barin ignored them. Finally on the evening of May 1st Aurobindo 'called Barin and ordered him' to hide everything. Barin carried out these orders only at the Garden (*Banglay Biplab* 270). Barin did not mention the incident in his account of the searches in *Atmakahini*.

Gupta, still groggy with sleep, felt a hand gripping his shoulder and heard a voice commanding 'Come.' Soon thirteen drowsy terrorists had been arrested: Barin, Nolini, Indu Bhusan Roy, Ullaskar Dutt, Sisir Kumar Ghose, Sachin Kumar Sen, Paresh Chandra Mallick, Kunja Lal Saha, Bijoy Kumar Nag, Narendra Nath Bakshi, Purna Chandra Sen, Hemendra Nath Ghose and Bibhuti Bhusan Sarkar. Police searching outside hauled in two Oriya gardeners and two boys from the neighbourhood who had chosen the wrong morning to take a stroll. Terrified they pleaded their innocence in vain.[10]

As the young men stood in line, guarded by abusive rifle-wielding constables, the officers started to search the house and grounds. After a number of hours they succeeded in finding only a few spent shells and the previous day's *Empire* with the Muzaffarpur article marked in blue. 'Interesting news, isn't it?' a sergeant asked Barin. The constables taunted them, saying, 'Why didn't you fire at us? We would have run.' In fact the captives never had a chance. Before Frizonni knocked on the door, fifty constables had formed a cordon around the house. Escape would have been impossible. Not realizing this, the boys were happy to think that Upen had got away. Then Frizonni violated his lumber-room purdah. Upen leaped out into the arms of a constable. 'Isn't it funny,' quipped a European sergeant when he saw the pathetic figure.[11]

As the search went on Barin was tortured by the thought that he and he alone was responsible for the debacle. It hurt him to see young boys like Sachin bullied by the police. Making up his mind to take the blame on himself, he declared that the youngsters knew nothing. He alone knew all and was willing to tell. Grabbing a piece of paper he scribbled out a statement. Aware that this would be valueless in court, one of the officers was sent to fetch a magistrate. While he was gone the search was halted. After a couple of hours the officer returned to say that no magistrate was available. The search resumed, this time with Barin's assistance. Going out to the yard he pointed out some patches of fresh soil. A few strokes of a spade uncovered the society's exiguous arsenal: three sporting rifles, two double-barrelled shotguns, nine revolvers, fourteen boxes of cartridges, and three bombs, one ready for use. Also discovered were twenty-five pounds of dynamite, dynamite cartridges, large quantities of picric acid and other chemicals, two bombshells and a forge for casting them. Documents discovered included a copy of the Paris explosives manual, several textbooks on the same subject, books on military training and 'numerous papers and correspondence indicating the existence of a secret society'. These included organizational plans (with the members' initials) and the letter sent by Prafulla from Muzaffarpur in which he spoke of Kingsford as 'the bridegroom'. A coat, claimed by Indu, had a notebook in the pocket with an entry giving the date and time of the attempt to kill the mayor of Chandernagore. There was also a record of revolver repairs with the name 'Indra'. The collection and burning of the previous night had not been very thorough.[12]

The same time the police were carrying out their unexpectedly successful searches at the Garden, another posse was busy at 134 Harrison Road, the site of the chemist's shop owned by Ullaskar's friends Nagendra Nath and Dharani Nath Gupta. Arresting these two and their companions, Bijoy Ratna Sen Gupta, Ashok Nandi and Motilal Bose, the police began to search the premises. In the shop's outer room they found only a few bottles of innocuous medicines. But in a storeroom they came across the three locked trunks and locked basket that Ullaskar had dropped off the previous week. The police asked Nagendra what the trunks contained. 'Books and clothing', he replied. He and his friends then watched silently as the police opened the trunks. The first two contained chemicals, but not the sort usually sold in pharmacies. All told there were twenty-two cartridges of gelignite and a pound of picrate of potash (all highly unstable and soon afterwards destroyed), five additional boxes of gelignite, a bucketful of dynamite and 'mixed explosives' amounting to around thirty pounds. There were also large quantities of strong acids and other chemicals used to make explosives, and a collection of glass tubes, retorts, etc. It was later calculated that the materials found in the trunks were enough to make two hundred small bombs. The basket contained six live bombs ready for use. One, described by the government's explosives examiner as a 'peculiarly handy little bomb' was 'made of the brass knob of a bedstead filled with picric acid'. Others consisted of ball cocks from cisterns filled with lyddite (fused picric acid). Such bombs had been used successfully by Irish terrorists. Among the documents discovered was a treatise on artillery and an article from an English newspaper about the attempt to blow up the king and queen of Spain, with a diagram of the bomb employed.[13]

Not far from Harrison Road, at the *Nabashakti* office, the police pounded at the door at around four-thirty. When no one answered they decided to resort to a ruse. A sub-inspector knocked on the door crying out 'open up, a thief is inside'. At length Aurobindo's sister came down the stairs to find out what was the matter. Opening the door she saw men with guns in their hands. As she screamed a dozen policemen, lead by Superintendents Creagan and Clarke, ran past her and up the staircase in the back. Entering Aurobindo's room they found him sleeping on the floor with his wife. When he opened his eyes he saw he was surrounded by armed policemen. After exchanging a few words with Creagan, he signed the search warrant. Creagan then declared that he was under arrest and had him handcuffed and bound.* At the same time an inspector downstairs was arresting Abinash and Sailen.[14]

For the next six hours Aurobindo and his companions looked on while the police ransacked the house, seizing hundreds of letters and papers: literary writings, articles, press matter, etc. A particularly interesting find was the letter Barin had written at Surat, telling Aurobindo that it was now 'time for sweets all over India'. Aurobindo apparently had pocketed this compromising document, carried it across Maharashtra to Calcutta and from the house in Scott's Lane to the *Nabashakti* office. Another exciting discovery was a bicycle with a Kushtia label, Kushtia being the site of a recent attack on a British missionary. Despite these finds the police were disappointed by the haul at the house of the society's 'ringleader'. They discovered no arms, ammunition or explosives; the nearest thing to a dangerous substance was a lump of what looked like clay. This was a piece of the hut of Ramakrishna Paramahansa that a follower of the yogi had given to Aurobindo. The police thought of sending it for analysis, but finally decided against this.[15]

Four other houses in north Calcutta were raided at the same time. At 38/4 Naba Krishna Street the police arrested Hem Das

* In *On Himself* (p. 52) Aurobindo says that he was tied but not handcuffed. Most contemporary accounts including Aurobindo's own *Karakahini* (1909) and an interview Aurobindo gave to the *Bengalee* the same year says that he was both handcuffed and tied. In the sessions court Superintendent Creagan said under oath that he had Aurobindo handcuffed but not tied (ABT records XI).

and seized his chemical apparatus, books on chemistry and assorted correspondence. Much more would have been found a week earlier. The same is true of 15 Gopi Mohan Dutt's Lane, where the police found only some chemical debris and a notebook containing the formulas of nitroglycerine, picric acid and fulminate of mercury. Here they arrested Nirapada Roy and Kanailal Dutt. At 30/2 Harrison Road the police found a few documents. At 4 Harrison Road and 23 Scott's Lane they found nothing and made no arrests.[16] The next day the Calcutta searches and arrests were completed when Dindayal Bose, Sailen's brother, was taken into custody at his workplace and some correspondence was seized from his residence at 80 College Street.[17]

The only unsuccessful parts of the whole operation were the searches and arrests in Midnapore. The local police superintendent, whose information about the society had been the cause of its penetration, was unable to decipher the telegram sent from Calcutta directing him to search the houses of Satyen Bose and others. Sometime on the 2nd Satyen received word that some arrests had been made in Calcutta. Immediately he destroyed all the documents he could lay his hands on. When the police came the next day all they could find was an old gun and a couple of swords. These were seized and Satyen, his brother Jnan and two others were arrested.[18]

Once the searches of the 2nd in Calcutta were over, the men arrested were taken to various police stations and then either to the headquarters of the Calcutta police or of the CID, where they were locked up. The police did not go out of their way to treat the captives kindly. Roughly handled, deprived of food, their resolution failed them. Barin was singled out from the others and interrogated closely. The CID officers, particularly Superintendent Ramsaday Mukherjee, were adept at the 'good cop–bad cop' style of questioning and they were able to draw out a good deal of information from the leader. But Barin refused to make a full statement till he had consulted with Upen, Ullaskar, Hem and some others. Upen and Ullaskar were brought to headquarters the next morning. The police used all the persuasion and deceit at their disposal to make them confess. Finally the three decided that those connected with known attempts should take full responsibility.[19] If they did so, they thought, 'the innocent' would be let off. By 'the innocent' they had in mind the younger boys at the

Garden, who of course were far from innocent, as well as people with no connection with the society, such as the Narayangarh coolies, the men arrested at Harrison Road, and the bystanders arrested at the Garden. It seems likely that Ramsaday promised the penitents leniency or release in exchange for statements.[20] This induced Barin, Ullaskar, Upen and Indu Bhusan to give him written confessions.* Barin provided a detailed account of the derailment attempts at Chandernagore and Narayangarh and the bomb-throwing attempts at Chandernagore and Muzaffarpur. His description of the activities at the Garden was somewhat low-key, but he did not dissemble in regard to the society's purpose. The people of India wanted 'one successful political murder'. He and his companions, 'though unwilling', were 'compelled to take up the task and work it out to its bitter end'.[21]

The confessions of the others followed the pattern set by Barin. Each men related something of his early history, admitted to taking part in one or more actions, and attempted to exculpate 'the innocent'. They mentioned no one unconnected with known attempts, but did speak rather freely about some who had been arrested but were not badly incriminated, such as Hem Das,† or who had not yet been arrested, such as Narendra Nath Goswami. None of the five implicated Aurobindo, though Barin and Upen did mention that he visited the Garden once in answer to a dinner invitation. Aurobindo himself, along with the rest of those arrested in Calcutta, refused to make a statement.[22]

On the morning of the 4th, thirty prisoners were produced before the commissioner of police at Lal Bazar. The twelve arrested in Calcutta were remanded for further inquiry. Of the eighteen arrested at the Garden, four, the gardeners and neighbours, were released on bail. The other fourteen were sent to the magistrate's court at Alipore. This south Calcutta suburb was the headquarters of the 24 Parganas, the district in which the Garden lay. At Alipore the prisoners were placed before Mr Leonard

* Some accounts mention that Bibhuti Bhusan Sarkar also confessed to Ramsaday Mukherjee. If he did, his was the only confession that was not published. Bibhuti certainly made a statement before Birley on the 4th.

† Many years later Barin claimed that he and the others mentioned Hem's participation only after Ramsaday Mukherjee showed them a piece of paper which he declared was Hem's own confession (B. Ghose, *Atmakahini* 54). Hem in fact never confessed anything.

Birley, the officiating district magistrate, who took down the confessions of Barin, Upen, Ullaskar, Indu and Bibhuti in proper legal form. From the magistrate's court the fourteen Garden prisoners were taken to Alipore Central Jail.[23]*

It was of course extremely stupid for Barin and the others to give statements to the CID and the magistrate. When Aurobindo learned his brother had done so he exclaimed, 'Has Barin gone off his head?'[24] Though the confessions were later withdrawn they formed the basis of the prosecution's case. The CID used them to carry out subsequent investigations and the government quoted from them freely in a series of reports on terrorism in India. Whatever his motives for confessing, Barin provided his enemies with a body of extremely useful data. According to the rules of the society the penalty for such indiscretion was death and at least one terrorist thought Barin ought to pay it.[25]

Barin made a point of telling Birley that the party 'was divided as to propriety of disclosing these facts'. He persuaded his comrades to confess 'because I believe that as this band was found out, it was best not to do any other work in the country, and because we ought to save the innocent'. The second part of this explanation is unobjectionable and won Barin plaudits from friend and foe alike. But the first part amounts to little more than 'after us the Flood'. At the time of his arrest Barin announced, 'My mission is over.'[26] This is not the statement of a disciplined revolutionary.

Still, Barin's confession was not ignoble. As a judge later remarked, if his object 'was to save the innocent' he deserves 'full credit for it'. The fact remains however that the case against him 'was so strong' that he 'had little hope of escape, confession or no confession'. The judge went on to comment that Barin did not disclose the name of anyone not already incriminated, 'not that this concealment indicates depravity, rather the contrary'. Moreover 'the ordinary motive for a confession, to save one's skin at the expense of others' was 'entirely absent'.[27] A police official thought that Barin's purpose was 'to lead the police into believing that the revolutionary plot did not extend outside the party which had been arrested'.[28] This may have been at least partly true. But more important was the motive that Barin openly admitted: 'to

* The Alipore Central Jail was later transformed into the Presidency Jail, which still exists at the same location.

place the details of our workshops before the country so that others may follow in the [*sic*] footsteps'. Indu Bhusan put it more pithily if less elegantly: 'The main object of my sacrificing my life,' said the eighteen-year-old, 'is to set examples in the country.'[29] Scholars agree that 'publicity is an essential factor in the terrorist strategy'.[30] Barin and his cohorts proved this axiom true. After reading the confessions in the newspaper on the 5th, Hemendra Prasad Ghose noted in his diary: 'Their statements are really startling and show that these young men belong to a higher class than those ordinarily found in the underground movements [of] Europe & America. One cannot help admiring their courage of conviction & honesty of purpose.' Police later cited the publicity given to the Alipore prisoners as an important factor in the continuation of terrorist activity in Bengal.[31]

While Barin, Ullaskar and the rest were making a clean breast of their involvement, 'the innocent', as agreed, were denying any knowledge of what was going on. Dynamite supplier Sisir Kumar Ghose declared he 'had only been in Calcutta for two months, and knew nothing at all about the affair'. Former bomb-maker Nolini Kanta Gupta said he was 'oblivious of the reason for which he was charged'. Fifteen-year-old Sachindra Kumar Sen, who may in fact have been free of involvement though not of guilty knowledge, said he 'had not the faintest idea of what went on in the house'. He added that his father 'would be terribly upset if he knew the circumstances in which he has been arrested'. Naren Bakshi, Purna Sen, Bijoy Nag and the other teenagers told similar stories. The police were unimpressed.[32]

On the morning of 5 May, Aurobindo and the others arrested in Calcutta were produced before the commissioner of police. The five who had been apprehended at 134 Harrison Road were remanded to await trial before the chief presidency magistrate for violations of the Arms Act. The other seven were sent to the magistrate with a request that they be transferred to the court of the district magistrate, Alipore, to be tried with the Garden prisoners. Requests for bail were not heard. The charges did not permit it.[33] On the afternoon of the 5th the seven were taken in police vans to Alipore. At the district magistrate's court an officer obtained an order by which the prisoners were remanded to custody. A short while later the Black Marias were driven through the gates of Alipore jail.

16

The Trial Begins

The moment that Leonard Birley, officiating district magistrate of the 24 Parganas, learned of the nefarious deeds being done in his district, he decided he was the man to set things right. His eagerness to have the case leads one to suspect that he saw himself as a sort of Defender of the Empire: as Lawrence in Lucknow, as Kitchener in Khartoum, so Birley in Bengal. In the normal course of affairs the case would have gone to the police court of Sealdah, in east Calcutta, which had jurisdiction over the suburbs. But Birley 'made up his mind' to try the accused and arranged for the case to be transferred to his file. Having heard from his neighbour Superintendent Clarke of the arrest of Aurobindo and the others, Birley wrote on 3 May to Police Commissioner Halliday saying that the prisoners should be sent to him for inquiry. The next day he took the unusual step of going to CID headquarters to encourage Deputy Superintendent Plowden to send him the arrested persons as soon as possible. While at headquarters Birley read the statements that Barin and the others had given to Ramsaday Mukherjee. When the prisoners were produced before the commissioner on the 4th, Halliday, in accordance with Birley's wishes, sent those arrested at the Garden to the magistrate's court at Alipore.[1] There five of them gave statements to Birley. 'Sitting high in his chair', with a face 'that was like a polished slab of marble', he seemed to the prisoners to be 'an embodiment of the machinery of government itself'. At one point he looked down at them contemptuously and asked, 'You think you can govern India?' One of them answered, 'Sir, were you governing India a century and a half ago?' Birley left this comment out of the record.[2]

When the seven Calcutta prisoners were transferred to Alipore the next day, Birley did not even bother to see them, but simply signed the order remanding them to custody. In the days that followed, as the police investigated clues found in the documents and confessions, they made a number of searches and arrests in the districts of both Bengals. All of the persons arrested were brought to Alipore and placed before Birley. The first to arrive was Narendra Nath Goswami. The police had no trouble finding this landowner's son, whom both Barin and Indu had mentioned in their confessions and who in any case was known to the CID. Arrested and brought to Alipore on the 5th, Naren gave a statement admitting his role in the attempt to kill the mayor of Chandernagore. On the 10th Hrishikesh Kanjilal was arrested in Serampore and Sudhir Sarkar in Khulna. The following day both made statements before Birley. Between then and the 16th five more persons were taken into custody: Birendra Nath Ghose in Jessore, Kristo Jiban Sanyal in Malda, Sushil Sen and his two brothers in Sylhet. Documentary and material evidence was found in all these places. In Sylhet police seized some makeshift weapons and a bag of black powder that Biren Sen candidly explained was 'not yet an explosive'.[3] Additional searches were carried out at the Garden, at Sil's Lodge in Deoghar, and at Subodh Mullick's house in Benares.[4]

The Muzaffarpur killings and subsequent events 'sent a thrill of horror throughout the length and breadth of the land'. Calcutta in particular was 'stirred to its depths' by the arrests and discoveries. People found it hard to believe that Bengalis had performed such dreadful exploits. 'Could anyone ever think it probable that the Bengali, who had been ever maligned as cowardly, would, regardless of all care for life, try to kill an official?' wrote one paper. The *Indian World* noted that the character of the accused 'reveals not only a striking amount of boldness and determination, but also a certain degree of heroism which constitutes the real essence of patriotism. 'Say what you may, the paper observed, 'all this is a glorious vindication of Bengalee character.' More than one editor commented that by Khudiram's act 'the Bengalee has been avenged upon Macaulay'![5]

Meanwhile the Anglo-Indian community,* in the opinion of

* Here and elsewhere I use 'Anglo-Indian' in the sense current in 1908: '(of) the British settled in India'.

Lord Minto, was becoming 'hysterical' over the news. Was it going to be Cawnpore and Lucknow all over again? Loyalist bodies passed resolutions demanding the restoration of law and order. Native newspapers should be censored, meetings prohibited, the Arms Act amended, offenders deported without trial.[6] The viceroy kept his head, writing to Secretary of State Morley of 'irresponsible talk and war fever'. Yet he could not but reflect that if the disclosures had been delayed he might have had to deal 'with something in the nature of organized simultaneous outrages throughout India'.[7] Both Barin and Upen had declared in their confessions that if they had not been caught they would have organized 'numerous outrages all over the country'. Papers and diagrams found at the Garden showed that these claims were not just empty boasting. Hrishikesh Kanjilal spoke of plans to enlist the sympathy of the frontier tribes.[8] It is unlikely that Minto took this seriously, but it must have given him food for thought. He was in fact more concerned at the time with the Amir of Afghanistan and the restive tribes of the North-West Frontier than with the doings of a race he considered effeminate and incapable of revolution. Britain's geopolitical interests, particularly the 'Great Game' in central Asia, was always uppermost in his mind.* Morley remained cool in his London office but even he admitted that the situation in Bengal helped make for some 'pretty anxious days. The Amir, the Tribes, the Bombs,—any of the three would have been troublesome enough by itself; and to have them all three together is really too bad.'[9]

Other Britons had varying reactions to the Calcutta discoveries. Labour M.P. Keir Hardie called the outbreak of terrorism 'the natural outcome of the policy now being pursued in India'. William Wedderburn made the same point aphoristically: 'As in

* See Morley papers, Minto-Morley correspondence for May 1908, etc. The 'Note on the Military Policy of India' contains, for example, this comment: 'If Russia were allied with France, would it be possible to count on being able to send reinforcements within the first six months of war?' (MSS Eur D 573/37). A spokesman of the Minto-Morley administration was in no way untypical when he wrote 1910: 'Should Great Britain remove her support, Russia would pour her hordes over the wide plains of Hindusthan. This horror of a Russian invasion is no mere phantasm, got up by Britain to awe India into submission. The Frontier Provinces have had proofs of its reality; the fertile Punjab has before now been blighted with the shadow of the fear, when the Afghan barrier seemed likely to turn into a Russian war basis' (Major 177–8).

Russia, so in India.' On the other hand J. D. Rees, a Tory who had served in India, said the outrages 'were the result of too little repression'.[10] In India British opinion was almost exclusively of this type. *Capital*, an Anglo-Indian paper, cried: 'Anarchists and anarchy must be mercilessly extirpated if human society is to hold together. . . . The anarchist should be brought swiftly to his doom.' *Asian*, another voice of Anglo-India, went still farther: 'In any other country both the man who has been arrested as one of the actual perpetrators, and the men who have been so cleverly caught at the bomb factories in Calcutta by the Police, would have been lynched and probably burnt.' The paper admitted that such methods were barbarous, 'but in cases such as these, it is understandable how they sometimes meet with the approval of even the most sober minded. The non-official white public is now-a-days a strong body, and in the present case it is only waiting to see what measures the Bengal Government propose to adopt before taking action itself.' Three measures ought to be put into effect immediately: 'house to house visitation for arms', 'summary suppression of every seditious native rag of a newspaper', and 'deportation under the old Regulation' in order to 'permanently obliterate those against whom it is issued'. In the long term, 'Bengal should be treated and governed with the utmost harshness and rigour by a ruler who is not afraid to put his heel down—and keep it there.' Before finishing, *Asian* offered some practical advice to Douglas Kingsford:

> We recommend to his notice a Mauser pistol, with the nickel filed off the nose of the bullets or a Colt's Automatic which carries a heavy soft bullet and is a hard-hitting and punishing weapon. We hope Mr. Kingsford will manage to secure a big 'bag' and we envy him his opportunity. He will be more than justified in letting daylight into every strange native approaching his house or his person.[11]

Asian's ravings were doubtless extreme—indeed they could hardly have been bettered by a Ku Klux Klansman—but even respectable Anglo-Indian newspapers like the *Pioneer* of Allahabad resorted to sabre-rattling when commenting on the 'first appearance' of the bomb 'on the social stage in India'. Indian nationalists should remember, the Allahabad paper warned, that 'the British people have not the remotest intention of retiring from India and still less from being driven out of it by bombs.'[12] After reading the *Pioneer*'s observations, *Bande Mataram* reminded its editor of what he had written about a Russian bomb incident of 1906: 'The horror of such crimes is too great for words, and yet it has to be acknowledged, almost, that they are the only method of fighting left to a people who are at war with despotic rulers, able to command great military forces against which it is impossible for the unarmed populace to make a stand.'[13] It does not appear that the *Pioneer* replied to *Bande Mataram*'s apt comparison.

Throughout the month of May, wrote Hemendra Prasad Ghose, Anglo-India had a case of 'bomb on the brain'—and not without reason.[14] On the 5th or 6th a north Calcutta neighbourhood was startled by an explosion in the house of Colonel Nandi, IMS, on College Street. Inside, the colonel's son Indra, a friend of the Garden society, had been trying to unload a bomb when it blew up. The explosion carried his hand to the roof of an adjoining building. A dozen surprised neighbours tried to find out what had happened. Doctor Nandi treated his son while his wife pleaded with the neighbours not to talk. But such an occurrence could hardly be hushed up.[15] Ten days later four people were injured when a municipal dust cart ran over a bomb on the Grey Street tram line. Two days after that, on Sunday the 17th, police removed another bomb from the steps of a Native Christian church on Upper Circular Road.[16] For weeks people in the city could talk of nothing but bombs. The police questioned anyone who looked the least bit out of the ordinary. One constable's suspicions were aroused by a boy carrying something wrapped up in his *chaddar*. When he followed him, the boy took flight. After a short chase, seeing that escape was impossible, the boy cried out, 'Touch the thing beneath my arm and we are both dead!' The constable backed off and called for help. Soon afterwards the desperate lad was surrounded. He reached inside his chaddar, took out a ripe quince, threw it at his pursuers and disappeared.[17]

On the 17th, the day the bomb was removed from the church on Upper Circular Road, CID inspector Purna Chandra Biswas submitted a first information report mentioning five distinct crimes: the two attempts to blow up the lieutenant-governor's train near Chandernagore, the attempt to do the same at Narayangarh, the attempt in Chandernagore against Mayor Tardivel, and the Muzaffarpur murders. The report charged the thirty-one revolutionaries so far arrested under eight sections of the Indian Penal Code, including Sections 121, 121-A, 122 and 123. The most important of these, Section 121, reads as follows: 'Whoever wages war against the King, or attempts to wage such war, or abets the waging of such war shall be punished with death, or transportation for life, and shall forfeit all his property.'[18] 'Waging war against the King' was the Indian equivalent of high treason—traditionally considered by Britons to be the most heinous of crimes. An offence under this section was 'the most serious in the [Indian] Penal Code except that of murder by a life convict'.[19] Sections 121A was an 'amplification' of Section 121, punishing conspiracy to wage war against the King with transportation for life or another term. Sections 122 and 123 covered preparations to wage war and concealment of a design to wage war, both being punishable by long periods of imprisonment.[20]

Since all of these offences were crimes against the state, the sanction of the Government was necessary before proceedings could be instituted. Both the 'local government' (i.e. the Government of Bengal) and the imperial government (the Government of India) were interested in the charges, though only the local government actually could frame them. Between the 8th and the 10th the viceroy and other members of the imperial government considered the possibility of charging Barin, Ullaskar and Hem with abetment of the murders at Muzaffarpur, those connected with the Narayangarh and Chandernagore bombs with attempted murder, and all the members of the society with abetment of murder 'in general terms' so that if connection with the death of the Kennedy ladies could be proved all would be 'liable to sentence of death'. Minto was afraid that the charge of conspiracy under Section 121A would be of 'doubtful validity'. But he decided to wait to see what the Government of Bengal would do, remaining 'fully prepared to make suggestions if we are not satisfied with the Lieutenant-Governor's report'.[21]

Before writing to the Government of India, Andrew Fraser talked the situation over with his advocate-general. The two men concluded that 'the confessions which have been made by various members of this gang . . . clearly indicate a conspiracy to overthrow the local Government and even to wage war' as this phrase was interpreted in a certain British case. The advocate-general therefore recommended that, provided sufficient evidence could be produced, the accused should be tried under Sections 121-A, 122 and 123. These offences fell under Chapter IV of the Penal Code, which meant that they were 'not triable by jury'. Other charges were possible including two under the Arms Act; but such charges would necessitate a separate trial by jury. Since it 'would be inconvenient' to try 'both classes of offences at one time', it was thought best to rely 'solely on charges under sections 121-A, 122 and 123'. Those who had admitted to taking part in actual outrages could later be 'tried separately for such offences'; but it was 'essential that they should first be tried jointly with the rest, so that their statements may be used . . . to prove the conspiracy under section 121-A of the Penal Code'.[22] Thus all the accused, whether arrested in the Garden or Calcutta, whether connected with specific incidents or suspected only of conspiracy, would be tried in a single trial by the sessions judge of Alipore.

The report of the Government of Bengal was sent to the Government of India on 17 May. The same day Bengal sanctioned the prosecution of thirty-three of the thirty-five persons already in custody: the fourteen arrested at the Garden, the twelve arrested in Calcutta, six of those arrested in the mofussil, and Khudiram Bose, who was awaiting trial in Muzaffarpur. All were accused 'of organizing a band for the purpose of waging war against the Government by means of criminal force' and charged under sections 121-A, 122, 123, 124 of the Indian Penal Code. (Later all of them also were charged under Section 121 while the charges under Section 124 were dropped.)[23] Included on the list of persons charged were the five prisoners arrested at 134 Harrison Road, who were already being tried under the Arms Act. Afraid that these men would get off with at most a year or two of prison, the Government of Bengal hoped to prove their complicity in the conspiracy. Also on the list were three prisoners that Bengal hoped would not have to be brought to trial at all: Aurobindo and the two arrested with him at the *Nabashakti* office. The previous day Bengal had submitted a request to the Government of India for permission to deport these men under Regulation III of 1818.[24]

It will be recalled that Bengal had drafted a similar request the day before the arrests. This had been laid aside while the materials seized during the searches were being evaluated. Disappointed by the finds at the *Nabashakti* office, Andrew Fraser decided to have the proposal redrafted and submitted to India for approval. Anglo-Indian sentiment in Calcutta was strongly in favour of deportation. This public opinion was cited in the report; but it is clear that Bengal's intention to deport had more to do with the sentiments of the lieutenant-governor, who understandably was indignant that he had three times been the target of bomb-wielding assassins.

Bengal's lengthy report on deportation was written by E. A. Gait, chief secretary to the government. 'The facts that have been adduced' against Aurobindo, Gait wrote, 'are not such as would constitute clear legal proof' that he was what Fraser was convinced he was: 'the ringleader of the whole movement'. Accordingly 'if a prosecution were instituted' against Aurobindo 'it is more than probable that it would end in an acquittal.' This would be a grave misfortune, for there could be no doubt that this 'fluent and impressive writer', this 'organizer of great ability and ingenuity' was 'the master mind at the back of the whole extremist campaign in Bengal'. Conviction of the other members of the society would be 'of no avail if Arabinda were set free' for this 'irreconcilable' would then 'lose no time in starting a fresh conspiracy' and all the work of the police and the government 'would be altogether in vain. In the interest of peace and good government,' Gait concluded, 'it is absolutely necessary that this man should be removed from the political arena.' He and the two men arrested with him, Abinash Bhattacharya and Sailendra Nath Bose, should forthwith be confined in 'a fortress, jail or other place' outside the province of Bengal.[25]

Three days later Fraser sent two letters to Minto. One, a confidential note running to four pages in printed form, summarized the history of the society and suggested a number of ways to contain the danger. In this note Fraser gave special prominence to Aurobindo, who, he reiterated, 'appears undoubtedly to be the ringleader of the gang'. In a covering letter, Fraser urged Aurobindo's deportation in the strongest possible terms. The man, wrote the lieutenant-governor, was 'able, cunning, fanatical'.

These qualities have their vigour in him which they not infrequently have in the man who is not quite sane. . . . He is regarded and spoken of by all as the disciples regard a great Master. He has been in the forefront of all, advising seditious writing and authorizing murder. But he has kept himself, like a careful and valued General, out of sight of the 'enemy'. We cannot get evidence against him such as would secure his conviction in a

Court. But we have been fortunate enough to get papers which show his connection with the conspiracy, and information as to his action, quite sufficient to convince the reasonable mind and justify deportation.

I earnestly hope no sentiment will be allowed to prevent this.[26]

The 'sentiment' Fraser referred to was the traditional British dislike of arbitrary government. Suspension of due process of law, resort to *lettres de cachet* and *ukases*, were just what liberty-loving Britons professed to despise in tyrannical regimes on the continent. But Britons in India were likely to forget such feelings when they confronted the reality of imposing government by force on seventy million people.

However convenient it may have been to nervous administrators, deportation was rarely effective. Denzil Ibbetson deported Lala Lajpat Rai and Ajit Singh at the first sign of disturbance in Punjab. He succeeded only in making martyrs of them. Protests in the press and Parliament brought about their swift release. This episode made the viceroy wary of acceding to such requests and he had turned a deaf ear when Fraser and his East Bengal counterpart called for the deportation of Bipin Pal and Aswini Kumar Dutt. The case of Aurobindo appeared to fall in the same category.

Minto's chief advisors on the India Council, Sir Harold Stuart and Sir Harvey Adamson, were also against deporting Aurobindo. Stuart thought there was a good chance of obtaining his conviction in court, particularly if one of the prisoners could be induced to turn King's Evidence. But even if Aurobindo was certain to go free, Stuart would not recommend deportation. The proposal would create too many political problems in London, and even in India would be counterproductive: 'on the one hand [it would] fail to strike terror' in the minds of the disaffected and 'on the other [would] excite much sympathy, cause great irritation, and provoke hostility to the Government'. Adamson underlined this point by writing that deportation 'would not in the slightest degree frighten the others, and it would alienate from us many who are ready to support us'. Stuart concluded, 'In matters such as this we must rely on the police . . . and I believe that in this particular case, when once the easy solution by deportation is banished, the police may be able to secure a conviction under the ordinary law.' After reading the file Minto declared himself less averse from deportation than Stuart and Adamson, but he agreed that it would be 'infinitely preferable that prisoners should be convicted by the ordinary law'.[27]

Fraser learned of Minto's attitude before receiving his reply and was bitterly disappointed. On the 24th he fired off a cipher telegram that concluded: 'To release Arabinda is to ensure recrudescence and further spread of the evil.' Stuart was not impressed. He told the local government to put the idea of deportation out of its head and to direct 'every endeavour . . . to the complete presentation of the evidence against [the prisoners] before the regular courts'.[28] After receiving Stuart's reply, Gait wrote to L. Morshead, the inspector-general of Police, to follow up 'every clue tending to connect' Aurobindo 'with the conspiracy' and to make 'every effort . . . to procure a conviction in court'.[29]

The government's efforts to do so had begun the previous week. Before the case could go to the sessions judge, the accused had to be committed by the magistrate. The hearing before Birley began on Monday, 18 May. From early in the morning the premises of the magistrate's court were teeming with young Bengalis anxious to catch a glimpse of the prisoners. Mounted policemen rode through the crowd attempting to keep order. Thirty constables armed with swords and rifles with fixed bayonets guarded the courthouse. The public was not allowed in. At around one o'clock two police carriages drove up and twenty-six prisoners got down. They were made to stand in two rows, one headed by Aurobindo and the other by Barin. All the onlookers were struck by the prisoners' untroubled faces. To *Bande Mataram*'s correspondent they 'looked—one and all—bright, cheerful, even smiling, as though conscious of their innocence. . . . Calm resignation was stamped on their faces but not defiance.' The *Empire*'s reporter found them 'a very happy-go-lucky lot', their expressions seeming to indicate 'that not a soul of the gang had a care in the world'.[30] All were in bare feet except Aurobindo who, when he noticed this disparity, 'doffed his slippers and stood barefooted like the rest'. After their names had been checked the prisoners were marched into the courtroom to await the magistrate. At around one-thirty Mr Birley made his appearance and the preliminary hearing of the Alipore Bomb Case began.[31]

Informing the Bengal Government on the evening of the 18th that the hearing was at last underway, the inspector-general of Police noted: 'it is anticipated that this evidence [concerning the finds in the Garden] will take three days to record'.[32] If this created the impression that the case would soon be ready for commitment, the government was destined to be disappointed. It took the prosecution more than three months to present all its evidence. The hearing proceeded slowly because of the number of persons charged, the amount of evidence to be recorded and, above all, the government's anxiety that the trial be brought to a successful conclusion. 'The interests of Government', a high official later admitted, 'were very deeply involved in its success'.[33] A successful prosecution was necessary to placate the unruly Anglo-Indian community and to satisfy Tory interests at home. The 'native' Indian community had to be shown that the government would deal mercilessly with revolt, but reassured that all would be done by due process of law. Liberal and Labour members of Parliament were ready to cry foul at any irregularities and it would not be difficult for them to get the ear of the Liberal secretary of state.

When the Sen brothers were brought down from Sylhet, the number of prisoners in Alipore jail rose to thirty-four. The government had to prove the involvement of each of those arrested—those who had taken part in overt acts as well as those who had not. This explains the extraordinary number of exhibits introduced, more than one thousand documents and objects, and the extraordinary number of witnesses examined, precisely 222. The prosecution had its hands full keeping track of all this evidence. One mistake in handling or introducing an exhibit would give the defence the opportunity of declaring it inadmissible. Working against the need for care was the government's demand for speed. The longer the case lasted, the more popular sympathy for the prisoners would grow. Signs of commiseration were noted by the East Bengal Government as early as mid-May. Even the sort of people 'who would not actively sympathise' with persons supporting violent revolt, were yet inclined 'to regard them in the light of patriots who are sacrificing themselves for the good of the country'. This feeling became particularly 'prominent among the younger members of the educated classes'. In Kishoreganj little children adulated Barin and the rest and played 'bomb-making' instead of their usual games.[34]

In order to assure itself the best chances of success the government engaged the services of Eardley Norton, one of the most successful trial lawyers in India. Norton had won his reputation in the Madras High Court: a Bengali colleague called him the 'Demosthenes from the benighted province'.[35] Ironically this man who became the bugbear of Indian nationalism was, like the bereaved Pringle-Kennedy of Muzaffarpur, an early supporter of the Indian National Congress. Norton not only attended the 1888 session as a delegate, but was also appointed a member of a high-level committee (the other members were Allan O. Hume, W. C. Bonnerjee, Surendranath Banerjea and R. N. Mudholkar) that was sent to represent the views of Congress in England. Seventeen years later he could still find time to write on Indian politics and to review Indian poetry in *The Indian Review*.[36] Hearing that this man had accepted to lead the prosecution, Sister Nivedita called him 'a renegade patriot' and bitterly criticized the fees the government paid him—rumoured to be as high as a thousand rupees a day.[37] Norton was aided by a colleague named Barton, by the public prosecutor Ashutosh Biswas, and by all the men and resources the government and the police could place at his disposal. The accused on the other hand were represented by a team of rather undistinguished pleaders. One of them, however, was sharp enough to teach a lesson in law to Norton and to Birley as well. After the first day's evidence was recorded, Babu Sarat Chandra Sen objected that the magistrate could not take cognizance of the case before the police had made a formal complaint. The objection was well taken and the next day CID inspector Biswas was called in to make a complaint and to resubmit the government's sanction. Then the over-eager magistrate had to re-record the evidence of the day before.[38]

The hearing went forward without incident until 22 May, when it was adjourned for two weeks. During this period the Harrison Road Arms Act Case, in which six of the Alipore prisoners were involved, was taken up by the chief presidency magistrate. At the same time police were combing through the mountains of material seized on 2 May, looking for anything that could help them win their case.

17

In Jail and in Court

In the Alipore Central Jail the thirty-four men accused in the Bomb Case joined some two thousand other prisoners, the usual assortment of murderers, rapists, and thieves that fill any big city prison. As undertrial prisoners they ought to have been treated better than the convicts, but because of the gravity of their charges they were treated worse. All of them were put in an old ward where they could be 'completely segregated and cut off from communication with other prisoners'.[1] In the ward were two blocks of cells resembling kennels. These were known, after the number of cells in each, as 'the 44 degrees' and 'the six degrees'. Most of the Bomb Case prisoners were lodged in groups of three in the 44 degrees. The men the government feared most, Hem Das and Aurobindo, were placed in solitary confinement, Hem in the 44 degrees and Aurobindo apart from everyone else in the six degrees. The cells of both blocks were approximately nine feet long and six feet wide. This made for crowded conditions when the prisoners were kept in groups, but none of them envied the prisoners kept separately. The cells had no windows, only barred iron doors in front. The only furnishings were tar-covered baskets that did duty for latrines. These were emptied on occasion by convict-sweepers; other convicts brought food—watery tasteless gruel—twice a day. At night the prisoners were roused by the warders whenever the guard was changed. In the morning they were wakened from unquiet sleep by the wailing of the prison siren.[2]

The fortnight before the hearing was a time of acute psychological suffering for all the prisoners. Even Aurobindo, accustomed as he was to seclusion, found solitary confinement difficult to bear.[3] After the excitement of the period of arrests had passed, the young men found that they had nothing to do but reflect on the hopelessness of their condition. The very walls they stared at, Upen wrote, seemed to tell them: 'You are prisoners, prisoners.'[4]

Once the hearing began and the men could see one another again they recovered their customary spirits. Each morning they were driven to the court in a pair of horse-drawn carriages. All the way they talked and joked and sang. At the courthouse they were awaited by policemen and lawyers and onlookers and reporters and even the occasional photographer. 'All the precaution, pomp and pageantry that are necessary for a State trial . . . were gone into without a single omission.'[5] Inside, they were made to stand in the dock when the magistrate was present. But it soon proved impossible to continue this day in and day out, and the magistrate eventually allowed them to sit on the floor. Spectators and reporters were astounded by the prisoners' cheerful demeanour and their 'apparent disregard for the proceedings against them'. Regarding the trial as a farce, they paid scant attention to the testimony.[6] Instead they chatted and laughed, making jokes about the magistrate's bad Bengali or the witnesses' bad English. But they had to be careful: if the din became too loud the magistrate ordered them to stand. At the end of the day they were driven back to jail, as happy as students released from school.

They were still in high spirits when the trial was resumed in June, although some, Aurobindo among them, had begun to look rather pale. This was apparently due to 'the excessive heat' which, *Bande Mataram* noted, 'becomes more oppressive to those confined in dark and dingy cells'.[7] But on 13 June conditions in the jail changed markedly for the better. Convinced that the accused were really not so dangerous, the authorities transferred them all to a ward consisting of one large room and two attached smaller ones. The prisoners could move freely between the three rooms, the courtyard and the veranda. When they discovered that they would be kept together night and day, the young men exploded with delight. Before long they had arranged themselves in three compatibility groups: Aurobindo and the contemplatives in one of the side rooms; Hem Das and the rationalists in the other; and in the central hall the intellectuals led by Upen.[8]

One of those staying with the contemplatives was Narendra Nath Goswami. Although not really interested in spiritual practice—he spent most of his time chatting and singing—Naren enjoyed Aurobindo's company and from time to time engaged him in conversation. A rich man's son, Naren found jail life impossible to bear. He told Aurobindo that his father was going to get him out. It was just a simple matter of hiring lawyers and buying witnesses. Aurobindo listened but said nothing. Around this time Naren's father began to visit the jail frequently in the company of CID detective Shamsul Alam. Alam and Naren had a number of conversations, after which Naren 'developed a tendency to ask questions'. One day he admitted to Aurobindo what Aurobindo had already surmised: the police were trying to make him turn King's Evidence. They kept on asking questions: Who were the men who supported the society? Who were the leaders in the other parts of India? Naren asked Aurobindo what to do. Aurobindo suggested he tell them that the head of the secret society was Sir Andrew Fraser.[9]

Naren had similar talks with his fellow-townsman Hrishikesh, who together with Upen decided to have some fun. The two concocted some names of 'conspirators' in Gujarat, Tamil Nadu and elsewhere and fed them to the gullible Naren, who promptly passed them on.* But the thing soon passed a joke. One day Naren got into a fight with Upen and some of the others. After this the authorities placed him in another ward.[10]

Between the 6th and 22nd of June the Bomb Case was heard five or six times. During this period little of note took place. Several witnesses deposed, some of them identifying or misidentifying men, documents or handwriting samples. On the 23rd the case

* This incident is told in the reminiscences of Upen, Barin and Aurobindo (*Nirbasiter Atmakatha* 44; *Atmakahini* 73; *Karakahini*, pub. *Bangla Rachana* 296) and in several secondary sources. The disturbing thing about it is that at least three of the names supplied by Upen and Hrishikesh were rather accurate. They said that the leaders in Gujarat, Madras, Baroda and Satara were 'Professor Bhat', 'Viswambaram Pillay', 'Krishnaji Rao Bhau' and 'Purushottom Patekar'. In fact Dr V. M. Bhat was an active revolutionary who had attended Barin's Surat meeting in December (B. Majumdar 93). 'Viswambaram Pillay' was obviously an echo of Chidambaram Pillay, the Madrasi Extremist who (it transpired at the Alipore trial) had been in correspondence with Aurobindo. 'Krishnaji Rao Bhao' is uncomfortably close to Keshavrao Deshpande, Aurobindo's revolutionary friend of Baroda, whose name was found in Aurobindo's correspondence and who was later investigated by the police. One would think that Upen and Hrishikesh might have gone to a little more trouble to pick innocuous names.

again was taken up. Waiting for the hearing to begin the prisoners were their usual jolly selves. The magistrate put in his appearance at ten o'clock. Then Norton addressed the court: 'I have the honour to apply to the Court under Section 137 of the C. P. C. to tender pardon to Narendranath Gosain for his turning approver.* We believe that Narendranath Goswami, the accused, is going to make a full confession. . . . He ought to be released on bail and kept apart from the other prisoners.' This was followed by some discussion between Norton and the court concerning the discharge of the approver, for he could not be an accused and a witness at the same time. When this talk was over Naren was produced. 'All the prisoners stood up and heard him in breathless silence.' His sell-out had been expected but the naked fact of his betrayal was still a shock. The court asked the approver: 'Are you willing to disclose truly everything about the conspiracy against the State and about every person whether as a principal or an abettor?' Naren answered, 'Yes sir, I shall disclose all that I know.'[11] There followed more discussion between Norton and Birley on the technicalities of Naren's pardon. During this interval the approver 'kept looking downwards' as the prisoners glared menacingly at him. Never daring to look 'any of his comrades in the face', Naren 'went on stroking his moustaches'.[12] At length the Court announced that he was discharged. Sworn in as a witness he began his deposition.

Goswami talked all morning and all afternoon. He related how he had met friends of Jatindra Nath Banerji in 1905, how they had told him of a secret society whose leader was Aurobindo Ghose, how he came in contact with Aurobindo's brother Barin and Bhupendra Nath Dutt around the time *Jugantar* was launched in 1906. Along the way Naren identified Aurobindo, Barin and Hem Das, whose mission to France he revealed. He spoke of the early days of *Jugantar*, of Aurobindo's arrival in Calcutta, and of his meetings with him, Subodh Mullick and Charu Chandra Dutt. He gave detailed accounts of the failed dacoity in Rangpur in 1906 and of a planned dacoity in Bankura a year later. While he spoke the prisoners stood silently, unable to express their feelings except by

* The term 'approver' was used constantly in court and in the newspapers. I retain it in my narrative even though it does not occur, in the sense of King's Evidence, in any modern dictionary. 'Gosain' is a variant of 'Goswami'.

spitting on the floor. During the lunch break however they 'chatted merrily with the police sergeants as if nothing had taken place'.[13]

For five days Naren told the magistrate everything he knew about the society's organization and activities. His revelations caused a stir in Calcutta. Never at a loss for a cliché, Hemendra Prasad Ghose observed that 'truth is strange—stranger than fiction' and wrote that the approver's confession 'reads like a romance'.[14] Many thought it to be nothing more than that; but there can be little doubt that it represented the truth as Naren knew it. Mindful of the magistrate's warning that his pardon would be withdrawn if he said anything false, he does not appear to have told a deliberate lie. To be sure some of his information was incorrect. He repeated the false or partly false names of the leaders in other parts of India as though they were gospel truth. But most of his testimony was accurate. His accounts of the five 'overt acts' with which the society was charged were richly detailed—no surprise since he was involved in three himself. As promised he incriminated not only those on trial but scores of others, some of whom were promptly arrested. Indra Nandi and Nikhileswar Roy Maulick were hauled in the day Naren began deposing. At the time of his arrest Indra was asked what had happened to his hand. He explained that it had been amputated after a cast iron safe had fallen on it. The police, who had learned of the College Street explosion, were not deceived. In the weeks that followed Jatindra Nath Banerji, Bijoy Bhattacharya, Provas Deb, Haridas Das and Balkrishna Hari Kane were rounded up. These seven, together with Debavrata Bose and Charu Chandra Roy, who had been arrested a little earlier, and Satyen Bose, who had been convicted under the Arms Act in Midnapore, were formed into a second batch of accused. Their hearing was put off until the first batch was disposed of. In the meantime they joined the others in Alipore jail.

The new arrivals made it impossible for the Bomb Case prisoners to be kept together in their three-room ward. At the suggestion of the prison doctor they were shifted to Ward 23, a single hall capacious enough for all forty. Here the young men passed their time in an ever-changing round of amusements. There were games like 'word-making and word-taking', acting, caricature, and Ullaskar's ventriloquism. In the evenings there were songs by Debavrata, Ullaskar and Hem. Young Sachin knew no exhaustion and was capable of making life intolerable for the authorities and the prisoners as well. Aurobindo spent most of his time reading or practicing yoga; but occasionally even he took part in the fun. If the party inside got too wild one could always take a stroll in the courtyard. There was a tap there so bathing was no problem and the kitchen was near at hand. Food from outside was now permitted and the prisoners got fish, sweets, biscuits, and more fruit than they could eat. All this, along with fresh *dhotis* and shirts, was brought by relatives and friends who thronged to the jail each Sunday. During visiting hours there was so much talk and tears and embracing that one could almost forget that a barred iron window separated the visitors from the inmates.[15]

Meanwhile the hearing continued. The prisoners brought the merriment of Ward 23 into the courtroom. If they ran out of amusements they could always watch the performance of Messrs Birley and Norton. Birley had long since ceased to look like a marble-faced embodiment of Justice. He was in fact a young and inexperienced magistrate, unduly concerned with courtroom etiquette. If the men in the dock talked too much he told them to stand up. If a defence lawyer raised too many objections he told him to sit down. But such treatment was never accorded to the eminent Mr Norton, who was allowed to examine an almost unlimited number of witnesses, trying to draw out information on the aims and extent of the conspiracy. Once, one of the witnesses mentioned Drona, a personage in the *Mahabharata*. Norton immediately demanded details, certain he had discovered another member of the conspiracy.[16]

Not everyone enjoyed Norton's performances. Towards the beginning of July he received the first of many letters threatening him with death. One day after court Norton asked Barin whether he approved. Barin 'courteously informed me', the barrister later wrote, 'that there was no personal objection to myself but that I was an obstruction to justice from the point of view of the accused and that much as he would regret my disappearance he could not forbid it.' Still, Norton was 'but "small fry", a mere parasite'. Barin predicted (quite accurately) that there would soon be an attempt at bigger game, a viceroy perhaps. Norton objected 'that there was an indefinite number of noblemen to whom the position of a Viceroy and his emoluments would more than overcome the dread of assassination.' Barin replied 'without heat' that 'the supply would in time prove insufficient to meet the demand.'[17] On 14 July, after still more threats were received, a Scottish regiment stationed in Calcutta wrote a note to the beleaguered barrister saying in part: 'if a hair of your head is harmed or if another European is killed we the men of the Gordon Highlanders will have a massacre for seven days, and slaughter every Bengali we come across without any discrimination whatsoever.' Norton later rewarded the regiment with breakfast at his expense. He tried to laugh off the threats, but from this point till the end of the trial he kept a loaded revolver on his brief.[18]

The hearing continued, with occasional adjournments, through July and the first part of August. The adjournments were necessary because the police needed time to investigate the links of the conspirators to men in Bombay and northern India. Closer to home the second batch of prisoners had to be dealt with. They were produced before the court on 22 July and their trial was scheduled to begin the following week; but before the week was out the High Court took up the trial of the Harrison Road Arms Act Case. Many of the witnesses and lawyers in the Alipore case had to be present there as well. Despite these complications the trial against the first batch went ahead. There were still many witnesses to be called—police detectives to detail their shadowing, persons from Midnapore and Muzaffarpur to make identifications. Everyone but Norton began growing weary of the whole affair. Even a columnist in the Anglo-Indian paper *Capital* wrote that the trial was 'fast degenerating into a farce' and that Norton's enormous fees were 'a wanton and wicked waste of public money'. Despite his lack of sympathy for the accused the columnist maintained that they too were 'entitled to justice. This prolongation of, after all, what is only an inquiry, seriously prejudices them financially. The case is bound to be committed to the Sessions. Why then this delay?'[19] The Governments of Bengal and of India felt the same way. When Lord Minto heard that 'the preliminary inquiry [was] not to be completed until August' he 'twice impressed upon the home department the imperative necessity of avoiding unnecessary delay.'[20] The home department doubtless found ways to put pressure on Birley, but the magistrate sat firm and allowed Norton to call witness after witness. Narendra Nath Goswami was called several times more to amplify his evidence.

One day he took the witness box attired in a fresh white *punjabi* and looking, *Bande Mataram* sneered, 'just like a bridegroom'.[21] His appearance contrasted starkly with that of his former comrades, who looked more and more bedraggled and unhealthy as the case wore on.

The Harrison Road Arms Act Case came to an end on 7 August. The jury found Ullaskar Dutt and the Gupta brothers guilty but acquitted the other three accused. The three convicts and one of those acquitted, Ashok Nandi, also were accused in the Bomb Case and now joined the others in the Alipore magistrate's court.

Finally, on 15 August the last scheduled witness was heard. That morning Birley received an application from the Crown asking him 'to exercise [his] discretion and stop the enquiry'. The previous day two pleaders had applied for permission to cross-examine Narendra Nath Goswami on behalf of nine of the accused. When they renewed their application on the 15th Birley passed an order refusing their request. He had already 'made up his mind to commit the accused', and he 'did not want it to last forever'. The pleaders did not press the matter. They would be able to cross-examine in the sessions court. The same day the prosecution informed the magistrate that it had more evidence to produce. Birley replied that 'sufficient evidence has already been given before me to justify commitment of the accused and I wish to commit them without further delay.'[22] He therefore closed the evidence and adjourned the hearing until 19 August. On that day he committed thirty of the thirty-five accused of the first batch to the court of sessions, charging them with offences under Sections 121, 121A and 123 of the Indian Penal Code. The five who were not committed were Khudiram Bose, who had been hanged, Narendra Nath Goswami, who had been pardoned, two of the men arrested at Harrison Road, who had been discharged, and Barin Ghose, whom Birley charged with abetment of the Muzaffarpur murders. The Magistrate told Barin, who had been born in a London suburb, that as a European British subject he was entitled to a trial by jury before the High Court. Barin declined to claim the privilege. He preferred to stand trial with his comrades.[23]

18

Retribution

Barin had not lost his boldness but he was subject to fits of depression. Often while the others were amusing themselves in the ward, he lay between his blankets oblivious of what was going on.[1] But soon he would rise and again be possessed by one of his enthusiasms. Eventually an idea took form in his brain. He and some of the others would break out of jail! It would not really be difficult. They would contact friends outside who would organize everything. The friends would get them weapons, a car, maybe even a bomb. Visitors would smuggle in revolvers, wax (to make impressions of the keys) and acid (for throwing on the guards). The prisoners would smuggle out the formula for picric acid and a diagram of the jail. When everything was ready they would shoot their way to the walls and climb over using rope-ladders thrown from the other side. Then they would be driven to the river where a boat would take them to the impenetrable jungles of the Sundarbans, just as in Bankim's *Devi Chaudhurani*. Or else they could go to the hills of central India where Barin had searched for the site of his temple to Bhawani. There they could stay or else continue on to Afghanistan, perhaps returning at the head of a liberating army.[2]

The most amazing thing about this imaginative scheme is that part of it actually materialized. Through the lawyer B. C. Chatterjee the prisoners got in touch with the revolutionaries of Chandernagore, who agreed to help. Srish Ghose and Basanta Bannerjee looked around the French settlement for some weapons. They succeeded in finding a Royal Irish Constabulary .45 Webley. On 23 August a sympathizer named Sudhangshu Jiban Roy went to the jail and applied for permission to visit

Barin. When the leader came to the visitors' veranda Sudhangshu embraced him through the bars. The guards had been paid a half-rupee to look the other way. Besides by now they were used to emotional demonstrations. Nobody interfered with Sudhangshu's embrace and nobody examined the rolled-up *kurta* that Barin took with him back to his cell. Undertrial prisoners had the right to wear anything they liked. What if tins of tobacco or packs of opium entered the jail along with gifts of clothing? The guards would get their share.[3]

Once the revolver was inside it was an easy matter to hide it. Nolini Kanta Gupta, who was the custodian of another weapon, simply hollowed out a hole in the mound of brick and earth on which he slept. When the pistol was slipped in and the hole was covered over no one could tell a thing.[4] Nolini was one of the four chosen by lot to take part in the jailbreak. By the end of August he and his confederates were ready; but before they could go ahead they had to ask Aurobindo's permission. Barin sent a messenger to the jail hospital where Aurobindo was staying. After hearing the messenger out he said simply, 'I mean to stand trial.' Characteristically however he did nothing to prevent his brother from proceeding.[5] But there were a number of prisoners who no longer were willing to go along with Barin's harebrained notions. The leaders of this dissident faction were Satyendra Nath Bose and Hem Chandra Das.

Satyen, it will be recalled, had been arrested on 3 May and put on trial for violations of the Arms Act. He was kept in police custody until 20 June and then released on bail. Two weeks later he was convicted and sentenced to two months' imprisonment; but before his term was over he was sent up to Alipore. The informer had mentioned him more than once as a leading member of the secret society. Satyen was ill when arrested and he remained ill during the weeks that followed. He spent most of his time in the jail hospital. Here he learned that Narendra Nath planned to implicate many new people when the hearing was resumed.[6] It would be pointless to try to tell Barin that this was more important than the jailbreak.

Hem and Satyen needed another man to help them with their plans and they decided to take Kanailal Dutt into confidence. Since his arrest the bright sensitive Kanai had become more and more depressed. He avoided the fun and frolic, spending most of the day lying on his earthen mound. Even the news that he had passed his B.A. examination did not cheer him up. He was often heard to say that jail-life was not for him; he could never stand twenty years of it.[7] A few days after the Webley .45 had been smuggled in, Hem told Kanai to take it to Satyen in the hospital. Satyen said it was too big and asked Kanai to bring another. When Kanai realized what was afoot, he insisted on joining the plot.[8]

Nobody likes to be unpopular, and Narendra Nath Goswami was more unpopular than most. During his last days in the witness box he had been listless and morose, always conscious of the hateful glances from the dock. No doubt his future looked bright. The government had promised to send him to England when the trial was over. There he could start a new life. But would he be safe even there? In the courtroom the prisoners often hissed to him that his fate was sealed. He told a reporter that he was haunted by 'a peculiar, inexplicable feeling' regarding 'the fatal outcome of the trial'. Pressed to describe this feeling he could only add that he 'certainly felt very nervous'.[9] But really he had nothing to worry about. Since the day of his pardon he had been staying in the European ward. A convict-warder was assigned to look after him. Yes, he and his family would go to England and start life afresh. Someday, perhaps, he might even live down the shame of betraying his comrades.

Narendra Nath did not know Satyen well, but when he heard on the 29th that Satyen wanted to see him, he was delighted. In the hospital the ailing prisoner told Naren that he too wanted to turn King's Evidence. After all, it was just the smart thing to do. Naren told Satyen that he would speak with the authorities. Warned by them that it was dangerous for him to mix with the Bomb Case prisoners, Naren, a wrestler, answered, 'What do I care for them. I can manage fifty of them.' The next day, Sunday, 30 August, Naren returned to the hospital and told Satyen that the government was favorably inclined to his proposal. Then the two discussed the revelations that they would make when the hearing began the next day.[10]

The 30th was visiting day at Alipore. That morning Srish Ghose came from Chandernagore carrying an Osborne .38 in his pocket. He was able to pass this to Barin as easily as Sudhangshu had passed him the Webley the previous week. Barin took the five-chambered pistol back to the ward and gave it to Kanailal. He of course did not know Kanai and Satyen's intentions. That evening Kanai complained of chest pains and fever. Sent to the hospital he gave the Osborne to Satyen, taking from him the .45 horse-pistol.[11]

At six-thirty the next morning Satyen told a watchman that he wanted to see Narendra Nath Goswami. The watchman went to the European ward and delivered the message. At seven or seven-fifteen Naren and convict-warder Higgins walked to the hospital. Both were anxious for Satyen to turn King's Evidence: Goswami to have a companion in disgrace, Higgins to earn credit-points that might lead to a reduction of his sentence. To avoid being refused they did not report their visit to the authorities.[12] As they walked across the courtyard Higgins looked up and saw Satyen watching from the veranda.

After they climbed the stairs to the dispensary, Naren asked Higgins to fetch Satyen. But as the European turned to the door Satyen entered along with Kanai. After a moment's consultation, the three Bengalis went to the veranda. Five minutes passed. Then suddenly a shot rang out. Naren ran into the dispensary crying, 'My God, they are going to shoot me.' Higgins leapt to Naren's aid but found himself facing two revolvers.* He closed with Kanai and in the struggle was shot through the wrist. Naren meanwhile 'was shivering in the corner of the room'. Kanai broke free and took a shot at him, wounding him in the hip. Then a hospital assistant and some prisoners rushed in. Kanai threatened them and fired in their direction and they rushed out again. The hospital assistant ran to inform the jailor. In the confusion Naren and Higgins stumbled down the stairs. After a brief delay Kanai and Satyen followed. Terrified and weak from their wounds, Naren and Higgins staggered out of the hospital courtyard. Supported by one or two others they moved along slowly in the direction of the jail offices. At the corner of the weaving shed they met the jailor, some of his assistants and a prisoner named Linton. Just then Kanai and Satyen caught up with them from behind. Kanai held up his revolver and shouted: 'Get out of the way or I'll shoot you all.' Everyone obeyed except Linton who grabbed Satyen and attempted to disarm

* In his own account Higgins says that Kanai was holding two revolvers and Satyen one. Other testimony also pointed to three guns, but the third if it existed was never found.

him. During the scuffle Kanai aimed at Naren and fired. The bullet pierced him through the spine. Spinning around from the force of the blast, the informer 'fell dying into the drain'. As he lay there Kanai and probably also Satyen fired again. Then, with all but one of their bullets expended, they quietly submitted to capture. As they were led off Naren was taken to the hospital where a short while later he was pronounced dead.[13]

At seven-thirty that morning most of the Bomb Case accused were out for a stroll in the courtyard. Suddenly they heard the alarm bell followed by the wail of the siren. An upcountry prisoner rushed in crying like a madman, 'Naren Goswami is finished! Naren Goswami is finished!' Before they could find out what had happened a squad of armed policemen and soldiers swarmed into the courtyard. The prisoners were driven back into the ward, which was carefully searched. Then, deprived of everything but the clothes they were wearing, they were marched off to the 44 degrees. This time each prisoner was confined to a separate cell, which was changed every five or six days. The warders were supplemented by a squad of Gordon Highlanders—no doubt in recognition of their bellicose letter. The Scotsmen were armed with rifles and had orders to shoot.[14]

For most of the accused this was a time of mental suffering as bad as or worse than after their arrest. Denied every form of recreation, able to see no one but the orderlies who brought them their food and emptied their latrines, many succumbed to depression and despair. After a while the authorities relented a little and allowed them to leave their cells for exercise and meals. Still forbidden to talk, they at least could see one another. Before long they learned to communicate by tapping, the universal language of jails. By this means and through messages sent through the sweepers they were able to keep up with courtroom news.[15] During September and October there were two main stories: the trial of Kanai and Satyen, and the hearing of the case against the second batch of prisoners.

On the afternoon of the murder Kanai and Satyen were brought before W. A. Marr, the district magistrate. After recording the statements of Linton, Higgins, the jailor and some others, Marr asked Kanai if he had anything to say. In an attempt to dispel the notion that there were three guns (and three gunmen), Kanai said: 'I and Satyendra Nath Bose and we two alone were responsible for the attempt.' Asked if he wished to admit taking part in the shooting, he declared: 'I wish to state that I did kill him. I don't wish to give any reason why I killed him. No, I do wish to give a reason. It was because he proved a traitor to his country.' Satyen reserved his statement. Marr charged both with murder and committed them to trial by the court of sessions.[16]

The Alipore Jail Murder Case began on 9 September 1908. Kanai made no statement; Satyen pleaded not guilty. Satyen's friend Hem had persuaded him that it was his duty as a revolutionary to survive any way he could.[17] For two days the judge and jury heard various witnesses. Then the judge asked Kanai if he wanted to add anything to his statement. With 'remarkable' poise, he said he wanted to retract 'the part in which I said that I and Satyendra were responsible for the murder of Narendra. I wish to say that I alone am responsible and no one else.' Satyen made no further statement. The five-man jury (two Europeans and three Indians) were unanimous in finding Kanai guilty but divided over Satyen, whom they found not guilty by a majority of three to two. The judge accepted the verdict against Kanai but referred Satyen's case to the High Court.[18] Then turning to Kanai he said, 'The one sentence against you is that you will be hanged from the neck till you are dead.' Kanai, according to *Bande Mataram*, 'laughed a laugh of merry scorn and his looks became as steady and unconcerned as before. Everyone in the court,' the paper continued, 'was overwhelmed at the sight of Kanai's self possession.' The judge was anxious to have the sentence executed as quickly as possible. He was reminded that the prisoner had the right to an appeal. 'If you refer an appeal you will have to do it in seven days,' he said. 'There shall be no appeal,' Kanai answered.[19]

Satyen's reference was heard by the High Court from 15 October, Kanai's sentence being sent for confirmation at the same time. On the 21st the two judges ruled that 'with respect to Kanai' they had 'no alternative but to confirm the sentence of death in his case'. In respect to Satyen they had 'no doubt that Satyendra and Kanai were acting in full concert'. Though it appeared that all the shots fired by Satyen's 'small and untrustworthy weapon' had missed their mark, 'there can be no doubt that he did not fail to kill Gossain for the want of trying.' They therefore found him guilty and sentenced him to death.[20] The nationalist press was bitterly critical of this decision. 'In a British law-court the verdict of not-guilty passed by a majority of the jury would have resulted in the prompt acquittal of Satyendra', complained the *Howrah Hitaishi*. Instead the sessions judge had referred the case to the High Court and, despite the reservations of Mr Justice Sharfuddin, the court had sentenced him to death. The verdict, wrote *Anushilan*, 'leads one to think that their Lordships held a brief for the prosecution'.[21]

Kanailal Dutt's execution was set for 10 November. On the 9th the sentries allowed the other prisoners to see him. To Upen Kanai's face seemed more peaceful than a saint's, without 'a line of care or shadow of despondency'. The next morning people began gathering around the jail long before dawn. Three hundred armed policemen were brought from Fort William to deal with any demonstration. Promptly at six the bolts of Kanai's cell clanked open. The twenty-year-old walked briskly to the gallows in a procession that was led by Police Commissioner Halliday and the district magistrate. According to the *Bengalee* Kanai stood firm and erect as the noose was adjusted around his neck. A 'serene smile' lingered on his lips until the last moment. A European who witnessed the hanging later asked Barin: 'How many boys like this do you have?'[22]

After being kept suspended for an hour Kanai's body was cut down and made over to his relatives. Placing it on a flower-decked charpoy, they started off in the direction of the Ganges. Thousands of barefoot mourners joined the procession, probably the largest and certainly the most memorable that Calcutta had ever seen. On the rooftops women wailed while on the streets spectators and marchers cried 'Jai Kanai' and 'Bande Mataram'. As they passed Kalighat temple a wizened Brahmin came out and garlanded the weaver-caste hero. Special prayers were offered to the goddess. At the burning ghat countless mourners were waiting, among them hundreds of high-caste women who had left the seclusion of purdah to be present. Some anointed Kanai's limbs with sandalwood paste and vermillion while others filled his mouth with *charanamrita*, a mixture of milk, coconut water and other ingredients blessed by the goddess Kali. His body was 'smothered under heaps of flowers'. Copies of the Gita and other scriptures were placed open upon his breast. His hair was shorn, locks being kept as relics. The mourners sang patriotic songs and shouted 'Bande Mataram'. At length Kanai's body was laid upon a pyre of sandalwood. His brother applied the sacramental fire to his mouth and others scrambled up to torch the pyre. After the body had been consumed hundreds pushed forward to take handfuls of bone and ashes. So many reliquaries were filled that 'nothing was left for throwing in the Ganges'.[23]

For days afterwards the city's 'native quarter' was plunged in gloom. The demand for Kanai's ashes was so great (claimed a police official) that 'the supply was made to suit the demand'. The British, shaken by the 'wild scene' at the ghat, decided that nothing like it should ever happen again. When Satyendra Nath Bose was executed on 21 November, the authorities made his relatives cremate his body in the jail courtyard.[24]

The assassination of the approver and the martyrdom of Kanai and Satyen 'introduced an element of exaltation that upheld public morale'. After three months the Bomb Case had 'lost the charm of novelty' and people were 'beginning to doze over it'. Now it was again the talk of the town, the assassins' daring the subject of general admiration.[25] When news of the death of the traitor reached one small village a thanksgiving service was held and the women blew conch-shells for joy. Similar celebrations were held in other places, including Narendra Nath's hometown of Serampore. One Anglo-Indian paper reported with some shock that 'not a single expression of sorrow was heard for Narendranath'. The Bengali community seemed to be 'well pleased at the outcome of this deed of blood'.[26] Even the nationalist press was nonplussed by the dramatic evidence of Bengal's changed mood. In distant Lahore the *Punjabee* commented: 'That Hindu boys, Bengalis in particular, would be led to adopt methods and means so dangerous and desperate . . . would not have been even dreamed a twelve-month ago.' The blood-lust, wrote the *Amrita Bazar Patrika*, was the result of 'the materialism of the West'. The British-owned *Statesman* blamed it on oriental craftiness. The murder of the approver was, it said, the 'cowardly assassination of an unarmed man by men who were provided with deadly weapons'.[27] But other Anglo-Indian editors found something to admire in Kanai and Satyen's self-sacrifice. Replying to the *Statesman*, the editor of the *Pioneer*, no friend of Indian nationalism, wrote in a remarkable but not un-British vein:

'Cowardly' the deed most certainly was not. An act of this kind committed within the four walls of a jail allows no hope of escape: the only alternative left is between suicide and the gallows. Such a crime may be properly described as desperate action, but it is fatuous to call it a cowardly one. Murder though it has only one punishment has many degrees of blackness, and on any fair view this Alipore crime approaches the hue of grey as much as any action of the kind can do. . . . The law will take its course doubtless none the less, and justice indeed is particularly bound to avenge the informer, whom the executive Government has failed to protect: but when we come to ethical judgments we are clear of the Codes, and instead of burying the question in a heap of jargon it is better to endeavour to put things in their true light. . . . If the Bengalis like to enthrone these two young men hereafter in popular remembrance as another Harmodius and Aristogeiton it is not easy to see how anyone could justly object to the selection.[28]

The *Pioneer*'s editorial sparked off a furious debate in the press, British and Muslim writers condemning, nationalist writers applauding the paper's outspokenness. *Sandhya* observed: 'What would the Sarkar Bahadur [British Government] have done if any Native newspaper had published such an article? It would certainly have been caught in the net of sedition. Oh, what a difference colour makes.'[29]

In the days that followed the assassination both Anglo-Indian and nationalist newspapers speculated on the effect it would have on the trial. One thing was certain: there would be no King's Evidence against the second batch. Narendra Nath 'was to have gone into the box and told of all that he knew relating to the deeds of these men' on the 31st, observed the *Bengalee*. He therefore had to be 'got rid of immediately' if the second batch 'were to benefit by his death'. By killing him when they did Kanai and Satyen saved the necks of many of their comrades. The question remained as to 'what use the Crown can make of Gossain's [Goswami's] testament in the Sessions trial' against the first batch of prisoners. 'Some have gone so far as to suggest' reported the *Bengalee* on 3 September, 'that the confession of Goswami will not be admissible since the accused had put in a petition to cross-examine'. If this were true it would show that 'the crime was well thought out and that the accused are as versed in law as in bomb-making'.[30] The *Empire* however wrote that it was 'the opinion of Members of the Calcutta Bar that Gossain's depositions can be put in before the Judge', since 'the pleaders representing the accused, in every instance, so far as can be recalled, reserved the right of cross-examination of Gosain, intending to put him to the test in the Sessions Court.' But the *Empire* also mentioned that it was 'said in a certain quarter that Mr Birley, the Committing Magistrate, in one instance refused the right of cross-examination'. Had he done so the approver's testimony would be inadmissible. But since there appeared to be no record of such a blunder, it seemed certain that 'the remarkable testimony of Gossain will be put in and accepted in the case brought against the Manicktolla and Harrison Road group of prisoners.' The *Empire* foresaw however that 'the point will be one round which a wordy legal battle will be fought.'[31]

One certain result of Goswami's killing was the abandonment or failure of several cases brought against persons he mentioned in his testimony. The most important of these was the planned prosecution of three men of wealth and position: C. C. Dutt, Subodh Mullick and Abinash Chakrabutty. Unfortunately for the government the approver's testimony was the only significant evidence against them and when he died the proposed cases were allowed to drop. Dutt, a judge in Bombay Presidency, remained under suspicion—a senior civil servant who investigated his case was 'convinced of the moral certainty of his complicity'—but after an enforced two-year leave he was allowed to resume his duties. Transferred to Upper Sind the 'disloyal judge' completed his term in closely watched obscurity. Abinash Chakrabutty also remained under suspicion and was dismissed from his position as government *munsif*. Subodh Mullick, after repeated searches and harassment, was deported in December under Regulation III and spent fourteen months in jail.[32]

The death of the approver also had an immediate effect on the case against the second batch of prisoners. The depositions of witnesses continued until 14 September, but without Narendra Nath's testimony the prosecution's case foundered. Still, the magistrate committed all but one of the eight men before him.[33] The exception was Swami Niralamba alias Jatin Banerji. The former leader had been an impressive sight in the courtroom, clothed in saffron robes and bearing 'a most striking aspect'.[34] His discharge aroused suspicions that he had come to an agreement with the police; but this impression was unfounded. The revolutionary swami kept his interest in the struggle, giving advice in later years to terrorists like Jatin Mukherjee and Jadugopal Mukherjee.

While the hearing of the case against the second batch was under way the magistrate had also to deal with the case against Barindra Kumar Ghose. Barin had been charged in August only with abetment of the murders of Mrs and Miss Kennedy. The prosecution wanted him also to be committed under the Chapter VI (non-jury trial) sections with which the others had been charged. Birley refused, saying that Barin could be tried later under these sections if it proved necessary. The government was not happy with this decision. If Barin were not tried with the others the prosecution might not be able to use his confession to prove the charge of conspiracy. There was even a chance that if he was acquitted of abetment he might be let off altogether. The government therefore instructed Norton to move the High Court to intervene. On 2 September the court ordered Birley to discharge Barin or to commit him for trial under Sections 121, 121A and so forth. Birley chose to commit him under these sections. Since Barin still declined the privilege of being tried as a European-born British subject, Birley directed him to appear along with the others in the Alipore court of sessions.[35]

19

Before Mr Beachcroft

The Alipore Bomb Case was given to Charles Porten Beachcroft, additional district and sessions judge of 24 Parganas and Hooghly. Ironically the judge and the principal accused had been at Cambridge together, Beachcroft at Clare College and Aurobindo at neighbouring King's. Both had passed into the Indian Civil Service in 1890, Aurobindo standing eleventh, Beachcroft thirty-sixth among the selected candidates. In the entrance examination Beachcroft had done particularly well in Greek, being bettered in that subject only by Aurobindo. But, to give a further twist to the tale, Beachcroft did better than Aurobindo in Bengali, a language they both learned during their ICS studies at Cambridge. In 1892, the year Aurobindo was rejected from the service, Beachcroft began his career in the Bengal cadre of the ICS. After rising to the grade of magistrate and district collector he switched to the judicial side and in 1905 was appointed district and sessions judge, third grade. He must have been surprised when he heard that his old classmate had been charged with a capital offence. During their Cambridge days Aurobindo had been anything but a firebrand. When the case fell to Beachcroft no one suggested that he should refuse it on account of his acquaintance with one of the accused. During his years on the bench he had impressed the government, the Bar and the public with his 'inflexible sense of justice'.[1]

Beachcroft and Aurobindo may have got a glimpse of one another on 26 September, when Aurobindo, guarded by several armed sergeants, was driven to the court to meet his *vakil*.[2] This man was part of the defence team that had been handling the case in the magistrate's court. In the sessions court a barrister of stature would be needed; but barristers of stature cost money. Aurobindo's uncle Krishna Kumar Mitra, a Moderate politician and editor, had been trying to collect funds for Aurobindo's defence since early June. An appeal published over the name of Aurobindo's sister had been carried by nationalist newspapers across the country. Early response was encouraging; within a few days Rs 15,000 were received.[3] Papers like *Bande Mataram* printed heart-warming stories of contributions by persons of small means, most notably a blind beggar of Calcutta named Chintamani. Five- and ten-rupee subscriptions were sent from as far away as Poona, Pondicherry and Durban, South Africa. The rich were not so generous, but one man of Calcutta tore a gold-mohur ornament from his chain and offered it to the fund.[4] Despite such gestures only Rs 23,000 had come in by August. A bare minimum of Rs 60,000 was needed. People evidently were afraid that the authorities would be displeased if they gave monetary assistance to 'anarchists'. The CID in fact did keep track of contributors and the Calcutta police harassed Krishna Kumar Mitra, searching his house and carrying away some papers. Six months later the Bengal Government deported Krishna Kumar and eight others under Regulation III of 1818.[5]

After a number of postponements the Bomb Trial opened on 19 October 1908. Unprecedented security precautions were observed. Early that morning a squad of policemen took positions around the courtroom. At nine-thirty the accused were brought from the jail and half an hour later were made to stand in the dock. Sachin Sen, ill with fever, was allowed to lie in a stretcher. There were thirty-seven prisoners in all, thirty from the first batch and seven from the second. All of them, reported *Bande Mataram*, were 'pale and emaciated', particularly Aurobindo who 'looked like the ghost of his former lean self'. Fifteen barristers, pleaders and vakils appeared for the defence. Chief among them was Byomkesh Chakrabarti, a leading member of the Calcutta bar, who had been engaged to appear for Aurobindo. P. Mitra, the pugnacious barrister who six years earlier had helped to found the secret society, appeared on behalf of Ashok Nandi, Indra Nandi and Debavrata Bose. The prosecution was led by Eardley Norton, assisted by Messrs Barton and Withall and the Public Prosecutor Ashutosh Biswas. Several members of the police force were at their disposal, notably CID detective Shamsul Alam. At eleven-twenty-five the judge mounted the bench and the trial began.[6]

Setting a precedent that would be followed by both prosecution and defence in the months to come, Chakrabarti spent most of the first day raising technical objections, all of which were set aside. Not until the second day were the accused persons charged. All of them pleaded not guilty. Barin Ghose then announced that he wished to withdraw the statement he had given to the magistrate after his arrest. The other surviving men who had given statements followed suit. This caused a flurry of excitement in the court. The prosecution's case was based on these confessions and it was not immediately apparent how their withdrawal would affect the course of the trial. The next order of business was the selection of the assessors, the men who would 'advise' the judge in this trial without a jury. Two Bengalis, Guru Das Bose, a schoolmaster, and Kedar Nath Chatterjee, a clerk, were selected.[7] Once these preliminaries were over, Norton began his presentation of the government's case. He explained the meaning of the sections under which the accused persons were charged. If they 'by any overt act did something to subvert the British rule', they were guilty of an offence under Section 121 and liable to the supreme punishment. If they conspired together against the government they were guilty under Section 121A and liable to imprisonment for a term extending to life. Norton took a considerable amount of time to explain the meaning and implications of conspiracy in Indian law. 'If two or more persons have associated together' for an illegal end and an 'overt act' has taken place, that was conspiracy. If this could be proved, 'whatever has been done or spoken or written by anyone will not only incriminate him but will incriminate all the rest'. It was the government's contention that all thirty-seven men in the dock had conspired together and all therefore were incriminated in four illegal acts: the three attempts to mine the lieutenant-governor's train and the attempt against Kingsford that resulted in the deaths of Mrs and Miss Kennedy. (The Chandernagore bombing, which took place in French territory, was left out of consideration.) Norton dealt more briefly with the other two charges. If the prisoners made preparations to overthrow the government or concealed a design to do so they were liable to a term of imprisonment under Sections 122 or 123.[8]

For the rest of the 20th and for all of the five days that followed the prosecution presented the history of the secret society. Court was then adjourned for several days due to the ill health of Sachin Sen and Narendra Nath Bakshi. In the interim the authorities devised more rigorous security measures. Fearful that the revolutionaries 'would jump out and murder the judge', the police enclosed the dock in a framework of wood and wire netting. To enter this cage the prisoners had to pass through a gate that was locked behind them. An armed sentry was posted at the entrance. European sergeants holding rifles with fixed bayonets stood by the dock and at every door of the courtroom.[9] The situation got worse before it got better. Once the police discovered that a hole had been cut in the netting. From the next day the prisoners were made to wear handcuffs even while sitting in the dock. Later a chain was passed through the manacles.[10] It was quite illegal to treat undertrial prisoners like this and a question was asked in Parliament. The Government of Bengal replied disingenuously that the handcuffs and chains were removed when the prisoners reached the courthouse.[11] In any event they were not used in the courtroom for long. For one thing the prisoners soon discovered how to undo them. One day counsel for the defence drew the judge's attention to the fetters and chains. With a great clanking of iron the prisoners raised their hands. The judge protested his inability to interfere with the arrangements made by the police. Thereupon the prisoners lowered their hands, undid the handcuffs and held them up again. 'If in any case they can release themselves, of what value is this arrangement?' asked Beachcroft.[12] Eventually the police came to feel the same way; but they were never entirely at ease with the prisoners. One day a piece of metal resembling a chisel was found in the dock. It was explained that this was 'used by the boys for cutting their nails'. The authorities were not amused.[13]

The prisoners were not unhappy about the new set-up. Inside the cage they could go about their business as though nothing unusual was happening. Occasionally they listened to the depositions, particularly if the witness was entertaining; but for the most part they read, talked or otherwise diverted themselves. Split up into batches of four or five according to temperament, they talked of revolutionary politics or spiritual philosophy. Sometimes these discussions became rather animated, particularly when rival factions disagreed. If the commotion in the dock became too loud the judge cried out, 'Less noise. Less noise there.' If the prisoners did not comply he threatened them with handcuffs and if this failed with the ultimate punishment: 'If you don't stop, your tiffin will stop.' This never failed to produce the desired result, for lunch in court was the prisoners' principal meal. Relatives and friends brought *luchis*, potatoes, fritters and sweets—quite a contrast from the gruel given in jail. Once the police had inspected the food for bombs and revolvers they handed it over to the hungry young terrorists.[14]

Early in November two important questions concerning the admissibility of evidence were resolved. On the 6th the prosecution applied to put in the testimony of the assassinated approver, Narendra Nath Goswami. The defense objected on the grounds that it had not been allowed to cross-examine him. Magistrate Birley was called in to depose. He claimed that the pleader who put in the application to cross-examine 'did not know what was in it'. The defence had desired to cross-examine only 'on a few points' and did not consider it particularly important. When he refused permission 'the defence did not push it and I did not push it' and the matter was allowed to drop. In fact by refusing the application Birley had 'violated the law'.[15] In the ordinary course of events it would not have mattered since the approver would have been cross-examined in sessions. But now the approver was dead. Beachcroft considered the question for two days and when court reopened on the 9th said that as 'sufficient opportunity was not given to the accused to cross-examine', the approver's testimony was invalid.[16] This ruling changed the whole complexion of the trial.

In the wake of Beachcroft's decision people speculated that Kanai and Satyen had killed Narendra Nath with the deliberate intention of invalidating his testimony.[17] It is highly unlikely that they did. It is part of the unwritten code of revolutionaries that the penalty for treachery is death. Kanai and Satyen were willing to carry out this sentence. Their act was not so minutely considered as legend would have it, but this in no way diminishes their heroism.

Beachcroft's ruling in regard to the other question of admissibility of evidence was less favourable to the defence. In regard to the confessions he declared that their withdrawal affected their value but not their admissibility.[18] These freely given statements remained the core of the government's case and all but assured the conviction of the men who gave them. On account of this Norton spent comparatively little time dealing with them. What was difficult from the government's point of view were the cases against the men who had not confessed, had not been mentioned in the confessions and could not be connected directly with any overt act. In sessions the prosecution made a long-drawn-out effort to prove the complicity of persons in this category, particularly Aurobindo. To this end Norton recalled most of the witnesses who had deposed before the magistrate. All told 206 persons were examined and cross-examined and 1438 exhibits were filed. Those like the viceroy who hoped for a swift verdict soon resigned themselves, not without complaining, to a long winter.[19]

It would prove to be a season that the government would not look back on with pleasure. On 7 November the outgoing lieutenant-governor, Sir Andrew Fraser, went to address a public meeting at Overtoun Hall. A student named Jatindranath Raichaudhuri went up to him, pulled out a pistol and fired twice at point blank range. Miraculously both shots missed fire. Questioned as to his motives, Jatindranath explained: 'If we kill one L-G other L-G's will listen to our grievances.' He added, 'We don't scruple to commit murders; the British themselves have got the country by blood-shed. Murder is not a sin when it is a necessity.' It transpired that the young man was from Arbelia, the home town of Abinash, Sailen and Dindayal, all of whom he knew. He also claimed to be a relative of Aurobindo and Satyen. Their arrest and Khudiram's hanging 'brought a spell of fanaticism' in his mind, causing him to volunteer for his dangerous mission.[20]

Bengali terrorists had a bad habit of missing British targets. They were more successful in killing their own countrymen. On 9 November, two days after the attempt on Sir Andrew, Nandalal Banerjee, the sub-inspector who had earned Rs 5000 for tracking Prafulla Chaki to his doom, was shot dead in a Calcutta street. After he fell his assailants 'stooped over his prostrate body and discharged shot after shot into it'. Four days later Sukumar Chakrabarti, a member of the Dacca Anushilan who had agreed to give evidence against Pulin Das, the *samiti*'s leader, was found brutally murdered and decapitated. In both cases the police could make no arrests.[21] Frustrated by the inability of the law to prevent such outrages, the viceroy asked the secretary of state for permission to deport suspects 'without previous sanction'. Morley was reluctant, but fearing the effect that Minto's threatened resignation would have on the reforms they were getting ready to announce, gave his consent to the deportation 'of the instigators'.[22] Minto responded by deporting not just Pulin Das and his lieutenant Bhupesh Nag, but also seven other Bengali leaders, among them Aswini Kumar Dutt and Krishna Kumar Mitra, who had no connection with the terrorists. This arbitrary use of Regulation III soon became a nettlesome issue in Parliament.

Fortunately for the Alipore prisoners Krishna Kumar had been able to make arrangements for their defence before his deportation. Since few of the prisoners' relatives had enough money to engage legal help, it was decided to use Aurobindo's defence fund for as many of them as possible. But the fund was in fact too small to satisfy even one experienced barrister. After representing Aurobindo for a month, and taking all but Rs 6000 of the fund, Byomkesh Chakrabarti told Krishna Kumar that he would have to engage someone else. In desperation Krishna Kumar went to Chittaranjan Das, then a briefless barrister with little courtroom experience. Das had known Aurobindo since their student days in England and like him had long been involved in nationalist politics. In 1902 he had been a member of Aurobindo's short-lived revolutionary council. Krishna Kumar offered him the Rs 6000 that remained and begged him to take up the case. Das agreed and threw himself into the defence.[23] He first appeared in the courtroom along with Chakravarti on 16 November.[24] From that point, though Chakrabarti showed up occasionally for several weeks, the defence was in Das's hands.

Das's strategy was to minimize the importance of the overt acts and challenge the legitimacy of the testimonial and documentary evidence. In regard to the charge that the prisoners had waged war, he insisted that the various attempts at assassination were isolated acts done 'for the purpose of redressing private wrongs'. Despite Beachcroft's decision with regard to the confessions, he insisted that they ought not to be used. He and other defence lawyers raised innumerable objections on points of law, subjected the prosecution's witnesses to very lengthy and minute cross-examination, and objected to 'practically every document' that could not be shown 'to be in the writing of some one or other of the accused'. This last tactic was used often in the case of

Aurobindo, particularly in regard to the 'sweets letter'.[25]

Throughout the presentation of the evidence, the prosecution kept trying to bring Aurobindo into the picture, generally without success. During December Norton called a number of witnesses from Midnapore and made them relate the story of the previous year's conference in the minutest detail. All he could show was that Aurobindo was the leader of the Extremists. This of course was not an offence, though to Norton the Extremist Party was part of an insidious conspiracy that had spread to every corner of the land. In Bengal its tentacles included Chhatra Bhandar, the 'student's store' whose prospectus Aurobindo had signed; *Bande Mataram*, *Jugantar* and other Extremist papers; the 'bomb factory' at Harrison Road and of course the Garden. Through December and January Norton attempted to unravel the threads of this widespread plot.

Meanwhile outside the courtroom the actual revolutionary movement—not as romantic as Norton's but more dangerous to the Empire—was vigorously expanding. In western and northern India action was confined for the most part to riots and petty acts of vandalism. But in Bengal the seed Aurobindo, Barin and their associates had planted was bursting out in almost every district. There were bomb-finds in Nadia, Midnapore and Chandernagore and dacoities in Dacca, Hooghly, Malda and Mymensingh. The government responded by passing emergency legislation and banning suspect organizations.[26] But neither this nor the nine deportations could stem the tide. After a lull at the beginning of the year the revolutionaries brought terrorism to the very door of the Alipore Sessions Court. On 10 February Ashutosh Biswas, public prosecutor in the Bomb Case, had some work to do at the nearby magistrate's court. As he was leaving that courtroom a youth named Charu Chandra Bose walked up and pumped five bullets into his body. Charu Chandra succeeded where Jatindranath Raichaudhuri had failed even though one of his hands was crippled. He simply strapped the pistol to his bad hand and used the other to pull the trigger. At four-thirty an orderly went to the sessions court and announced that Ashutosh Biswas was dead. 'In an unnatural falsetto' a stunned Beachcroft blurted out: 'Ashu Babu, the Public Prosecutor, is shot?' '*Han Huzur*,' confirmed the orderly.[27] Court was adjourned for the day. As the prisoners were driven back to the jail, they had the satisfaction of knowing not only that the work they had started was prospering, but also that the man some considered the mainstay of the prosecution (Norton being more bluff than brains) would no longer be using his skills against them.[28]

But now the case was approaching its close. On 12 February, owing to objections from the defence, Beachcroft reformulated the charges against the thirty-six remaining accused. (The thirty-seventh, Charu Chandra Roy of Chandernagore, had been released at the instance of the French Government.) The accused did not benefit from the changes, since the judge made the terms more explicit. Two weeks later, after the last of the evidence was heard, Beachcroft called each of the accused to the witness box. Most said nothing beyond their name, father's name, caste, occupation and address, adding that they had given full instructions to their attorneys. Some like Nolini Kanta Gupta refuted specific pieces of evidence with a series of false statements. Sushil Sen did not bother to do even this. To the amusement and chagrin of the assembled lawyers, he declared that he would not make any statement since 'anything I say might be twisted into law'.[29]

On 4 March Norton closed his evidence and began his concluding statement. It took him more than two weeks to present the government's case. Most of his oration was given over to an elaborate attempt to prove Aurobindo's complicity. This man, Norton asserted, though 'possessed of qualities far above the ordinary run', had been driven by religio-political fanaticism to launch a conspiracy against the King-Emperor. He could not be shown to have taken part in any illegal act, but he was unquestionably 'the guiding spirit of the whole gang' and must be convicted. If it had not been for the murder of Narendra Nath Goswami, Aurobindo's complicity would not be in question. But even without that testimony there was a convincing mass of circumstantial evidence against him. The 'school' at the Garden, of which he was part owner, was structured on lines laid down in his *Bhawani Mandir*. It was impossible to believe that Aurobindo did not know what was going on there. The initials 'A.G.' appeared in an incriminating context in a notebook found at the Garden. Aurobindo's brother was the group's acknowledged leader. Another conspirator, Abinash Bhattacharya, looked after Aurobindo's household Documents like the 'sweets letter' and the 'scribblings' provided incontrovertible proof that Aurobindo was involved in the plot. Norton spent whole days trying to prove Aurobindo's connection with known conspirators. He gave less time to the cases of Barin and the rest. The confessions, the arms and explosives found at the Garden, and the testimony of numerous witnesses showed conclusively that Barin had led the others in an abortive insurrection against the legally constituted rulers of India.[30]

Norton finished his address on 21 March. Immediately afterwards the first defence lawyer, R. C. Bonnerjea, began his statement. Speaking for Barin and eight others, Bonnerjea could do little more than raise a series of technical objections. The confessions were induced, the charges misjoined, the evidence inadmissible. As for the arms found at the Garden, 'eleven revolvers, four rifles and one gun' could hardly be said to constitute a 'preparation for waging war'.[31] Bonnerjea spoke for two days, after which Das began his address on behalf of Aurobindo. This 'masterly specimen of forensic eloquence' lasted for more than a week. It was, in the words of a contemporary, 'nervous, compact, closely argued and with that touch of genuine passion which is the essential characteristic of great oratory'.[32] Courtroom eloquence tends to become overwrought. Das's oration suffers from this defect. It is also filled with statements that he knew to be untrue. But for all that it was both impassioned and well-argued. The case of the Crown, Das said, 'is that Arabinda was the head of the conspiracy'. Norton 'has credited Arabinda with vast intellectual attainments and with vast powers and organization and his case was that he was directing this conspiracy and was working from behind.' But even if the evidence established the existence of a conspiracy, it was at best a 'childish conspiracy —a toy revolution'. It was altogether 'impossible that Arabinda could ever have believed in his heart of hearts that by bombing one or two Englishmen, or some Englishmen in different places, they would ever have been able to subvert the British Government. If you credit him with intellectual powers and say that he has a brilliant mind, it is not open to you at the same time to say that he was the leader' of such a bungling effort. In his conclusion Das adopted the first person to present his client's 'whole case':

If it is an offence to plead the ideal of freedom, I admit having done it—I have never disputed it. It is for that that I have given up all the prospects of my life. . . . If that is my offence let it be so stated and I am cheerful to bear any punishment. It pains me to think that crimes I could never have thought of or deeds repellent to me, and against which my whole nature revolts, should be attributed to me and that on the strength, not only of evidence on which the slightest reliance cannot be placed, but on my writings which breathe and breathe only of that high ideal which I felt I was called upon to preach. . . . I felt I was called upon to preach to my country to make them realise that India had a mission to perform in the comity of nations. If that is my fault you can chain me, imprison me, but you will never get out of me a denial of that charge.

Das then added his much-quoted peroration, which concludes: 'My appeal to you therefore is that a man like this who is being charged with the offences imputed to him stands not only before the bar in the Court but stands before the bar of the High Court of History.'[33]

The addresses of the other defence counsels occupied the court until 13 April—the hundred and twenty-fifth day of the proceedings. When the last vakil had had his say, Norton rose and asked the judge, 'Will your honour hear me further on law points?' 'No. I don't wish to hear you any further,' Beachcroft answered.[34] The two assessors were then asked for their opinions. Unlike jurymen they were not on oath: their duty, as another judge told other assessors, was 'merely to offer advice which need not bind me as Judge'.[35] On the 14th the two Bengalis who had been selected to discharge this decorative function gave their verdicts. Neither believed that there had been a conspiracy to wage war; the only section that had been violated was 122: collecting arms and men. Eight of the thirty-six accused were guilty of offences under this section: Barin, Upen, Ullaskar, Hem Das, Indu Bhusan, Bibhuti Bhusan, and two others. The other twenty-eight were not guilty. The judge 'congratulated the assessors at having arrived at the end of their labours' and informed the court 'that he would take a month to write his judgement'.[36]

20

Judgment

Early in 1907 Lord Minto wrote that he, along with the 'great majority of the population', viewed Bengalis with 'supreme contempt'. Two years later, after the murders of the Kennedys, Narendra Nath Goswami, Nandalal Banerjee, Ashutosh Biswas and several others, after four attempts to kill Sir Andrew Fraser and one claimed attempt on Minto himself, the viceroy had learned to temper his contempt with prudence.[1] Several days before Beachcroft's judgment was to be delivered Minto's chief secretary wrote to the Government of Bengal that it should take 'such police precautions . . . as will render impossible any disorder or attempt at rescue, and will ensure the safety of the Judge and of all concerned.' In compliance with these orders F. L. Halliday, Calcutta's commissioner of police, and F. C. Daly, his deputy inspector-general, arranged for a contingent of military police to be sent down from Hooghly and 'for a large body of European sergeants to be ready in case of necessity'.[2] For reasons of security the date of Beachcroft's judgment was not made public. Even the superintendent of Alipore jail was kept in the dark until eight o'clock on the morning of 6 May 1909, when a company of Gordon Highlanders marched up to his gate and informed him that they had orders to convey the prisoners to the court. By ten o'clock five hundred military policemen 'were patrolling the many roads and by-lanes leading from the jail to the Court'. Roads within a half-mile of the courthouse were 'practically impassable'. Noticing the unusual activity, the people of the city realized that the long-awaited day had come. Soon it was all the police could do to keep the crowds in order. Shortly after ten o'clock the prison vans, guarded by European armed police, drove up and discharged thirty-five of the thirty-six accused. Ashok Nandi, dangerously ill with tuberculosis, was brought in an ambulance and carried on a stretcher to the veranda of the court. After being divested of their manacles the other prisoners were conducted to the dock.[3]

At ten minutes to eleven the judge put in his appearance. As he mounted the bench a 'sudden hush fell upon the court and the prisoners pressed eagerly to the front of the netted dock'. After five minutes of silence, without making a preliminary speech, Beachcroft read out the names of those he had convicted.[4] According to one of the accused, the judge was 'very grave. For a moment he seemed to have lost that composure of mind which should belong to a dispenser of Justice, and there was a perceptible tremor in his voice as he pronounced the death sentences.'[5] This is what he said:

> Accused Barindra Kumar Ghose and Ullaskar Dutt are sentenced to death under sections 121, 121A, and 122 I.P.C. and they are informed that if they wish to appeal they must do so within one week. Accused Hem Chandra Das, Upendra Nath Banerjea, Bibhuti Bhusan Sirkar, Hrishikesh Kanjilal, Birendra Chandra Sen, Sudhir Kumar Ghose [*a mistake for* Sarkar], Indranath Nandy, Abinash Chandra Bhattacharjee, Sailendranath Bose are sentenced to transportation for life under Sections 121, 121A and 122 I.P.C. Accused Indra [Indu] Bhusan Roy is sentenced to transportation for life under sections 121A and 122 I.P.C.

Seven more—Paresh Mallick, Sisir Ghose, Nirapada Roy, Ashok Nandi, Balkrishna Kane, Sushil Sen and Kristo Jiban Sanyal—were sentenced to from ten years to one year of transportation or imprisonment. All the rest of the accused were 'acquitted and to be set at liberty'.[6]

Barin said nothing when the judge pronounced his doom. Ullaskar muttered 'Thank you very much.' Otherwise, according to F. C. Daly, 'the sentences were received in silence—that is, silence compared to the turmoil that there has usually been in the Dock. Arabinda, as usual, looked stoically indifferent,' but 'Hem Das for the first time looked seriously depressed.' It appeared to Daly that Hem 'was disappointed at not being sentenced to death'.[7]

Having delivered his sentences and handed his judgment to the authorities, Beachcroft rose and left the court. As the police executed warrants for the nineteen convicts, the other men crowded round and embraced them. The sentences, especially the sentences of death, were painful, but the young men were beside themselves with joy over Aurobindo's acquittal. Aurobindo told his brother, 'You will not be hanged' and assured Abinash, 'You will come back soon.' Then he walked to the Bar library where he talked with a jubilant C. R. Das and the other lawyers. The liberated leader was 'treated with great respect', a British observer noted, adding with distaste that one or two pleaders went 'so far as to touch their foreheads with the dust from his feet'.[8] Asked for his reactions by a newspaper reporter, Aurobindo 'expressed no surprise at his release or the verdicts generally'. 'This is one year out of the world,' he commented, 'and a year out of my life.' Precisely twelve months before he had been taken to Alipore Jail. He and the other acquitted persons would not have to return. But even as he spoke twenty-two of his comrades were put in handcuffs and led to the van, the condemned men forming the principal pair.[9]*

After everyone else had left the premises, G. C. Denham of the Special Branch sat with barrister Eardley Norton taking notes from Beachcroft's 354-page judgment. Two days earlier Denham's superior F. C. Daly, basing himself on the opinion of detective Shamsul Alam, had informed the Bengal Government that only nine of the accused, none of them important, were 'at all likely to be acquitted'. Needless to say both the police and the government were unhappy over the actual result. Daly was astonished that several of the men arrested along with Barin and Ullaskar at the Garden were found not guilty. But the main blow was the acquittal of Aurobindo, which had come 'to everyone's surprise'. When details of the judgment were rushed to Sir Edward Baker, the new lieutenant-governor of Bengal, his only comment was: 'But Mr Daly's informant [Shamsul Alam] was wrong about Arabindo!'[10] Baker's aides immediately telegraphed a list of the sentences to the viceroy in Simla. Minto received it while writing to the secretary of state and added a summary to his letter: 'Arabinda Ghose acquitted, two death sentences and some long transportations. . . . There will now be an appeal.'[11] He was referring to the expected appeal by the men who had been convicted; but the

* Two of the seventeen acquitted, Nagendra Nath and Dharani Nath Gupta, had already been convicted in the Harrison Road Case. A third, Proves Chandra Deb, was immediately rearrested on a sedition charge.

Government of Bengal was already thinking of filing an appeal of its own. Before going home that evening Norton informed Denham that Aurobindo had been acquitted because Beachcroft had 'introduced in his Judgment many hypotheses' that neither he nor the defence had put forward. There was, the barrister asserted, 'an excellent case for appeal'.[12]

It was not just the government that was surprised at Aurobindo's acquittal. To most of his countrymen it was 'totally unexpected' and as the news spread through Calcutta 'much rejoicing' broke out—so much that a rumoured attack on the European quarter did not come off.[13] In the days that followed, detectives going through the Calcutta native press found that most 'attention was focussed on the acquittal of Arabindo Ghose'. 'Various theories' were put forward to explain the verdict, some attributing it 'to personal fear on the part of the Judge and some to policy on the part of the Government'.* All in all, an official concluded, Aurobindo's escape from prison—or scaffold—had 'given considerable satisfaction in Bengali patriotic circles, which is balanced by a great deal of talk about the "ferocity" of the sentences passed on those convicted.'[14] The reaction was similar in other parts of the country. The *Mahratta* of Poona considered the verdict 'a great triumph for Indian Nationalism' and declared that Beachcroft had 'undoubtedly done a great service to the State by thus rehabilitating the confidence of the people in the sense of British Justice'. *The Gujarati Punch* was happy to report the acquittals but sorry that so many of the accused, 'mostly young boys', had been convicted. 'Cannot anything be done', it wondered, 'towards making these sentences deterrent rather than vindictive?' Anglo-Indian opinion was less clement. *The Eastern Bengal and Assam Era* was 'sorry that such a pretentious trial should have terminated in results so paltry and meagre, so morally powerless for good' and disappointed that 'some offenders of those who have escaped' were not awarded 'long terms of transportation and imprisonment'. *The Madras Mail* was happy that at least some of the malefactors had been suitably punished: 'At last the time has come when the dark pages of contemporary

* It may have been at this time that the theory was first proposed that during the trial the judge supplied C. R. Das with information to help him secure the acquittal of his old Cambridge friend. A version of this fantastic tale was published as late as 1980, needless to say without reliable documentation. See *A&R* 6 (1982): 233–5.

history can be turned over with satisfaction that the promoters of atrocious conspiracy have not escaped penalties they deserved.'[15]

The provincial and imperial governments showed as much interest as the public in the results of the trial. So many officials in Calcutta and Simla wanted to study Beachcroft's judgment that a special edition had to be printed for them.[16] In the year since the bombing at Muzaffarpur dozens of men had been arrested in connection with terrorist incidents. Beachcroft's judgment was the first to address this growing problem and it was certain to set legal precedents. As soon as printed copies were available administrators and legal experts began to scrutinize it.

Beachcroft began his judgment with a discussion of the history of the case. After dealing with the overt acts the sites, the searches and discoveries, the confessions, and the writings of various newspapers, he summed up: 'We have then the connection of 15, Gopi Mohan Dutta's Lane, 134, Harrison Road, and the garden established. We have further Baren's explanation [in his confession] of the collection of arms and ammunition, that it was in the anticipation of a far off revolution. We have his description of the attempts to rouse the people of India, and the starting of the *Yugantar* for the purpose.' The articles of this journal, Beachcroft remarked, 'exhibit a burning hatred of the British race, they breathe revolution in every line, they point out how revolution is to be effected.' What they advocated was for the country's youth 'to forcibly expel the British from India, in other words to wage war on the King and deprive him of the Sovereignty of British India'. Nor was Barin content simply to preach this doctrine. He turned the Maniktola Garden into a revolutionary school and workshop following more or less exactly 'the methods advocated by the paper'. 'In the face of the evidence', the judge concluded, 'I do not see how any reasonable man can doubt the connection between the two', that is between the ideal of revolution put forward in *Jugantar* and other papers and the steps actually taken at the Garden. Since it was clear from the evidence that Barin was not alone in his efforts, but 'was assisted in his design by others', there could be 'no question of the existence of a conspiracy to commit the offence of waging war and to deprive the king of the Sovereignty of British India'. All persons who could be shown to be members of that conspiracy were therefore guilty under section 121-A.[17]

'Those responsible for this conspiracy did their work well', Beachcroft observed. 'They realized that their best chance was to get hold of the youth of the country and inflame them by appealing to their sense of religion and their sense of chivalry, and to this end they have prostituted the teaching of their sacred books and represented that under English rule the chastity of their mothers and sisters is not safe.' Underlining a point that both Das and Norton had made during their arguments, Beachcroft declared: 'No Englishman worthy of the name will grudge the Indian the ideal of independence.' But he added immediately: 'No Indian of decent feeling but will deprecate the methods sought to attain it.'[18]

Coming to the sentences, Beachcroft wrote that according to the prosecution five overt acts had been committed by members of the conspiracy. Of these one took place in French India outside his court's jurisdiction. Another was directed against Mr Kingsford, a magistrate who had handed down several judgments inimical to the members of the society. The attempt to kill him might, as the defence maintained, be considered more 'an act of revenge than one in furtherance of the conspiracy'. But this could not be said of the attempts to mine the train carrying Sir Andrew Fraser. 'An attempt to blow up a Lieutenant-Governor for following a certain line of policy is just as much an act of war as an attempt to blow up Parliament.' Therefore all involved in the Mankundu and Narayangarh incidents were guilty under Section 121 of waging war against the king; all who were members of the conspiracy at the time of the Narayangarh attempt were guilty under the same section of abetment of waging war.[19]

Beachcroft found eleven men guilty under Section 121. All of them were liable to the supreme punishment. He distinguished however between the three leading members—Barin, Ullaskar and Hem—and the other eight. Hem had not been in India when the overt acts were committed, so the judge thought it right to 'stretch a point in his case' and sentenced him to transportation for life. He showed similar leniency in the cases of the eight subordinates. But Barin and Ullaskar deserved no mercy and Beachcroft sentenced them 'to be hanged by the neck till they are dead'.[20]

With one exception the judge devoted only a page or two of his judgment to the men he acquitted. The exception was Aurobindo, who required fifty pages. The judge left 'his case till last of all' because he was 'the most important accused', that is, 'the accused, whom more than any other the prosecution are anxious to have convicted'. 'But for his presence in the dock,' Beachcroft observed, 'there is no doubt that the case would have been finished long ago.' The prosecution had based its case against Aurobindo 'almost entirely, upon association with other accused persons'.[21] The judge therefore had to sift through the mass of evidence produced by the Crown to determine if this association was conspiratorial. In great detail Beachcroft considered Aurobindo's letters, speeches, and writings; letters and documents in which he was mentioned; and the testimony of spies and others. The prosecution laid great stress on his letters to his wife, particularly the one in which he declared, 'What would a son do if a demon sat on his mother's breast and started sucking her blood? Would he quietly sit down to his dinner, amuse himself with his wife and children, or would he rush out to deliver his mother? I know I have the strength to deliver this fallen race.' The judge wrote in reference to this: 'If we start with the knowledge that the writer of this letter is a conspirator, we can find passages in it that are suspicious. Viewing it in an unprejudiced way, there is nothing in it that really calls for explanation.' Other letters too contained 'some passages which may be suspicious, but which are also capable of an innocent explanation.'[22] A few somewhat violent statements in Aurobindo's speeches might be excused in view of his habit of indulging in hyperbole and other rhetorical devices. Those of his writings that were somewhat dubious were never published. Thus the only 'really important documents' against Arabinda, were the 'sweets letter' and the 'scribblings'. The judge went over each of these in detail. The prosecution maintained that the 'sweets letter' was written to Aurobindo by Barin and that the word 'sweets' referred to bombs. There were other examples of such argot in the society's correspondence. The defence raised numerous objections in regard to this damning piece of evidence. The greeting read: 'Dear Brother'. No younger brother in India would address an elder brother like that. The text contained the misspelling 'imergencies'. Barin was not so stupid. There were besides a number of legal irregularities about its discovery and filing. It was in short a forgery.[23] Das's performance was convincing. While not doubting that the letter was discovered at Aurobindo's house, Beachcroft wrote that he found it 'of so suspicious a character that I hesitate to accept it. Experience tells us that in cases where spies are employed documents do find their way into the homes of suspected persons [before their arrest] in a manner which cannot be explained by the accused.'[24] This was a notable victory for Das, particularly because the letter, as Barin later admitted, was precisely what the government claimed it was.[25]

The 'scribblings' were the passage in one of Aurobindo's notebooks in which Barin, Sudhir, Prafulla and other conspirators were mentioned along with 'a small charge of the stuff'. Beachcroft looked upon 'this piece of evidence as the most difficult point in this case'. The defence maintained that it had been forged in the notebook after its discovery. Beachcroft thought this unlikely but added that 'the scribbling bears no resemblance to his [Aurobindo's] writing; being such 'as any one might write'. He therefore declined to consider it proof of complicity.[26] This was another stroke of luck for Aurobindo, since the writing certainly was his.* Taking the evidence against Aurobindo as a whole Beachcroft was 'of the opinion that it falls short of such proof as would justify one in finding him guilty of so serious a charge.'[27]

The government was not of the same opinion. 'The whole result of the Manicktolla bomb case is rather puzzling as a guide as to what will and what will not secure a conviction in an Indian court of law', wrote F. C. Daly two years later in his influential *Note on the Growth of the Revolutionary Movement in Bengal*. Daly was aghast that 'seventeen out of 36 persons placed on trial, some of whom had been actually arrested in the garden' were able to escape conviction. He certainly was not wrong in disbelieving the pleas of Sachin Sen, Nolini Gupta and the other 'younger men found in the garden' that 'they were ignorant of the true nature of the place and had gone there for religious instruction'. Unfortunately for Daly and for the Government of Bengal, the British legal system, by placing the burden of proof on the prosecution, made it difficult to convict persons not caught or observed in the execution of a crime.[28]

* The author, who has helped edit Sri Aurobindo's writings since 1972, has no doubt that the 'scribblings' were written by him. The lack of resemblance to his normal hand was due to the fact that the 'scribblings' were examples of 'automatic writing'.

Whatever Extremist polemic might allege, British India was not imperial Russia. The judiciary was independent and—until hobbled by emergency regulations—bound by the principles of habeas corpus and 'innocent until proven guilty'. Even Aurobindo expressed grudging admiration of the British legal system a few months after his release: 'The European Court of Justice is also a curious and instructive institution', he began. 'In one aspect it is an exhilarating gamble, a very Monte Carlo of surprising chances.' The accused 'looks eagerly, not to the truth or the falsehood of the evidence for or against him, but to the skill with which this counsel or the other handles the proofs or the witnesses and the impressions they are making on the judge or jury.' But, he concluded, after all, praise must be given where it is due, and the English system must be lauded for not normally exposing the accused to the torture of savage pursuit by a prosecuting judge [as in France] or the singular methods of investigation favoured by the American police. If the dice are apt to be loaded, it is on both sides and not on one.'[29]

Aurobindo had more reason than most to appreciate these doubly loaded dice. He had just escaped imprisonment for an offence that he unquestionably had committed. Not only was he a conspirator, he was the originator and first organizer of a conspiracy whose declared aim was to drive the British from India. His counsel had of course denied any suggestion of this, but he could hardly deny what was common knowledge: that Aurobindo was a leader of a party that demanded political independence (also the proclaimed goal of the conspirators) and that he advocated the use of active methods for its attainment. Aurobindo was the brother of the admitted leader of the society and could be shown to have been in constant touch with him and other conspirators at the time the overt acts were committed. He was, according to the slain approver, fully cognizant of some of these acts. He was part owner of the land where the society established its headquarters and was mentioned in documents found on the spot. A search at his own house uncovered several compromising letters, including one that referred to bombs by a transparent metaphor and a piece of writing that spoke of known terrorists and terroristic acts. All in all, as Daly wrote in his confidential *Note*,

it is hard to see how on the evidence laid before the Court the Judge could have believed that Arabindo had no guilty knowledge of what was going

> on and that it did not have his tacit approval, if not enthusiastic encouragement. Though Arabindo may be regarded as a man too clever and foreseeing to believe that success would attend a little effort of this kind of revolution, he possibly believed that an open demonstration of murder by bombs and an exhibition of the audacity to which Bengali youths had been brought to by the new system of [revolutionary] training, would have a stimulating effect on the spirits of others and would excite the minds of the young men throughout India and develop in them a spirit of reckless daring that would be of great use in the big venture which he possibly had in his mind's eye and for which he intended to wait a suitable opportunity, such as the embarrassment of England in a big foreign war.[30]

One has to admire the penetration of Daly's analysis, the accuracy of which is borne out by Aurobindo's retrospective statements.[31]

Daly's *Note* was published in 1911. On the afternoon of 6 May 1909, the writer had too many tasks on his hands to concern himself with the terrorists' long-term goals or the vagaries of the British legal system. He had to arrange for the protection of the judge and several others; he had to organize the shadowing of the fourteen men who had been released; and he had to find a way to put Aurobindo, whose release was 'considered as of serious importance', safely back in jail.[32]

21

Appeals

On the afternoon of 6 May 1909 Daly's detectives followed Aurobindo from the court's Bar library to the house of C. R. Das in Bhawanipur, Calcutta. From there he went to 6 College Square, the house of his uncle Krishna Kumar Mitra, where he took up residence with his aunt and her three children. Krishna Kumar was still being detained in Agra under Regulation III of 1818.[1] While Aurobindo was settling in that evening, his Special Branch nemesis dashed off his last letter of the day. Writing to F. W. Duke, chief secretary to the Government of Bengal, Daly communicated Norton's opinion that an appeal of Aurobindo's acquittal would have an excellent chance of success. Four days later Duke asked Daly 'to look into this possible contingency'.[2] The first step was to submit the case to Bengal's legal remembrancer, E. P. Chapman. After an 'exhaustive study', Chapman wrote to Duke on 21 May that 'Mr Beachcroft's judgment is assailable on several material points.' Chief among them was the judge's failure to realize that Aurobindo's mission was not the 'innocent' dissemination of Vedantic ideas. Aurobindo was religious to be sure but his 'religion was (to use a loose phrase) the expulsion of the English from India'. After several pages of legal analysis, Chapman summed up: 'I am disposed to think that if I had tried the case, I would have convicted. . . . *BUT* the issue of such a case especially in the form of an appeal against acquittal cannot be otherwise than doubtful.' The legal remembrancer, who evidently knew his Carlyle, considered Aurobindo 'a hero of the spiritual type'. Even if the Crown succeeded in 'getting him sentenced to imprisonment', what would be the result? He would simply 'develop into a myth'. If on the other hand the government allowed him to remain free 'he may be actually less dangerous', for 'in the wear and tear of actual life his unpracticality is certain to disclose itself'. Accordingly Chapman concluded: 'On the whole my advice is against an appeal.' Transmitting this opinion to Sir Edward Baker, Duke expressed his own doubts 'as to whether an appeal should be filed'. Nevertheless he suggested that the case be sent to a Bombay expert for a second opinion. On 29 May the lieutenant-governor agreed to this course of action, which enabled him to put off taking a decision for almost three months.[3]

Unaware of the government's machinations against him, Aurobindo passed the month of May quietly at home. He received many visitors, among them the inevitable police spies who reported that he spent 'most of his day in study of religious books and in writing'.[4] This information doubtless was correct; but despite his absorption in study and spiritual practice Aurobindo had not lost interest in politics or revolution. Visitors and friends soon brought him up to date in both areas. For several months the Extremist party had been leaderless and inactive. Tilak was serving a six-year jail sentence in Burma; Lajpat Rai and Bipin Pal were self-exiled in the West. The nine deportations of 1908, besides depriving Bengal of many of its leaders, had taught the value of discretion to the others. The Moderates meanwhile were basking in the government's approval, with men like G. K. Gokhale and Surendranath Banerjea openly co-operating with high officials. Banerjea eventually went so far as to court the lieutenant-governor's favour by 'deliberately resiling' from his 'support of the boycott movement' in his influential daily, *The Bengalee*.[5]

The government had won over these and other Moderate leaders by convincing them that if they helped keep the country quiet they would gain what they had been crying for since 1885: a package of administrative reforms. This scheme, the Indian Councils Act (known popularly as the Morley-Minto Reforms), had been announced in December 1908. It was to consist of a reorganization of the legislative councils and to be accompanied by the appointment of 'native' members to the councils of the viceroy and of the secretary of state. Moderate spokesmen competed with one another to find the most fulsome words of praise for the proposed reforms. They were 'a great step forward . . . in the grant of representative government' and 'a step worthy of the noble traditions of the Government which has given us liberty of thought and speech, high education and good government'.[6] The sponsors of the measure (with London to answer to) were quick to set the record straight. 'We have distinctly maintained,' said Minto, 'that Representative Government, in its Western sense, is totally inapplicable to the Indian Empire and would be uncongenial to the traditions of Eastern populations.' Morley told the House of Commons: 'If it could be said that this chapter of reforms led directly or necessarily up to the establishment of a Parliamentary system in India, I, for one, would have nothing at all to do with it.'[7] Soon even the Moderates realized that the Act did not represent a change for the better in any real sense. Its principal effect was negative. By institutionalizing communal electorates it drove a wedge between Hindus and Muslims, splitting the movement and encouraging the growth of that sectarian brand of politics which remains the curse of the subcontinent.

The government combined its policy of 'rallying the Moderates' with a harsh campaign of repression against the Extremists. In the wake of the Muzaffarpur incident lawmakers had rushed through the Explosives Substances Act and the Newspapers (Incitement to Offences) Act. The latter measure made it dangerous to publish anything remotely resembling sedition—as the editors of *Bande Mataram* soon learned. The silencing of this journal in November 1908 left the Bengal Extremist Party without an organ. It was planned to hold a national Extremist Congress but this was prohibited by executive order. When the Moderate Convention that had taken the place of the Congress met in December, the President, Minto's friend Rash Behari Bose, declared that sometime 'in the distant future' when the Indian people had 'proved themselves fit for self-government' they might witness 'the extension to India of the colonial type of Government'.[8] This utter betrayal of the ideals of the Calcutta Congress was heard by fewer than 600 delegates.

Despite the government's repression, an outbreak of revolutionary activity had come on the heels of the Muzaffarpur incident. With the breaking up of the Garden society, the Dacca Anushilan became the chief revolutionary samiti in Bengal. During the second half of 1908 it carried out a number of dacoities and other actions including the beheading of the informer Sukumar Chakravarti. In response the government passed the Indian Criminal

Law Amendment Act, which provided for summary trials and 'the prohibition of associations dangerous to the public peace'. Under this measure the Dacca Anushilan and four other East Bengal samitis were outlawed in January 1909.[9] The Dacca Anushilan survived and eventually prospered as an underground society; but the proscription, the deportation of its leaders and other effective countermeasures made it necessary for the group to cut back on its activities temporarily. By May 1909, when Aurobindo was released, Lord Minto could write to the secretary of state: 'Politically things continue satisfactorily, and there is the feeling of a calm after a storm.' But Minto was too much of a realist not to add: 'Still we must never be surprised if it starts to blow hard again.'[10]

Aurobindo's own reading of the situation was similar to the viceroy's. It was impossible to deny that the enthusiasm of 1905–8 had been replaced by 'a general discouragement and depression'. But closer observation convinced him that 'the feeling in the country had not ceased but was only suppressed and was growing by its suppression.' He therefore 'determined to continue the struggle'.[11] The first necessity was to reawaken nationalist sentiment through open propaganda, the second to continue the secret revolutionary work. As in the period before his arrest, Aurobindo gave most of his attention to the open movement. In June he launched a weekly newspaper, *Karmayogin*, and began to appear regularly on the public platform. His first speeches and writings showed a definite spiritual slant, but as time went by they became more explicitly political. Simultaneously he began quietly to rebuild the revolutionary network, encouraging leaders like Jatin Mukherjee and Satish Bose to continue recruitment, training and, when possible, action.[12]

The first issue of *Karmayogin* was published on 19 June. The same day a copy was sent to the central office of the CID; before the end of the month it had reached Lord Minto's office. After leafing through the newspaper Minto's chief secretary H. A. Stuart, a former CID director, advised putting pressure on the Bengal Government to prefer an appeal of Aurobindo's acquittal, there being 'no political reasons' against this course of action. A week later Stuart was for taking even more aggressive measures. In a circular letter to his colleagues on the viceroy's council, he pointed out that Aurobindo 'has been most active since his release'. This was something of an exaggeration since so far he had only brought out three issues of his journal and delivered a half-dozen speeches. Nevertheless, said Stuart, 'If he is allowed to go on he will very soon have the country in a blaze again.' Stuart recommended calling 'the attention of the local [provincial] governments of the two Bengals' to Aurobindo's 'dangerous campaign and inquire what steps they propose or recommend to stop it'. Venturing the optimistic opinion that 'at this juncture the Secretary of State would probably give us a fairly free hand', he concluded: 'I would not hesitate to deport Arabindo if he cannot be silenced in any other way.' Minto agreed to this proposal, but when he wrote to the secretary of state the same day he made no mention of deportation, which Morley had ruled out except for cases of 'extreme urgency'.[13]

The Governments of Bengal and Eastern Bengal and Assam were informed of Stuart's proposal. Not that they needed to be told that Aurobindo's presence on their soil was 'dangerous'. Indeed the epithet became something of a cliché in the months that followed. Officials in Dacca, Calcutta and Simla all agreed that Aurobindo was, as F. W. Duke put it, 'the most dangerous of our adversaries now at large'.[14] The problem was to find a way to get rid of him—and someone who wanted to do it. There were three possible methods of proceeding: a conventional prosecution for an offence such as sedition, an appeal of the Alipore acquittal, and deportation. The Governments of India and Bengal agreed that something ought to be done; but both suffered from the functional disorder of bureaucracies: the fear of being held responsible for a wrong decision. The result was a complicated game of administrative juggling, the two governments tossing the three proposals back and forth until they landed, one after another, on Edward Baker's desk. The lieutenant-governor, with his eyes turned to London, considered each of them in turn and in the end sent them all back to Simla.

The most attractive of the possibilities was a prosecution for an infraction of the existing law. It was this Minto had in mind when he wrote to the secretary of state on 7 July: 'I only hope he will sufficiently commit himself for us to prosecute.'[15] If Aurobindo wrote or said anything expressing 'disaffection' of the government he could be indicted for sedition and put in jail for a very long time. But Aurobindo was a cautious speaker and a master of writing between the lines. Police spies took down every word he spoke in public; police officials scrutinized these transcripts together with published versions of the speeches and the texts of every article that appeared in *Karmayogin*.[16] Aurobindo disappointed them. His speeches, as a Government of India official acknowledged, were 'not actually seditious' though of a 'distinctly inflammatory character'. Once Daly set off a flurry of activity by suggesting that Aurobindo had made a 'distinctly violent speech' in Calcutta on 11 July. The passage the deputy inspector-general found offensive was this: 'Imprisonment in a righteous cause was not so terrible as it seemed; suffering was not so difficult to bear as our anticipations made it out. The prize to which they aspired was the greatest to which a nation could aspire, and if a price was asked of them, they ought not to shrink from paying it.' It is difficult to see what Daly found indictable in this passage, particularly when Aurobindo concluded the speech in almost Gandhian terms: 'On their fidelity to *Swadeshi*, to Boycott, to passive resistance, rested the hope of a peaceful and spiritual salvation. On that it depended whether India would give the example, unprecedented in history, of a revolution worked out by moral force and peaceful pressure.' Bengal's legal remembrancer, after some hesitation, said he was unwilling to advise a sedition prosecution on the basis of this speech. Bengal's chief secretary, Duke, agreed. On 22 July he informed the Government of India on Baker's behalf that none of Aurobindo's utterances were 'such as to afford a reasonable probability of a conviction being obtained under any section of the existing law'. He added that the lieutenant-governor was 'considering whether any further action in regard to him is possible.[17]

This was a reference to the question of deportation, which was then under consideration. Procedurally this was the simplest of the three methods, since neither warrant nor legal process were needed to 'restrain' a man under Regulation III. Politically however the measure was dynamite. In May a group of Liberal, Labour and Irish members of Parliament had begun corresponding with the prime minister about the detention of the nine deportees.[18] The secretary of state was not anxious for more questions in Parliament and he certainly would have opposed further deportations. In order to act, the Government of India would have to obtain a strong recommendation from Bengal making it clear that Aurobindo advocated the forcible overthrow of the British Raj.

Nothing he had said or written was so imprudent. Informing Baker that 'the time had not yet come' for deportation, Duke could only hope that 'length of rope may induce him to cross the border line', that is, permissiveness induce him to commit a serious blunder. Accepting the chief secretary's advice, Baker wrote to the Government of India on 23 July, the day after he refused to prosecute Aurobindo for sedition, that he was 'not prepared to recommend that Arabindo Ghose be deported under Regulation III of 1818'.[19]

With prosecution and deportation eliminated, the only remaining means of putting Aurobindo out of action was to appeal his Alipore acquittal. Informing Baker that it 'accepted for the present' his decision in regard to deportation, India's Stuart added: 'the real reason . . . for not deporting Arabinda Ghose at this moment is that the question of appealing against his acquittal has still to be decided and that we cannot prejudice the case by deporting him in the meanwhile.' The absurdity of this statement —Aurobindo's case would be more than 'prejudiced' if he was whisked away to Burma!—shows how foggy bureaucratic thinking was becoming in the matter of the dangerous Aurobindo. Ten days earlier Duke had informed Stuart that Chapman, Bengal's legal remembrancer, was against an appeal of Aurobindo's acquittal. To obtain a second opinion, the case had been sent to T. J. Strangman, the advocate-general of Bombay. After three weeks of study, Strangman arrived at an opinion very similar to Chapman's. He believed that there was 'a fair chance of a conviction against Arabindo Ghose being obtained in appeal'. The most important piece of evidence, the 'sweets letter', should not have been rejected. If it were held proved 'there can be little doubt that Arabindo Ghose was in the conspiracy.' But all things considered Strangman was not prepared to say that the appeal would have 'a two to one chance of success'—the only odds on which Bengal was prepared to undertake the gamble.[20] In accordance with Strangman's opinion Baker had his officiating Chief Secretary write to Stuart that while Aurobindo remained 'one of the most dangerous factors in the present situation' he had decided not to prefer an appeal of his acquittal. Such a course would 'certainly cause a revival of public feeling against Government . . . and, if the appeal should fail, that price would have been paid for nothing.' India accepted Baker's decision, but did not abandon the hope of an appeal. On 26 August it informed Bengal that Aurobindo's case should be reconsidered after the appeals against the convictions of Barin and the other Alipore convicts had been decided by the High Court of Calcutta.[21]

The Court had taken up these appeals earlier the same month. Ullaskar Dutt had not wanted to challenge his sentence of death, but Barin convinced him via tapping telegraphy that it was their duty as revolutionaries to do so.[22] After the two condemned men filed their appeals the rest of the convicts followed suit. The case opened before Sir Lawrence Jenkins, the chief justice, and Mr Justice Carnduff, on 9 August. The adversaries at the bar were the same as in the court of sessions: Eardley Norton representing the Crown, C. R. Das and others representing the prisoners. Even more than in the sessions trial the two counsels concerned themselves with legal technicalities. Did the Alipore court have jurisdiction to take cognizance of the offences? Did Birley take down the confessions in proper form? Were the confessions, once withdrawn, admissible as evidence? And, most important for Barin and Ullaskar, was there a valid complaint under Section 121, in accordance with which the sentences of death were awarded? The consideration of these and matters occupied the Court until 12 October.

When the Government of India instructed the Government of Bengal to reconsider the question of Aurobindo's appeal after the other appeals had been heard, it suggested that the Crown bring up the 'sweets letter' during the hearing of the case in the High Court. According to Chapman and Strangman the question of Aurobindo's guilt or innocence hung on this document. If the High Court considered it genuine, the case against Aurobindo would be considerably strengthened. Accordingly on the thirty-first day of the proceedings Norton referred to the letter and to Beachcroft's opinion of it. But the chief justice was on to the barrister's game. Jenkins commented: 'If your case against Barin rests upon this letter I can understand your argument. If it is merely for the purpose of showing that the Judge and the Assessors were wrong in their view as to Arobinda then you are in mistake.'[23] This was a blow to the government's plans but did not dampen the hopes of the police, who more than anyone else wanted Aurobindo's case to be appealed. As the High Court trial dragged on into September they became increasingly nervous. If nothing was done before 6 November, the six-month statute of limitations would be overpassed and an appeal of the case become impossible. Three days before the deadline there was a last spasm of activity, the Crown's solicitors submitting their case to the Government of Bengal for immediate consideration. No decision was reached and the case against Aurobindo was allowed to lapse.[24]

Two weeks later, on 23 November, the High Court delivered its verdict on the appeals of the Alipore convicts. Their Lordships held that there was convincing proof of the existence of a conspiracy to wage war, but accepted the defence's arguments that there had been no valid complaint under Section 121.[25] Barin and Ullaskar thus escaped the gallows. The chief justice considered the question of the punishment to be given to be 'one of considerable difficulty' since 'those who have been convicted are not ordinary criminals; they are for the most part men of education, of strong religious instincts, and in some cases of considerable force of character.' On the other hand 'they have been convicted of one of the most serious offences against the State.' Their punishments had therefore to be 'in proportion to the gravity of the offence'.[26] Barin Ghose and Ullaskar Dutt were sentenced to transportation for life, sharing this punishment with Hem Das and Upendranath Banerjee, whose sentences were not reduced. All the other prisoners except one benefited from the High Court's judgment. Bibhuti Bhusan Sarkar, Indu Bhusan Roy and Hrishikesh Kanjilal had their terms of transportation reduced from life to ten years; Sudhir Sarkar and Abinash Bhattacharya from life to seven years; and Paresh Mallick from ten years to seven. The ten-year terms of transportation awarded to Sisir Ghose and Nirapada Roy were reduced to five years' rigorous imprisonment while the seven-year term against Balkrishna Hari Kane was overturned and Kane released. The two judges differed over the cases of the five remaining convicts—Indra Nandi, Kristo Jiban Sanyal, Sushil Sen, Biren Sen and Sailen Bose—Jenkins declaring himself in favour of acquittal, Carnduff in favour of retaining or reducing their sentences. The cases of these five men were referred to a third High Court justice for decision. The only prisoner who did not profit from the three-month deliberations was Ashok Nandi, who succumbed to his illness while the case was being heard.[27] The verdict in the appeal was a great victory for C. R. Das, whom Jenkins singled out for special praise. He also had good words for the mainstay of the prosecution, CID inspector Shamsul Alam, whose 'industry and perseverance' in 'mastering the details of this case' were, Jenkins said, 'deserving of great commendation'.[28]

The energetic inspector did not bask long in his glory. On 24 January 1910, after a day of piloting the government's case in the Alipore Appeal Reference, Alam left the courtroom and strode across the veranda. As he reached the staircase a youth named Birendranath Datta Gupta sprang from the crowd, drew a Webley .38 and shot him in the back. The hated detective tumbled down the stairs, mortally wounded. Birendranath dashed from the building and across the courtyard. Finding his path blocked by mounted policemen he fired wildly but was overcome and arrested.[29] His accomplice Satish Sarkar managed to get away from the Court and ran to inform Jatindra Nath Mukherjee, who had arranged the shooting. Jatin directed Satish to tell Aurobindo Ghose.* Running at once to the *Karmayogin* office Satish gave the welcome information to the man who was still regarded as the secret society's supreme leader. According to Nolini Kanta Gupta, Aurobindo was 'very happy' when he received the news.[30]

After a suitable interval the hearing of the Appeal Reference was resumed without the inspector's assistance. For seventeen days Justice Sir Richard Harrington heard the arguments of the barristers and vakils representing Indra Nath Nandi and four others about whose cases the High Court had been divided. The Crown was represented by the newly arrived advocate-general. The case was concluded on 2 February and sixteen days later Justice Harrington delivered his judgment. He upheld the convictions of Biren Sen and Sailen Bose, but reduced their terms of transportation from life to seven years and five years respectively. The three other prisoners, Sushil Sen, Kristo Jiban Sanyal and Indra Nandi were acquitted and released. An astounded F. C. Daly considered the verdict in the case of the bomb-maimed Nandi 'one of the luckiest that ever favoured an obviously guilty person'.[31] Totalling up his Alipore scorecard Daly could not but feel discouraged. Of the thirty-eight persons committed by the

* According to Jadugopal Mukherjee, Satish went first to Abinash Chakrabutty and then to Aurobindo. Prithwindra Mukherjee (a scholar who is Jatin's grandson) wrote in 1971 that Satish told him personally that he went first to Jatin and then Aurobindo. This seems probable, since it is certain that it was Jatin who gave the job of killing Alam to Birendra Nath and Satish (P. Mukherjee 532).

magistrate only half had been convicted by the sessions judge. Of those nineteen only fourteen had to serve their sentences. Three of these received short terms of imprisonment. The other eleven were condemned to 'transportation', the British euphemism for banishment to a penal colony. For Indian convicts this did not mean starting a new life in Georgia or New South Wales but 'penal servitude' in the green hell of the Andaman Islands.

PART FOUR

The Aftermath

22

Exiles

The shooting of Shamsul Alam marked an era in the history of the revolutionary movement in Bengal. The year 1909 had been distinguished by several spectacular terrorist 'actions': the assassination of Ashutosh Biswas in February, the assassination of Sir William Curzon-Wyllie in London in July, an unsuccessful attempt against the viceroy in Ahmedabad in November, and the assassination of M. T. Jackson, district magistrate of Nasik, in December. But the gunning down of the deputy superintendent 'publicly, in daylight, under the eyes of many and in a crowded building', broke 'the silence which had settled on the country' and had immediate repercussions that radically altered the situation in Bengal. Writing in *Karmayogin* a few days afterwards Aurobindo said that he could 'feel a menace in the air from above and below'—from the government and from the terrorist societies —and could 'foresee the clash of iron and inexorable forces in whose collision all hope of peaceful Nationalism will disappear, if not for ever, yet for a long, a disastrously long season.'[1] In the paper's next issue Aurobindo returned to the same theme. 'An organized party of armed Revolution in Indian politics' was now 'a recognized factor in the situation'. It had arisen because of the failure of the national movement: 'In five years [from the beginning of the movement in 1905] everything has been struck to the earth. Boycott has almost disappeared, Swadeshi languishes under sentence of arrest, Arbitration died still-born, National Education is committing suicide.' He and others could only look with amazement 'on the ruins of the work our labour and our sacrifice erected'. And on those ruins grim, wild-eyed, pitiless to itself and to others, mocking at death and defeat with its raucous and careless laughter Revolution rises repeating the language of the old-world insurgents, cherishing a desperate hope which modern conditions deny, grasping at weapons which the Slav and the Celt have brought into political warfare.[2]

Aurobindo could not of course express all his ideas on this subject in the columns of a newspaper. But by laying special stress on one point in his article he demonstrated that his thinking had undergone a fundamental change. It was necessary to point out, he wrote, 'the immense difference between Indian conditions in modern times and the historical precedents on which the revolutionists rely'. In other words the successes of the Irish and Russian terrorists could not be duplicated in India. The military resources at the government's disposal were too great. Already the Anglo-Indian press was crying for retaliatory measures. Eventually the government would be forced to respond. Aurobindo did not 'believe in a remedial system which suppresses symptoms and leaves the roots untouched'; but given current conditions all he could do was 'to stand aside and let the physician try his system'. So long as the way 'to healthy political development in India' was 'barred by the legislator and the Terrorist', he would abstain from 'comment on current Indian politics'.[3]

Four days later the 'legislator' finalized his first bar: the Indian Press Act of 1910. Under the provisions of this measure printers and publishers were made liable to deposit a security that could be seized if they printed 'obnoxious matter', the nature of which could be determined by the government.[4] This together with the extension of the Seditious Meetings Act and the Indian Criminal Law Amendment Act effectively interdicted the free expression of opinion in the press or on the platform.

The day after the Press Act was passed the government announced the release of the nine deportees. But at the same moment the Government of Bengal, shaken by Alam's assassination and the continuing wave of terrorism, was preparing a file recommending the deportation of fifty-three 'leading agitators' of the province.[5] Aurobindo was of course on the list. It was quite a turnabout for Sir Edward Baker, who seven months earlier had been unwilling to recommend the deportation of Aurobindo alone. This time however the Government of India, which in July had been anxious to see Aurobindo deported, insisted 'on legal procedure'. In January Home Secretary Stuart had asked the Government of Bengal to investigate the possibility of prosecuting Aurobindo for sedition for articles published in *Karmayogin*. On 12 February Bengal's advocate-general gave his opinion that a prosecution had a good chance of success and Baker's aides began preparing the government's case.[6] A month later Baker gave sanction to prosecute. A warrant was issued but could not be served, for Aurobindo had left the province.

Sometime after 15 February one of Aurobindo's associates came to the *Karmayogin* office and warned him that the government planned to deport him. After a moment's reflection he resolved to go to Chandernagore,* the French enclave up the Hooghly that had developed into a centre of anti-British activity. He departed from Calcutta that night and reached Chandernagore early the next morning. His old comrade and fellow-accused Charu Chandra Roy refused to take him in, so he took refuge with Motilal Roy, the leader of another faction of revolutionaries. After a stay of about a month Aurobindo left Chandernagore for Pondicherry, another parcel of French territory situated a hundred miles south of Madras. He intended to stay in this asylum for a year or two at most. As it turned out he remained the rest of his life.

Four months before Aurobindo began his voluntary exile from British India, his brother and several others became exiles of another sort against their will. During the hearing of their appeal the convicted Alipore prisoners had been lodged in the 44 degrees. Barin and Ullaskar had the distinction of occupying two of the block's first cells, which were reserved for prisoners condemned to death. The others spent the day carding jute, but were permitted to leave their cells for eating, bathing and exercise. Barin and Ullaskar, confined all day to their cells, had nothing to do but dwell on their impending doom, fearing death and yet longing for its release. Encouraged by Aurobindo, with whom he communicated by surreptitious notes, Barin threw himself into the practice of yoga. Soon he was passing much of the day in meditation.[7] The only people he spoke to were the jail superintendent, who wanted

* Aurobindo himself said he received an *adesh* (command from God) to go to Chandernagore. In the present context the source of the impulsion is of no particular importance. I have discussed the question of the *adesh* at some length in *A&R* 11 (1987): 220–24.

to learn yoga, and the head warder, who delivered sermons on the Supreme Father and the repentance of sinners. On 23 November Barin and Ullaskar learned that they would not be executed. Those of their associates whose sentences of transportation or imprisonment were confirmed were taken off jute-carding. The authorities did not want them to escape punishment by hanging themselves.[8]

On the morning of 12 December seven prisoners were roused from sleep and herded into the courtyard of Alipore jail. Clad only in short-sleeved kurtas and knee-length dhotis, they sat shivering by the prison gate. Around their necks were iron halters from which dangled wooden identification 'tickets'; around their ankles were iron bar-fetters. Seeing each other in this state, it was all they could do to keep from laughing. At length they were ordered into the van. As before, as soon as the doors were closed they all started talking at once. But this time they were bound not for the Alipore courts but for the docks at Kidderpore. Here they were put on board the S. S. *Maharaja*, the ship that plied the 'black waters' between the mainland and the Andamans. The seven Alipore prisoners who were making the voyage were Barin Ghose, Ullaskar Dutt, Hem Chandra Das, Indu Bhusan Roy, Bibhuti Bhusan Sarkar, Hrishikesh Kanjilal and Abinash Chandra Bhattacharya. Three of their companions—Upendranath Banerjee, Sudhir Sarkar and Paresh Mallick—had been left behind in Calcutta on account of illness. Two of these joined the others after six weeks. And a month later, after the hearing of the Reference, Biren Sen raised the number of Bomb Case convicts in the Andaman Islands to ten.*

The six-hundred mile voyage from Calcutta to Port Blair took four days. The pioneers spent most of the time in the hold, their handcuffs fastened to a chain. The food was perhaps the worst they had ever eaten. Using the toilet meant squatting over a bucket in full sight of everyone else. But all was not misery and degradation. Through a porthole they could see a piece of the ocean and the irrepressible Hem and Ullaskar displayed their talents as singers and comedians. On the morning of the fourth day they were taken on deck, where they got their first glimpse of the

* In their accounts of life in the Andamans, Barin and Upen spoke of only ten Bomb Case prisoners. Neither of them mentioned Paresh Mallick, who apparently was not transported.

beautiful hills of South Andaman Island. 'As yet,' one of them later commented, 'we knew nothing about the soul of the place.'[9]

Before the coming of the British the Andaman archipelago was inhabited only by fierce tribes of hunter-gatherers. Some eight to ten thousand of these men and women lived on the islands in 1910. They had never signed a treaty with the British. Adept with bow and arrow, they would shoot at any alien they encountered. But few of these 'savages' were seen in the neighbourhood of Port Blair. There in the prison and surrounding settlements lived fourteen thousand prisoners, most of them male, and a free population of two thousand. The colony had first been used for detention after the Revolt of 1857, but since 1863 ordinary prisoners had predominated over rebels. Each year the *Maharaja* brought some twelve hundred more, most of them dacoits and murderers. Before the arrival of the men from Alipore the colony had received no political prisoners for a number of years. As the first to be transported in a terrorist case they were accorded special treatment. The jail officers tried to cow these 'anarchists' down with a great show of fetters and regulations. They did not realize that the anarchists were much more frightened than they, and with better reason.

After a week in quarantine the prisoners were taken to the famous Cellular Jail, a unique monument in the annals of penology. From a looming central watchtower radiated seven blocks of cells—only cells and no barracks, hence the name. After registration the new inmates were introduced to the jailor, Mr Barry. He told them, 'If you disobey me, may God help you, at least I will not, that is certain. Remember also that God does not come within three miles of Port Blair.'[10] Thus initiated the prisoners were divested of their fetters and issued prison dress and vessels. After a meal served on rusty, oil-smeared plates, they were marched off to Block No. 5. Here each of the 'bombers' was assigned a separate cell. Between them were four or five cells holding ordinary prisoners. The warders had strict orders not to allow the Bengalis to talk with one another. After a few days the prison blacksmith fastened rings around their necks from which dangled their new 'tickets' like bullocks' bells. These tags were inscribed with their numbers, dates of conviction and terms of sentence. Their circular shape declared that the wearers had been convicted of a crime against the state. Murderers wore rectangular tickets; those who attempted escape, triangular.

The next morning the newcomers were taken for physical examinations. They did not know their fates hung on the result. A week later when they went to Barry for work-assignment, he distributed tasks according to the doctor's ratings. The economy of the Andamans revolved around the fruit of the coconut-palm. To turn this plentiful crop to profit the authorities had at their disposal a glut of the cheapest possible labour. These slaves—for the prisoners were nothing but that—were given one of three toils: rope-making for the weakest, coir-pounding for the sturdy and oil-pressing for the brawny or disobedient. Rope-making, to which Barin and Abinash were assigned, consisted of twisting coir-fibres into progressively larger 'wicks', which ultimately were plaited into ropes. It was, Barin said, a skill to be learned like any other. If the prisoner managed to produce three pounds of rope by the end of the day he could go back to his cell without being punished and enjoy his usual ration. The coir-pounders had it much worse. Each was given the husks of twenty coconuts that had to be beaten with a mallet until the fibres of coir came loose. Two pounds of this fluffy material had to be produced before evening. It was, Sudhir Sarkar explained, 'a really tough job'; sometimes 'we could not even close our bruised and stiffened palms in order to put a morsel in our mouths'. But this was nothing compared to the sufferings of the oil-pressers. Yoked to millstones like bullocks or horses, men assigned this work had to trudge around in circles from six in the morning till six in the evening. During this period they had to turn out thirty pounds of oil. The quota for bullocks was sixteen.[11] So terrible was the oil-presser's lot that even cultured Brahmins used to beg to be given the work of scavenger instead. All in all, observed Barin, 'if the sheer weight of punishment were taken into consideration, we should stand as far bigger avatars than Ram Chandra. If anybody does not admit this', he added, 'I would earnestly request him to pay a visit to Mr. Barry's kingdom and do the oil-grinding and coir-pounding for a week only. One week would be sufficient to make him feel what another avatar felt on the cross.'[12]

During the first six months of their imprisonment the Alipore convicts were spared the agonies of oil-pressing. But they enjoyed in full the thousand petty torments of prison life. Everything had to be done to order: working, eating, stripping, bathing, defecating. The sadistic guards took pleasure in making them dance at their command and then showering them with abuse. Bribery was the only way to placate these demons. After the head warder of his block had polished off Barin's special ration of milk, he would wipe his beard, smack his lips and exclaim, 'What a wonderful thing God has created!'[13] Disobedience was punished with reduced rations, then bar-fetters or 'separate confinement'. There was no possibility of appeal to the authorities for ill-treatment. Once when Upen was serving a stretch of separate confinement he had a heated exchange with one of the warders. The man grabbed his neck-ring and slammed his head against the bars. This filled Upen 'with such a blind rage' that he retaliated the only way he could. Seizing his tormenter's hand he 'bit it till it ran blood'. There would have been more trouble if a sympathetic petty officer had not hushed up the incident. In the face of such oppression most of the 'politicals' stuck together and helped each other out whenever they could. But most of the ordinary prisoners were bad to begin with and had been further corrupted by years of imprisonment. They could punish anyone they disliked by stealing his quota of work or reporting him for a minor infraction. And in the unnatural environment of the colony every form of moral depravity flourished.

Towards the end of 1910 a number of political prisoners arrived from Maharashtra. The newcomers and the Bengalis did not get along very well, being divided by provincial rivalry and political factionalism. Around the same time a new superintendent decided that it was time for the Bengalis to take up oil-pressing. They did their best for a number of days until at last the infirm Abinash broke down. It was only with the help of Indu Bhusan that he was able to fulfil his quota. Another man who found the oil-mill not to his liking was the Punjabi nationalist editor Nanda Gopal. He refused to fulfil his quota and was punished with fetters and confinement. The politicals struck work in sympathy. The authorities resorted to every form of punishment they knew: penal diet, increased quotas, solitary confinement and fettering to the wall. Weakened by fasting and lack of exercise the prisoners fell prey to the diseases endemic to the colony: malaria, dysentery and so forth. At length the authorities relented. On the occasion of the Coronation Durbar of 1911 they sent some of the Bengalis to work in the islands' 'settlements'. This turned out to be more difficult than oil-pressing, with the additional problems of stolen rations, exposure to the elements and non-existent medical care. One by one all of the prisoners came back to Cellular Jail, where conditions remained unbearable.

In April 1912 Indu Bhusan, fed up with the humiliations of jail life, made a noose with his shirt and hanged himself.[14] Two months later Ullaskar Dutt went mad overnight after developing a fever while fettered to the wall of his cell. The politicals again struck work. An important figure in this phase of the strike was Nani Gopal Mukherji, a Bengali terrorist who had been sent to the colony after attempting to kill G. C. Denham of the Calcutta CID. The teenager went on a hunger-strike and stuck to it for more than a month. Even in his emaciated state the authorities did not hesitate to fetter him to the wall. News of Indu Bhusan's death, Ullaskar's insanity and Nani Gopal's sufferings eventually found their way to the mainland. The Calcutta press launched a campaign against the prisoners' inhuman treatment. A commission was sent to investigate. At this time Charles Tegart of the CID came to interrogate the prisoners. Offered reduced sentences in exchange for information, some of the Alipore prisoners gave fairly extensive statements. But Hem Das remained as uncommunicative as ever. Questioned about bomb-making he replied that all he knew about the subject he had picked up from the testimony of Major Smallwood, the expert witness at Alipore.[15]

As a result of the investigation the political prisoners' conditions were improved. The 'term convicts', those who had been sentenced to a term less than life, were sent back to India and confined in conventional prisons. (The insane Ullaskar had already been sent to an asylum in Madras.) The only Alipore convicts left on the islands were Barin, Upen and Hem. These three were promised the privileges enjoyed by ordinary convicts, such as the right to cook their own food. And after ten years their cases would be reconsidered.

During the early part of the First World War the prisoners prayed for a German victory. Perhaps the enemies of Britain would invade the islands and free them! Instead of liberators came more captives: four dozen Sikhs arrested in the 'Ghadr conspiracy' and fifteen or twenty Bengalis. After a period of relative quiet Port Blair again was a lively place. The Sikhs did not appreciate the jail food and discipline and before long many struck work. Several died of diseases contracted during the strike. Anywhere else,

Upen commented, this sort of thing would have created an uproar, 'but in Port Blair it was an everyday affair.'[16]

During the War the superintendent sometimes talked politics with the Bengalis. They used the occasion to let him know just what they thought of the British government. One day the jailor told Upen that the superintendent was noting their opinions in the reports he sent to the mainland. These would be used to determine the suitability of setting them free in the amnesty that might follow a British victory. Upen thought about it and decided that prison was not the best place to ventilate his views on British imperialism. The next time he and the superintendent had a talk he spoke mostly about the villainy of the Germans. The superintendent was impressed by his change of heart. Since the strike of 1912 the Bengali prisoners had generally been co-operative and had been rewarded with light and useful work. Hem helped out with a geographical survey of the islands; Barin worked in the prison library. All of them got good marks in their annual reports, and in February 1919 the superintendent recommended their release. Reluctantly the Government of Bengal agreed.[17] On 23 December 1919 the king gave his Royal Assent to a Government of India Act granting amnesty to selected political prisoners. There followed a number of anxious weeks while the convicts awaited developments. Finally in January several prisoners, among them Barin, Upen and Hem, were told that they would be sent to the mainland and released. Early in February they boarded a ship which carried them to the same Kidderpore docks from which they had left for the Andamans ten years earlier. From Kidderpore they were taken under guard to Alipore jail. After the formalities of release had been completed the superintendent asked them if they had a place to spend the night. They did not but replied that they did and a moment later they found themselves free men in the streets of Calcutta.

23

After Alipore

Eardley Norton left Calcutta as soon as the arguments in the Alipore Bomb Case Appeal had been heard. On 3 November 1909 he wrote to F. W. Duke from the Hôtel Meurice in Paris asking if Sir Edward Baker would recommend him for 'silk'—the robes of King's Counsel—which represented his 'only ambition in life'. Sir Edward was amenable and directed Duke to draft a letter. Addressing the barrister on 28 November, five days after the High Court's judgment had been delivered, the chief secretary expressed 'high appreciation for your services to Government in piloting the very complicated and difficult Alipore conspiracy case to a successful conclusion. It was', Duke added, 'a prosecution of a new order and probably of a more serious character than we have ever had in Bengal.'[1]

Duke's letter was a thoughtful gesture on the part of the Government of Bengal, especially considering the fact that the outcome of the trial was a disappointment to many. Even Duke was lukewarm when he sent Norton's request to Baker, commenting only that the trial had had a 'fairly successful issue'. Two months later, when the Chief Secretary proposed the deportation of fifty-three Bengalis, he admitted that if 'first Alipore Bomb Case [had] resulted in a more complete success', it would have been followed by another case in which among others Abinash Chandra Chakrabutty would have been arraigned.[2] As it was this case was allowed to drop and the fortunate Abinash escaped prosecution for the second time in six months.

The partial success of the Alipore Bomb Trial continued to haunt the Bengal Government for a number of years. In 1917 J. C. Nixon, author of the official *Account of the Revolutionary*

Organizations in Bengal other than the Dacca Anushilan Samiti, wrote that while the convictions dealt a 'severe blow' to the terrorist organization, 'it cannot be said that the heart of the movement was crushed', 'inasmuch as Arabinda Ghosh . . . was acquitted'. Nixon went on to observe: 'during the three years following the arrests in the Alipore case, what is known as Western Bengal passed through a phase of very severe anarchical crime'. There were, Nixon thought, 'six causes which contributed to this' development, of which the first three were: '(1) The protracted nature of the trial and the publicity it gave to revolutionary methods and to the ostensible strength of the conspiracy. (2) The character of martyrdom which was popularly given to the accused, and particularly to those who had been hanged for murder. (3) The still violent attitude of the newspapers.'[3] It is clear that the confessions of Barin and his confederates and the self-sacrifice of Kanailal and Khudiram had not been in vain.

Despite Nixon's gloomy assessment, his ICS colleague J. C. Ker, also writing in 1917, was able to view the results of the trial in a sufficiently positive light to characterize it as a 'success'. The eradication of the Maniktola society and the imprisonment of most of its leaders had, after all, resulted in the break up of 'the Calcutta branch of the revolutionary movement for the time'. But it could not be denied that this did not result in a cessation of terrorist activity in the province. On the contrary there was an upsurge, emanating at first mostly from Dacca, where (as Ker observed) 'the Anushilan Samiti was becoming active and dangerous'. West Bengal lagged behind for a while but then rebounded with new vigour. The two nodes of activity in this part of the province were the society based in Chandernagore and a more amorphous group that as yet had neither headquarters nor name, but would soon become known as the Jugantar Party. All three of these organizations were related to the Maniktola society: the Dacca Anushilan as a sister, the Jugantar Party as a daughter and the Chandernagore group as a little of each. An index of their indebtedness to the original organization set up by Jatin Banerji and Aurobindo Ghose in 1902 is the fact that both Jugantar and Anushilan claimed Aurobindo as founder or co-founder and one section of the Chandernagore group regarded him as its head.[4]

The Calcutta Anushilan Samiti was outlawed in October 1909

and thereafter declined in importance. The Dacca branch remained strong despite its earlier proscription and in 1910 it moved its headquarters to Calcutta.[5] From this point onwards the name Anushilan Samiti was applied to the all-Bengal organization that grew out of the Dacca branch. The formation and activities of the Dacca Anushilan have been referred to often in previous chapters. From the first the personality of Pulin Behari Das was impressed upon his creation, giving it the character it kept till the end: tight discipline and rigid organization. The government made many attempts to get rid of Pulin, first by deporting him, then by arresting him in the Dacca Conspiracy Case and finally by transporting him to the Andamans. It is a tribute to his methods that the group he established not only survived but flourished. But Pulin's authoritarian methods did not appeal to all prospective terrorists. The loose organization favoured by Barin Ghose and others was in many ways more congenial to the Bengali temperament. With Barin this looseness led to negligence that resulted in the downfall of him and his associates: but in more capable hands flexible leadership had better results. The greatest exponent of this style of command was Jatindra Nath Mukherjee, who became the leader of the West Bengal organization after the Muraripukur debacle. Jatin probably was behind the shooting of Nandalal Banerjee and Ashutosh Biswas in 1908 and 1909 and he unquestionably instigated the assassination of Shamsul Alam in January 1910. Before being executed on 21 February of that year, Shamsul's assailant Birendranath Datta Gupta mentioned Jatin and other unnamed 'leaders' (Aurobindo obviously being one) as cognizant of the murder plot. This led to Jatin's arrest and prosecution in the Howrah Conspiracy Case, a long and complex trial from which he was eventually discharged.[6]

It was during the hearing of the Howrah Conspiracy Case that the name 'Jugantar gang' was first publicly used; but the term already had a history. After the split between Barin and Nikhileswar Roy Maulick over the running of *Jugantar* in the summer of 1907, those who remained on the staff of the paper became known as the '*Jugantar* group'.[7] This term was picked up by the police, who used it first to designate Barin's rather than Nikhileswar's faction. In a letter written just before the Maniktola arrests, the chief secretary of the Bengal Government referred to Barin's secret society as the 'Yugantar Party' and 'Yugantar boys'.[8] A year later, after Barin's society had been eliminated, the same government used 'the Jugantar Gang' to indicate the group that had been publishing *Jugantar* at the time of the arrests and subsequently continued its activities in secret.[9] This 'gang' was given its first complete description by F. W. Duke in his proposal of March 1910 to deport fifty-three persons. The name 'Yugantar Gang', he wrote, could be used to describe 'a large number of people who used constantly to meet at the office of the *Yugantar* paper and even after the dissolution of the paper used to congregate at certain common rendezvous in Calcutta and its suburbs'.[10] Prominent among them were Kartik Dutt and others indicted in the Howrah Case. To distinguish Kartik's group from the other eleven batches in that case, the prosecution referred to it as the Jugantar Gang or Group.[11] The 'gang' so differentiated had in fact no formal existence. What was gradually taking form was a loose federation of revolutionary societies in various parts of Bengal that stood apart from the Dacca Anushilan. In the northern and eastern parts of the province this federation was known to Anushilan as 'the other party' or 'the Company'.[12] Elsewhere it was nameless; but as time passed the court's label was pressed into service and the 'Jugantar Party' was born. By the 1930s the term was so well established that it was used retroactively to refer to the group founded by Aurobindo and Jatin Banerji a quarter-century earlier. Barin himself came to accept this identification, writing of himself and his former associates as 'the first pioneers called the Jugantar Party'. It should be kept in mind, however, that the term 'Jugantar Party' did not come into general use until around 1915, and that the group never had a formal party structure.[13]*

The origins of the Jugantar Party are hard to pin down since, unlike the Anushilan Samiti, it had no formal inauguration. Arun Chandra Guha, a leading member of Jugantar, gave a half-dozen different accounts of its beginnings in his authoritative *First Spark*

* I have gone into such detail concerning the origin and history of the name 'Jugantar (Party)' in order to avoid imprecision in speaking of this historically important but nebulous organization. From this point I will use the name to refer to the party composed of the remnants of the Aurobindo-Barin organization and other non-Anushilan groups in different parts of western and eastern Bengal. It should be remembered however that the name was not in general use until after the period I deal with in this chapter.

of Revolution.[14] The same sort of vagueness is apparent in the accounts of Jadugopal Mukherjee, an important Jugantar leader, in his *Biplabi Jibaner Smriti.*[15] What is clear from both writers' accounts is that Jugantar took form gradually, partly in opposition to Anushilan, though never totally at odds with it. In the beginning the two groups were 'generally on good terms' (in the opinion of the CID's J. E. Armstrong), 'exchanging members from time to time and occasionally acting in co-operation'. But even at this time, despite similarities of origin and aim, the two groups were 'sometimes in rivalry' and this mutually antagonistic attitude soon became the rule.[16] Except for two brief periods Jugantar and Anushilan could not pull together and the later 'history of revolutionary terrorism in Bengal' was largely, as Gopal Haldar has commented, 'the history of wasteful rivalry between these two principal groups'.[17]

In 1910 and 1911 both Anushilan and the still unnamed Jugantar were hamstrung by conspiracy trials. Despite the limited success of the Alipore Bomb Case, the government initiated a number of similar prosecutions because the conspiracy law was the only way it could deal with men suspected of involvement in dacoities and other terrorist crimes. As Ker explained: 'As it was practically impossible as a rule to obtain sufficient evidence to satisfy the courts in specific cases of dacoity, an attempt was made, where the evidence showed that several dacoities were the work of one gang, to prosecute the whole gang for conspiracy, and to rely on the cumulative effect of the information collected on different occasions implicating the same people.'[18] Unfortunately for the government it proved frustratingly difficult to obtain convictions on the count of conspiracy. As the verdicts in the Alipore case showed, the courts were loath to sentence men under Section 121-A unless they could be shown to have participated in overt acts. Until the law was altered to permit summary trials, most conspiracy cases fared ill in the courtroom; but they did enable the police to keep the accused out of action for the duration of the trial.

During 1910 and 1911 Pulin Das and other members of the Dacca Anushilan were involved in the Dacca Conspiracy Case. Ostensibly concerned with several East Bengal dacoities, the case soon 'resolved itself into an investigation of the Anushilan Samiti' in all its aspects. The High Court found that the Samiti was 'a criminal society the object of which was to conspire to wage war against the King-Emperor', but it confirmed the convictions of only fourteen of the forty-four accused.[19] The Howrah Conspiracy Case, heard between March 1910 and April 1911, had a similar outcome: only six of the forty-six men sent up were convicted. As in the Dacca case the cognizable offences were dacoities but the government's purpose in instituting proceedings was to break the back of the West Bengal organization. As it turned out this strategy backfired. During his year-long confinement as an undertrial prisoner, Jatin Mukherjee was able to bring together the 'disjointed threads of the organization', becoming after his release the unchallenged leader of a more coherent party.[20] Both the Howrah and Dacca cases were followed by related prosecutions: the Khulna Conspiracy Case in western Bengal and the Barisal Conspiracy Case in the East. Neither of these was a notable success for the Government, though in Barisal plea-bargaining lead to the imprisonment of twelve men while the trial kept the eastern branch of Anushilan busy until the beginning of 1914.[21]

During this period of legal embarrassment for Anushilan and Jugantar the centre of Bengal's revolutionary activity shifted to Chandernagore. Charu Chandra Roy, the founder of the party in the French enclave, was still regarded as its overall head; but by 1911 most decisions were being taken by Srish Ghose and Motilal Roy. Both these men had had contacts with the Maniktola society. Srish, it will be recalled, arranged for the supply of the pistols that were used to kill Narendra Nath Goswami. Motilal was Aurobindo's host during the latter's stay in Chandernagore and subsequently kept in touch with the exiled leader. Another member of the Chandernagore group was Suresh Dutta, a college chemistry professor who helped make Chandernagore the principal centre of bomb manufacture in India. One of Suresh's first creations was the bomb used by Nani Gopal Mukherjee in his bid to kill Denham of the Special Branch in March 1911.[22] A year and a half later, on 13 December 1912, another bomb made in Chandernagore was used in an attempt against Abdur Rahman, the Midnapore informer. This was a prelude to an even more daring action.

Since the formation of the revolutionary party the dream of the terrorists had been to assassinate a really important official. What better target could there be than the viceroy and what better occasion than an ostentatious ceremony? On 23 December 1912 Lord Hardinge was scheduled to make his state entry into the newly designated capital of Delhi. Srish and other Chandernagore terrorists resolved to take advantage of this opportunity. One of their associates was Rash Behari Bose, a relative of Srish's who like him had been in contact with Barin's society. After the arrests at the Garden, Rash Behari went to Dehra Dun and got a job as a clerk in the Imperial Forestry Institute. Here he discharged his duties assiduously, impressing his British employers with his 'exemplary character'. At the same time he got in touch with a party of Punjabi revolutionaries in Lahore. Towards the end of 1911 Rash Behari paid a visit to Chandernagore. During a conversation Srish brought up the idea of killing Lord Hardinge. Rash Behari volunteered for the job, declaring: 'Better to shoot an elephant than to get your hands dirty swatting flies.' Motilal introduced him to two aspiring assassins. Rash Behari chose one of them, twenty-one-year-old Basanta Kumar Biswas, and took him back with him to Dehra Dun. During the next twelve months Rash Behari gave Basanta the political indoctrination and practical training he needed to carry out his mission. As the date of the state entry approached, Rash Behari took Basanta to Lahore and arranged for him to stay with his Punjabi associates. On 22 December, the two men met in Delhi. Rash Behari brought a picric-acid bomb made by Suresh Dutta using a shell cast by Amritlal Hazra of Anushilan. On the 23rd Rash Behari and Basanta went to the gaily decorated Chandni Chowk, the city's principal thoroughfare. Dressed in woman's clothing, Basanta went to a rooftop overlooking the viceroy's route that was reserved for ladies. According to legend, he told the other spectators that his name was Lakshmibai—an allusion to the famous Rani of Jhansi.[23]

The state entry was planned to match the imperial durbars in pomp and brilliance. Lord Hardinge and Lady Hardinge, like Lord Lytton and Lady Lytton thirty-five years earlier, were seated in a howdah on the back of a richly caparisoned elephant. As the procession passed the rooftop where 'Lakshmibai' was waiting, a bomb sailed down and exploded behind the viceroy. An Indian attendant who was sitting there was killed at once. Lord Hardinge was gravely injured but he ordered the procession to proceed. It was not until Lady Hardinge saw that her husband was semiconscious and the attendant dead that she gave the order to stop. The viceroy was taken to the hospital, where it was discovered that several shell-fragments had entered his body. It took him a number of months to recover.[24]

As soon as his job was done Basanta dashed down to the street, threw off his sari and disappeared into the crowd. Rash Behari also managed to escape. Back in Dehra Dun the exemplary clerk attended a condolence meeting for the viceroy, himself proposing the president to the chair. Basanta returned to Punjab where he continued his terrorist activities. In 1913 he placed a bomb near Lahore's European club, which killed an Indian messenger who cycled over it. Inquiries set in motion by the incident led to the arrest of Basanta and some of his associates. In the resulting trial he and two others were found guilty of murder and sentenced to death.[25]

Developments after 1912 can only be sketched in brief. In November 1913 the police arrested Amritlal Hazra and three others in Raja Bazar, Calcutta. The mystery of the common origin of the bombs used against Denham, Abdur Rahman and the viceroy was solved. But the arrests did little to stop the spread of terrorist violence, particularly in Bengal. In 1914 men of Anushilan and Jugantar were involved in six murders or attempted murders and sixteen dacoities or attempted dacoities in different parts of the province. The first incident of 1914 demonstrated how difficult it was for the authorities to deal with such crimes. On 19 January inspector Nripendra Nath Ghose was shot dead in Shobha Bazar, Calcutta. The deed was witnessed by numerous persons, including some members of the police. One of the assailants, Nirmal Kanta Roy, was captured moments after the shooting. When arrested he was carrying a revolver with spent cartridges in its chambers. In the resulting trial he was defended by two lawyers better known as antagonists: Eardley Norton and C. R. Das. Norton, who never did get his 'silk', had settled in Calcutta and become a leading member of the Bar. Das, whose career had skyrocketed after his Alipore successes, was now the most successful barrister in the metropolis. In the Nirmal Roy Case the two men had to deal with a crushing burden of evidence ably marshalled by the advocate-general S. P. Sinha. But by discrediting key witnesses they were able to obtain acquittals in two successive trials and ultimately to force Sinha to enter *nolle proseque* ('I will not prosecute') on behalf of the Crown.[26]

Accepting the time-honoured wisdom of the formula 'the enemy of my enemy is my friend', Indian revolutionaries viewed the outbreak of the First World War as a God-given opportunity. The leaders of the terrorist movement had always dreamed of transforming it into a militant uprising. This was Aurobindo's original idea and before the secret societies turned to terrorism he and others had made some efforts to spread disaffection in the army. Even during the trial of the Alipore Bomb Case, Bengali revolutionaries made 'an organized attempt to tamper with the loyalty' of the 10th Jats, a regiment then stationed at Alipore. The government viewed this development with the utmost alarm and disciplined the offenders severely.[27] Few efforts in this direction were made over the next four years, but in 1914 a group of Sikh militants, working together with Rash Behari Bose and Vishnu Ganesh Pinglay, formulated an ambitious plan for simultaneous risings to take place in Punjab and elsewhere in February 1915. Unfortunately for the conspirators the plan leaked out at the last moment. No risings took place except in Singapore, where the isolated troops were quickly subdued. Many of the participating Sikhs were tried and sentenced to transportation. Pinglay was caught and condemned to death while the elusive Rash Behari managed to give the police the slip and eventually made his way to Japan.[28] His attempts to enlist the help of that country had little immediate result, but a quarter-century later bore fruit in vastly changed global circumstances.

During the First World War Indian hopes for foreign help were pinned not on Japan but Germany. Even before 1914 nationalists from different parts of the country had established themselves in Berlin, Paris, San Francisco and other places, where they worked in different ways to spread propaganda, obtain arms and collect money. The Berlin group succeeded in making contact with the German Foreign Office and obtained a promise of monetary and material assistance. It is beyond the scope of this book to trace the ramifications of the resulting 'Indo-German Plot'. It will be enough to suggest its seriousness, extent and final failure by looking briefly at an important episode involving members of the Jugantar group.

After his release from the Howrah Conspiracy Case in 1910 Jatin Mukherjee went to Jessore and set himself up as a law-abiding contractor. For the next two years he and his associates worked quietly to rebuild the Jugantar organization. Under Jatin's direction revolutionaries like Amarendra Nath Chatterjee (a man previously associated with Upendranath Banerjee and Aurobindo Ghose) set up dummy enterprises in Calcutta and the districts to serve as fronts for the transmission of funds and information. After the War broke out Jatin and his friends laid plans for procuring German money and arms. Jatin's lieutenant Narendra Nath Bhattacharya went to Batavia (Jakarta) to make arrangements for money to be sent to Calcutta in the name of Harry and Sons, a dummy Jugantar enterprise. Sometime earlier a subsidiary of Harry and Sons had been established in Balasore, Orissa, near one of the projected sites for the landing of German matériel. In 1915 Jatin moved to a village near Balasore to await the arrival of one of the hoped-for shipments. Searches in Calcutta led the police to Orissa, where they obtained information on Jatin's whereabouts. Pursued by a well-armed body of police, Jatin and his companions took refuge in the jungle. On 16 September they were surrounded by their adversaries. A battle ensued, the Bengalis firing with Mauser pistols, the government's vastly superior forces answering with rifles. Three of the Bengalis including Jatin were hit. Chitta Priya Roy Chaudhuri died on the spot, Jatin the following day. In his report to the government G. C. Denham of the Special Branch paid tribute to Jatin by calling him 'perhaps the boldest and the most actively dangerous of all Bengal revolutionaries'.[29]

The discovery of the wartime conspiracies prompted the imperial government to pass the Defence of India Act, under which hundreds of suspected terrorists were interned without trial for the duration of the war. This did not prevent the occurrence of numerous murders, dacoities and other 'actions'. Most of these were carried out by Anushilan, which as usual was acting in opposition to its rival. (Jugantar thought such isolated operations would be a needless and conspicuous distraction while the Indo-German plot was being hatched.) Eventually the internments under the act had the desired effect. There were thirty murders and dacoities in Bengal in 1915, twenty in 1916 and only seven in 1917.[30] The success of the programme convinced the government that some of the provisions of the act should be continued even after the war. In July 1918 a committee was constituted 'to investigate and report on the nature and extent of the criminal conspiracies connected with the revolutionary movement in India', 'to examine the difficulties' that these conspiracies had created and 'to advise as to legislation, if any, necessary to enable Government to deal effectively with them'. The report of the committee, named after its president, Mr Justice Rowlatt, was issued towards the end of 1918. It traced the growth of 'revolutionary crime' from the Chapekars in Poona and Barin Ghose in Calcutta to the Indo-German plot and beyond. It recommended, briefly, that the wartime emergency measures should be continued. In 1919 some of the committee's recommendations were embodied in the so-called Rowlatt Act. The agitation against this measure led to the Non-Co-operation Movement, which marked the emergence of M. K. Gandhi as India's foremost political leader.

From this point onwards non-violent mass protest was the principal strategy of the Indian national movement; but terrorism remained always a significant undercurrent. Between 1918 and 1947 there were three main outbreaks of revolutionary violence: the North Indian eruption of 1920–30 in which Chandrashekhar Azad and Bhagat Singh played prominent roles, the Bengali surge of 1930–33 which culminated in the Chittagong Armory Raid, and the country-wide upheaval that followed the arrest of Gandhi and other Congress leaders in 1942. That same year the terrorists' old dream of taking part in a militant uprising came closer to fulfilment when Rash Behari Bose announced the formation of the Indian National Army (INA). Made up of Indian soldiers captured by the Japanese in South-East Asia and by other Indian men and women of the region, the INA, under the leadership of Subhas Chandra Bose, played a minor role in the Japanese invasion of Assam. It is a sign of the enduring influence of the pioneers of the revolutionary movement that when Rash Behari Bose issued a series of open letters explaining his actions as 'Representative of Indians in Greater East Asia', the first one addressed to an individual was a 'salute to Sri Aurobindo', 'whose inspiring call' was responsible for 'the birth of positive Indian nationalism'.[31]

24

Conclusion: Terrorism and the Struggle for Freedom

The Alipore Bomb Conspiracy Trial was regarded by contemporaries as a landmark in at least three respects. The event that brought it about was 'the first occasion in which an Indian had used this product of modern science [the bomb] with murderous effect'; the men who plotted that attack constituted 'the first criminal conspiracy of any magnitude that the revolutionary party started'; and the resulting trial was 'the first State Trial of any magnitude in India'.[1] Lord Minto underlined the significance of the conspiracy when he wrote to the Secretary of State: 'We must remember that up to the murders at Muzufferpore we thought we were dealing with sedition as represented by treasonable speeches and writings, but that the Manicktola Garden discoveries shed an entirely new light on the dangers we had to face.'[2] Officials in later viceroyalties continued to assign priority to the Alipore conspiracy and trial. Most official histories of terrorism prepared by the Government of Bengal began with a description of the work of Aurobindo and Barin Ghose and their associates. J. C. Ker's authoritative *Political Trouble in India 1907 to 1917* devoted an entire twenty-page chapter to what Ker called 'The Manicktola Bomb Conspiracy' —more space than he gave to any other conspiracy. Reflecting this emphasis the Rowlatt committee's celebrated *Report on Revolutionary Conspiracies in India* began its treatment of Bengal with Barin's 'first campaign' and devoted a whole section to the Muzaffarpur murders and Alipore trial.[3]

Basing themselves largely on these and other official sources, most English-language historians of the Indian freedom movement have given considerable attention to the Alipore conspiracy and trial. Writers in Indian languages, memorialists as well as academics, have also treated them in detail. But even without this scholarly attention the Alipore trial would remain perhaps the best known conspiracy trial of the freedom movement period. A fairly complete selection of the court proceedings was published in 1922; in the next decade it was selected as one of ten *Notable Indian Trials*. Since then numerous commemoratory articles have appeared in the Indian popular press.[4] The trial's renown is due in part to its historical priority but perhaps more to the drama of its events both inside and outside the courtroom. Two of the principal actors, Aurobindo Ghose and C. R. Das, are famous in their own right as politicians of the pre-Gandhian era. Aurobindo has also won international renown as a philosopher and yogi. Many of the subordinate figures have been forgotten, but few of the hundreds of revolutionaries who gave their lives for the country have a stronger hold on the imagination of the Indian people than Khudiram Bose and Kanailal Dutt.

The priority and celebrity of the Alipore conspiracy are enough to justify the detailed reconstruction in the foregoing chapters; but to assess its historical significance it is necessary to view it in perspective. The Maniktola conspirators were active for only two years, from the beginning of 1906 to April 1908. During this period they undertook ten 'actions', with the following results:

ACTIONS UNDERTAKEN BY THE MANIKTOLA SECRET SOCIETY[5]

Year	*Month*	*Place*	*Target*	*Type*	*Result*
1906	?	East Bengal	Fuller	Assassination	Aborted
1906	? August	Rangpur	a widow	Dacoity	Aborted
1907	? August	Bankura	a *mahant*	Dacoity	Aborted
1907	October	Darjeeling	Fraser	Assassination	Aborted
1907	November	Mankundu	Fraser	Derailment	Failure
1907	November	Mankundu	Fraser	Derailment	Aborted
1907	December	Narayangarh	Fraser	Derailment	Failure
1908	January	Calcutta	Kingsford	Assassination	Failure
1908	April	Chandernagore	Tardivel	Assassination	Failure
1908	April	Muzaffarpur	Kingsford	Assassination	Wrong persons killed

Clearly if the conspiracy is judged from the point of view of immediate effectiveness, it would have to be considered a failure. But the conspirators never believed that assassinations and dacoities would themselves bring about India's liberation. Aurobindo's original idea was to prepare for 'an open armed revolution' in which rebel soldiers would join forces with the insurgent populace. He thought it might take thirty years for the men of the country to develop the necessary attitudes and skills. During this period terrorism might have a place as a 'subordinate movement'. Its purpose would be 'to prepare the young men to have some sort of a military training, to kill and get killed.'[6]

Barin Ghose also considered terrorist activity 'a means to educate the people up for facing death and doing anything for their country's sake'.[7] But when he became the active head of the organization, he got the bit of terrorism between his teeth and ran. Aurobindo thought Barin's strategy of attacking officials 'very childish', but (as he said in 1938 in a passage already quoted) he did not rein him in because 'it is not good to check things that have taken a strong shape. For something good may come out of it.'[8]

Something good did come out of the Maniktola catastrophe. The example of the terrorists, publicized by the press, immortalized in song and spread by word of mouth, made revolutionary action an attractive alternative to men and women impatient with the tardy pace of constitutional reform. The bulk of the population, who were never associated with terrorism, condoned or even celebrated the acts of the terrorists. The public reaction to the Muzaffarpur incident and to the shooting of Narendra Nath Goswami make it clear that many people regarded the assassins not as criminals but martyrs to a noble cause.

Any act of political terrorism is meant chiefly as a message to the rulers and its effectiveness can be judged by its influence on government decision-making. Less than a year after the Muzaffarpur incident the British Government enacted the Indian Councils Act (Morley-Minto Reforms). Soon it was 'common talk in Calcutta that the Council reforms and the appointment of the Hon'ble Mr Sinha [to the viceroy's council] were the direct results of the [Alipore] conspiracy. It is said that the Congress begged for twenty years and got nothing, but one year of bombs has brought all this reform.'[9] These claims were of course exaggerated—the Reforms had first been proposed in 1906—but they did contain a kernel of truth. Before May 1908 progress on the proposals was slow and the results unimpressive. The pace accelerated from the moment the Alipore conspiracy was unearthed. Five days after the arrests in the Garden, Morley wrote to Minto: 'We must persevere with liberal and substantial reforms, perhaps wider than those in your original sketch. . . . Reforms may not save the Raj, but if they don't, nothing else will.' Two weeks later Morley informed Minto that British opinion favoured reform: 'The Bomb (here at least) has made old John Bull waken up and rub his eyes; he won't be satisfied with mere Police Vigour (though we may throw him judicious morsels of this sort); he will want rational endeavors to set right whatever may be amiss.' In the same letter he urged the viceroy to appoint an Indian member to his council.[10]

Minto's response was slow and circumspect. He viewed Indian 'anarchism'—as he insisted on calling it—as a law-and-order problem imported from Europe and he refused to admit that the bombs of Bengal were 'the efforts of a people struggling to relieve themselves from an oppressor'.[11] Like many of his contemporaries, Indian as well as British, he believed that 'the maintenance of British rule is necessary for the good of India, and in the interest of the people entrusted to his charge' he was 'determined to suppress all attempts to subvert his authority.'[12] While willing to let the reforms go ahead, he was concerned that a generous response might be seen as an 'ignoble concession to unlawful agitation or to unjustifiable nervousness'.[13] When in July he submitted a draft reform proposal, it was far from being 'liberal and substantial', and Morley's response was immediate and angry: '*India can't wait*', he wrote. 'It [the draft] will have to be extended immensely.'[14] When the final proposals were tabled a half-year later they were much closer to what Morley had intended and, despite the opposition of many in India, were accompanied by the appointment of Sinha to the council.

More important than its effect on any particular decision was the influence of the party of physical force on the course of Indian politics. Even before the existence of terrorism was acknowledged, Extremist politicians were prepared to make use of the leverage it might provide. 'Even diplomacy must have some compelling force behind it to attain its ends,' observed a *Bande Mataram* writer in 1908, and 'peaceful means can succeed only when these imply the ugly alternative of more troublesome and fearful methods, recourse to which the failure of peaceful attempts must inevitably lead to.'[15] Several years had to pass before this leverage could be effectively applied. In the aftermath of the Surat split and the terrorist discoveries, the government virtually stamped out the Extremist Party. For a decade the Moderates had a monopoly on the Congress movement. But eventually the Extremists rejoined the organization and before long succeeded in driving the Moderates out.

By this time the principal Congress leader was M. K. Gandhi. At no time did this apostle of non-violence compromise his ideals by co-operating with terrorists; but he knew that much of his strength came from being regarded by the British as a lesser evil. At the Round Table Conference of 1931, while declaring that he held 'no brief for terrorists', he made it clear that if the government refused to work with him it would have the terrorists to deal with. 'If you will work [with] the Congress for all it is worth you will say good-bye to terrorism, then you will not need terrorism'. But if the government refused to co-operate, the terrorists might get the upper hand and create endless trouble for everyone. It was up to the British to decide: 'Will you not see the writing that these terrorists are writing with their blood? Will you not see that we do not want bread made of wheat, but we want bread made of liberty; and without that liberty there are thousands today who are sworn not to give themselves peace or to give the country peace.'[16]

When Gandhi and other leaders were imprisoned in 1942 the terrorists emerged from the shadows and made the ordinary governance of the country impossible for several weeks. At the same time the Indian National Army was taking form in South-East Asia. Militarily insignificant, the INA's campaign was thrust into prominence after the War when some of its officers were court-martialled. The public outcry against these proceedings together with a localized revolt of the Royal Indian Navy convinced the government that the armed services could no longer be counted on to protect British interests in India. Shattered by the War, Britain had neither the resources nor the will to impose its rule upon India any longer. Within two years it pulled out of the country for good.

In his judgment in the Alipore Bomb Trial, C. P. Beachcroft observed: 'The danger of a conspiracy such as this lies not so much in its prospect of success as in its fruition. When once the poison had entered into the system it is impossible to say where it will break out or how far-reaching will be its effects.'[17] He spoke more prophetically than he knew. During the first two decades of India's independent existence there was little organized terrorism in the country. But during the late sixties left-wing Bengali insurgents began resorting to terrorist methods to achieve their revolutionary aims. The eighties saw the rise of separatist terrorist groups in Punjab, Kashmir and Assam as well as among ethnic Indian Tamils in Sri Lanka. Some of these groups are distinguished by the use of brutal methods, including indiscriminate murder, and by aims that sometimes seem more criminal than political. Writers on terrorism often point out the immense moral gulf that separates European terrorist groups of the nineteenth century, such as the Narodnaya Volya, from contemporary groups like the Baader-Meinhof Gang.[18] A similar abyss would appear to divide the Bengali revolutionaries of the early twentieth century from their less idealistic descendants in contemporary India.

Appendixes

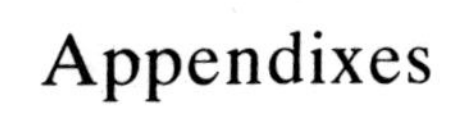

Appendix 1
Textual Notes

1. The prototypal group referred to is the Anushilan Samiti. Its early history and that of its predecessors is very imperfectly documented. Accounts by former participants and observers are vague and contradictory and the government reports (based on hazy information from informers) lack their usual precision. A Government of India file of 1910 states: 'It would appear that in about 1900 P. Mitter [Mitra], Miss Sarala Devi and a Japanese, Okakura, met in Calcutta and founded a secret society, of which one of the principal objects was the assassination of officials and persons who prevented the progress of any society towards its final goal—the independence of India.'[1] This would appear to be an attempt to pin down to a single place and time a series of developments that were actually much less definite: the early efforts of Sarala Devi and Mitra, the influence of Okakura and the gradual turn of the samiti towards terrorism. If the conjectured meeting took place at all (and this is far from certain) it must have been in 1902, the only year before 1912 that Okakura was in India. It should be noted that all Bengali memorialists say that Sarala Devi and P. Mitra were against assassination. The account in the Nixon Report, written six years after Daly's, is more believable: 'At the beginning of 1902 three distinct *akharas* existed in Calcutta respectively associated with the names of—(1) Jatindra Banarji, (2) P. Mitter, (3) Miss Saralabala Ghosal. The second of these was later known as the Calcutta *Anushilan Samiti*, and P. Mitter was its President and Satish Chandra Basu its Secretary.'[2] This evidently refers to the situation around March 1902. The roles assigned in these government records to Sarala Devi, P. Mitra and Okakura are confirmed in general terms by the oral statements by Aurobindo cited below. In a written statement Aurobindo says that 'the special cover used by Mitter's group was association for lathi play which had already been popularised to some extent by Sarala Ghosal in Bengal'.[3]

It is significant that in this passage and in all related passages of his autobiographical writings, Aurobindo never refers to the Anushilan Samiti by name, speaking rather of various small groups without a strong central organization.[4] In this connection it may be noted that Sarala Devi writes of her groups as being separate from Anushilan; that Hem Chandra Das writes of Anushilan as being separate from the Jatin-Aurobindo group, of which he was an early member; and that Abinash Bhattacharya, another member of the same group, writes of the various Anushilan centres as being set up by Satish Bose *after* the foundation of the Upper Circular Road group.[5] Abinash, who was recruited no earlier than the end of 1902, was evidently not fully in the know. But the fact that two members of the Upper Circular Road group thought of Anushilan as a separate organization is significant. It seems clear that the situation in Calcutta around the time of the founding of Anushilan was a good deal more complex than what is projected by the official histories of the Samiti (N. Roy, J. Haldar). In later years Anushilan became a political party. It seems likely that the writers of its history have replaced its inchoate and undocumented origins with a coherent but over-simplified account.

The role played by Okakura in the formation of Anushilan or the groups that preceded it is far from clear. All that can be said with certainty is that he is often mentioned as having something to do with the start of Bengal's first revolutionary secret society. But his part seems to have been short-lived and largely inspirational. He is mentioned in various sources cited in this note, but only one informant, Aurobindo Ghose, gives him any real importance. In two oral statements of 1940, Aurobindo said that Okakura was the founder of the revolutionary party in Bengal.[6] Two years earlier Aurobindo said that the party was started by P. Mitra and Sarala Ghosal under Okakura's inspiration.[7] There are a number of reasons to doubt these statements. To begin with, Aurobindo's knowledge of Okakura was second-hand. There is no evidence that he ever met the Japanese and it is unlikely that he did. (The fact that Pulin Das included Aurobindo in his list of those present at the meeting at the Indian Association Hall is insignificant, since Pulin, who was not himself present, named just about every important nationalist sympathizer in Calcutta.) Aurobindo's remarks were made to contradict statements that he was the be-all and end-all of the movement. It would appear that in attempting to set right this misrepresentation, he attached undue importance to Okakura, who arrived in Calcutta years after Sarala Devi had begun her work.

Three other men who became important in the movement from 1902–3 gave Okakura much less importance than Aurobindo. Barin Ghose speaks of the Japanese along with Rajnarain Bose as an early (and ineffective) precursor of the movement.[8] Since Barin was active in Calcutta less than a year after Okakura's arrival, it is clear that Okakura's influence was quickly forgotten. Hem Chandra Das, writing in the context of a 1903 visit to Calcutta, gives only passing mention to Okakura and scoffed at the idea that Japan had anything to do with India's liberation.[9] Abinash Bhattacharya, who joined the Calcutta society early in 1903, knew nothing at all about Okakura.[10] The statements of these men make it clear at least that Okakura's role, whatever its importance, was of brief duration.

In her biography of Okakura, Horioka speaks nowhere of her subject having any political interests or taking part in political activities in India other than addressing Indian youths on the subject of 'protecting and restoring Asiatic modes [of life]'.[11] In an article published in India, Horioka writes that there is no evidence of Okakura's involvement in Indian politics in any Japanese source, and that without evidence the involvement 'remains unproven'.[12] The impression one gets from Horioka's biography is that Okakura came to India on a religious and artistic mission with the further intention of inviting Vivekananda to Japan. In addition he seems to have been generally disgusted with the art scene in Tokyo and may have been fleeing the unhappiness occasioned by the false report of the death of his former mistress. Okakura spent less than a year in India. After his departure in October 1902 he did not return to India for a decade.

Two writers who have given much importance to Okakura's involvement in Indian politics (in which Nivedita is said to have shared) are Nivedita's biographer-advocates Lizelle Reymond and Sankari Prasad Basu. Reymond, a highly romantic writer, cites mysterious 'reliable sources' to support her claims. We may with Horioka dismiss the claims until the sources are revealed. Basu's work is filled with interesting citations, none of which prove a political involvement on Okakura's part. He admits that Nivedita's letters (his main primary source) suggest no reason for Okakura's visit other than his wish to persuade Vivekananda to come to Japan. He also admits that there is no mention of any revolutionary activities by Okakura in Surendranath Tagore's *Smritikatha*. (Neither is there any mention in Surendranath's 'Kakuzo Okakura'.) Nevertheless in the beginning of his chapter on Okakura, Basu says without hesitation that the main reason for Okakura's visit to India was revolution. Later he writes that he feels certain that Okakura must have come to India for a different reason than the one given in Nivedita's correspondence, namely, to found, with Nivedita, Bengal's revolutionary society.[13] I can find no reason to support these suppositions.

2. Hem Chandra Das refers to the founder of the group only as 'A-babu', whom he describes as one who had known 'K-babu' (certainly Aurobindo Ghose) from the latter's childhood and as the former sub-editor of certain English journals.[14] This description fits Rajnarayan's eldest son Jogindranath Bose and perhaps no one else. In his account of the revolutionary years, Barin Ghose writes: 'In the meantime my two maternal uncles [*mama*s] Jogendra Bose and Satyen Bose formed a secret circle out of a youth group there [in Midnapore].'[15] This passage would appear to support my reading of Hem Chandra. Jogendra is a common variant of Jogindra just as Baren(dra) is of Barin(dra). Barin's relation to Jogin and Satyen was somewhat different (the former was his mother's brother, the latter the son of another brother of his mother) but the word *mama* is flexible enough to apply to both.

Other accounts say that the brothers Jnanendra and Satyendra Bose were the co-founders of the Midnapore society. These two names are the first listed under Midnapore in Denham's chart of Bengal's revolutionary organization in the Daly Report. Sumit Sarkar (citing Hem Chandra's biographer Benoyjiban Ghosh) and Arun Chandra Guha also say that the joint founders of the Midnapore society were Jnanendra and Satyendra Bose.[16] If it is true that A-babu knew Aurobindo from his childhood it does not seem possible that Jnanendra Nath Bose could be A-Babu. (I do not know the date of Jnanendra's birth, but he does not seem to have been much older than his brother Satyendra Nath, who was born in 1882). It is known that Aurobindo's mother's brother Jogindranath knew Aurobindo before he departed for England at the age of seven in 1879.[17] In the same chapter of *Agnijug* in which

Barin mentions Jogen as the founder of the Midnapore society, he speaks of Jnan Bose simply as a brother of Satyen who was also connected with the Midnapore society.[18]

Incidentally, Satyen and Jnan are often referred to as the 'uncles' of Aurobindo and Barin. This is confusing—Aurobindo was ten years older than Satyen—and also technically incorrect. The proper way to state the relationship in English is to say that Aurobindo and Barin were first cousins once removed of Jnan and Satyen. In the text I have referred to Satyen as Aurobindo's 'uncle' (using inverted commas) because of the familiarity of this imprecise term.

While the available evidence seems to indicate that Jogin Bose was A-Babu, that is, the founder of the Midnapore secret society, this does not necessarily mean that he was an ardent and dangerous revolutionary. The references to him in Purani and in D. Roy's *Aurobindo Prasanga* portray him as an amiable avuncular person. Aurobindo's letter to him of 15 August 1902 contains a lot of jokes and no reference to revolutionary work.[19] Aurobindo never spoke of Jogin as a revolutionary (and never, I believe, spoke of Jnan Bose at all). Jogin is not mentioned in any government or police report. He appears in any case to have been dead by November 1907.[20]

3. It is difficult to determine when Barin arrived in Baroda or how long he stayed there. He certainly was in the city before the Ahmedabad Congress of December 1902; not long afterwards he returned to Bengal.[21] Since he seems to have stayed a reasonably long time in Baroda, one would imagine he arrived there at least a month before December. In a statement made to the police in 1908 Barin said that he spent 'a year' in Baroda before returning to Bengal. In *Atmakatha* he gives a detailed description of his activities there. These accounts would seem to presume a stay of at least several months. He may however have been conflating two or more stays. In *Agnijug* Barin says that he arrived in Baroda about six months after Jatin Banerji left that city for Calcutta. This probably happened late in 1901 and certainly before March 1902 (see Chapter 4 of the present book). It seems clear from Barin's writings that he never met Jatin in Baroda.

On the basis of the above information one is led to conclude that Barin came to Baroda sometime in the middle of 1902. Aurobindo, however, did not mention Barin in letters to his wife of July and August 1902 or in the letter to his uncle of August 1902. This would tend to indicate that Barin was not then in Baroda, since Aurobindo's letters to family members were invariably full of family news. (There does not seem to be any reason why Aurobindo would not have wanted to mention Barin's presence in Baroda in 1902. He did not hesitate to mention the presence of Jatin Banerji, who was then in Baroda.) In writing about Sister Nivedita's visit to Baroda in October, Barin did not indicate that he was there at that time. Of course he would not necessarily have met her. All things considered it seems best to say that Barin arrived in Baroda sometime in 1902, probably towards the end of the year.

4. Aurobindo mentions only Nivedita by name.[22] In his account of the origins of the Anushilan Samiti, Satish Bose says that the first officers of the samiti (not of Aurobindo's council) were P. Mitra (president), C. R. Das and Aurobindo (vice-presidents), and Surendranath Tagore (treasurer) ('Bibriti' 181). If Nivedita is added to this list the total comes to five, the number mentioned by Aurobindo. These five names (with certain variations) appear in most secondary sources as the officers of Aurobindo's council or of the Anushilan Samiti or of the Bengal revolutionary movement in general, the three not being distinguished.[23] The same list appears in certain primary sources; but it should be noted that none of the authors of these accounts had important positions in the Calcutta organization at the moment in question.[24] They may well have got their information at second hand, possibly from a printed source. Indeed one of the writers, Bhupendranath Dutt, says elsewhere that his informant was Lizelle Reymond, a notoriously unreliable writer, who according to Dutt received her information from Aurobindo.[25] But Aurobindo's only communication to Reymond was the letter cited at the beginning of this note. In fact there is no unimpeachable authority for any of the names of the members of Aurobindo's council except Nivedita's. It is clear from the accounts of Aurobindo and others that Mitra was the head of the organization. The other three names are quite plausible, and the list may be accepted as having the authority of established tradition. I feel less confident about the offices, however. They make the secret society look like a branch of the Lions Club.

5. There has been for several decades a lively and unprofitable controversy over the extent of Nivedita's involvement with the

revolutionaries. Three of Nivedita's biographers, Lizelle Reymond, Girijashankar Raychaudhuri and Sankari Prasad Basu, have put her forward as an extremely active leader, more important perhaps than those to whom credit has been given. This extreme view has been rejected by all professional historians who have considered it.[26] The most capable of Nivedita's advocates, Sankari Prasad Basu, has done commendable work in gathering source materials; but even he admits that there is no real documentary evidence to support his view either in government files or in the revolutionaries' memorial writings.[27]. His contention that the absence of documents is due entirely to Nivedita's cleverness in avoiding detection is unconvincing.[28]

No one denies that Nivedita was active in the national movement or that she was closely connected with the revolutionaries. That she was is attested to by two undoubted leaders: Aurobindo and Barin Ghose. Aurobindo says simply that she was 'one of the revolutionary leaders'; Barin writes that she was deeply connected with the secret society and that he spoke about revolutionary work with her more than once.[29] (Contrast with this a comment by Abinash Chandra Bhattacharya: 'Nivedita had no connection or relation with our revolutionary party'. This may refer to a later period.)[30] Bhupendranath Dutt, who was closely associated with Nivedita and with Aurobindo and Barin as well, also speaks of her as being connected with the revolutionaries. But in one of his books he writes that at a certain point Nivedita requested members of the party 'not to tell her anything of the secret [terrorist] movement'.[31] Elsewhere Bhupendranath characterizes Reymond's account of Nivedita the revolutionary as a 'fairy tale'.[32] A good example of Reymond's story-telling is provided by her treatment of the episode in which Nivedita arranged with Jagadis Chandra Bose for revolutionaries to carry out experiments in bomb-making in a university laboratory.[33] Compare Reymond's romantic narrative with the accounts of Nolini Kanta Gupta, the person actually involved: see N. Gupta, *Smritir Pata* 31, and the following note, reproduced here for the first time from Nolini's papers (Sri Aurobindo Ashram Archives):

When it was found that some laboratory experiment was necessary for bomb-making Sister Nivedita spoke about it to her friend Jagadis Chandra Bose, the great scientist, then professor of Physics, Presidency

College. Jagadis Chandra took the matter up with Prafulla Chandra Roy, another great scientist and Professor of Chemistry at the same College, who agreed to arrange for Nolini Kanta's experiment in his College laboratory. But this did not materialise as Nolini Kanta had to go out of Calcutta for some work of the Centre.

The incident apparently took place early in 1907, as Nivedita left India for two years in August of that year.

6. In her autobiography Sarala Devi gives a lengthy account of an episode in which (she claims) Jatin Banerji came to her with a plan to kill a rich old woman for her money. Sarala asked him who had ordered him to do this. He replied that the order had come from Tilak. Sarala Devi said she would not believe this unless she heard it from Tilak's lips. She rushed to Poona and spoke to the Maharashtrian leader, who told her that he was vehemently opposed to this sort of thing.[34] While reading this passage it is good to keep in mind Sumit Sarkar's comment that 'it is difficult to take too seriously . . . Sarala Debi's naively pretentious account of how revolutionary leaders like Jatindranath Banerji danced attendance on her'.[35] She can however be trusted as to the general course of events in which she was involved. In regard to the Jatin-Tilak incident, she wrote (in English) to Girijashankar Raychaudhuri that Tilak told her that 'he did not approve of the dacoities, much less authorise them, if for nothing else simply on the score of their being practically useless for political purposes.' Tilak however added that 'looking to differences in human nature and the varying processes of evolution suited to different temperaments, he did not condemn them openly.' Sarala Devi informed Raychaudhuri that the incident involving Jatin, her and Tilak took place in September 1902.[36]

7. Bhupendranath is listed as the printer and publisher in the table of declarations used as part of the evidence in the Alipore Bomb Trial.[37] In a statement of October 1910, Upendranath Bannerjee said that *Jugantar* was started jointly by Barin, Debavrata, Bhupendra and Abinash.[38] In his memoirs Upen spoke of Debavrata as the principal editor and Barin as the man who ran the paper, mentioning Bhupen as being 'also on the editorial staff'.[39] In his pre-trial confession, Barin named besides himself only Abinash and Bhupendranath, who were by then so closely connected with the paper that further incrimination could

not hurt them.[40] Abinash wrote that the main men were Barin, Upen and himself.[41] (All but Abinash make it clear that Abinash was a general factotum and not an editor or writer.) Only Hem Das, who was not directly connected with the paper, included Bhupen in his list of the first editors, giving the other two as Debavrata Bose and Sakharam Deuskar, and saying that these two (but not Bhupen) were good writers.[42] Aurobindo was emphatic that Bhupen was neither an editor or writer, but only 'an obscure hand' or 'a member of the sub-editorial staff'.[43] Aurobindo also provided the most complete statement of *Jugantar*'s editorial and writing staff: 'The real editors or writers of Yugantar (for there was no declared editor) were Barin, Upen Banerji (also a sub-editor of *Bande Mataram*) and Devabrata Bose'.[44]

8. A Hindu sub-inspector of Jamalpur testified in court that Hindu Volunteers went to the mela 'in a body . . . and damaged the articles of [Muslim] shopkeepers'. He also testified: 'it was never the case that the police took the side of the Mahomedans'.[45] Few Bengali Hindus believed this. During the Alipore Bomb Trial, political leader A. C. Banerjee deposed: 'There was a belief that the East Bengal Government was responsible for the aggressiveness of the Mahomedans; for instance for the desecration of the temples at Jamalpur'.[46] This belief is still common among Hindu writers and the Hindu public. Arun Chandra Guha's account is representative. He makes the destruction of property by Hindu volunteers at the Jamalpur *mela* (which set off the riots) seem trivial: 'In their enthusiasm for the boycott of foreign goods, the people destroyed some foreign-made toys, salt etc.' Then he devotes a long paragraph to the desecration of the image, the attacks on Hindu property and the wounding of Hindu men.[47] Some of Guha's examples of the unresponsiveness of the police do seem convincing, but more convincing still is the account of Nirad Chaudhuri, who was living in nearby Kishorganj when the riots broke out. He begins: 'Heaven preserve me from the dishonesty, so general among Indians, of attributing this conflict to British rule, however much the foreign rulers might have profited by it. Indeed they would have been excusable only as gods . . . had they made no use of the weapon so assiduously manufactured by us, and by us also put into their hands'.[48]

Appendix 2
The Composition of the Maniktola Society

All but one of the members of the secret society led by Barindra Kumar Ghose were Bengalis.* The exception, Balkrishna Hari Kane, was a trainee sent from the Central Provinces. The thirty-five Bengalis came from thirteen districts, principally the cluster of western districts surrounding the capital:

MEMBERSHIP OF THE MANIKTOLA SECRET SOCIETY BY DISTRICT[1]

Bengal		*Eastern Bengal and Assam*	
Calcutta	4	Dacca	4
Hooghly	3	Faridpur	2
French Chandernagore	1	Malda	1
Jessore	4	Rajshahi	1
Khulna	2	Sylhet	3
Midnapore	2	Tipperah	2
Nadia	3		
24 Parganas	3		
Total	22	Total	13

The preponderance in favour of western Bengal was greater than appears from this table. Four men not included in the sample were from the western districts (Midnapore, Hooghly (2), Chandernagore) while two of the East Bengal men were not

* In this appendix I take the society to consist of the 36 men whose dossiers are included in Government of Bengal political confidential file 24/1909: 'Photos and descriptions of the accused in the Alipore Bomb Case'. These are the men on whom judgment was passed in the Alipore Sessions Court. The file does not contain dossiers of Narendranath Goswami, Kanailal Dutt, Satyendranath Bose or Charu Chandra Roy. The actual membership of the society is problematical. Not all the members were arrested and not all those arrested were members.

actually connected with the society. Moreover all the important leaders were from the western districts.

All the members of Maniktala society were Hindus. (Some were nominal Brahmos.) Practically all of them belonged to the 'respectable' or *bhadralok* class. The word bhadralok has been variously defined. In its ordinary sense it is the Bengali equivalent of the English 'gentleman'; in a more restricted sense it denotes a class of cultivated Bengalis, described as follows in the Rowlatt Report: 'They are mainly Hindus and their leading castes are Brahmins, Kayasthas and Vaidyas; but with the spread of English-education some other castes too have adopted *bhadralok* ideals and modes of life.'[2] The writers of the Rowlatt Report and other British officials found it convenient to speak of the freedom movement as a bhadralok conspiracy motivated in part by the class's diminishing employment opportunities as non-bhadralok Bengalis began to avail themselves of English education.[3] Several historians have made use of the term bhadralok to characterize the Bengali revolutionary movement as an affair of social élites rather than a mass movement.[4] Leonard Gordon has criticized this use of the term as imprecise and denigratory.[5] It is also misleading. If one confines oneself to manifest evidence one has little reason to believe that bhadralok individuals furthered their interests by becoming terrorists. Rather the opposite was true: they sacrificed their prospects by dropping out of school and university and exposing themselves to arrest or death. However this may be, 'bhadralok' remains useful as a general description of the social class to which most of the members of the Maniktala society belonged. Of the 36 persons on whom judgment was passed in the Alipore case, 33 or 92 per cent were Bengali bhadralok in the restricted sense of the term.[6] The breakdown by caste is as follows: 9 Bengali Brahmins, 14 Kayasthas, 10 Baidyas, 2 members of 'inferior' Bengali castes, and 1 Maharashtrian Brahmin. This bhadralok dominance remained constant through the first ten years of the Bengal terrorist movement. Statistics published in the Rowlatt Report on the 186 persons 'convicted in Bengal of revolutionary crimes or killed in commission of such crimes during the years 1907–17' show 165 or 89 per cent as belonging to the three chief bhadralok castes (65 Brahmins, 87 Kayasthas and 13 Baidyas). Of the remainder, 15 were from 10 'inferior' Bengali castes, 2 were non-Bengali and 4 were Eurasians or Europeans engaged in arms traffic. This predominance of higher classes is typical of urban revolutionary groups everywhere.[7]

All 36 members of the Maniktala group could be counted as bhadralok in the ordinary sense, that is, men of good breeding and culture. But they were not especially gentlemanly in their conduct. Rather they tended to be 'bad boys': unruly and rebellious, though with 'more stuff' than the 'ordinary steady' students.[8] Studiousness and application are such valued qualities among the bhadralok that publicists sometimes felt impelled to promote and defend the rebels' wayward ways. In April 1912 Amarendra Nath Chatterjee, a terrorist who had been associated with the Maniktala group, gave a public reading of an essay which (according to a police report) dealt with 'the superiority of youths of even loose morals (who cherish nationalism at heart) over educated men devoid of national feelings'.[9] A dozen years later Subhas Chandra Bose wrote in one of his 'Prison Diaries': 'Those who are considered good boys in the society are in fact nothing but eunuchs. . . . The Bengali will never become manly unless the so-called good boys are totally uprooted.'[10]

Like terrorists in all countries and periods,[11] the members of the Maniktala society were young, many of them no more than boys. The average age of the 36 Alipore prisoners at the time of their arrest was 22. This sample may be divided into two groups: 6 leaders (Aurobindo Ghose, Barin Ghose, Hem Das, Upen Banerjee, Debavrata Bose and Nikhileswar Roy Maulick) with an average age of 32, and 30 rank-and-file members, with an average age of 20. Age, like class, remained a constant factor during the first ten years of the movement. In the following table the 21 Alipore Sessions (and/or Harrison Road Bomb Case) convicts and the 186 Bengali 'revolutionary criminals' of 1907–1917 have been placed in 8 age-categories.

AGE OF BENGALI TERRORISTS, 1907–8 and 1907–17[12]

	10–15	*16–20*	*21–25*	*26–30*	*31–35*	*36–45*	*+45*	*Unrecorded*
Alipore sample	0	9	7	4	0	1	0	—
Rowlatt sample	2	48	76	29	10	9	1	11

The Maniktala society members (including those acquitted) were slightly younger on average than the terrorists in the Rowlatt ten-year sample. It is therefore not surprising that their leading occupation was 'student'. (Most of them were drop-outs at the time of their arrest.) Among the adults the leading professions were teacher, journalist, doctor and government servant. This is in line with the Rowlatt sample which shows 68 or 37 per cent as students, 16 or 9 per cent teachers, 5 or 3 per cent connected with newspapers or presses, 7 or 4 per cent doctors or compounders and 20 or 11 per cent in government service. The largest category after students in the Rowlatt sample was 'persons of no occupation'. Many of the Maniktala terrorists might have been assigned to that category at the time of their arrest. No one in the Maniktala sample, and only one man in the ten-year sample, was listed as a 'cultivator'.

Reference Notes
Bibliography
Index

Reference Notes

Officiai records are referred to by government or collection (abbreviated); the repository is given in the bibliography. Titles of official reports are reduced to a single word, generally followed by 'report'. Private papers are referred to by individual; the repository is given in the bibliography. Published primary sources are referred to by initials of title (italicized). Newspapers are referred to by title and date. Newspaper articles abstracted in Reports on Native Newspapers are referred to by place and date of first publication, followed by 'RNN' and an abbreviation of the province. Writings by participants, eyewitnesses, etc. are referred to by author's name and short title of book or article. Other books and articles are referred to by author's name, with date if more than one of the author's works is cited.

ABBREVIATIONS

ABT	The Alpore Bomb Trial; *The Alipore Bomb Trial*
AN	Archives Nationales, Paris
A&R	*Sri Aurobindo: Archives and Research*
B	Bengal
Bo	Bombay
BT	Bengal Terrorism (report)
CAOM	Centre des Archives d'Outre-Mer, Aix-en-Provence
CID	Criminal Investigation Department
CP	Central Provinces
EB&A	Eastern Bengal and Assam
EINC	*The Encyclopaedia of Indian National Congress*
GOB	Government of Bengal
GOI	Government of India
GOM	Government of Madras
INMSD	*The Indian Nationalist Movement: Select Documents*
IOR	India Office Records, London
Ker	J. C. Ker, *Political Trouble in India*
HD	Home Department (Series A, B or D)
M	Madras
NAI	National Archives of India, New Delhi

NMML	Nehru Memorial Museum and Library, New Delhi
P	Punjab
PJ	Public and Judicial (department)
pol. conf.	Political confidential file
q.	quoted in
RNN	Report on Native Newspapers
SAAA	Sri Aurobindo Ashram Archives
SMHFM	*Source Materials for a History of the Freedom Movement*
TNSA	Tamil Nadu State Archives
UP	United Provinces
VM	Victoria Memorial, Calcutta
WBSA	West Bengal State Archives, Calcutta

Chapter 1

1 Mehra 625–6; Weintraub 423.
2 Val C. Princep, q. Kaul 412.
3 Princep, q. Kaul 413; Mehra 185; Dutt 424; Sergeant 33.
4 q. Urwick 82.

Chapter 2

1 John Seeley, *The Expansion of England* (1883), Lecture I, q. *The Oxford Dictionary of Quotations* (New York: Oxford University Press, 1980): 419.
2 Temple to Lytton 9 July 1879, q. Nanda 13.
3 *SMHFM* 1: 82–3. Translated from the Marathi.
4 Ibid. 85–6.
5 Kedarnath 27, 58.
6 Phadke (1986) 31; Łatthe 327.
7 *SMHFM* 2: 965–80, 996–7, 1000–1. Translated from the Marathi.
8 Ibid. 982, 979.
9 Ibid. 993 (cited somewhat inaccurately in Rowlatt report par. 2).
10 Ibid. 1013–14.
11 *SMHFM* 1: 81–2.
12 *SMHFM* 2: 980.
13 Sandhurst to Elgin, 25 July 1897, q. Wolpert (1989) 90.
14 Wolpert (1989) 90–2; Keer 150, 159; Phadke (1985) 10; Nath 18–19.

Chapter 3

1 F. Gaekwad 1–25.
2 Sergeant 22–5; Allen 65–6.
3 Sri Aurobindo, *Collected Poems* 11, 15.
4 Sri Aurobindo, *On Himself* 17.
5 Sri Aurobindo, *On Himself* 4.
6 Sri Aurobindo, *Bande Mataram* 22.
7 Ibid. 22–3, 35.
8 Sri Aurobindo, *The Harmony of Virtue* 80.
9 *A&R* 8 (1983): 163.
10 Sri Aurobindo, *The Harmony of Virtue* 95–98.
11 Hunter 70–1. The first phrase is from an official letter of 1773.
12 B. Chatterjee, *Anandamath* (translated by Sri Aurobindo) 30–2.
13 Sri Aurobindo, *The Harmony of Virtue* 100–1.
14 Aurobindo Ghose to Mrinalini Ghose 20 August 1902, pub. *A&R* 1 (April 1977): 76.
15 B. Ghose, 'Sri Aurobindo as I Understand Him' 42.
16 Sri Aurobindo, *Bande Mataram* 75.

17 Sri Aurobindo, *On Himself* 23.
18 Gokhale papers, Deshpande to Gokhale 29 October 1895.
19 GOI HPD October 1909, 29: 5; GOM CID 4 (1909) 81.
20 See letter Aurobindo to Jogin Bose (uncle) 15 August 1902, pub. *A&R* 1 (April 1977): 72–3.
21 Sri Aurobindo, talk of 16 January 1939, pub. Purani, ed., *Evening Talks* 618. The quotation is from the unedited transcript of this talk.
22 Sri Aurobindo, *On Himself* 22.
23 T. Macaulay, 'Warren Hastings' (1841) in Macaulay 562.
24 Sri Aurobindo, *The Harmony of Virtue* 75, 88.
25 Ibid. 100.
26 B. Ghose, letter of 1955 in HFMP IV & V 41/2; B. Ghose, *Agnijug* 36, 49; A. Bhattacharya, 'Aurobindo' 831; B. Datta, 'Aurobindo Smarane' 60.
27 J. Banerjee, statement of July 1908 in IOR L/PJ/6/883; Ker 138; B. Ghose, *Agnijug* 36–7; B. Ghose, 'Sri Aurobindo as I Understand Him' 24.
28 J. Banerjee, statement of July 1908 in IOR L/PJ/6/883; cf. Ker 138.
29 K. G. Deshpande, preface to B. K. Kulkarni's *Sri Aurobindo* 8; C. C. Dutt, *Purano Katha-Upasanghar* 102. For the depression cf. 'Unity: An Open Letter', which was written around this time (Sri Aurobindo, *Bande Mataram* 57–8).
30 Sri Aurobindo papers, postcard to Bhuban Babu (SAAA).
31 B. Ghose, *Agnijug* 37.
32 Tilak papers vol. 3: 147, Yatindra Nath Banerjie to Tilak 15 October 1901.
33 Karandikar 97; Keer 71.
34 Wolpert (1989) 149; Karandikar 186–7; Keer 188.
35 Sri Aurobindo, *On Himself* 23
36 Ibid. 21.
37 Ibid.
38 Ibid. 23.

Chapter 4

1 Vivekananda, *Complete Works* 3: 220, 192.
2 Ibid. 224.
3 q. B. Datta, *Patriot-Prophet* vii.
4 Vivekananda, *Complete Works* 3: 180.
5 G. K. Gokhale, remark to M. K. Gandhi, q. Atmaprana 131.
6 Letter Nivedita to J. MacLeod 19 July 1901, pub. Nivedita, *Letters* 434–6.
7 B. Datta, 'Aurobindo Smarane' 59, reporting oral information from Sister Christine.
8 Avrich 67, 73; Cahm 92.
9 Nivedita to unknown recipient [18 August 1900], pub. Nivedita, *Letters* 381.
10 Atmaprana 125.
11 Horioka (1975) 30.
12 Letter J. MacLeod to O. Bull 30 October 1901, pub. Nivedita, *Letters* 454; Horioka (1975) 32.
13 Horioka (1963) 46.
14 Horioka (1975) 140–1; Vivekananda, *Collected Works* 5: 174–8; Dhar 1379.
15 E.g. S. Chaudhurani, *Jibaner Jharapata* 150; B. Datta, *Patriot-Prophet* 117: S. P. Basu (1985) 186; S. P. Basu (1394) 86.
16 Nivedita, introduction to Okakura, *The Ideals of the East* xix.
17 Atmaprana 243; S. Tagore, 'Kakuzo Okakura' 65–6.
18 P. Das, *Amar Jiban Kahini* 103; *Pioneer* reprinted in *Bande Mataram* daily 20 May 1908: 7. Cf. Ker 48; B. Datta, 'Aurobindo Smarane' 59; N. Ray 21–2.
19 B. Pal, *Memories* 246–8; 311–12,

266, 315; S. Sarkar 468–9, 397.
20 R. Tagore, *Jibansmriti* 86–91 ('Swadeshikta').
21 S. Chaudhurani, *Jibaner Jharapata* 134; P. Das, *Amar Jiban Kahini* 52; Daly report 3, 5; Ker 7; B. Pal, *Memories* 89–90.
22 Statement of Raghunath Bannerjee, HFMP I 55/2; I. Nandi, 'Atmonnati Itihas' 201; Armstrong report v.
23 B. Ghose, *Agnijug* 78.
24 P. Das, *Amar Jiban Kahini* 100.
25 GOI HPA March 1910, 33–40: 26, repeated in Daly report 5.
26 S. Bose, 'Bibriti' 179. Cf. B. Datta, 'Aurobindo Smarane' 59; J. Haldar 3.
27 S. Basu, 'Bibriti' 181. Cf. B. Datta, 'Aurobindo Smarane' 59; S. Sarkar (1973) 471–2. N. Ray 22–3
28 S. Basu, 'Bibriti' 181.
29 Sri Aurobindo, *On Himself* 23.
30 S. Chaudhurani, *Jibaner Jharapata* 178; information given by Sarala Devi to Girijashankar Raychaudhuri published in Raychaudhuri 340–1; B. Ghose, *Agnijug* 33, 47; J. Mukhopadhyay, *Biplabi Jibaner Smriti* 166.
31 S. Basu, 'Bibriti' 181; J. Mukhopadhyay, *Biplabi Jibaner Smriti* 165.
32 S. Basu, 'Bibriti' 181.
33 Sri Aurobindo, *On Himself* 23.
34 B. Ghose, *Agnijug* 72; A. Bhattacharya, 'Baiplabik Samiti' 191; J. Mukhopadhyay, *Biplabi Jibaner Smriti* 166; Atmaprana 180.
35 B. Datta, *Patriot-Prophet* 16, 119; B. Ghose, *Agnijug* 66; J. Mukhopadhyay, *Biplabi Jibaner Smriti* 166; Atmaprana 180; B. Majumdar 101.
36 A. Bhattacharya, 'Aurobindo' 831; B. Majumdar 100–1.
37 A. Bhattacharya, 'Aurobindo' 831–2; A. Bhattacharya, 'Baiplabik Samati' 191; B. Ghose, *Agnijug* 62.
38 Sri Aurobindo, *On Himself* 23.
39 H. Kanungo, *Banglay Biplab*, chapter 1.
40 A. Bhattacharya, 'Baiplabik Samiti' 190–1.

Chapter 5

1 BSR Huzur Order Book 1905–6: 97/1/1; 'Leave information' from Service Lists.
2 See Aurobindo's letter to his uncle of 15 August 1872 (*A&R* 1 [April 1977]: 70).
3 BSR Huzur Order Book No. 3, order of 19 April 1901; Civil List dated 31 July 1901.
4 Sri Aurobindo, *On Himself* 9–10; D. Ray, *Aurobindo Prasanga* 31. Letters and memoranda written by Aurobindo are found in the files of numerous Baroda State departments 1895–1906, e.g. Dewan Cutcherry, Vernacular Branch.
5 E. g. *SMHFM* 2: iii, 553 ff; F. Gaekwad 179 ff.
6 q. Cashman 110; Morley Papers, letter Minto to Morley 5 August 1909.
7 Chirol 193.
8 q. Sergeant 105.
9 *Memoranda on the Native States of India 1905*, 12.
10 Sardesai, *Sri Sayajirav Gayakwad* 25–6; BSR confidential files: 'Lord Curzon's Visit to Baroda in 1900'; 'Protest proposed to be sent against the Viceroy's Circular re the visits of Indian Chiefs to Europe 1905'.
11 Sergeant 106.
12 BSR confidential files: 'Protest . . . against the Viceroy's Circular', undated draft in reply to resident's letter 11 February 1903.

13 q. Sergeant 94.

14 F. Gaekwad 188; *SMHFM* 2: 575; GOM CID circular 2/1909, CID report, vol. vii: 80–81.

15 Sri Aurobindo, talk of 7 April 1926, pub. Purani, ed., *Evening Talks* 277.

16 Letter Aurobindo Ghose to Mrinalini Ghose 25 June 1902, published in Sri Aurobindo, *Bangla Rachana* 330.

17 Letter Nivedita to Brahmananda 18 July 1902 and notice in *Amrita Bazar Patrika* 19 July 1902: both q. Atmaprana 141–2.

18 Atmaprana 147.

19 Sri Aurobindo, *On Himself* 58, 69; Sri Aurobindo, talk of 21 January 1939, pub. Purani, ed., *Evening Talks* 636; B. Ghose, 'Sri Aurobindo as I Understand Him' 20–1.

20 Jadugopal Mukhopadhyay, HFMP I 1/2; B. Datta, *Patriot-Prophet* 10.

21 Atmaprana 147; Sri Aurobindo, talk of 21 January 1939, pub. Purani, ed., *Talks* 636; Sri Aurobindo, *On Himself* 58.

22 Sergeant 114.

23 B. Ghose, *Amar Atmakatha* 164–65. Cf. B. Ghose, 'Sri Aurobindo as I Understand Him' 19.

24 Birth Certificate. Croydon, County of Surrey. No. 335 of 1880; B. Ghose, *Amar Atmakatha* 14–15.

25 Beveridge papers, letter Annette Akroyd to Fanny Akroyd 22 January 1873, pub. *A&R* 14 (1990): 97.

26 This and the four paragraphs that follow are based on Barindrakumar Ghose, *Amar Atmakatha*, chapters 1–17; see also 'Sri Aurobindo as I Understand Him' 19.

27 Moshel 14–18.

28 *Atmakatha* 163–65; B. Ghose, 'Sri Aurobindo as I Understand Him' 19.

29 ABT 22; GOI HPA May 1908, 112–50: 13, 25.

30 Sri Aurobindo, *On Himself* 17.

31 Ibid. 14. See also GOI HPD, August 1911: 11; GOI HPD October 1909, 29: 2; Daly report 4.

32 Sri Aurobindo, *On Himself* 4.

33 Ibid. 14.

34 Sri Aurobindo, talk of 12 December 1940, pub. Nirodbaran, ed., *Talks* 4: 279; B. Ghose, *Agnijug* 40–50.

35 Sri Aurobindo, *On Himself* 23.

36 B. Ghose, letter of 1955 in HFMP IV & V 41/2; B. Ghose, *Agnijug* 40. Cf. *Bande Mataram* weekly, 28 June 1908: 2 (deposition of Narendra Nath Goswami).

37 *A&R* 14 (1990): 60.

38 Ibid. 65.

39 Sri Aurobindo, *On Himself* 17.

40 *EINC* 4: 328.

41 *EINC* 4: 410.

42 Sri Aurobindo, talk of 6 March 1926, pub. Purani, ed. *Evening Talks* 446.

43 Sri Aurobindo, *On Himself* 25.

44 Sri Aurobindo, talk of 21 January 39, pub. Purani, ed. *Evening Talks* 637.

45 *A&R* 7 (1983): 51–2.

46 *A&R* 2 (1978): 23–30.

47 H. Kanungo, *Banglay Biplab* 2.

Chapter 6

1 B. Ghose, *Agnijug* 40, 51.

2 A. Bhattacharya, 'Aurobindo' 831. Cf. A. Bhattacharya, 'Baiplabik Samiti' 190; B. Ghose, *Agnijug* 58.

3 BSR BROC 21/Poli Hall, file 4, letter from A. Ghose dated 14 February 1903; BCR 64: 124–8,

letter from A. Ghose dated Srinagar 4 June 1903.

4 Sri Aurobindo, *On Himself* 23, 5, 69.

5 Atmaprana 156.

6 Mary Minto 385; Sri Aurobindo, talk of 21 January 1939, pub. A. B. Purani, ed., *Evening Talks* 636.

7 A. Bhattacharya, 'Baiplabik Samiti' 196.

8 S. Chaudhurani, *Jibaner Jharapata* 134.

9 A.C. Banerjee papers, letters Sarala Ghosal to Banerjee 20 and 23 October 1902.

10 S. Chaudhurani, *Jibaner Jharapata* 179–81; A. Bhattacharya, 'Baiplabik Samiti' 191.

11 A. Bhattacharya, 'Aurobindo' 832–3.

12 Sri Aurobindo, talk of 14 December 1938, pub. A. B. Purani, *Evening Talks* 541; H. Sarkar 55; GOB History Sheet 679; J. Mukhopadhyay, *Biplabi Jibaner Smriti* 166; J. Mukhopadhyay, HFMP I 1/2.

13 GOI HPA March 1910, 33–40: 12; Daly report 6.

14 GOB History Sheet 602: 2–3; GOB History Sheet 603: 2–3.

15 H. Kanungo, *Banglay Biplab* 19–20; Sri Aurobindo, talk of 27 February 1939.

16 GOI HPA May 1908, 112–50: 13, 25; Midnapore note 2; Nixon report 1; B. Ghose, *Agnijug* 76; Sri Aurobindo, talk of 21 January 1939, pub. Purani, *Evening Talks* 635.

17 B. Ghose, *Agnijug* 77, 69.

18 B. Ghose, *Agnijug* 65.

19 H. Kanungo, *Banglay Biplab* 29.

20 B. Ghose, *Swadesh* 1338, q. G. Raychaudhuri 283.

21 S. Deuskar, *Desher Katha*, note to the fifth edition.

22 Midnapore note 2 citing letter Debabrata Bose to Indra Nandi 29 April 1904; H. Kanungo, *Banglay Biplab* 40, 75.

23 S. Sarkar (1973) 473; N. Ray 25.

24 B. Ghose, 'Sri Aurobindo as I Understand Him' 37.

25 H. Kanungo, *Banglay Biplab* 37.

26 Ibid.

27 N. Ray 25.

28 B. Ghose, *Agnijug* 111–2.

29 Sri Aurobindo, *On Himself* 16; Sri Aurobindo, *Bande Mataram* 658; Sri Aurobindo, talk of 1 July 1926.

30 Potdar. The author reproduces and translates parts of a letter from the Russian consul in Bombay to his superior in St Petersburg dated 5/18 March 1905. Cf. Keer 250.

31 Tilak papers, Tilak to Krishnavarma 14 July, 4 August and 25 August 1905, 9 February and 14 December 1906 (15:1,2,3,4,11); Aurobindo to Mrinalini Ghose 3 October 1905, pub. *Bangla Rachana* 326; Ker 385–6.

32 Sri Aurobindo, *Bande Mataram* 658; Sri Aurobindo, talk of 1 July 1926.

33 Sri Aurobindo, *Bande Mataram* 57–8.

Chapter 7

1 Rowlatt report par. 22; cf. Tegart 6.

2 BSR Dewan Cutcherry Vernacular Branch 1905–6, letters Aravind A. Ghose to Gaekwar 29 March 1905, letter Ghose to Dewan 12 December 1904 and correspondence Khangi Kharbhari and Dewan March to September 1905.

3 Letter Sri Aurobindo to Mrinalini Devi 22 October 1905 (SAAA collection of ABT records: this

court translation has 'never sits quiet'); Sri Aurobindo, talk of 27 Feb 1940, pub. Nirodbaran, ed., *Talks* 2–3: 253.

4 J. Banerjee, statement in IOR L/PJ/6/883 (source of Ker 138); Barin Ghose in *Dawn of India*, q. G. Raychaudhuri 355; cf. Nixon report 1.

5 J. Mukhopadhyay, *Srimat Niralamba Swami* 12; J. Mukhopadhyay, *Biplabi Jibaner Smriti* 23, 255–6; Sri Aurobindo, *Karmayogin* 174; A. Bhattacharya, 'Baiplabik Samiti' 200.

6 Tegart 6–7; Natesan 1; Lyall in Chirol, *Indian Unrest* ix.

7 Kakuzo Okakura, *The Book of Tea*, q. Penguin Dictionary of Modern Quotations (Harmondsworth: Penguin, 1984): 253.

8 Natesan 1. Cf. H. Kanungo, *Banglay Biplab* 71.

9 P. Mitra papers, Mitra to A. C. Banerjea 29 February 1904; S. Chaudhurani, *Jibaner Jharapata* 146–7; Tilak papers 17: 30.

10 *Bengalee* 14 June 1905, q. S. Ghose 90.

11 Note by H. H. Risley 6 December 1904, q. S. Sarkar (1973) 18.

12 Nevinson 171–2.

13 Sri Aurobindo, *Bande Mataram* 76–7.

14 Letter Aurobindo to Mrinalini Devi, 30 August 1905, pub. Sri Aurobindo, *Bangla Rachana* 319–23.

15 B. Chatterjee, *Ananda Math* 30 (translation by Sri Aurobindo).

16 A. Bhattacharya, 'Aurobindo' 833–4; A. Bhattacharya, 'Baiplabik Samiti' 193–4. Cf. B. Ghose, *Agnijug* 115.

17 Ranade, *Rise* 11.

18 Sri Aurobindo, *Bande Mataram* 61–74.

19 This paragraph is based on a comparison of the preamble of the Servants of India Society, reproduced in Hoyland 103–5, and the text of *Bhawani Mandir*, pub. Sri Aurobindo, *Bande Mataram* 61–74.

20 Sri Aurobindo, *On Himself* 51.

21 Ker 30 ff, 128; Rowlatt report par. 30; Ronaldshay 128; Tegart 7.

22 See e.g. the opinion of Eardley Norton (ABT 296).

23 Rowlatt report par. 30; Ronaldshay 128.

24 Chirol, *Indian Unrest* 31.

25 Daly report 3; GOI Foreign and Political, General, Conf. B of 1914, 2: 9; Edwardes 210.

26 H. Kanungo, *Banglay Biplab* 58, 244–5; see chapters 4, 5 and 15 of this book for Hemchandra's full argument.

27 M. N. Roy, *India in Transition* (1922) in *Selected Works*, vol. 1, 332–4; R. K. Ray 70, 64; S. Sarkar (1973) 486.

28 Speech of 19 January 1908, pub. Sri Aurobindo, *Bande Mataram* 652.

29 Chirol, *Indian Unrest* 341.

30 Aurobindo Ghose, 'The Age of Kalidasa'. *The Indian Review* (July 1902) 349; revised version Sri Aurobindo, *The Harmony of Virtue* 228.

31 Sri Aurobindo papers, notebook G10: 75 (SAAA); Sri Aurobindo, *The Harmony of Virtue* 174.

32 Eagleton 215; cf. Nanda passim.

33 Sri Aurobindo, *On Himself* 50, 81, 98.

34 *A&R* 2 (1978) 198.

35 See e. g. Sri Aurobindo, *On Himself* 403, 406.

36 Ibid. 51; Sri Aurobindo, talk of 27 February 1940, pub. Nirodbaran, ed., *Talks* 2–3: 253.

37 Barin Ghose to Girijashankar Raychaudhuri 12 June 1943, q. Raychaudhuri 410–11; Sri Aurobindo papers, talk of 27 February 1940; pub. Nirodbaran, ed., *Talks* 2–3: 253; confession of Hrishikesh Kanjilal GOI HPA May 1908, 112–150: 35.

38 Letter Aurobindo Ghose to Mrinalini Ghose 22 October 1905 (SAAA collection of ABT records).

39 GOI HPA September 1910, 33–40: 43–44; C. C. Dutt, 'Narmada Valley'; C. C. Dutt, 'My Contact'; C. C. Dutt, *Purano Katha-Upasanghar* 15.

40 GOI HPD October 1909, 29: 2; GOM CID 7 (1909): 80–1; Sri Aurobindo papers, statement by R. N. Patkar, 1956 (SAAA).

41 C. Dutt, 'Narmada Valley'.

42 BSR Huzur English Office, political file 36/10.

Chapter 8

1 Aurobindo Ghose to Mrinalini Ghose, 3 October and November-December 1905, pub. Sri Aurobindo, *Bangla Rachana* 326–7.

2 *Sanjivani* 13 July 1905 (RNN-B).

3 *Indian Mirror* 10 August 1905 (RNN-B).

4 Mukherjee and Mukherjee (1957) 29–32; GOB History Sheet 723: 3.

5 *Kesari* 3 October 1905; Aurobindo Ghose to Mrinalini Ghose 3 October 1905, pub. *Bangla Rachana* 326.

6 Sri Aurobindo, *On Himself* 30–1.

7 Deb, 'Sri Aurobindo'.

8 B. Ghose to Girijashankar Raychaudhuri 12 June 1943, q. Raychaudhuri 410–1. Cf. B. Ghose, *Agnijug* 115.

9 VM ABT records III.6.Ex 1226. This is an English translation used in the Alipore trial.

10 English translation printed in *Empress* in September 1906, reprinted in S. Basu (1395) 114–6.

11 *Bengalee* 1 and 3 April 1906; deposition of Nagesh Chandra Mukherjee, P. W. 58 in Alipore sessions trial, ABT records XIII; H. Kanungo, *Banglay Biplab* 109; Midnapore note 3–4.

12 *Sandhya* 9 August 1905 (RNN-B).

13 Sri Aurobindo, *On Himself* 24; cf. Barin's 1909 confession: GOI HPA May 1908, 112–50: 13, 25.

14 Sri Aurobindo, *On Himself* 24.

15 B. Ghose, 'Sri Aurobindo as I Understand Him' 43; ABT 81, 96, 293–4; deposition of A. C. Banerjee in Alipore sessions case, VM ABT records IV. 5. 420–1.

16 Upendranath Banerjee's statement in GOI HPD 9: 6; Sri Aurobindo, *On Himself* 24.

17 Sri Aurobindo, *On Himself* 41–2; N. Gupta, *Smritir Pata* 77.

18 Chirol, *Indian Unrest* 94–5 (citing two Bengali authorities).

19 *Jugantar* 18 March 1906 (WBSA Freedom Movement papers file 104).

20 *Jugantar* 8 April 1906 (Mukherjee and Mukherjee, *Jugantar Patrika* [see next note] 55–60); article ascribed to Aurobindo by Bhupendranath Dutt ('Aurobindo Smarane' 55).

21 The source of most of my citations from *Jugantar* is the text of the articles making up *Mukti Kon Pathe* as published in Mukherjee and Mukherjee, eds., *Bharater Swadhinata Andolane 'Jugantar' Patrikar Dan*. *Mukti Kon Pathe* was made up of articles reprinted from *Jugantar* and published January 1907. Citations in this paragraph: *Jugantar Patrika* 62, 78, 131, 72–3, 190.

22 *Jugantar* 17 June 1906 (date from Ker 65). Text *Jugantar Patrika* 160.
23 *Jugantar* 6 May 1906 (NNR-B); *Jugantar* 29 April 1906 (WBSA Freedom Movement Papers file 104).
24 Sri Aurobindo, *On Himself* 24, 69.
25 BT report 4; GOB History Sheet 55: 6; Ker 141, 140.
26 BT report 4: Nixon report 9; Tegart 8.
27 *Hemendra Kishore Acharyya Chaudhury* 14; GOB pol. conf. 266 of 1908, dossier on Manoranjan Guha Thakurta 4.
28 Armstrong report 27; N. Chaudhuri, *Autobiography* 254.
29 B. C. Pal, *Leaders of the Nationalist Movement* 94–5; 'Pictorial India of Today' (1908), HFMP IV & V 94/2.
30 Nevinson, *The New Spirit* 14–15.
31 GOI HPA June 1906, 152–68.
32 *Sandhya* 20 April, *Jugantar* 22 April 1906 (RNN-B).
33 Sri Aurobindo, *On Himself* 27, 46; Sri Aurobindo, talk of 27 July 1926, pub. *Sri Aurobindo Circle* 35 (1979) 17; Deb, 'Sri Aurobindo'; Nixon report 37; Armstrong report v.
34 B. Ghose, *Agnijug* 148.
35 B. Ghose, *Atmakahini* 58; GOI HPD September 1911, 9: 13.
36 H. Kanungo, *Banglay Biplab*, chapter 9.
37 H. Kanungo, *Banglay Biplab* 156.
38 Narendra Nath Goswami, statement to magistrate (ABT 41); GOI HPA September 1910, nos. 33–40: 18.
39 GOI HPA September 1910, 33–40: 18.
40 H. Kanungo, *Banglay Biplab*, chapter 10.
41 H. Kanungo, *Banglay Biplab*, chapter 11.
42 H. Kanungo, *Banglay Biplab* 97.
43 H. Kanungo, *Bangluy Biplab* 158.
44 Avrich 35; Laqueur 112.
45 Sri Aurobindo, talk of 18 December 1938, pub. Nirodbaran, *Talks* 1: 43–4.
46 Sri Aurobindo, talk of 28 February 1940, pub. Nirodbaran, ed., *Talks* 256.
47 B. Ghose, 'Sri Aurobindo as I Understand Him' 36; Barin Ghose to Girijashankar Raychaudhuri 20 June 1943, q. Raychaudhuri 448n. Cf. ibid. 659, 709, 729.
48 C. C. Dutt, *Purano Katha-Upasanghar* 22.
49 For Hem's account see above in the text; for Narendranath's GOI HPA September 1910, 33–40: 18. Sri Aurobindo, talk of 11 September 1943.
50 B. Datta, 'Aurobindo Smarane' 53.
51 B. Ghose, 'Sri Aurobindo as I Understand Him' 36–40.
52 Sri Aurobindo, *On Himself* 22.

Chapter 9

1 Upendranath Bannerjee, *Nirbasiter Atmakatha* 3.
2 H. Kanungo, *Banglay Biplab* 176–80.
3 Kanungo, *Banglay Biplab*, 196–7.
4 Ibid. 198; Gharpurey 412–13.
5 Kanungo, *Banglay Biplab*, 199–200.
6 Kanungo, *Banglay Biplab*, 198–208.
7 Ibid. 209–11.
8 AN F/7/12894, n° 1.
9 Letter Préfet de Police to Président du Conseil, 16 December 1907 (AN F/7/12894, n° 1); Minto papers, telegram Morley to Minto 30 December 1907. Cf. Ker, 130.
10 Ker, 131; Kanungo, *Banglay*

Biplab 218.

11 Khaparde papers, diary 12 June 1906.

12 Hemendra Prasad Ghose papers, diary 21 July 1906.

13 Pal, *Leaders* 119–20; Sri Aurobindo, *On Himself* 42–3; Hemendra Prasad Ghose papers, diary 30 July and 5 August 1906; H. Ghose, *Prophet* 11–12; Deb, 'Political Leader' ix; Deb, 'Sri Aurobindo'.

14 *On Himself* 28.

15 Letter Banerjea to Naoroji 25 October 1906, q. Argov (1967) 119.

16 Sri Aurobindo, *On Himself* 42. Cf. ibid. 28, 45.

17 *Times* (London) 10 September 1906. The issue of *Bande Mataram* in which the article appeared has been lost.

18 Sri Aurobindo, *On Himself* 24.

19 Prabhakar Mukherji 113.

20 A. Bhattacharya, 'Aurobindo' 931; Jadugopal Mukherjee (HFMP I 1/2); H. Sarkar 6–7.

21 Armstrong report i, 1, 11–12.

22 VM ABT records III.6.1362; ABT 122; GOB pol. conf. 266 of 1908 ('Ex parte . . .') paras 14 and 17; Nixon report 2; Statement of Raghunath Banerjee (HFMP I 55/2: 1).

23 Nixon report 2, 4; Daly report 10, 8; J. Haldar 12; GOB pol. conf. 279 of 1910 (Sl. 1–5) 1.

24 Jadugopal Mukherjee statement (HFMP I 1/2); Guha, *Aurobindo and Jugantar* 20; A. Bhattacharya, 'Baiplabik Samiti' 194.

25 Ranade, *Rise* 225; Ker 6; Keer 121; Sri Aurobindo, *On Himself* 25, 15n.

26 Khaparde papers, diary 31 December 1906; Statement by Malaviya in Bapat 170–1; Tahmankar 122.

27 Khaparde papers, diary 31 December 1906.

28 'The Congress', *Mukti Kon Pathe* (official English translation), VM ABT records III.9.157–8; *Jugantar* 7 April 1907 (RNN-B).

29 *Mukti Kon Pathe* (official English translation), VM ABT records III.9.178; *Jugantar Patrika* 147; *Jugantar* 14 October 1906 (WBSA Freedom Movement Papers file 104).

30 *Jugantar* 26 August 1906 (date from WBSA Freedom Movement papers file 104), text *Jugantar Patrika* 94–99. The last paragraph was apparently omitted from the text published in *Mukti Kon Pathe*.

31 U. Bannerjee, *Nirbasiter Atmakatha* 2–3.

32 q. R. West (1986) 369.

33 U. Bannerjee, *Nirbasiter Atmakatha* 3.

34 *Jugantar Patrika* 147–50, 160–166 (date WBSA Freedom Movement papers file 104).

35 English translation q. Ker 66.

36 *Indian Nation* 15 April 1907.

37 B. Ghose, 'Sri Aurobindo as I Understand Him' 43; Ker 65.

38 Hemendra Prasad Ghose papers, diary 8 June 1907.

39 ABT records XII: 726–8: ABT 71–2. Cf. Hemendra Prasad Ghose papers, diary 3 July 1907.

40 Hemendra Prasad Ghose papers, diary 23 July 1908.

41 Government of India Home Department June 1908, 126–9 (reproduced in HFMP B 153/2).

42 Sri Aurobindo, *On Himself* 41, 24; A. Bhattacharya, 'Aurobindo' 840; statement reproduced in *Bande Mataram* weekly, 28 July 1907: 7.

43 *Indian Empire* reproduced in *Bande Mataram* weekly 28 July

1907: 11; Hemendra Prasad Ghose papers, diary 23 July 1908; B. Datta, *Patriot-Prophet* 112–13; Macdonald, *Awakening* 125; Nivedita, *Letters* 912.

44 Morley papers, telegram Minto to Morley. 1 August 1907.

45 Sri Aurobindo papers, talk of 23 February 1940, pub. Nirodbaran, ed., *Talks* 226.

46 Sri Aurobindo, *On Himself* 30.

47 *Times of India* 19 August 1907; *Pioneer* 18 August 1907. Both these papers were considered to be quasi-official.

48 Sri Aurobindo papers, talk of 23 February 1940, pub. Nirodbaran, ed., *Talks* 226 (in the published version 'all false', the phrase used in the original transcript, was emended to 'rather made up').

49 GOI HPA March 1910, 33–40: 63.

50 Government of India, Home Department, June 1908, 126–9 (reproduced in HFMP B 153/2).

51 Hemendra Prasad Ghose papers, diary 2 and 5 September 1907; GOB Judicial Dept file 260 reproduced in HFMP I 47/2.

52 ABT 259; Government of India Home Department June 1908, 126–9 (reproduced in HFMP B 153/2); Ker report 71; Hemendra Prasad Ghose papers, diary 23 September 1907; q. B. Majumdar 109.

53 U. Bannerjee, *Nirbasiter Atmakatha* 6; U. Banerjee, statement in GOI HPD August 1911, 9: 11–12; *Note on the Jugantar Gang* 1; GOI HPA May 1908, 104–11: 7; GOI HPA September 1910, 33–40: 28.

54 GOI HPD July 1907, 66: 1; Minto papers, telegram Minto to Morley 26 May 1908; Chirol, *Unrest* 22.

55 GOI HPD August 1911, 9: 11–12; GOI HPA May 1908, 104–11: 7; GOI HPA June 1908, 130–1, 4.

56 B. Ghose, *Atmakahini* 55–6; H. Sarkar, *Revolutionaries of Bengal* 6 (Barin informant).

57 *Jugantar* 19 August 1907 (NNR-B). This is the official government translation, the Bengali text does not seem to have survived. Barin never named the title of the article in which he made the announcement, but 'Our Hope' is the only article published around the time of the second *Jugantar* trial that answers his description.

Chapter 10

1 *Bande Mataram* daily 9 May 1908: 6; description by Beachcroft reported in *Bengalee* 7 May 1909; ABT 147; GOI HPA May 1908, 112–50: 11; GOI HPA June 1908, 130–1: 11; GOI HPD May 1908, 17: 1; A. Bhattacharya, 'Aurobindo' 835.

2 Nevinson, *New Spirit* 16–17; N. Chaudhuri 234–40.

3 ABT records XIII: 713–15; S. Sarkar (1984) 281.

4 *Bande Mataram* daily 1 May 1907: 1.

5 Hemendra Prasad Ghose papers, diary 27 April 1907; ABT records XII: 713–4; GOI HPD March 1908: 1; GOB History Sheet 709: 3–4.

6 Hemendra Prasad Ghose papers, 4–9 May 1907.

7 I. Nandi 204–5.

8 I. Nandi 204–05; Sri Aurobindo to Motilal Roy 29 August 1914, pub. *Supplement* 464.

9 Hemendra Prasad Ghose papers, diary 26 April 1907.

10 Nevinson, *New Spirit* 17–19; Telegram Minto to Morley 8 May 1907, pub. Mary Minto 124–5;

Wolpert (1967) 111–12. Comments in the native press, e.g. RNN-UP, lasted well into August.

11 Sri Aurobindo, *Supplement* 49; *Jugantar* 16 July 1907, official translation q. Ker 67.

12 ABT records XII: 729–30; Ker report 65; Hemendra Prasad Ghose papers, diary 7 August and 5 September 1907.

13 Biren Sen papers, 'The Late Sushil Kumar Sen' 6–7; *Bengalee* 28 and 28 August 1907; *Bande Mataram* daily 28 and 29 August 1907; GOI HPD March 1908, 1: 15; Ker 123–4; ABT 7, 96.

14 U. Bannerjee, *Nirbasiter Atmakatha* 3.

15 B. Ghose, 'Sri Aurobindo as I Understand Him' 49.

16 B. Ghose, 'Sri Aurobindo as I Understand Him' 49–50; B. Ghose, *Atmakahini*, chapter 2; Upendranath Bannerjee, *Nirbasiter Atmakatha* 6–8.

17 N. Gupta, *Smritir Pata* 28–39; Nolini Kanta Gupta papers, unpublished statement dealing with the Nivedita-Bose incident (see Appendix 1, note 5); ABT 442–3.

18 U. Bannerjee, *Nirbasiter Atmakatha* 10–11.

19 Ibid.; N. Gupta, *Smritir Pata* 32–3; Statement by Biren Ghose in HPA May 1908, 112–50: 38.

20 GOI HPD May 1908, 17: 5–6.

21 H. Kanungo, *Banglay Biplab*, chapter 2.

22 Ker 134–5, 53–5.

23 *Bartaman Rana-Niti* (official translation) VM ABT records III. 10; Ker 47–50; GOB pol. conf. 279 of 1910: 2; Rowlatt report, par. 94; N. Gupta, *Smritir Pata* 33.

24 *Mukti Kon Pathe* (official translation) VM ABT records, III.9.x; BT report 2.

25 Ker 135; GOI HPA May 1908, 104–11, 6; ABT 440, 445.

26 GOI HPA September 1910, 33–40: 40; ABT 31, 37; GOI HPA May 1908, 112–50, 39; GOI HPD August 1911, 9: 13.

27 GOI HPD August 1911, 9: 13; Daly report 7.

28 U. Bannerjee, *Nirbasiter Atmakatha* 9–10.

29 GOI HPD May 1908, 17: 3.

30 GOB pol. conf. 194 of 1909 (9).

31 Daly report 9, 10; ABT 88, 145; N. Gupta, *Smritir Pata* 32.

32 A. Bhattacharya, 'Aurobindo' 835; ABT 23; GOI HPD May 1908, 17: 1.

33 Sri Aurobindo, *On Himself* 17, 28, 21.

34 B. Ghose, letter of 1955 in HFMP IV & V 41/2; Sri Aurobindo, talk of 21 Jan 1939, pub. Nirodbaran, ed., *Talks* 1: 220–1.

35 N. Gupta, *Smritir Pata* 35.

36 B. Ghose, confession in GOI HPA May 1908, 112–50: 27; U. Bannerjee, *Nirbasiter Atmakatha* 17.

37 B. Ghose, *Atmakahini* 58–9; B. Ghose, *Wounded Humanity*, 46–47; GOI HPD August 1911, 9: 13. cf. H. Kanungo, *Banglay Biplab* 98, 118.

Chapter 11

1 C. C. Dutt, *Purano Katha-Upasanghar* 22–4; GOI HPA September 1910, 33–40: 42; HFMP IV & V 36/2.

2 *Sandhya* 6 May 1907, official translation reprinted in Ker 74.

3 Biren Sen papers, 'The Bengal Revolutionaries—Evolution of the Bomb' 3–5 typed version; H. Kanungo, *Banglay Biplab*, chapter 9.

4 *Statesman* 15–16 November 1905; *Bengalee* 15–16 November 1905;

N. Gupta, *Smritir Pata* 25; U. Datta, *Kara-Jibani* 3.

5 U. Datta, *Kara-Jiban* 3–5; ABT 23; GOI HPD August 1911, 9: 12.

6 Biren Sen papers, 'The Bengal Revolutionaries—Evolution of the Bomb', 6–7 typed version.

7 Andaman note 8; ABT 62; Midnapore note 27.

8 GOI HPD August 1911, 9: 12–13; Daly report 14.

9 GOI HPA May 1908, 112–50: 26; Chandernagore note 4; Daly report 8.

10 *Bande Mataram* daily 1 November 1907.

11 GOI HPA May 1908, 112–50: 14, 23, 26, 32; ABT 39; GOI HPD August 1911, 9: 12; Andaman note 4.

12 GOI HPA May 1908, 112–50: 7, 14, 26, 32; ABT 24, 28; *Bengalee* 2 October 1908.

13 GOI HPD, August 1911, 9: 12.

14 GOI HPA May 1908, 112–50: 7, 14, 26, 32.

15 GOB. pol. conf. 51 of 1908. sl. 21: 2–3; GOB 1910/123: 5.

16 ABT 24, 28; GOI HPA May 1908, 112–50: 32; GOI HPD August 1911, 9: 12.

17 GOI HPA May 1908, 112–50, 26; *Bande Mataram* weekly 26 July 1908: 10.

18 GOI HPB February 1908, 92–94: 5–13.

19 GOB pol. conf. 123 of 1910: 3, 5.

20 GOB pol. conf. 112 of 1908 (A): 1; Daly report 10.

21 Midnapore report 4–5; Midnapore note 13–22.

22 GOI HPA May 1908, 104–11: 5; GOB pol. conf. 170 of 1908, letter Halliday to Chief Secretary 16 May 1908.

23 GOI HPA May 1908, 112–50: 11.

24 U. Bannerjee, *Nirbasiter Atmakatha* 19–23; GOI HPA March 1910, 33–40: 82.

Chapter 12

1 Khaparde papers, diary 31 December 1906. Cf. Karandikar 235.

2 Letter Tilak to Aurobindo 11 December 1907 (ABT records I).

3 Midnapore note 6.

4 Hemendra Prasad Ghose papers, diary 9 December 1907.

5 Letter Aurobindo to Mrinalini Ghose, 6 December 1907, pub. *Bangla Rachana* 325.

6 Sri Aurobindo papers, notebook G15: 4–10 even (SAAA).

7 Sri Aurobindo, *On Himself* 65.

8 Hemendra Prasad Ghose papers, diary 11 December 1907.

9 Hemendra Prasad Ghose papers, diary 14 and 15 December 1907; GOI HPD March 1908, 1: 25–26.

10 B. Ghose, 'Sri Aurobindo as I Understand Him' 44.

11 Minto papers, Morley to Minto 26 December 1907.

12 Nevinson, *New Spirit* 238.

13 Gokhale papers: A. Chaudhuri to Gokhale 16 November 1907; Mudholkar to Gokhale 17 December 1907; S. Banerjea to Gokhale, 12 December 1907.

14 Tilak to Motilal Ghose 2 December 1908 (ABT records I); *Prayag Samachar* 17 December 1907 (RNN-UP).

15 Tilak to Motilal Ghose 2 December 1908 (ABT records I); *Times of India* 25 December 1907.

16 q. Feroz Chand 210–11.

17 Nevinson, *New Spirit* 243–4.

18 Nevinson, *New Spirit* 248.

19 B. Ghose, *Atmakahini* 20.

20 Nevinson, *New Spirit* 249–53.

21 Sri Aurobindo, talk of 23 February 1940, pub. Nirodbaran, ed., *Talks* 226.

22 This is the famous 'sweets letter,'

which will be referred to often below. Reproduced *A&R* 5 (December 1981), Plate 4

23 B. Ghose, letter of 1955 in HFMP IV & V 41/2; B. Majumdar 93.

24 B. Ghose, *Atmakahini* 29–30; B. Ghose, letter of 1955 in HFMP IV & V 41/2.

25 B. Ghose, letter of 1955 in HFMP IV & V 41/2.

26 Sri Aurobindo, *On Himself* 48; Hemendra Prasad Ghose papers, diary 10 January 1908; B. Ghose, 'Sri Aurobindo as I Understand Him' 48; Government of Bombay, Abstract of Intelligence XXI (1908): 20.

27 P. Heehs (1989) 85–93.

28 Aurobindo Ghose to Mrinalini Ghose, 17 February 1908 [misdated 1907], pub. Sri Aurobindo, *Bangla Rachana* 324.

Chapter 13

1 Purani, *Life* 100, 292.

2 Ker 132; GOI HPA May 1908, 112–50, 12, 30, 32.

3 H. Kanungo, *Banglay Biplab*, chapter 13; VM ABT records II.7.25; Andaman note 4.

4 H. Kanungo, *Banglay Biplab*, chapter 14.

5 GOI HPD May 1908, 16: 1–7; GOI HPA May 1908, 112–50: 6, 16, 19; ABT 82–5; Ker 129–30; S. Sarkar (1973) 479.

6 GOI HPB March 1909, 181–2: 1–5; H. Kanungo, *Banglay Biplab* 262–4; Daly report 9; N. Gupta, *Smritir Pata* 54–5; Biren Sen papers, 'Evolution of the Bomb' 10.

7 U. Bannerjee, *Nirbasiter Atmakatha* 24: GOI HPA March 1910, 33–40: 82; ABT 76–7, 290–1, 312; *Bengalee* 8 June 1908.

8 N. Gupta, *Smritir Pata* 40–7; U. Bannerjee, *Nirbasiter Atmakatha* 24–5; Andaman note 8.

9 U. Bannerjee, *Nirbasiter Atmakatha* 24–5; H. Sarkar (Barin informant) 5–6.

10 U. Bannerjee, *Nirbasiter Atmakatha* 25–7: B. Ghose, *Atmakahini* 37–40; N. Gupta, *Smritir Pata* 42; Phadke (1985) 33–4, citing Bombay Abstract of Intelligence, 3 April 1909: 263.

11 VM ABT records III.5.774; ABT records III: 125; ABT 261.

12 ABT records X: 213.

13 ABT 57, 88–9; HPA June 1908, 130–1: 5.

14 A. Bhattacharya, 'Aurobindo' 834–5; Chandernagore report 14; GOB History Sheet 728: 3; VM ABT records II.7.26; ABT records XI: 437.

15 Rowlatt report, par. 36; Chandernagore report 8, 9; HPA September 1910, 33–40: 28–9; GOI HPD August 1911, 9: 12; VM ABT records II.7.26.

16 A. Bhattacharya, 'Aurobindo' 843.

17 Hemendra Prasad Ghose papers, diary 21 February 1908; Deb, 'Sri Aurobindo'.

18 A. Bhattacharya, 'Aurobindo' 835.

19 ABT 40: A. Bhattacharya, 'Aurobindo' 843.

20 Ker 364; Phadke (1985) 90; Keer 293.

21 ABT records XI: 429; ABT records XIV: 1132–4, 1233.

22 GOI HPA May 1908, 112–50: 28, 34; ABT 15, 32, 59–60, 89, 101; Andaman report 8; HFMP I 46/2; *Bengalee* 16 April 1908; VM ABT records II.7.26.

23 ABT 58; GOB pol. conf. 170 of 1908, letter Halliday to Chief Secretary 16 May 1908: 1; CAOM Affaires politiques, Governor to Minister 28 April 1908.

24 ABT 60, 88: ABT records XIV: 1138.

25 ABT records XV: 1302; ABT 92, 97.

26 VM ABT records II.7.25; GOI HPA, March 1910, 33–40, 84; GOI HPA, 104–11: 9; GOI HPA, 112–50: 27, 33; ABT 60, 86, 140, 146.

Chapter 14

1 A. Bhattacharya, 'Aurobindo' 843; GOI HPA September 1910, 33–40: 30; GOI HPD August 1911, 9: 13.

2 *Bande Mataram* weekly 24 May 1908: 11.

3 B. Ghose, *Agnishishu Khudiram* 47; B. Ghose, statements to Girijashankar Raychaudhuri in G. Raychaudhuri 709, 729.

4 J. Mukhopadhyay, *Biplabi Jibaner Smriti* 240. Subsequently cited (without Jadugopal's qualification: 'this is what I have heard') in many secondary accounts, for example Guha, *First Spark* 130 and B. Majumdar 111.

5 Sri Aurobindo, talk of 28 February 1940, pub. Nirodbaran, ed., *Talks* 2 & 3: 256–9.

6 C. C. Dutt, *Purano Katha-Upasanghar* 22; Narendranath Goswami, statement of 1908 in GOI HPA September 1910, 33–40: 16 ff; H. Kanungo, *Banglay Biplab* 156, 171.

7 A. Bhattacharya, 'Aurobindo' 843.

8 See P. Heehs, 'Aurobindo Ghose as Revolutionary'. *South Asia* 15 (December 1992), for a full discussion of this question.

9 Biren Sen papers, 'The Late Sushil Kumar Sen' 8–9; GOB History Sheet 252: 7, 12, 16; GOB pol. conf. 265 of 1910, Denham's report of interviews in the Andamans 22 July 1910; H. Kanungo, *Banglay Biplab* 242.

10 *Bengalee* 5 June 1908.

11 N. Gupta, *Smritir Pata* 35.

12 VM ABT records VI.1.43 (Ex 150) (court translation).

13 ABT Records XV: 1505–8 (testimony of Kishori Mohan Bannerjee); VM ABT records II.7.26; Biren Sen papers, 'The Late Sushil Kumar Sen' 8; court testimony of Khewan Kakar, reported *Bande Mataram* weekly 31 May 1908: 14.

14 Biren Sen papers, 'The Late Sushil Kumar Sen' 9; GOB History Sheet 252: 7; Letter Biren Sen to Aurobindo Ghose 26 April 1908 (VM ABT II.7.34).

15 VM ABT records II.7.25: GOI HPA May 1908, 112–50: 20, 33; ABT 84.

16 *Bengalee* 2 October 1908; *Bande Mataram* weekly 31 May 1908: 16.

17 A. Bhattacharya, 'Aurobindo' 843; GOI HPA May 1908, 104–11: 9.

18 ABT records XIV: 1207, 1220; A. Bhattacharya, *Purano Katha*; B. Ghose, *Atmakahini* 59.

19 ABT records vol. XXI: Halliday to Armstrong 20 April 1908; GOB pol. conf. 170 of 1908, letter Halliday to Chief Secretary 16 May 1908: 1; GOI HPA May 1908, 112–50: 5, 11, 49; Daly report 9.

20 A. Bhattacharya, 'Aurobindo' 843–4.

21 GOI HPA March 1910, 33–40: 84.

22 Sri Aurobindo, *Bande Mataram* 890–1.

23 ABT records XXI; Daly report 9.

24 ABT records XXI: Khudiram's statement to magistrate; depositions of Fayazuddin and Tehsildar Khan; judgment; Tegart

papers, 'Charles Tegart' 75.

25 *Bande Mataram* weekly 10 May 1908: 16; ibid. 24 May 1908: 11.

26 ABT records XXI (statements of syce and coachman); IOR l/PJ/6/871; *Bande Mataram* weekly 24 May 1908: 12.

27 ABT records XIX, depositions of Kingsford and Armstrong; ABT records XI: statement of Woodman; GOB pol. conf. 170 of 1908, letter Halliday to Chief Secretary, 16 May 1908.

28 ABT records XIX and XXI: especially statements of Khudiram Bose, depositions of Armstrong, Fateh Singh and Shiv Pershad Misri in sessions court, High Court judgment.

29 This paragraph and the two that follow are based primarily on the records of the Muzaffarpur trial, especially the depositions of Nandalal Banerjee and others (ABT records XIX). The telegrams from and to Nandalal are in vol. XXI.

30 IOR L/PJ/6/871.

31 ABT records vol. XIX: statement of Khudiram Bose, 3 May 1908; *Bande Mataram* daily 7 May 1908: 2.

32 ABT records XIX (quotation from cross-examination of Public Witness 4).

33 *Bande Mataram* weekly 16 August 1908: 4.

Chapter 15

1 GOB pol. conf. 266 of 1908, file marked 'Spare copies etc.', draft letter Gait to Chief Secretary 1 May 1908.

2 ABT records X: 219–20; ABT records XI: 530; GOB pol. conf. 170 of 1908, letter Halliday to Chief Secretary 16 May 1908; GOI HPA May 1908 104–11: 5–6; ABT 58; *Empire* 1 May 1908; *Bande Mataram* weekly 10 May 1908: 17 (reproducing *Statesman*).

3 *Empire* 1 May 1908.

4 Sri Aurobindo, *Karakahini*, in *Bangla Rachana* 257.

5 B. Ghose, *Atmakahini* 43, 45.

6 ABT 97; N. Gupta, *Smritir Pata* 53.

7 N. Gupta, *Smritir Pata* 52; B. Ghose, *Atmakahini* 44; U. Bannerjee, *Nirbasiter Atmakatha* 30.

8 B. Ghose, *Atmakahini* 44.

9 N. Gupta, *Smritir Pata* 53; U. Bannerjee, *Nirbasiter Atmakatha* 30.

10 B. Ghose, *Atmakahini* 44; N. Gupta, *Smritir Pata* 53; U. Bannerjee, *Nirbasiter Atmakatha* 30–1; ABT 147.

11 B. Ghose, *Atmakahini* 45.

12 B. Ghose, *Atmakahini* 46; ABT 196–7, 63–67; GOB pol. conf. 170 of 1908, letter Halliday to Chief Secretary 16 May 1908; GOI HPA May 1908, 104–11: 6, GOI HPA 112–50: 6, 11; *Bande Mataram* weekly 20 September 1908: 11; VM ABT records II.7.17.

13 ABT records XI: 645–7; VM ABT records IV.5.338; GOI HPA May 1908, 112–50: 11, 19–20, GOI HPA June 1908, 130–31: 7; ABT 83; *Bande Mataram* weekly 2 August 1908: 15.

14 ABT records XI: 512–8; ABT records XI: 539–40; *Bande Mataram* weekly 24 May 1908: 18.

15 Sri Aurobindo, *Karakahini*, in *Bangla Rachana* 258–9; ABT 60–61; GOI HPA June 1908 130–1: 6: Sri Aurobindo, *On Himself* 59; ABT records XI: 512–8.

16 GOI HPA June 1908 130–1: 6–7; GOB pol. conf. 170 of 1908, letter Halliday to Chief Secretary 16

May 1908; ABT 14.

17 GOB pol. conf. 170 of 1908, letter Halliday to Chief Secretary 16 May 1908.

18 Midnapore report 6; *Bande Mataram* weekly 10 May 1908: 12.

19 B. Ghose, *Atmakahini*, chapter 10; U. Bannerjee, *Nirbasiter Atmakatha* 32–34.

20 H. Kanungo, *Banglay Biplab* 277 ff.

21 GOI HPA May 1908, 112–50: 25–27.

22 GOB pol. conf. 170 of 1908, letter Halliday to Chief Secretary 16 May 1908; GOI HPA May 1908, 112–50: 27–33; Sri Aurobindo, *Karakahini*, in *Bangla Rachana* 263.

23 ABT 21–34, 197; IOR L/PJ/6/907 (court proceedings reproduced in *Englishman* of 12 November 1908); GOB pol. conf. 170 of 1908, letter Halliday to Chief Secretary 16 May 1908; GOB J9 of 1910 (report of inquiry 2).

24 A. Bhattacharya, 'Aurobindo' 846.

25 Andaman report 9.

26 ABT 27; U. Bannerjee, *Nirbasiter Atmakatha* 36.

27 C. P. Beachcroft, extracts from judgment, reproduced HFMP I 46/2.

28 Daly report 10.

29 GOI HPA May 1908 112–50, 27; ABT 32.

30 Laqueur 143. Cf. Rapoport 660, 666.

31 Hemendra Prasad Ghose papers, diary 5 May 1908; Nixon report 7.

32 *Bande Mataram* daily 5 May 1908: 5.

33 *Bande Mataram* daily 5 May 1908: 2; GOB pol. conf. 170 of 1908, letter Halliday to Chief Secretary 16 May 1908.

Chapter 16

1 VM ABT records II.4.2; VM ABT records IV.4.23–7; GOB pol. conf. 170 of 1908, letter Halliday to Chief Secretary 16 May 1908; IOR L/PJ/6/907 (court proceedings reproduced in *Englishman* of 12 November 1908); ABT 108, 197.

2 U. Bannerjee, *Nirbasiter Atmakatha* 35.

3 ABT records XI: 593; GOI HPA June 1908, 130–1: 8; GOB History Sheet 252: 3.

4 ABT records X: 369; ABT records XII: 789.

5 *Observer* (Lahore) 13 May 1908 (RNN-P); *Bande Mataram* daily 5 May 1908: 2; *Sanjivani* (Calcutta) 7 May 1908 (RNN-B); *Indian World* May 1908, quoted in *Review of Reviews* 38 (July 1908): 37; *Mahratta* 17 May 1908.

6 Morley papers, Morley to Minto 7 May 1908 (quoting Minto), cf. Wolpert (1967) 113; GOI HPA May 1908, 104–11: 10–15; HPD March 1909, 1: 6.

7 Morley papers, Morley to Minto 7 May 1908, Minto to Morley 8 July 1908.

8 GOI HPA May 1908, 104–11: 6; GOI HPA June 1908, 130–1: 9; GOI HPA May 1908, 112–50: 35.

9 Morley papers, Morley to Minto 21 May 1908.

10 *India* (London) 8 May 1908.

11 *Capital*, reprinted in *Bande Mataram* daily 9 May 1908: 7; *Asian*, reprinted in *Bande Mataram* daily 12 May 1908: 7.

12 *Pioneer* 7 May 1908.

13 Reprinted in *Bande Mataram* weekly 17 May 1908: 10.

14 Hemendra Prasad Ghose papers, diary 12 May 1908.

15 I follow Indra Nandi's own

account (*Atmonnati Samitir Itihas* 205–6) for everything but the date, where I follow ABT 88. See also ABT 61, 353.

16 GOI HPA May 1908, 112–50: 20; *Bande Mataram* weekly 17 May 1908: 11–12.

17 *Bande Mataram* daily, 20 May 1908: 7.

18 GOB pol. conf. 170 of 1908, letter Halliday to Chief Secretary 16 May 1908; Indian Penal Code, cited in *Bande Mataram* daily 7 May 1908: 2.

19 Marius 196; R. West (1985), passim; ABT 184.

20 Indian Penal Code cited in *Bande Mataram* daily 7 May 1908: 2; ABT 53–4, 177–9.

21 GOI HPA May 1908, 112–50: 7–8; IOR L/PJ/6/867, Minto telegram to India Office 6 May 1908.

22 GOI HPA May 1908, 104–11: 14–15.

23 ABT 17–19, 53–4.

24 GOI HPA May 1908, 104–11: 5–10, 15.

25 GOI HPA May 1908, 104–11: 7–9.

26 Minto papers, Fraser to Minto 19 May 1908, enclosing Confidential Note.

27 GOI HPA May 1908, 104–11: 1–2.

28 GOI HPA May 1908, 104–11: 2, 18: GOB pol. conf. 266 of 1908, cipher telegram of 24 May 1908.

29 GOB pol. conf. 266 of 1908, letter Gait to Morshead 2 June 1908.

30 *Bande Mataram* daily, 19 May 1908: 7; *Empire*, apparently of 19 May, reprinted in *Bande Mataram* daily 20 May 1908: 7.

31 *Bande Mataram* daily 19 May 1908: 5.

32 GOI HPA June 1908, 130–1: 12.

33 GOB pol. conf. file 194 of 1909 (13), letter Duke to Norton.

34 GOI HPA June 1908, 147: 3; N. Chaudhuri, *Autobiography* 253.

35 J. Bannerji, 'Aravinda Ghose' 486.

36 *Indian Review* 6 (1905): 834–40.

37 Nivedita, *Letters* 998.

38 ABT 17–21, 182, 199.

Chapter 17

1 GOB jud. conf. 130 of 1908: 1–3.

2 U. Bannerjee, *Nirbasiter Atmakatha* 40; Sri Aurobindo, *Karakąhini* in *Bangla Rachana* 264, 272; B. Ghose, *Atmakahini* 64.

3 Sri Aurobindo, *Karakahini* in *Bangla Rachana* 276–9.

4 U. Bannerjee, *Nirbasiter Atmakatha* 41.

5 *Bande Mataram* daily 19 May 1908: 5.

6 *Englishman*, q. *Bande Mataram* daily 13 July 1908: 7; Sri Aurobindo, *Karakahini* in *Bangla Rachana* 292–3; U. Bannerjee, *Nirbasiter Atmakatha* 50.

7 *Bande Mataram* weekly 14 June 1908: 12.

8 GOB J9 of 1910 (report of inquiry 2); N. Gupta, *Smritir Pata* 68–9; *Bengalee* interview with Aurobindo Ghose, 21 May 1909; U. Bannerjee, *Nirbasiter Atmakatha* 45–6.

9 Sri Aurobindo, *Karakahini* in *Bangla Rachana* 293–5.

10 B. Ghose, *Atmakahini* 73–4.

11 *Bande Mataram* daily 24 June 1908: 5.

12 *Bengalee* 24 June: 4.

13 *Bande Mataram* weekly 28 June 1908: 3.

14 Hemendra Prasad Ghose papers, diary 23 and 24 June 1908.

15 U. Bannerjee, *Nirbasiter Atmakatha* 46–9; N. Gupta, *Smritir Pata* 71; Sri Aurobindo,

On Himself 33–4, 67; GOB jud. conf. (Jails) 130 of 1908: 6.

16 Sri Aurobindo, *Karakahini*, in *Bangla Rachana* 288; *Bande Mataram* weekly 19 July 1908: 11.

17 ABT iii.

18 *Bande Mataram* daily 15 July 1908: 4; ABT iv.

19 q. *Bande Mataram* daily 27 July 1908: 7.

20 Morley papers, Minto to Morley 17 June 1908.

21 *Bande Mataram* daily 14 July 1908: 5.

22 IOR L/PJ/6/907 (court proceedings reproduced in *Englishman* of 12 November 1908); VM ABT records II.4.6 and IV.4.25.

23 VM ABT records II.4.6; ABT 44–8.

Chapter 18

1 U. Bannerjee, *Nirbasiter Atmakatha* 48.

2 B. Ghose, *Atmakahini* 82–4; N. Gupta, *Smritir Pata* 69–70; Daly report 13–14; Chandernagore note 10–11.

3 Daly report 14; GOI HPA August 1909, 44–52: 11; GOB J9 of 1910 (report of inquiry 33); U. Bannerjee, *Nirbasiter Atmakatha* 54–5; B. Ghose, *Atmakahini* 82–4.

4 N. Gupta, *Smritir Pata* 72.

5 N. Gupta, 'Sri Aurobindo Jibandhara' 24–5; N. Gupta, *Smritir Pata* 70.

6 H. Kanungo, *Banglay Biplab* 323.

7 U. Bannerjee, *Nirbasiter Atmakatha* 51; N. Gupta, *Smritir Pata* 72; B. Ghose, *Atmakahini* 89–90; *Bande Mataram* weekly 5 July 1908: 17.

8 H. Kanungo, *Banglay Biplab* 323–4; Daly report 14; GOI HPD August 1911, 9: 14.

9 *Bengalee* 1 September 1908; *Pioneer* 2 September 1908 (quoting *Statesman*); *Empire* 2 September 1908.

10 GOI Home Jails-A February 1909, 29–32: 62–64; HFMP I 30/2; commitment order reproduced in *Bande Mataram* weekly 6 September 1908: 17.

11 GOI HPD August 1911, 9: 14; Andaman report 4, 9; *Bande Mataram* weekly, 6 September 1908: 16: GOI HPA August 1909, 44–52: 11.

12 GOB jud. conf. (jails) 130 of 1908: 4; GOI Home Jails-A February 1909, 28–32: 62–64; GOB J9 of 1910 (report of inquiry 19–22, Emerson's statement 8).

13 GOB pol. conf. 160 of 1908, letter Halliday to Chief Secretary 31 August 1908; GOI HPB December 1908, 96–110: 29 (including account printed in the *Pioneer* 10 September 1908); HFMP I 30/2; commitment order reproduced in *Bande Mataram* weekly 6 September 1908: 17; *Bande Mataram* daily 4 September 1908: 6–7, 9 September 1908: 4–5, 10 September 1908: 4–5.

14 N. Gupta, *Smritir Pata* 73; U. Bannerjee, *Nirbasiter Atmakatha* 52; B. Ghose, *Atmakahini* 89; Daly report 14; Interview with Aurobindo Ghose, *Bengalee* 21 May 1908.

15 N. Gupta, *Smritir Pata* 73; B. Sen, 'Sri Aurobindo' 19.

16 HFMP I 30/2.

17 H. Kanungo, *Banglay Biplab* 327.

18 HFMP I 30/2; *Bande Mataram* daily 8 September 1908: 4–5, 10 September 1908: 4–5.

19 *Bande Mataram* weekly 13 September 1908: 13.

20 HFMP I 30/2.

21 *Howrah Hitaishi* 31 October 1908;

Anushilan 30 October 1908 (both RNN-B).

22 U. Bannerjee, *Nirbasiter Atmakatha* 57–8; *Bengalee* quoted in *Englishman* 12 November 1908. Cf. Daly report 14: Kanailal 'went to his execution without flinching'.

23 *Sandhya* 11, 12, 13 November 1908 (RNN-B); *Englishman* 12 November 1908 (including report reproduced from *Bengalee* 11 November 1908); Daly report 14; Hemendra Prasad Ghose papers, diary 11 November 1908; J. Bannerji, 'Aravinda Ghose' 486; G. Bannerjee 16.

24 Daly report 14, 19.

25 Deb, 'Sri Aurobindo'; Hemendra Prasad Ghose papers, diary 5 August 1908.

26 *Empire* 1 September 1908; *Sandhya* 2 September 1908 (RNN-B).

27 *Punjabee 5 September 1908 (RNN-P); Amrita Bazar Patrika* 1 September 1908, quoted in *Empire* of same date; *Statesman* quoted in *Pioneer* 4 September 1908.

28 *Pioneer* 4 September 1908. Cf. comment of the *Madras Times* reproduced in *Bande Mataram* daily 11 September 1908: 6.

29 *Sandhya* 5 September 1908 (RNN-B).

30 *Bengalee* 2 and 3 September 1908.

31 *Empire* 1 September 1908: 5.

32 HFMP IV & V 36/2; GOI HPA March 1910, 33–40: 49–50; A. De 129.

33 Commitment order reproduced in *Bande Mataram* weekly 20 September 1908: 9–10.

34 *Bande Mataram* weekly 26 July 1908: 12.

35 *Bande Mataram* weekly 23 August 1908: 12–13; *Bande Mataram* weekly 30 August 1908: 12–13; ABT 45–6, 208.

Chapter 19

1 Bengal History of Services (WBSA); Sri Aurobindo, talk of 3 January 1939, pub. Nirodbaran, ed., *Talks* 1: 114; obituary in *Times* (London) 17 May 1927.

2 *Bande Mataram* daily 28 September 1908: 4.

3 B. Chakrabarti, *Amader Aurodada* 780–1.

4 Bombay Abstract of Intelligence XXI (1908): 554; Letter Sarojini Ghose to H.I. Joshi, 22 October 1908 (SAAA); *Bande Mataram* daily 27 July 1908: 4.

5 Bombay Abstract of Intelligence XXII (1908): 534, 554, 575, 602–3; *Bande Mataram* daily 26 June 1908: 7; K. Mitra, *Atmacharit* 242–3.

6 *Bande Mataram* daily 20 October 1908: 5.

7 *Bande Mataram* daily 21 October 1908: 6; VM ABT records I.1.232, 236.

8 *Bande Mataram* daily 21 October 1908: 6.

9 Interview with Aurobindo Ghose in *Bengalee* 28 May 1908; N. Gupta, *Smritir Pata* 26, 57; Sri Aurobindo, talk of 3 January 1939, pub. Nirodbaran, ed., *Talks* 1: 114; B. Sen, 'Sri Aurobindo' 21.

10 Interview with Aurobindo Ghose in *Bengalee* 28 May 1909: 4.

11 GOI HPB June 1909, 22–34: 8–11.

12 A. Bhattacharya, 'Aurobindo' 847–8.

13 Interview with Aurobindo Ghose in *Bengalee* 28 May 1909: 3.

14 U. Bannerjee, *Nirbasiter Atmakatha* 59; N. Gupta, *Smritir Pata* 58; B. Sen, 'Sri Aurobindo' 19; interview with Aurobindo Ghose *Bengalee* 28 May 1909: 4.

15 IOR L/PJ/6/907.
16 ABT 58; IOR L/PJ/6/907.
17 N. Gupta, *Smritir Pata* 73–4. Cf. H. Kanungo, *Banglay Biplab* 327.
18 IOR L/PJ/6/907.
19 Morley papers, Minto to Morley 9 November 1908.
20 GOI HPA February 1909, 1: 3–4; GOB jud. conf. 16 of 1909; Daly report 15.
21 Daly report 15; *Times* (London) 11 November 1908; Ker 150.
22 Wolpert (1967) 121–2.
23 U. Bannerjee, *Nirbasiter Atmakatha* 58; B. Chakrabarti, 'Amader Aurodada' 781; K. Mitra, *Atmacharit* 240–4; Sri Aurobindo, *On Himself* 34.
24 *Bengalee* 17 November 1908.
25 ABT 183, 152, 305.
26 Ker 415–19.
27 Guha, *First Spark* 164; Daly report 16; *Bengalee* 11 February 1908.
28 Nivedita, *Letters* 989, 998.
29 *Bengalee* 28 February 1908.
30 *Bengalee* 5–22 March 1909, 21 and 22 October 1908.
31 ABT 107; *Bengalee* 21 March 1908.
32 J. Bannerji, 'Aurobindo Ghose' 486.
33 ABT 137, 138, 140.
34 *Bengalee* 14 April 1909.
35 *Bande Mataram* daily 15 June 1908: 7 (the judge to the assessors in the Muzaffarpur murder case).
36 GOB pol. conf. 194 of 1909; ABT 144; *The Hindoo Patriot* 16 April 1908: 3–4.

Chapter 20

1 Minto papers, Minto to Morley January 1907 (item 1 of 1907 'From Minto'); Minto to Morley 18 August 1908, q. Mary Minto 248.
2 GOB pol. conf. 194 of 1909, letters Allen to Duke 28 April 1909 and Daly to Duke 6 May 1909.
3 *Hindoo Patriot* 7 May 1909.
4 *Hindoo Patriot* 7 May 1909.
5 B. Sen, *Sri Aurobindo* 21.
6 ABT 145.
7 B. Ghose, *Atmakahini* 102; GOB pol. conf. 194 of 1909, letter Daly to Duke 6 May 1909.
8 A. Bhattacharya, 'Aurobindo' 848; GOB pol. conf. 205 of 1909 (3): 1.
9 *Hindoo Patriot* 7 May 1908.
10 GOB pol. conf. 194 of 1909 (10), copy of letter Daly to Halliday 4 May 1909 and handwritten note by Baker 6 May 1909; Tegart papers, 'Charles Tegart': 81.
11 GOB pol. conf. 194 of 1909, copy of telegram; Minto papers, Minto to Morley 6 May 1909.
12 GOB pol. conf. 194 of 1909, Daly to Duke 6 May 1909.
13 GOI HPA July 1909, 40–41: 3; GOB pol. conf. 194 of 1909, letter Halliday to Duke 7 May 1909.
14 GOI HPA July 1909, 40–1: 3.
15 *Mahratta* 9 May 1909; *Gujarati Punch* 9 May 1909 (RNN-Bo); *Eastern Bengal and Assam Era* 15 May 1909: 4; *Madras Mail* 7 May 1909, reproduced in *Bengalee* 8 May 1909.
16 GOB pol. conf. 194 of 1909, letter Daly to Duke 13 May 1909.
17 ABT 151.
18 ABT 184.
19 ABT 179, 178.
20 ABT 184–5.
21 ABT 154.
22 Sri Aurobindo, letter to Mrinalini Ghose 30 August 1905, pub. *Bangla Rachana* 321; ABT 156, 158.
23 ABT 168. Cf. ABT 136–7, 198, 233; Daly report 11.
24 ABT 172.

25 B. Ghose, statement cited by G. Raychaudhuri 670.
26 ABT 173.
27 ABT 177.
28 Daly report 11.
29 Sri Aurobindo, 'European Justice'. Cf. *The Harmony of Virtue* 446–7, a defective text reproduced from *The Standard Bearer*; my text has been corrected against the author's manuscript.
30 Daly report 11.
31 See *inter alia On Himself* 21–3.
32 GOB pol. conf. 194 of 1909, Daly to Duke 6 May 1909.

Chapter 21

1 GOB pol. conf. 205 of 1909 (3): 1.
2 GOB pol. conf. 194 of 1909, Daly to Duke 6 May 1909; same to same, handwritten note of same date; Duke to Halliday 10 May 1909.
3 GOB pol. conf. 205 of 1909 ('Case against Arabindo Ghose'; Chapman's note of 21 May 1909 and sequel).
4 GOB pol. conf. 205 of 1909 ('Arabindo Ghose and his Speeches'): 2.
5 GOB pol. conf. 142 of 1910: 2.
6 Wolpert (1967) 153; Williams, ed. 267.
7 q. Mary Minto 372; J. Morley, speech of 17 December 1908, pub. *INMSD* 32.
8 q. Major 69.
9 Ker 418–9.
10 Minto papers, Minto to Morley 6 May 1909.
11 Sri Aurobindo, *On Himself* 34.
12 GOI HPA September 1909, 56–7: 4.
13 GOI HPA October 1909, 230–48: 2–3; GOI HPA February 1909, 137–99: 1; Morley papers, Minto to Morley 7 July 1909.
14 GOB pol. conf. 205 of 1909, letter Duke to Baker 16 August 1909.
15 Morley papers, Minto to Morley 7 July 1909.
16 GOB pol. conf. 205 of 1909 ('Arabindo Ghose and his speeches').
17 GOB pol. conf. 205 of 1909 (1): 1; ibid. (3): 24–6; GOI HPA October 1909, 230–48: 29.
18 Major 125.
19 GOI HPA October 1909, 230–3: 31.
20 GOI HPA October 1909, 230–48: 11; GOB pol. conf. 205 of 1909 ('Case against Arabinda Ghose', Serial No. 19).
21 Ibid. (Serials 20–1).
22 Ullaskar, q. H. Sarkar 31–2.
23 ABT 304–5.
24 GOB pol. conf. 205 of 1909 ('Case against Arabinda Ghose', Serials 19–27).
25 ABT 361–3.
26 L. Jenkins, Judgment 23 November 1909 (transcript SAAA).
27 ABT 383–4, 397.
28 L. Jenkins, Judgment 23 November 1909 (transcript SAAA).
29 GOI HPA March 1910, 118–23: 5–6.
30 J. Mukherjee, *Biplabi Jibaner Smriti* 267; P. Mukherjee 532; N. Gupta, *Smritir Pata* 89; information given by Nolini Kanta Gupta to author, May 1975.
31 Daly report 11.

Chapter 22

1 *Karmayogin* 29 January 1910.
2 *Karmayogin* 5 February 1910.
3 *Karmayogin* 5 February 1910.
4 Ker 59.
5 GOI HPA March 1910, 33–40.
6 Minto papers, telegram Baker to

Minto 18 April 1910; GOI HPA December 1910, 14–42.

7 B. Ghose, 'Sri Aurobindo as I Understand Him' 59; B. Ghose, *Atmakahini* 107.

8 B. Ghose, *Tale of My Exile* 2–6; Upendranath Bannerjee, *Nirbasiter Atmakatha* 68. The remainder of this chapter is based almost entirely on these two books. Except in the case of direct quotations further references to them will not be given.

9 Upendranath Bannerjee, *Nirbasiter Atmakatha* 72.

10 B. Ghose, *Tale of My Exile* 52.

11 M. Sarkar, ed. 63–65.

12 B. Ghose, *Tale of My Exile* 50.

13 B. Ghose, *Tale of My Exile* 73.

14 IOR L/PJ/6/980; B. Ghose, *Tale of My Exile* 97.

15 Andaman note 8.

16 U. Bannerjee, *Nirbasiter Atmakatha*, passage in English translation in National Library, Calcutta (n.d., n.p.) 161.

17 GOI HPA October 1919, 129–39.

Chapter 23

1 GOB pol. conf. 194 of 1909 (13), letter Norton to Duke 3 November 1909; Duke to Norton 28 November 1911.

2 GOI HPA March 1910, 33–40: 50.

3 Nixon report 7.

4 Ker 139; J. Mukhopadhyay, *Biplabi Jibaner Smriti* 37, 220; S. M. Ghosh, *A Talk* 26; B. Bhattacharya, ed. (1979): xx, xxiv, 22–7.

5 Nixon report 9.

6 Ker 292–3.

7 J. Mukhopadhyay, *Biplabi Jibaner Smriti* 38.

8 GOB pol. conf. 266 of 1908, file marked 'Spare copies etc.', draft letter Gait to Chief Secretary 1 May 1908.

9 'Note on the "Jugantar" Gang'.

10 GOI HPA March 1910, 33–40: 46.

11 Rowlatt report, Annexure (1), 6.

12 Armstrong report iv.

13 BT report 3; B. Ghose, *Wounded Humanity* 52.

14 Guha, *First Spark* 102, 117, 141, 155, 190, 195, 249, 363. Cf. Guha, *Aurobindo and Jugantar* 33–4.

15 J. Mukhopadhyay, *Biplabi Jibaner Smriti* 37–9.

16 Armstrong report iv.

17 G. Haldar 243.

18 Ker 291–2.

19 Ker 151; Rowlatt report, Annexure (1), 5; Guha, *First Spark* 175–7.

20 Ker 292; Guha, *First Spark* 174.

21 Ker 151–2, 291–2, Guha, *First Spark* 368–9, 174–5; Rowlatt report, Annexure (1), 7 and 8.

22 HFMP B 8/2; U. Mukherjee 41; Chandernagore report 13; Nixon report 34; GOB pol. conf. 145 of 1933: 10.

23 Ker 324, 329–330; HFMP B 8/2 (statements of Pratul Chandra Ganguli, Jadugopal Mukherjee and Motilal Roy; the quotation is from Motilal Roy's Bengali statement.)

24 Ibid.

25 Ker 330–1.

26 Rowlatt report par. 66; S. C. Sarkar 1–15.

27 Daly report 18; Minto Papers, telegram Minto to Morley 15 June 1910.

28 Ker 332–6; Guha, *First Spark* 352–4.

29 Ker 251–6; Guha, *First Spark* 389–94.

30 Ker 290; Rowlatt report, par. 84 (I omit two failed murder attempts

from the Rowlatt total since such attempts apparently were not counted by Ker).

31 Letter dated Tokyo, 11 March 1942, q. Rath and Chatterjee 162–3.

Chapter 24

1 Chirol 96; Rowlatt report, Annexure (1) 3; ABT, Preface i.
2 Morley papers, Minto to Morley, 17 December 1908.
3 Daly report 1, 4, 6 ff; Nixon report 1ff; BT report 2: Ker 123–39; Rowlatt report, paras 22 ff.
4 S. C. Sarkar 98–124. Articles include Parchanivis (1957), Aiyar (1962) and Noorani (1988).
5 GOB pol. conf. 266 of 1908; ABT 16; Nixon report, Table A; GOI HPA September 1910, 33–40: 18–21, 42; GOI HPD August 1911, 9: 13.
6 Sri Aurobindo, talks of 18 December 1938 and 28 February 1940, pub. Purani, ed., *Evening Talks* 547, Nirodbaran, ed., *Talks* 2 & 3: 257.
7 GOI HPA May 1908, 112–50: 27.
8 Sri Aurobindo, talk of 18 December 1938, pub. Nirodbaran, *Talks* 1: 43–4.
9 GOI HPA July 1909, 40–41: 3.
10 Morley papers, Morley to Minto 7 May 1908 and 21 May 1908.
11 Morley Papers, Minto to Morley, 27 May 1908.
12 GOB conf. file of 1910 (without cover), circular letter Stuart to Chief Secretary East Bengal and Assam, 4 March 1910.
13 IOR J&P 929/1453 G.G.'s Council Progs, 29 March 1909, q. H. Chakravarti 49.
14 Morley papers, Morley to Minto 10 August 1908.
15 *Bande Mataram* daily 24 April 1908, pub. Mukherjee and Mukherjee (1964) 376.
16 M. K. Gandhi, 'Speech at Plenary Session of Round Table Conference' (1 December 1931), pub. *Collected Works* 48: 358, 365.
17 ABT 184.
18 E. g. Laqueur 4.

Appendix 1

1 GOI HPA March 1910, 33–40: 26; repeated in Daly Report 5.
2 Nixon report 1.
3 Sri Aurobindo, *On Himself* 23–4.
4 Ibid. 23 etc.
5 S. Chaudhurani, *Jibaner Jharapata* 134; H. Kanungo, *Banglay Biplab* 31; A. Bhattacharya, 'Aurobindo' 831–2.
6 Sri Aurobindo, talks of 28 February and 12 December 1940, pub. Nirodbaran, *Talks* 2 & 3, 256; *Talks* 4, 279.
7 Sri Aurobindo, talk of 18 December 1938, pub. Nirodbaran, *Talks* 1, 43.
8 B. Ghose, *Agnijug* 17–18.
9 H. Kanungo, *Banglay Biplab* 35.
10 A. Bhattacharya, *Baiplabik Samiti* 192.
11 Horioka (1963) 46, citing Okakura's *Ideals of the East*.
12 Horioka (1977) 121.
13 S. Basu (1394 Bengali era) 88–93).
14 H. Kanungo, *Banglay Biplab* 18; for Jogin's literary activities see D. Roy, *Aurobindo Prasanga* 6; B. Ghose, 'Sri Aurobindo as I Understand Him' 18; B. Ghose, *Agnijug* 25.
15 B. Ghose, *Agnijug* 73–4.
16 S. Sarkar, (1973) 470; A. Guha, *First Spark* 198.
17 Purani (1978) 3.
18 B. Ghose, *Agnijug* 76.
19 *A&R* 1 (April 1977): 68–74.
20 GOI HPA March 1910, 33–40:

62
21 B. Ghose, *Agnijug* 40.
22 Sri Aurobindo, *On Himself* 69.
23 See e.g. G. Haldar 238; Uma Mukherjee (1966) 12; N. Ray 23 (with Satish Bose and not Aurobindo); Nath 44–5 (with Jatin Banerji and not Surendranath Tagore).
24 J. Mukhopadhyay, *Biplabi Jibaner Smriti* 38 and HFMP I 1/2; B. Datta, 'Aurobindo Smarane' 51; and Raghunath Banerjee, HFMP I 55/2 (with Raghunath Bannerjee and not Aurobindo).
25 B. Datta, *Patriot-Prophet* 10.
26 R. C. Majumdar 412; S. Sarkar (1971) 475–6; H. and U. Mukherjee (1972) 195–202.
27 S. Basu (1394 Bengali era) 20, 22.
28 Ibid. 27.
29 Sri Aurobindo, talk of 21 January 1939, pub. Nirodbaran, ed., *Talks* 1, 220; B. Ghose, *Agnijug* 67.
30 A. Bhattacharya, handwritten note of 22 April 1957 (collection of Haridas Mukherjee).
31 B. Datta, *Patriot-Prophet* 118; cf. Atmaprana 194–5.
32 B. Datta, appendix to Mukherjee and Mukherjee (1961) 248ff.
33 L. Reymond, *Nivedita: Fille de l'Inde* 306.
34 S. Chaudhurani, *Jibaner Jharapata* 179–81.
35 S. Sarkar (1973) 466.
36 G. Raychaudhuri 319.
37 ABT 189.
38 GOI HPD August 1911, 9: 11.
39 U. Bannerjee, *Nirbasiter Atmakatha* 3.
40 GOI HPA May 1908, 112–50: 25.
41 A. Bhattacharya, 'Baiplabik Samiti' 198.
42 H. Kanungo, *Banglay Biplab* 106.
43 Sri Aurobindo, *On Himself* 41, 24.
44 Ibid. 42: cf. ibid. 24 and Sri Aurobindo papers, unpublished portion of talk of 6 January 1939 (SAAA).
45 ABT records XII: 715.
46 VM ABT records IV.5.423.
47 A. Guha, *First Spark* 259.
48 N. Chaudhuri, *Autobiography of an Unknown Indian* 234.

Appendix 2

1 GOB pol. conf. 24/1909.
2 Rowlatt report, par. 23.
3 Ibid.
4 See e. g. Broomfield; S. Sarkar (1984) 272; Laushay 3–4; G. Haldar 229–30.
5 Gordon 7.
6 ABT records, vol. VIII. The statements made before the sessions judge provide caste-membership for 31 of the 36 men in my sample. The castes of the others are evident from their surnames.
7 Laqueur 82–3.
8 U. Bannerjee, *Nirbasiter Atmakatha* 11.
9 GOB History sheet 608: 6.
10 q. Gordon 236.
11 Laqueur 77.
12 Alipore sample: GOB pol. conf. 24 of 1910. Rowlatt sample: Rowlatt report, Annexure (2). In both samples the age is that of conviction or death and not of arrest.

Bibliography

Primary Sources (unpublished)

Official Records

Alipore Bomb Trial Records [ABT records]
Collection of original records in Court of Additional District and Sessions Judge, Alipore, comprising records of:
(1) *Bande Mataram* Sedition Case (1907)
(2) Khudiram Bose Murder Case (1908)
(3) Alipore Bomb Trial, preliminary hearing in magistrate's court (1908)
(4) Alipore Bomb Trial, case in sessions court (1908–9)

Alipore Bomb Trial Records, Victoria Memorial collection [VM ABT records]
Printed records of the case in the magistrate's and sessions courts and original records of case in the Calcutta High Court (VM)

Government of India [GOI] (NAI)
Home Department Political Proceedings. Series A, B, D [HP (A,B,D)]
Home Department (Jails)

India Office Records, London [IOR]
Judicial and Public Department [PJ]

Government of Bengal [GOB] (WBSA)
History of Services
History sheets
Political department, confidential files [pol. conf.] [J = Jails Branch]
Judicial department, confidential files [jud. conf.]

Bombay Presidency Police
Abstract of Intelligence (Office of the Deputy Inspector General of Police, Intelligence (CID), Bombay)

Government of Madras [GOM]
Reports of Criminal Investigation Department [CID] (TNSA)

Records of [the erstwhile] Baroda State [BSR]:
(1) Confidential files (BRO)

(2) Ordinary files of various departments (BRO)
(3) Educational Department files (Baroda College Records) (SAAA)

Archives Nationales, Paris [AN]
Series F/7 (Police Générale)

Archives Nationales, Centre des Archives d'Outre-Mer, Aix-en-Provence [CAOM]
Affaires Politiques

Official Reports

Armstrong, J. E. *An Account of the Revolutionary Organization in Eastern Bengal with Special Reference to the Dacca Anushilan Samiti*. Calcutta: 1917 [Armstrong report] (WBSA).

Daly, F. C. *Note on the Growth of the Revolutionary Movement in Bengal*. Calcutta: 1911 [Daly report] (WBSA).

Ker, James Campbell. *Political Trouble in India 1907–1917*. Calcutta: Superintendent of Government Printing, 1917. Reprinted Calcutta: Editions Indian, 1973. [Ker] (My references are to the Calcutta reprint).

Memoranda on the Native States of India 1905. Simla: Government Central Printing Office, 1905 (NMML).

Memorandum on the history of terrorism in Bengal. Calcutta: Bengal Government Press, 1933 [BT report] (WBSA).

Nixon, J. C. *An Account of the Revolutionary Organizations in Bengal other than the Dacca Anushilan Samiti*. Calcutta: Bengal Secretariat Press, 1917 [Nixon report] (WBSA).

Note on the "Jugantar" Gang, subsequent to the Search of the Manicktola Garden. n.d. [1909] (WBSA).

Note on the Midnapore Revolutionary Conspiracy [Midnapore note] (WBSA).

Notes on Andaman Enquiry (August 1913) [Andaman report] (WBSA).

Report . . . on the Midnapore Conspiracy Case. Calcutta: Bengal Secretariat Press, 1909 [Midnapore report] (WBSA).

Rowlatt, S. A. T. and others. *Report of Committee appointed to Investigate Revolutionary Conspiracies in India*. London: His Majesty's Stationary Office, 1918 [Rowlatt report].

Tegart, Charles. *Note on the Chandernagore Gang*. Calcutta, 1913 [Chandernagore report] (WBSA).

Private Papers

Sri Aurobindo [Ghose] papers (SAAA):
(1) manuscripts
(2) transcripts of talks

(3) collection of biographical documents
A. C. Banerjee papers (NMML).
Beveridge papers (IOR) (MSS Eur C176)
Hemendra Prasad Ghose papers (Department of History, Jadavpur University, Calcutta)
G. K. Gokhale papers (NAI)
Nolini Kanta Gupta papers (SAAA)
History of the Freedom Movement papers [HFMP] (NAI).
G. S. Khaparde papers (NAI)
Minto papers (National Library of Scotland)
P. Mitra papers (NMML)
Morley papers (IOR) (MSS Eur D573)
A. B. Purani papers (SAAA)
State Committee for History of the Freedom Movement papers (WBSA)
Biren Sen papers (SAAA)
Charles Tegart papers (IOR MSS Eur C235/1)
Tilak papers (Kesari-Mahratta Office Library, Poona)

Primary Sources (published)

Collections of Documents etc.

Bose, Bijoy Krishna, ed. *The Alipore Bomb Trial*. Calcutta: Butterworth, 1922 [ABT].
Source Material for a History of the Freedom Movement in India. 2 vols. Bombay: Government Central Press, 1957–8 [*SMHFM*]
A. M. Zaidi and others, eds. *The Encyclopaedia of Indian National Congress*. 26 vols. New Delhi: S. Chand, 1976–87 [*EINC*].
B. N. Pandey, ed., *The Indian Nationalist Movement 1885–1947: Select Documents*. Delhi: Macmillan, 1979 [*INMSD*].

Newspapers

Bande Mataram (Calcutta, English daily and weekly)
Bengalee (Calcutta, English daily)
The Empire (Calcutta, English daily)
The Empress (Calcutta, English fortnightly)
The Englishman (Calcutta, English daily)
The Hindoo Patriot (Calcutta, English daily)
India (London, English weekly)
Jugantar (Calcutta, Bengali weekly) [no file of the paper exists; translated extracts in Report on Native Newspapers in Bengal (see below), some original articles reprinted in Mukherjee and Mukherjee, *Bharater Swadhinita Andolone 'Jugantar' Patrikar Dan* (see below under Secondary Sources)].

Karmayogin (Calcutta, English weekly)
Kesari (Poona, Marathi weekly)
Pioneer (Allahabad, English daily)
Reports on Native Newspapers [RNN]. Official intelligence reports containing paraphrases or extracts from the Indian press (original English or translated into English); reports of the following provinces consulted for the years 1906–10:
(1) Bengal [B]
(2) Bombay [Bo]
(3) Central Provinces [CP]
(4) Eastern Bengal and Assam [EB&A]
(5) Madras [M]
(6) Punjab [P]
(7) United Provinces [UP]
The Statesman (Calcutta, English daily)
The Times (London, English daily)

Writings by Participants, Eyewitnesses, etc.

Aurobindo, Sri [Aurobindo Ghose], *Bande Mataram: Early Political Thought I*. Pondicherry: Sri Aurobindo Ashram Trust, 1972.
———. *Collected Poems*. Pondicherry: Sri Aurobindo Ashram Trust, 1972.
———. *The Harmony of Virtue*. Pondicherry: Sri Aurobindo Ashram Trust, 1972.
———. *On Himself*. Pondicherry: Sri Aurobindo Ashram Trust, 1972.
———. *Sri Aurobinder Bangla Rachana*. Third edition revised and enlarged. Pondicherry: Sri Aurobindo Ashram Trust, 1982.
———. *Sri Aurobindo: Archives and Research*. Semi-annual review. Pondicherry: Aurobindo Ashram Trust, 1977– [*A&R*].
———. *Supplement*. Pondicherry: Sri Aurobindo Ashram Trust, 1973.
Bannerjee, Upendranath. 'Aurobindo Prasanga'. *Dainik Basumati* 20 Agrahayan 1357 Bengali era.
———. *Nirbasiter Atmakatha*. Calcutta: National Publishers, 1978.
Bannerji, Jitendra Lal. 'Aravinda Ghose—A Study'. *Modern Review* 6 (November 1909): 476–87.
Basu, Satish Chandra. 'Anushilan Samitir Utpatti Bishaye Satish Chandra Basur Bibriti' in Bhupendranath Datta, *Dwitiya Swadhinatar Sangram* [see below]: 179–89.
Bhattacharya, Abinash. 'Aurobindo'. *Galpa Bharati* 6 (1357 Bengali era): 829–50.
———. *Baiplabik Samitir Prarambh Kaler Itihas* in Bhupendranath Datta, *Dwitiya Swadhinatar Sangram* [see below]: 190–200.
———. 'Purano Katha'. *Dainik Basumati*. 28 Baishak 1359 Bengali era.

Chakrabarti, Basanti. 'Amader Aurodada'. *Galpa Bharati* 6 (1357 Bengali era): 776–85.

Chaudhurani, Sarala Devi, *Jibaner Jharapata*. Calcutta: Rupa and Company, 1982.

Chatterjee, Bankim Chandra. *Anandamath*. Translated by Sri Aurobindo and Barindra Kumar Ghose. Calcutta: Basumati Sahitya Mandir, n.d.

Chaudhuri, Nirad C. *The Autobiography of an Unknown Indian*. Bombay: Jaico Publishing House, 1951.

Chirol, Valentine. *Indian Unrest*. London: Macmillan and Co., 1910.

Das, Hem Chandra, *see under* Kanungo

Das, Pulin Behari. *Amar Jiban Kahini*. Calcutta: Anushilan Samiti, 1987.

Datta [Dutt], Bhupendranath, 'Aurobindo Smarane'. *Nirnay* (Paush-Magh 1357 Bengali era): 51–66.

———. *Dwitiya Swadhinatar Sangram*. Calcutta: Burman Publishing House, 1949.

———. *Swami Vivekananda: Patriot-Prophet*. Calcutta: Navabharat Publishers, 1954.

Datta [Dutt], Ullaskar. *Kara-Jibani*. Calcutta: Arya Publishing House, 1330 Bengali era.

Deb, Suresh Chandra. 'Sri Aurobindo as I Knew Him'. *Mother India* 2 (August 1950).

———. 'When He Was a Political Leader'. *Calcutta Municipal Gazette* 50 (20 August 1949): viii–ix.

Deshpande, K. G. Preface to B. P. Kulkarni, *Yogi Aravind Ghose* (Bombay, 1935): pp. 6–28.

Dutt, C. C. 'My Contact with Revolutionary Independence Movement'. *Mahratta* 1 August 1952.

———. 'A Pilgrimage to Narmada Valley'. *Amrita Bazar Diwali Supplement*, 9 November 1950.

———. *Purano Katha–Upasanghar*. Calcutta: Sanskriti Baithak, 1357 Bengali era.

Dutt, *see also under* Datta

Deuskar, Sakharam Ganesh. *Desher Katha*. Fifth edition. Calcutta: Mukherji and Company, 1908.

Gandhi, M. K. *The Collected Works of Mahatma Gandhi*, vol. 48. New Delhi: The Publications Division, Government of India, 1971.

Ghose, Barindra Kumar. *Agnijug*. Calcutta: Book Publishing Limited, 1355 Bengali era.

———. *Amar Atmakatha*. Calcutta: Arya Publishing House, 1338 Bengali era.

———. *Barindrer Atmakahini: Dhar-Pakader Jug*. Calcutta: D. M. Limited, 1379 Bengali era.

———. 'Sri Aurobindo as I Understand Him'. Unpublished manuscript (SAAA).

———. *The Tale of My Exile*. Pondicherry: Arya Office, 1922.

———. *Wounded Humanity*. Calcutta: privately published, n.d.

Ghose, Hemendra Prasad. *Aurobindo—The Prophet of Patriotism*. Calcutta: A. K. Mitter, 1949.

———. 'Reminiscences of Aurobindo Ghose'. *Orient Illustrated Weekly* 13 (27 February 1949): 10–12.

Ghosh, Surendra Mohan. 'A Talk by Surendra Mohan Ghosh'. *Mother India* 23 (1971): 25–31, 108–15.

Guha, Arun Chandra. *Aurobindo and Jugantar*. Calcutta: Sahitya Sansad, n. d.

———. *First Spark of Revolution*. Bombay: Orient Longman, 1971.

Gupta, Nolini Kanta. *Smritir Pata*. Calcutta: Sri Aurobindo Pathamandir, 1381 Bengali era.

———. 'Sri Aurobindo Jibandhara'. In *Shatabdir Pranam*. Calcutta: Sri Aurobindo Pathamandir, 1973; 20–30.

Kanungo, Hemchandra [Hem Chandra Das], *Banglay Biplab Pracheshta*. Calcutta: Kamala Book Depot, 1928.

Minto, Mary, Countess of, *India Minto and Morley: 1905–1910*. London: Macmillan, 1934.

Mitra, Krishnakumar, *Atmacharit*. Calcutta: Sadharan Brahmo Samaj, 1381 Bengali era.

Mukherji, Prabhakar. 'An Initiation'. *Mother India* 11 (December 1979): 111–14.

Mukhopadhyay, Jadugopal. *Biplabi Jibaner Smriti*. Calcutta: Academic Publishers, 1983.

———. *Srimat Niralamba Swami*. Calcutta: Niralamb Smriti Sabha, n. d.

Nandi, Indra. 'Atmonnati Samitir Itihas' in Bhupendranath Datta, *Dwitiya Swadhinatar Sangram* [see above]: 201–7.

Natesan, G. A. 'Japan: Its Message to India', *Indian Review* 4 (1905): 1.

Nevinson, Henry W. *The New Spirit in India*. London: Harper and Brothers, 1908.

Nirodbaran, ed. *Talks with Sri Aurobindo*. 3 vols. Calcutta, Madras, Pondicherry: 1986, 1985, 1989.

Nivedita, Sister [Margaret Noble], *Letters of Sister Nivedita*, ed. Shankari Prasad Basu, 2 vols. Calcutta: Navabharat Publishers, 1982.

Okakura, Kakuzo, *The Ideals of the East with Special Reference to the Art of Japan*. London: John Murray, 1920.

Pal, Bipin Chandra, *Leaders of the National Movement in Bengal*. London, n.p., n. d. [? 1910].

———. *Memories of My Life and Times*. Calcutta: Modern Book Agency, 1932.

Purani, A. B. ed. *Evening Talks with Sri Aurobindo*. Pondicherry: Sri Aurobindo Ashram Trust, 1982.

Ray, Dinendrakumar. *Aurobindo Prasanga*. Calcutta, Sri Aurobindo Pathamandir, 1379 Bengali era.

Roy, M. N. *Selected Works of M. N. Roy*, vol. 1. ed. Sibnarayan Ray. Delhi: Oxford University Press, 1987.

Sardesai, Govind Sakharam. *Sri Sayajirav Gayakwad yanchya Sahavasant*. Poona: S. Jagannath and Company, 1956.

Sarkar, Hemanta K. *Revolutionaries of Bengal*. Calcutta: The Indian Book Club, 1928.

Sen, Biren. 'Sri Aurobindo as I Remember Him'. *Mother India* 16 (April 1964): 16–24.

Tagore, Rabindranath, *Jibansmriti*. Calcutta: Visvabharati Granthavibhag, 1393 Bengali era.

Tagore, Surendranath. 'Kakuzo Okakura'. *The Visva-Bharati Quarterly* 2 (new series) (August 1936): 65–72.

Tegart, Charles. *Terrorism in India*. Supplement to the *Review of India*, November 1932.

Vivekananda, Swami, *The Complete Works of Swami Vivekananda*, 8 vols. Mayavati: Advaita Ashrama, 1989.

Secondary Sources

Aiyar, R. P. 'The Alipore Conspiracy Case'. *Blitz Newsmagazine*, 3 March 1962.

Allen, Charles, and Sharada Dwivedi, *Lives of the Indian Princes*. London: Arena, 1984.

Argov, Daniel. *Moderates and Extremists in the Indian National Movement*. Bombay: Asia Publishing House, 1967.

Atmaprana, Pravrajika, *Sister Nivedita of Ramakrishna-Vivekananda*. Calcutta: Sister Nivedita Girls' School, 1967.

Avrich, Paul. *Anarchist Portraits*. Princeton: Princeton University Press, 1988.

Bannerjee, Gobinda Lall. *Dynamics of Revolutionary Movement in India*. Calcutta: Sudhir Kumar Ghose, n.d.

Bapat, S. V. *Reminiscences and Anecdotes of Lokamanya Tilak*. vol. 3. Poona: 1928.

Basu, Sankari Prasad. *Lokmata Nivedita*. Calcutta: Ananda Publishers Private Limited, 1394 Bengali era (vol. 2) and 1395 Bengali era (vol. 3).

———. 'The Swadeshi Upsurge'. In *A Centenary History of the Indian National Congress (1885–1985)*. vol. 1. New Delhi: All India

Congress Committee (I), 1985: 180–262.
Bhattacharyỳa, Buddhadeva, ed. *Freedom Struggle and Anushilan Samiti*. vol 1. Calcutta: Anushilan Samiti, 1979.
Broomfield, J. H. *Elite Conflict in a Plural Society*, Berkeley: University of California Press, 1968.
Cahm, Caroline. *Kropotkin and the Rise of Revolutionary Anarchism 1872–1886*. Cambridge: Cambridge University Press, 1989.
Cashman, Richard T., *The Myth of the Lokmanya*. Berkeley: University of California Press, 1975.
Chakravarti, H. 'Morley, Minto and Unrest, 1905–9'. *Bengal Past and Present* 88 (January-June 1969): 34–60.
De, Amalendu. 'Raja Subodh Mullik and His Times'. *Bengal Past and Present* 98 (July-December 1979): 1–179.
Dhar, Sailendra Nath. *A Comprehensive Biography of Swami Vivekananda*. 2 vols. Madras: Vivekananda Kendra Prakashan, 1990.
Dutt, Romesh. *India in the Victorian Age: An Economic History of the People*. London: Kegan Paul, 1904.
Eagleton, Terry. *Literary Theory: An Introduction*. Minneapolis: University of Minnesota Press, 1989.
Edwardes, Michael. *High Noon of Empire: India Under Curzon*. London: Eyre & Spottiswoode, 1965.
Feroz Chand. *Lajpat Rai: Life and Work*. New Delhi: Publications Division, Government of India, 1978.
Gaekwad, Fatesinghrao. *Sayajirao of Baroda: The Prince and the Man*. Bombay: Popular Prakashan, 1989.
Gharpurey, V. S. 'Mystic Liaison: Senapati Bapat and Sri Aurobindo'. *Mother India* 20 (July 1968): 412–15.
Ghose, Sankar. *The Western Impact on Indian Politics (1885–1919)*. Bombay, Allied Publishers, 1967.
Gordon, *Bengal: The Nationalist Movement 1876–1940*, New Delhi: Manohar, 1979.
Haldar, Gopal. 'Revolutionary Terrorism'. In A. Gupta and J. Chakravorty, eds., *Studies in the Bengal Renaissance*. Calcutta: National Council of Education, 1977: 224–57.
Haldar, Jibantara. *Anushilan Samitir Sankshipta Itihas*. Calcutta: Anushilan Samiti, 1356 Bengali era.
Heehs, Peter. 'Aurobindo Ghose as Revolutionary'. *South Asia* 15 (December 1992).
———. 'Foreign Influences on Bengali Revolutionary Terrorism 1902–1908.' *Modern Asian Studies*. Forthcoming.
———. 'The Maniktala Secret Society: An early Bengali terrorist group'. *The Indian Economic and Social History Review* 29 (June-September 1992): 349–70.
———. 'Religion and Revolt: Bengal under the Raj'. *History Today* 43

(January 1993): 29–35.
———. *Sri Aurobindo: A Brief Biography*. Delhi: Oxford University Press, 1989.
———. 'Terrorism in India during the Freedom Struggle'. *The Historian* 55 (Spring 1993).
Hemendra Kishore Acharyya Chaudhury: The Revolutionary Leader. Calcutta: Hemendra Kishore Acharyya Chaudhury Birth-Day Celebration Committee, n. d.
Horioka, Yasuko. *The Life of Kakuzo: Author of The Book of Tea*. Tokyo: The Hokuseido Press, 1963.
———. 'Okakura and Swami Vivekananda'. *Prabuddha Bharata* 80 (1975): 30–34, 140–5.
Hoyland, John S. *Gopal Krishna Gokhale: His Life and Speeches*. Calcutta: Y.M.C.A. Publishing House, 1947.
Hunter, William, *Annals of Rural Bengal*. London: Smith, Elder and Co., 1897 (1970 reprint, London and New York).
Isherwood, Christopher. *Ramakrishna and his Disciples*. Calcutta: Advaita Ashrama, 1965.
Karandikar, S. L. *Lokamanya Bal Gangadhar Tilak: The Hercules & Prometheus of Modern India*. Poona: S. L. Karandikar, 1957.
Kaul, H. K. *Historic Delhi: An Anthology*. Delhi: Oxford University Press, 1985.
Kedarnath. *Kedarnath: Jivanna Ketlank Sansmarano*. Marathi text edited by Bhao Dharmadhikari, translated into Gujarati by Gokulbhai D. Bhatt. Ahmedabad, Navajivan Prakashan Mandir, 1980.
Keer, Dhananjay. *Lokmanya Tilak: Father of the Indian Freedom Struggle*. Bombay: Popular Prakashan, 1969.
Laqueur, Walter. *The Age of Terrorism*. Boston: Little, Brown, 1987.
Latthe, A. B. *Memoirs of His Highness Shri Shahu Chatrapati Maharaja of Kolhapur*, vol. 1. Bombay: The Times Press, 1924.
Laushey, David. *Bengal Terrorism & the Marxist Left: Aspects of Regional Nationalism in India 1905–1942*. Calcutta: Firma K. L. Mukhopadhyay, 1975.
Macaulay, Thomas B., *Critical and Historical Essays*, vol. 1. London: J. M. Dent, 1920.
Macdonald, J. Ramsay. *The Awakening of India*. London: Hodder and Stoughton, n. d.
Maitron, Jean, et al. *Dictionnaire Biographique du Mouvement Ouvrier Français*. vol. 13, Paris: Editions Ouvrières, 1975.
Maitron, Jean, *Le mouvement anarchiste en France*. vol. 1, Paris: François Maspero, 1983.
Major, E. *Viscount Morley and Indian Reform*. London: James Nisbet & Co., 1910.

Majumdar, Bimanbehari. *Militant Nationalism in India*. Calcutta: General Publishers and Printers, 1966.

Majumdar, R. C. *History of the Freedom Movement in India*. vol. 1. Calcutta: Firma K. L. Mukhopadhyay, 1971.

Marius, Richard. *Thomas More*. New York: Vintage Books, 1985.

Mehra, Parshotam, *A Dictionary of Modern Indian History 1707–1947*. Delhi: Oxford University Press, 1985.

Moshel, Vasudev. *Sakharam Deuskar o Bharatiya Swadhinata Juddha*. Calcutta: Pustak Bipani, 1979.

Mukherjee, Prithwindra. 'Some Documents on the Indian Revolutionary Movement and Sri Aurobindo'. *Mother India* 23 (1971): 531–4.

Mukherjee, Uma. *Two Great Indian Revolutionaries: Rash Behari Bose & Jyotindra Nath Mukherjee*. Calcutta: K. L. Mukhopadhyay, 1966.

Mukherjee, Uma and Haridas Mukherjee. *Bharater Swadhinata Andolane 'Jugantar' Patrikar Dan*. Calcutta: Firma K. L. Mukhopadhyay, 1972 [*Jugantar Patrika*].

———. *The Origins of the National Education Movement* (1905–1910). Calcutta: Jadavpur University, 1957.

———. *Sri Aurobindo and the New Thought in Indian Politics*. Calcutta: Firma K. L. Mukhopadhyay, 1964.

———. *Swadeshi Andolan o Banglar Nabajug*. Calcutta: Saraswati Library, 1961

Mukherji, Prabhakar. 'An Initiation'. *Mother India* 11 (December 1979): 111–14.

Nanda, B. R. *Gokhale: The Indian Moderates and the British Raj*. Delhi: Oxford University Press, 1979.

Nandy, Ashis. *The Intimate Enemy: Loss and Recovery of Self under Colonialism*. Delhi: Oxford University Press, 1988.

Nath, Shaileshwar. *Terrorism in India*. New Delhi: National Publishing House, 1980.

Noorani, A. G. 'Call to Arms'. *The Illustrated Weekly of India*. 27 March–1 April 1988.

Parchanavis. 'The Trial of Sri Aurobindo'. *Hindusthan Standard*. 15 August 1957.

Potdar, M. M. Datto Vaman. 'Tilakanchya "Asantoshacha" Prakhar Purava Rashian Lashkari Sahayy-Prapticha Prayatna'. *Kesari* 31 July 1966.

Phadke, Y. D. *Lokmanya Tilak ani Krantikar*. Poona: Srividya Prakashan, 1985.

———. *Shahu Chhatrapati ani Lokmanya*. Poona: Srividya Prakashan, 1986.

Purani, A. B. *The Life of Sri Aurobindo*. Pondicherry: Sri Aurobindo

Ashram Trust, 1978.
Purani, A. B., ed. *Evening Talks with Sri Aurobindo*. Pondicherry: Sri Aurobindo Ashram Trust, 1982.
Rapoport, David C. 'Fear and Trembling: Terrorism in Three Religious Traditions'. *American Political Science Review* 78 (1984): 658–77.
Rath, Radhanath and Sabitri Prasanna Chatterjee. *Rash Behari Basu: His Struggle for India's Independence*. Calcutta: Biplabi Mahanayak Rash Behari Basu Smarak Samity, 1963.
Ray, Niharranjan. 'From Cultural to Militant Nationalism: The Emergence of the Anushilan Samiti'. In Buddhadeva Bhattacharyya, ed., *Freedom Struggle and Anushilan Samiti*. Calcutta: Anushilan Samiti, 1979: 1–32.
Rajchaudhuri, Girijashankar. *Sri Aurobindo o Banglay Swadeshi Jug*. Calcutta: Navabharat Publishing, 1976.
Ray, R. K. 'Moderates, Extremists and Revolutionaries: Bengal 1900–1909' in *Congress and Indian Nationalism: The Pre-Independence Phase*. Richard Sisson and Stanley Wolpert, eds. Delhi: Oxford University Press, 1988.
Reymond, Lizelle. *Nivedita: Fille de l'Inde*. Paris: Victor Attinger, 1945.
Ronaldshay, Earl of. *The Heart of Aryavarta: A Study in the Psychology of Indian Unrest*. London: Constable and Co., 1925.
Sarkar, Mona, ed. *Ek Adamya Pran*. Pondicherry: Sri Sudhir Sarkar Birth Centenary Committee, 1990.
Sarkar, S. C. *Notable Indian Trials*. Calcutta: M. C. Sarkar & Sons, n. d.
Sarkar, Sumit. 'The Condition and Nature of Subaltern Militancy: Bengal from Swadeshi to Non-Cooperation, c. 1905–22'. In *Subaltern Studies III*, ed. Ranajit Guha. Delhi: Oxford University Press, 1984.
———. *The Swadeshi Movement in Bengal*. New Delhi: People's Publishing House, 1973.
Sergeant, Philip W. *The Ruler of Baroda*. London: John Murray, 1928.
Tahmankar, D. V. *Lokmanya Tilak: Father of Indian Unrest and Maker of Modern India*. London: John Murray, 1956.
Urwick, W. *India 100 Years Ago: The Beauty of Old India Illustrated*. London: Bracken Books, 1985.
Weintraub, Stanley. *Victoria*. New York: E. P. Dutton, 1987.
Wolpert, Stanley A. *Morley and India: 1906–1910*. Berkeley: University of California Press, 1967.
———. *Tilak and Gokhale: Revolution and Reform in the Making of Modern India*. New Delhi: Oxford University Press, 1989.
West, Rebecca. *Black Lamb and Grey Falcon*. New York: Penguin, 1986.
———. *The New Meaning of Treason*. New York: Penguin, 1985.
Williams, L. F. Rushbrook, *Great Men of India*. n.p.: n.d.

[illegible] Trust, 1977.

Purani, A. B., ed. *Evening Talks with Sri Aurobindo*. Pondicherry: Sri Aurobindo Ashram Trust, 1982.

Rapaport, David C. 'Fear and Trembling: Terrorism in Three Religious Traditions.' *American Political Science Review* 78 (1984): 658–77.

Rath, Radhanath and Sabitri Prasanna Chatterjee. [illegible] *for India's Independence*. Calcutta: [illegible] Sarat Samity, 1963.

Roy, [illegible]. 'From Cultural to Militant Nationalism: The Emergence of the Anushilan Samiti.' In Buddhadeva Bhattacharya, ed., *Freedom Struggle and Anushilan Samiti*. Calcutta: Anushilan Samiti, 1979: 1–52.

[illegible] *Calcutta*: [illegible] Publishing, 1966.

Ray, R. K. 'Moderates, Extremists and Revolutionaries: Bengal, 1900–1908.' In *Congress and Indian Nationalism: The Pre-Independence Phase*. Richard Sisson and Stanley Wolpert, eds. Delhi: Oxford University Press, 1988.

[illegible] *Paris*: Victor Attinger, [illegible].

Ronaldshay, Earl of. *The Heart of Aryavarta: A Study of the Psychology of Indian Unrest*. London: Constable and Co., 1925.

[illegible] Pondicherry: Sri Aurobindo [illegible] Birth Centenary Committee, 1980.

Sarkar, [illegible] *India*. [illegible] Calcutta: M. C. Sarkar & Sons, n.d.

Sarkar, Sumit. 'The Conditions and Nature of Subaltern Militancy: Bengal from Swadeshi to Non-Cooperation, c. 1905–22.' In *Subaltern Studies III*. Ranajit Guha, ed. Delhi: Oxford University Press, 1984.

———. *The Swadeshi Movement in Bengal*. New Delhi: People's Publishing House, 1973.

[illegible] London: John Murray, 19[illegible].

[illegible] London: John Murray, 19[illegible].

[illegible] London: [illegible] 1943.

[illegible] New York: [illegible] Dutton, 198[illegible].

Wolpert, Stanley A. *Morley and India, 1906–1910*. Berkeley: University of California Press, 1967.

———. *Tilak and Gokhale: Revolution and Reform in the Making of Modern India*. Delhi: Oxford University Press, 1989.

West, Rebecca. *Black Lamb and Grey Falcon*. New York: Penguin, 19[illegible].

———. *The New Meaning of Treason*. New York: Penguin, 1985.

Williams, L. F. Rushbrook. *Great Men of India*. n.p., n.d.

Index